Helen Spendlove

Applying Psychology: Understanding People

ROBERT C. BECK

Wake Forest University

Prentice-Hall, Inc. Englewood Cliffs, N.J. 07632

Library of Congress Cataloging in Publication Data

BECK, ROBERT C., (Date)
    Applying psychology.
    Bibliography: p.
    Includes index.
    1. Psychology. 2. Interpersonal relations. I. Title.
BF145.B42   158   81–17752
ISBN 0–13–043463–9   AACR2

To

Bettianne

Printed in the United States of America

10 9 8 7 6 5 4 3

Editorial production/supervision and interior design: Barbara Kelly
Cover art: Joel Beck
Cover design: Judy Matz
Manufacturing buyer: Edmund W. Leone

Cartoons by David A. Hills, Wake Forest University

ISBN 0-13-043463-9

Prentice-Hall International, Inc., *London*
Prentice-Hall of Australia Pty. Limited, *Sydney*
Prentice-Hall of Canada, Ltd., *Toronto*
Prentice-Hall of India Private Limited, *New Delhi*
Prentice-Hall of Japan, Inc., *Tokyo*
Prentice-Hall of Southeast Asia Pte. Ltd., *Singapore*
Whitehall Books Limited, *Wellington, New Zealand*

Contents

Part II

The Person: Motivation, Emotion, and Behavior Problems 61

Part III

The Social Animal: Personal Interactions   165

ν tot
  inc.

Part VI

Toward the Future: Creative Problem Solving 415

Preface

This book is the product of many years teaching introductory psychology as well as many different advanced courses. I have also benefitted greatly from the opportunity and pleasure of teaching in Western Electric Company Training Centers, working with men and women at all stages of career development and diverse job responsibilities. These classes have had a high level of student interest and participation and have given excellent feedback about much of the content contained herein.

In the typical introductory psychology course at the college level, one is concerned about trying to bring the material home to the students, so that the everyday application is made more pertinent. In the industrial situation there is somewhat the opposite concern, that is, to show general principles beyond the immediate specific situations facing employees or supervisors. The selection of material, the style of presentation, and the title APPLYING PSYCHOLOGY: UNDERSTANDING PEOPLE, reflect this concern with application in the broader context of understanding human psychology.

I have assumed that most students using this book have had little or no previous exposure to "formal" psychology and may have little or none hereafter. Hence, the writing is as free from technical detail and jargon as was feasible without becoming totally divorced from the academic background which spawned it. At the same time, one must be cautious not to oversimplify inherently complex problems and issues. The source material for every statement has not been given since this is even more burdensome to read than to write. Enough documentation and references have been provided however, so that the interested student can follow wherever curiosity might lead.

Chapters 17 and 18 are somewhat different than the rest of the text. These are a self-contained minicourse in creative problem solving, based on many years of teaching this material in industry. They stand on their own and some instructors might use them as the introduction rather than the culmination of a course. They utilize many principles discussed throughout the text, and students typically find the material enjoyable. The pace of the writing is somewhat different, because to be most effective the material should be *experienced,* especially through practice exercises, and not just read about.

A number of people deserve special mention for their contributions. John Isley of Prentice-Hall first proposed and has generously supported the project. Carol Lewis read and reread the hundreds of manuscript pages, diligently purged errors, corrected grammar, and checked references. David Hills' cartoons are much appreciated samples of his talents both as psychologist and artist. Bill Henry took or helped select and lay out photographs, Cecile Smith did original line drawings, and Joel Beck did the cover artwork. Both the formal and informal support of the Psychology Department at Wake Forest have been invaluable, but especially Jane Reade's secretarial skills. Martha Lentz copyedited and proofed the manuscript, and Barbara Kelly of Prentice-Hall pushed it through production.

I am grateful to the many professional colleagues who read and commented on either the complete manuscript or various chapters. Among these are: Gladys J. Baez-Dickreiter, St. Phillip's College; Robert C. Brown, Jr., Ph.D., Georgia State University; John M. Cozean, Central Piedmont Community College; John R. Dill, Lorain County Community College; Ed. J. Gunderson, M. A., formerly from Milwaukee Area Technical College; Ruth V. Kellar, Indiana Vocational Technical College; Thomas J. Kramer, Saint Louis University; Bernard Locke, Ph.D., Emeritus Professor, John Jay College of Criminal Justice; and Toni Powers, Dover Business College.

Finally, the aid and patience of my family must be acknowledged. I am best known in my part of the world as Bettianne's husband or as Joey's or Amy's or Meredy's or Davy's or Stevie's father. To each of them I am grateful.

Robert C. Beck
May 15, 1981

1

The Person:
Some Basic Ideas

1

The Art and Science of Human Behavior

Introduction

Around 1930 a study of work environments was undertaken at the Hawthorne, Illinois manufacturing plant of the Western Electric Company (Roethlisberger and Dickson, 1947). The orientation of the research was essentially biological. The question was, How would a change in the physical work environment affect productivity of assembly line workers?

The research began with a study of lighting. Two groups of female assembly line workers were isolated in separate workrooms. A maintenance worker came in weekly and increased light bulb sizes for one group, but not the other. Productivity steadily increased with both groups. The experimental subjects spontaneously made such comments as, "It really is easier to work with this better lighting."

But then the maintenance worker simply changed the light bulbs for new ones of the same size. Production still increased. Even a reduction in lighting led to higher production and morale. Obviously, the critical factor was not the change in illumination. Rather, those employees selected as subjects for the research were responding to the extra attention. This *social* factor affected production and morale.

A relatively straightforward study of the physical environment and behavior produced a whole new field: industrial *social* psychology. The importance of social relations on the job was dramatically unfolded in subsequent Hawthorne research. It had previously been assumed that people were *economic* creatures whose work could be completely manipulated by money, but in the Hawthorne experiments it became clear that the workers themselves were controlling production with a previously unsuspected *social pressure*. Money was only one of many influences on worker behavior.

We shall look at human relations from many viewpoints, including biological and social. We are biological creatures, and we do work, play, or survive in some environments better than in others. Our needs are usually met in a social context, however. To understand *human* relations we must know something about each of the following:

1. *The nature of the individuals involved,* including biological characteristics of people in general as well as individual past experiences, emotions, motives, attitudes, abilities, and personalities;

2. *The nature of social interactions,* including group dynamics, perception of others, interpersonal attraction, and prejudice; and

3. *The kinds of environments in which social interactions occur,* including the nature of the groups involved and the physical characteristics of the environment. (Some work environments foster productivity and others actually reward *not* being productive.)

In this chapter we shall first try to get an idea of what it means to think of people as biological-social (biosocial) individuals, and then move on to see how psychologists ask and answer questions about how people act.

The Biosocial Interaction

behavior depends on the person and the environment

Does biological inheritance or environment determine intelligence, personality, mental disorders, physical size, or aptitudes? The answer to such questions has always come in the same form: *Individual differences among people depend on both biological and environmental factors.* The genes (biological inheritance) passed to us by our parents develop one way in one environment and differently in another environment. The genes set certain limits to our capacities. The question is then rephrased: *How are specific genetic inheritances expressed in different environments?* A few examples will illustrate what this means.

1. *Physical characteristics* like eye and hair color are heavily determined by genetics; they are resistant to change in different environments. Even here the environment has an influence, however. Our hair may bleach in the sun and so-called "white" people range from pinkish-white to olive-brown, changing with the season.

2. The later adult *physical size* of a child can be predicted with some accuracy from knowledge of the parents' sizes, but such factors as diet and general state of health have a strong influence. Physical growth has even been found to be stunted by extreme social isolation.

3. *Intelligence* is affected by genetics, but also by *prenatal* environmental influences, such as the mother's health while pregnant. A well-known example is German measles, which if contracted by the mother during the first three months of pregnancy may produce blindness and deafness, as well as mental retardation in the child. After a child is born, its diet, social interactions, and sensory stimulation are all seemingly important for intellectual development.

4. *Personality characteristics* seem even more subject to social influence. We are rewarded and punished for different ways of behaving, as well as imitating others, and these learned behaviors become "part of us." It also appears, however, that there are genetic tendencies to be more or less fearful.

Major social decisions depend on our views of "nature versus nurture"—the question of whether genetics or environment is more significant in determining personality. Such federal programs as Headstart have assumed that improved opportunities for learning early in life will compensate for otherwise deficient learning environments. This is based on a belief in environmental importance. On the other hand, some people believe that genetic inheritance is the major influence on intelligence and learning ability. This has influenced past United States immigration policies and the treatment of minority groups generally. It is therefore *practical* to recognize that heredity and environment always work jointly.

the nature of the environment

By environment we usually mean whatever is *external* to us, our physical and social surroundings. Geographic characteristics are one part of the environment, but the friendliness of the people around us is also a part. Everyone lives in two environments, however: the *real environment,* as it physically exists, and the *perceived environment* that we are aware of.

The Real Environment. We are aware of mountains, lakes, clouds, buildings, smells, and so on. We are not normally aware of many other influences such as the pull of gravity, the pressure of air, x-rays, and ultraviolet light. But these things affect us. The problem of adjusting to weightlessness in space flight indicates how much we have taken gravity for granted in everyday life.

The Perceived Environment. The perceived environment is psychologically often more important than the real environment because it is the perceived environment we respond to consciously. We stop at a stop light *if* we see it. We smile back if we perceive a gesture to be friendly but react negatively if we perceive the same gesture to be hostile. It is not just the gesture which determines our response, but how we perceive it. Figure 1–1 has some simple perceptual illusions to show how a perceived situation differs from reality, even with very simple physical stimuli. Figure 1–1 also illustrates a social situation which can easily be misperceived. An important question is *why* do the real and perceived environments differ? We may think of this in terms of *perceptual filtering;* our perceptions are biased (filtered) by a "selective tuning" to the environment. This filtering process differs according to our biological structure, our past experiences and expectations, and our motives, emotions, and attitudes.

> **1.** *Perceptions are filtered through our sense organs.* Most mammals are color blind and hence must perceive the world quite differently than humans do. Dogs, bats, and porpoises hear much higher frequency sounds than do humans. Even among humans there is color blindness and sometimes "taste blindness." Some chemicals seem tasteless to most people but are bitter to others.

figure 1–1a. Six classic perceptual illusions. (A) In the Ponzo illusion the horizontal lines are actually the same length. (B) The two vertical lines are entirely straight. (C) The three diagonal line segments are continuations of the same straight line, not staggered. (D) The two crescents are exactly the same size. (E) The middle circles are the same size. (F) Lines 1 and 2 are the same length. If we can be so easily deceived with these simple perceptual illusions, what kinds of illusions might affect us in everyday life?

figure 1–1b. Allport and Postman (1947) showed this "subway scene" to people and had them describe the scene from memory to someone else. The second person then retells this description to a third person and so on. With successive retellings there was considerable distortion of the picture's content. See text for further detail. (Reprinted with permission of publisher.)

figure 1–1c. This progression of drawings gradually changes from a picture of the "wife" in A to the "mother-in-law" in C. If you see the "wife" first it is harder to see the "mother-in-law" in the middle drawing than if you saw the "mother-in-law" first. (Reprinted from Leeper, 1935.)

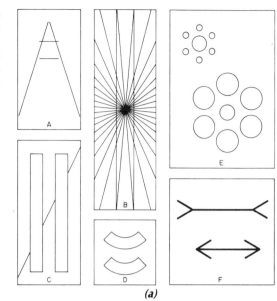

(a)

(b)

(c)

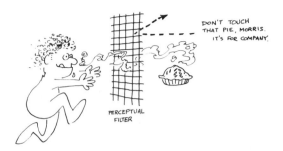

DON'T TOUCH
THAT PIE, MORRIS.
IT'S FOR COMPANY.

PERCEPTUAL
FILTER

2. *Perception is filtered by knowledge and expectations.* We often "see" what we *expect* to see as much as what is "really there." Look at the signs in Figure 1–2 before continuing.

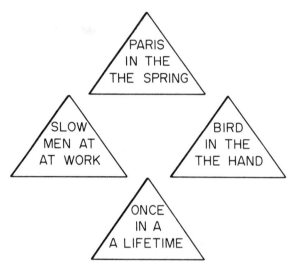

PARIS
IN THE
THE SPRING

SLOW
MEN AT
AT WORK

BIRD
IN THE
THE HAND

ONCE
IN A
A LIFETIME

figure 1–2. Read these signs. Read them again.

In the first sign did you see PARIS IN THE SPRING? If so, look again. The sign really says PARIS IN THE *THE* SPRING. We do not normally expect to see a sign with an article repeated because past experience tells us this does not fit the rules of English grammar. Now look at the rest of the signs in Figure 1–2. Did you misread these, too?

3. *Perceptions are filtered by motives, emotions, and attitudes.* We often see what we *want* to see or hear what we want to hear. We "see" the opposing team cheat without penalty while our team is harassed by biased referees. Similarly, we "see" the best in our friends and the worst in our enemies. We notice food more when we are hungry, and we notice small noises more when we are alone and afraid.

We cannot avoid seeing the world from our own individual perspectives. But we can *try* to see things from other peoples' points of view. We can also recognize that other people may not see things from our point of view.

the nature of the person: the self-concept

Meaning of Self-Concept. We may define the self-concept as the *sum total of a person's perceptions and evaluations of himself or herself.* These self perceptions are potentially subject to the same kinds of biases as any other perception. Our self-concept does not entirely determine our behavior, but it does play an important role. There are three important characteristics of this self-perception.

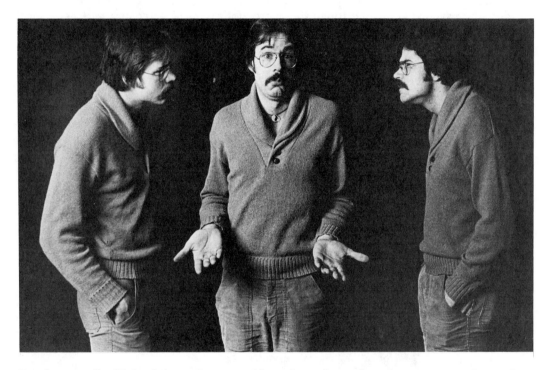

People generally think of themselves as stable and consistent, but there are exceptions. *(Photo by Bill Henry)*

1. *We perceive ourselves as separate entities,* not part of the environment or other people. In some sense, we often divorce our *self* from our *body.* We can lose parts of our body and still maintain a self-concept.
2. *We perceive ourselves as being consistent* over time. We do change and perceive change, but we tend to be remarkably stable. We may perceive ourselves as being competent, attractive, and honest over many years, even when others think we have changed.
3. *We strive for self-consistency.* Many psychologists consider this one of the most important motives. If something happens which is inconsistent with our self-concept we may feel a tension which we try to reduce. For example, if we

fail at a task which we think we should easily handle, we may feel tense and try to explain away the failure which is inconsistent with our self-concept. People who perceive a great similarity between how they are and how they would like to be, tend to be better adjusted than people who have a large difference in these perceptions.

Development of the Self-Concept. Young children have to learn that their bodies are not part of the environment. By touching and tasting and watching and smelling, they learn that their own hands and feet are not just "out there" but are parts of their own bodies. As the child further develops psychologically it distinguishes more subtle self-characteristics, such as personal appearance, aptitudes, knowledge, and character. We learn a great deal about ourselves from the way other people treat us; we learn that we are clever or attractive because we are treated as if we are clever or attractive. This information from other people may not always be accurate, but is nevertheless important to the development of our self-concept.

The Self as a Biological Entity. Our mental processes depend on our brains. Therefore, many biological factors affect our perception and performance. A few examples will illustrate.

1. Disease, injury, surgery, and drugs affect both our brains and our mental processes. Such mind-altering drugs as LSD, peyote, barbiturates, or amphetamines are close chemical cousins of naturally-occurring nervous system chemicals. The drugs alter natural body chemistry in unnatural ways. Under the influence of such drugs our perception of the environment or of the self may change drastically. Castaneda (1968) has given vivid first-hand descriptions of such effects.

2. With some forms of mental illness, a person may be very confused in thinking and may even lose the perception that he or she *is* a separate person. People sometimes perceive themselves as rotting or disintegrating and blending into the environment and becoming completely powerless. The fact that such drugs as Thorazine are effective treatment in such cases indicates the biological factor in the "mental" disorder.

3. If the two halves of the brain (right and left hemispheres) are surgically separated, a person may have two different and independent minds. The two minds correspond to the two hemispheres, have somewhat different abilities, and may actually learn things unknown to each other. The left hemisphere generally appears to be more concerned with logical, analytic thinking and speech, whereas the right hemisphere is more concerned with non-logical, non-sequential activities. The right hemisphere seems to take in things more "as a whole."

There is such an intimate relationship between mind and brain that we can profitably treat them as nearly, if not completely, the same thing. This permits us to look at mental processes, including self-perception, from a biological as well as a social, philosophical, psychological, or religious perspective.

freedom of choice: real or illusory?

We often perceive that our actions are initiated consciously by our minds, that our self is in control of our body. We believe that we have the free will to do anything within our capabilities. However, we also often say that we *had* to do something, that we had no choice. Or, we cannot explain why we did something and invent a plausible explanation. We really do act in ways we cannot understand and which therefore cannot have originated from a conscious free will. Sigmund Freud, the great Viennese physician who founded psychoanalysis, argued that there are *unconscious* causes determining (or partly determining) our behavior. A major goal of psychoanalysis is to find such hidden reasons.

Many real life examples indicate that outside forces cause us to behave one way rather than another. The very uniformity of behavior in certain situations shows the power of these situations. If I asked you the time, you would probably look at your watch (if you had one) and tell me. Think about all the other *possible* things you *could* do. But people almost invariably do the one predictable thing: They give you the time when asked.

If we knew *all* the causes and all the forces acting at a given moment we could probably predict behavior perfectly. The problem is that even if the preceding sentence were true, we *cannot know* all the causes for behavior or all the forces acting at the moment. It is still possible to predict behaviors for some important kinds of situations, however. Thus, I can predict pretty accurately that my students will (almost) all show up for class on the first day. This was even true for the first day of class with American students who had to travel to Italy for the course! We have considerable understanding about the effects of reward and punishment also, as well as many other determinants of behavior.

Research in Psychology

We can learn much about others by observing and talking with them. This is what most people do. We infer (or make a guess at) what is going on in their minds and how they are likely to behave on the basis of all sorts of cues which are observable to us. If John is slow to assert himself and we hear him say that he is not as clever as other people, we could infer that John has little self-confidence or a poor self-concept. Having inferred this much we might go on to explain other things about John and predict how he might act in new situations. We might explain his not joining clubs, not doing well in school, or not trying for a job promotion. We might argue that he does not do these things for fear of failing at them. Psychologists take much the same approach, although with more exacting procedures.

pure versus applied research

Pure and applied research differ only in that the former is done only because a problem is interesting and the latter has a practical goal in mind. For example,

1. One psychologist might be concerned generally with how people interact in groups and another with problem-solving groups in high-level management.
2. One researcher might be interested in chemicals in the nervous system while a second is concerned with reducing mental illness.
3. One researcher might be interested in how to attract people's attention while another is interested in advertising.

The same general "rules" for conducting and evaluating research are applicable in any case, and one form is not better or worse than the other. The two must come together at some point. Thus, the applied research necessary for the development of computers and other modern electronic equipment had to wait for the results of the pure research on semiconductors (transisters, diodes, etc.).

types of research approaches

Let us now look at some different research methods commonly used in psychology and other social-biological sciences.

Archival Research. Archival records include dates of birth, death, and marriage, as well as other records or artefacts that have survived a particular historical period. David McClelland (1961) examined children's stories in the nineteenth century for themes related to achievement motivation (working hard to get ahead). He then examined shipping records, manufacturing, and other indicators of economic activity. There was a systematic increase in achievement themes in the early part of the century, followed by a corresponding increase in economic indicators twenty-five years later. This, along with much other research, suggested that the achievement ideas presented to children influence their adult economic behavior. Such research would be almost impossible to conduct directly since the requisite events require fifty years to take place.

Naturalistic Observation. We can observe and record behavior in natural settings, with the observer as inconspicuous as possible. Philip Zimbardo (1969) watched people in a large city (New York) and a relatively small one (Palo Alto, California) as they came upon an apparently abandoned car. In New York the cars were quickly ravaged, but not by the "typical" vandal. They

Many school teachers-in-training use naturalistic observation to study the behavior of children in play areas.

were dismantled in broad daylight by well-dressed middle class people—sometimes by families on what appeared to be a Sunday outing. They simply stopped, stripped from the "abandoned" car what they wanted, and casually moved on. Abandoned cars in Palo Alto were not ravaged in this way. Zimbardo went on to discuss some of the effects of living in a large city.

In such observational research it is usually helpful to have some pre-established categories of behavior to observe. Before determining when children on a playground are aggressive or helpful toward each other we would have to define specific aggressive and altruistic behaviors. We could then tally the occurrences of these behaviors as we observed them under various conditions.

Case Histories. A psychologist trying to help a client gets as much information about the client as he or she can. This comes directly from the client through interviews and tests, and also from the client's family, school, physician, and other sources. One small piece of information may not be very useful in itself, but by putting many pieces of the puzzle together a better picture of the client is obtained.

Surveys and Polls. There are different kinds of surveys, of which polls are one. We shall use the terms interchangeably here. Surveys may be taken to determine voter preferences, TV viewing, or advertising effectiveness, for example. An important consideration in survey research is that the *sample* of selected individuals surveyed about some topic be *representative* of the whole *target population* from which the sample came. If we were interested in a target population of twenty-five to thirty-five-year-old males for an advertising campaign, we would want to survey a sample of individuals which is representative of this group. This usually involves a *random* choice of individuals to be in the sample. A notoriously *biased* sample was obtained in the 1936 presidential election year. A poll taken by the *Literary Digest* strongly indicated that

Alf Landon would defeat Franklin Roosevelt, who of course was an easy winner. What happened was that the individuals to be polled were selected from telephone books. At that time, the middle of the depression, many people did not have telephones. Those that did have them were more affluent, were more often Republican, and said they would vote for Landon. The sample was not representative of the voting population; it was overloaded with Republicans. Pollsters have since learned their lesson and have become very accurate.

Correlational Research. Researchers rely on statistics to help determine whether particular results are random occurrences or are meaningfully related to other events. The *correlation coefficient* is a number indicating the degree of relationship between two sets of events. For example, we might want to find out if the scores on a clerical aptitude test predict performance in a particular office job. We could give the test to a number of office workers (for one set of scores) and correlate these with independently-obtained supervisor's ratings for the same individuals (second set of scores). The correlation coefficient would tell us whether the test scores help predict job performance.

If there were absolutely no relation at all between the two sets of scores the correlation would be zero (0.00). This would mean that we could not tell from the test scores whether a person's supervisor rating was good, bad, or indifferent. If, however, the test were a *perfect predictor* of job performance the correlation would be +1.00. Individuals with high test scores would always get high ratings and those with low test scores would get low ratinges. Figure 1–3 shows some samples of *scatterplots* and their related correlation coefficients.

Correlations can take any value between −1.00 and +1.00. (The calculation procedures mean that values cannot be outside this range.) The interpretation is more complicated than we can go into here, but as a rule of thumb we may say that (a) correlations with absolute values (ignoring the + or − sign) between 0.00 and 0.30 are "low" and are not good predictors; (b) correlations

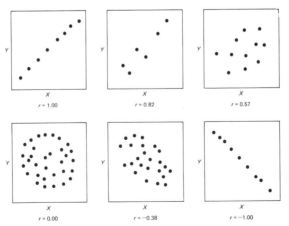

figure 1–3. Six hypothetical situations representing different degrees of positive and negative correlations. The straighter the line of points the higher the correlation. (From Runyon & Haber, 1980, Fig. 8.1 p. 120, reprinted by permission of publisher.)

between 0.30 and 0.70 are "medium" and are "reasonably good" predictors; and (c) correlations greater than 0.70 are "high" and are "very good" predictors. These rules of thumb are helpful for reading about correlations, but anyone wanting to use them would have to refer to a standard statistics book for the appropriate details.

Natural Experiment. When people are subjected to catastrophic events like fires, floods, accidents, riots, or bombings, which are *not* under the control of a researcher, a researcher can still take advantage of their occurrence to see how people react. Not all natural experiments involve disasters; the displacement of people for political reasons (as in Israel and surrounding areas) would also constitute a natural experiment, the effects of which can be studied.

Field Experiment. In a field experiment, the experimenter introduces a change into a natural situation and observes the effect on behavior. The Hawthorne study of illumination and productivity was a field experiment. The thing changed (illumination in this case) is called an *independent variable* and the thing observed (productivity) is called the *dependent variable.* Nothing but the independent variable should change systematically. If other conditions do change along with the independent variable we cannot tell what change produced any particular effect. Such an extraneous variable is an *uncontrolled* or *confounding* variable. This is what happened in the Hawthorne experiment: An important social factor was unknowingly changed along with illumination. It is almost impossible to completely control field experiments, but, almost for that very reason, such experiments are important. We would want to "field test" a new drug or other product before putting it on the market. Something that works in the laboratory may not work in the field, because important elements of "real life" may not have been introduced into the laboratory.

Laboratory Experiment. The laboratory experiment is the most elegant research method because it allows for the greatest possible control of the independent and of extraneous variables. There is also the greatest precision of measurement of the dependent variable. Pavlov studied animal learning in laboratories with four-foot thick concrete walls in a building surrounded by a moat. If there were going to be a stimulus presented, Pavlov wanted to know precisely what it was and who presented it. Seemingly unimportant factors can influence otherwise carefully controlled experiments.

There are many ways of setting up experiments. For example, we might administer a drug to an *experimental group* but not to a *control group* that is otherwise treated the same. We could then evaluate the results with confidence that it was the drug which produced any difference. We might administer different drug concentrations to different groups and compare their reactions. There would be no "control group" in this situation, but we would be comparing groups given different values of the independent variable.

some faulty methods for understanding behavior

(Photo by Bill Henry)

The research methods discussed up to now are commonly understood, and the methods and results of published research are available for any interested person to examine. Some other approaches to understanding behavior have repeatedly been shown to be unreliable. The methods we shall now discuss are not considered good methods for understanding or predicting behavior.

Phrenology. Phrenology is the study of bumps on the head and their relation to personality, thought and action. Arising in the early 1800s, this approach assumes that particular parts of the brain are the locations for such "faculties" as "benevolence, hope, and marvelousness," to quote from an 1834 list. Phrenology depends on three specific assumptions:

1. A particular faculty is located in a very specific part of the brain.
2. The more there is of the faculty, the bigger is that part of the brain.
3. The larger brain area produces a bump on the skull.

None of these assumptions is correct, and the approach is invalid. The early interest in phrenology, however, did stimulate the very research that showed phrenology to be wrong. "Localization of function" in the brain (for example, learning, memory) is still a lively topic, but it takes a far different form than phrenology did.

Facial Features. An Italian criminologist named Lombroso thought he could distinguish criminals from non-criminals by their facial features, or *physiognomy.* Unfortunately, when people try to sort photographs of criminals and non-criminals into separate stacks their accuracy is at a chance level. Furthermore, conventional wisdom tells us that a necessary characteristic of the successful confidence artist is to "look honest." Success in this crime specialty hardly supports the idea that we can accurately identify criminal "types" by their facial features. Unfortunately, many people still believe such myths as that a high forehead indicates intelligence or close-set eyes mean criminal tendencies.

AW, SHE CAN'T BE CHEATING...
WHY, LOOK AT THOSE TWINKLING
EYES, THAT MOTHERLY SMILE.

Astrology. The study of a supposed relation of the solar system to human behavior, astrology is notoriously unrelated to accurate predictions when put to rigorous tests. Astrological charts are so vague as to apply to practically anybody at any time and therefore do not make any contributions to our understanding of behavior. And few people would want to be classed with Attila the Hun on the basis of a common birthday.

Graphology. The study of handwriting, graphology can potentially be better than astrology. But in fact the bulk of interpretations (such as the meaning of *i*'s dotted with circles or letters with a backward slant) have little demonstrable relationship to personality or behavior.

Biorhythms. Our body functions *do* fluctuate rhythmically throughout the twenty-four-hour day-night cycle, and women do have menstrual cycles of *about* twenty-eight days. And, when our twenty-four-hour cycles get out of phase with the environment, such as with jet lag, our thinking may be unclear and our behavior erratic for a few days. The newest entry into the field of pretend-science is biorhythms, trading on the reputation of known

biorhythms but making fanciful extensions about personality and behavior which are entirely unwarranted and readily demonstrated to be inaccurate. Supposedly, by knowing your time of birth it is possible to predict your good and bad days *for your entire life*. This is said to result from the conjunctions of high or low points in three kinds of cycles: intellectual, emotional, and physical. You can put a quarter in a machine at a shopping mall to obtain this information. Research is exceptionally easy here, since it can all be archival (such as who batted how well in any past world series) and does not support any correlation between the supposed biorhythms and performance. Actually, there is no measurement of biorhythms, just the undocumented assertion that since you were born on a certain day the biorhythms have to be at certain points. The supposed biorhythms are nothing more than sine waves with different arbitrarily selected periods.

reasons for belief in unconventional predictive methods

How do such false methods gain a foothold on popular opinion and resist with such vigor any attempts to squelch them?

Exaggerated Claims by Promoters. Fortune-tellers, astrologers, or biorhythm computer salespeople are out to make a living and therefore promote their "products" with exaggerated claims. This is hardly new in advertising.

Lack of Standards for Evaluation. Most people are not trained to evaluate whether claims made by real science or pretend-science are valid. Modern soothsayers often use such scientific trappings as computer printouts, and to the unknowing this may seem to be sufficient proof.

The Self-Fulfilling Prophecy. If we believe in biorhythms or astrology, we might act differently depending on whether we believe today is supposed to be a "good" day: We might exert more energy, express more enthusiasm, exude more confidence, and therefore be more successful than otherwise. In research, however, when people do not know in advance what the biorhythm chart or horoscope says and hence cannot be affected by the self-fulfilling prophecy, the claimed relationships disappear into the mist.

Selective Attention to Positive Examples. People pay more attention to positive examples of what they believe (or want to believe) than they do to negative examples. The importance of examining both pro and con examples was pointed out by Francis Bacon in the sixteenth century. He illustrated this by a story in which a ship floundered during a storm and only one sailor was rescued. The sailor exclaimed: "I am a living example of the value of prayer; I prayed and I was saved." "That is very well," replied a cynic. "Now I would like to speak with all those who prayed and were drowned."

If a famous "psychic" accurately foretells the death of some eminent figure, this is given great publicity. Unsuccessful predictions are simply not reported because they are not newsworthy. Certainly the biorhythm "expert" or astrologer is not going to advertise failures.

Inaccurate Reporting or Intentional Falsification. There are many well-documented fraudulent mediums, faith healers, and fortune tellers. Even supposedly respectable researchers have "adjusted" their data to make them look better. Although J. B. Rhine, the highly respected and honest researcher in parapsychology, decried fakery, it nevertheless occurred in his own laboratory (clearly without his knowledge). An overzealous assistant falsified data so an experiment would come out "the way it ought to." The great stage magician Harry Houdini spent years looking for an honest medium (someone who could communicate with the dead), but he was only able to find cheats.

Truly accidental errors in data collection, recording, or analysis do occur. But we are less likely to detect a mistake in our favor than one against us. We don't look as hard for errors in favorable data. Scientists are prone to be careful in this regard because it is highly embarrassing to have someone else publicly point out errors in research.

Ambiguous Predictions. The Oracle (a seer into the future) at the Temple of Apollo in Delphi, Greece, was notorious throughout history for making predictions so ambiguous that no one could quite understand them. After an event occurred, however, the prediction could be interpreted as having been correct no matter what actually happened. This is still done. Read any newspaper horoscope carefully and ask whether it could be wrong under any circumstances. For example, "Today is a good time to make a wise investment" could hardly be false.

extrasensory perception

Extrasensory perception (ESP) refers to the alleged capacity to communicate with others, to see into the future, or to see objects, without using the normal sense organs (eyes, ears, etc.). ESP is a problem for most scientists because they are skeptical that it has been reliably demonstrated (for example,

Hansel, 1966). Yet, many would like to reserve the possibility that there may be as yet undiscovered sensory organs that people use. We deal with ESP as a separate topic because of the broad interest in it, but also because it has its own particular methods and difficulties.

Nature of ESP. ESP is subdivided into the three categories of *precognition* (knowledge of events before they occur), *clairvoyance* (perception of objects or events not directly influencing normal sense organs), and *telepathy* ("thought transference" from one person to another). There are three kinds of evidence claimed for ESP phenomena.

1. *Mediums.* We have already seen that mediums are highly unreliable sources of evidence.

2. *Anecdotal reports.* Aunt Suzy has a nightmare and wakes up with a strong feeling of anxiety. A few days later she finds that a relative had died the night of her nightmare. She believes she had a psychic experience and tells somebody about it. The following questions are important to ask about such anecdotal reports: (a) Did the dream really occur at the time of the accident? Aunt Suzy may have been hazy and "sharpened up" her memory after the fact. (b) How prone is Aunt Suzy to have such dreams? Perhaps she has them all the time but this was the first one she could relate to anything. (c) Even if this was the first such occasion for Aunt Suzy, how many *other* people have such dreams with no relation to anything else? Aunt Suzy's dream may have been improbable, but still a coincidence.

3. *Laboratory studies.* These are not considered experimental studies because ESP is usually *defined* to be independent of physical events and therefore uncontrollable. ESP studies are demonstrations, or possibly correlational studies. The standard way to study ESP for a number of years has been to use the so-called "Zener cards," first used by Rhine.[1] There are twenty-five cards to a set, five repetitions of five different symbols, shown in Figure 1–4. Under conditions corresponding to the type of ESP studied, a subject guesses which card will come up next in the shuffled deck. (a) *Precognition:* The subject guesses all twenty-five cards in advance of any being turned over. (b) *Telepathy:* A

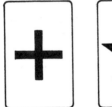    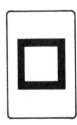

figure 1–4. Cards used by researchers to study extrasensory perception. The symbols were used originally rather than numbers or regular playing cards so that particular biasses in choosing one card rather than another might be eliminated.

---

[1] The use of computers, random radioactive decay processes, and the like in more recent research does not change the logic of this line of research. Such methods just reduce the problems of mechanical error and tedium.

person in one room looks at each card as it is turned and thinks hard on it (sending the message) while the subject in another room (the receiver) guesses what card the sender is looking at. (c) *Clairvoyance:* The cards might be put into separately sealed envelopes and the subject locates them by guessing.

A demonstration of ESP by any of these procedures is said to occur if there is a higher-than-chance number of "hits" (correct guesses). Since there are five symbols repeated five times, chance expectancy is taken to be 5/25, or 20 percent. The most famous, and generally considered one of the most definitive demonstrations of ESP, was by Soal and Bateman (1952). A good "sensitive" subject was Mrs. Stewart. In 13 runs (a run is eight times through the deck) over a period of four years she averaged 6.8 hits per 25 trials with a telepathy procedure and 4.9 with a clairvoyance procedure. These results are hardly dramatic but are statistically unlikely if chance is in fact 5/25.

Problems with ESP Research. There are four main reasons why psychologists are skeptical of ESP results (Hilgard, Atkinson and Atkinson, 1975).

1. There is general skepticism about extraordinary phenomena. We expect extraordinary proof for an unusual claim, but results reported thus far have not been very extraordinary.

2. There are serious statistical problems, some too complex to discuss here. We can point out two, however. (a) It is inappropriate to select only positive cases. If a large enough number of subjects is tested it is expected by chance that a few will perform unusually well, some unusually poorly, and most somewhere between. (b) Sometimes ESP researchers keep looking at the same data in many different ways and find an analysis which turns out to be "significant" (for example, the subject was "really" guessing ahead by one card, so if you look one card ahead the subject was doing well.)

3. In most research, better controlled procedures produce better results. In ESP, better procedures have generally led to worse results.

4. The phenomena are inconsistent; subjects gain and lose "the power" mysteriously, without warning.

In summary, there may be unexplored sensory avenues but the evidence for these from ESP research is weak at best. If the evidence becomes consistent and reliable it will have to be accounted for. Until then, most psychologists will remain skeptical.

SUMMARY

1. *Human relations* depend on the nature of the *individuals* involved, the nature of *social interactions,* and the kinds of *environments* in which social interactions occur.

2. *Individual differences* in thought and action are determined by both biological

and environmental factors. Biological factors may be expressed differently in different environments.

3. The *perceived* environment is often psychologically more important than the *real* (physical) environment. Perceptual filtering selectively creates the world which we see and respond to.

4. The *self-concept* is the sum total of a person's perceptions and evaluations of himself or herself. A person's self-concept plays an important part in the way that person acts, especially in striving for self-consistency from day to day.

5. Our mental processes depend on our brains. Biological factors, therefore, affect our perception and behavior.

6. We often *perceive* that we are free to act any way we choose, but our behavior is considered to be *determined* by internal and external events of which we may or may not be aware.

7. Different methods for the study of behavior are required for different purposes. Some are *non-experimental,* such as studying historical records (archives), studying people in their natural environments, case histories, surveys and polls, or behavior following unusual events such as earth-quakes ("natural experiments"). With *true experimental* methods the *experimenter* introduces a change in a situation. In the *field experiment,* for example, the change might be in a manufacturing plant.

8. The *laboratory experiment* gives the greatest possible control of an experiment. The experimenter introduces some treatment to one group (experimental group) but not to another group (control group). Both groups are treated identically otherwise, and any difference in behavior of the two groups can be attributed to the treatment introduced by the experimenter.

9. There are many *unreliable* approaches to the study of behavior. Among these are *phrenology* (study of bumps on the head and their relation to personality) and *physiognomy* (study of facial features). *Astrology, graphology* (handwriting), and *biorhythms* are also faulty approaches for understanding behavior.

10. People persist in believing in unreliable methods for a number of reasons: exaggerated claims by promoters, lack of standards for evaluation, self-fulfilling prophecy effects, selective attention to positive examples, inaccurate or intentional false reporting of data, and ambiguous predictions which "always come out right."

11. *Extrasensory Perception* (ESP) is the alleged capacity to communicate with others, to see into the future, or to perceive objects, without using the normal sense organs. Support for ESP comes from mediums, anecdotal reports, and some laboratory research, but the evidence is generally weak when examined closely.

EXERCISES

1. Can you think of anyone you have known whose mind seemed to be confused because of illness or injury? How did that person act? What does this suggest about the relationship between mind and body?

2. List all the situations you can think of where you could very reliably predict someone else's behavior. Can you predict the behavior of members of your family, or close friends, better than the behavior of strangers? Why do you think this is so?

3. Why do you think the perceived environment is more important with regard to behavior and the prediction of behavior of a particular person than is the "real" environment?

4. Think of a situation where your perception of events was very different from that of someone else. What were the circumstances? What do you think made your perceptions different? Did you think you were undoubtedly correct? Did the other person think he or she was also correct?

5. *Research Methods* (Different members of your class can do different things.)
   - *Case History.* Prepare a brief psychological case history of yourself. What kinds of materials do you think should be included? What were the significant psychological events in your life as you look back? (You can do this without getting too personal.)
   - *Naturalistic Observation.* Go to the library or an eating place. How do the people space themselves in the room? What does this imply to you? Do men or women spend more time at lunch? Do men or women tend to sit together more? You can count size of male, female, and mixed groups and record how long they stay for lunch.
   - *Survey.* Write a set of survey questions on some topic of local interest. Have the rest of the class evaluate these for clarity and relevance to the topic. Note especially whether questions which seem clear to you (the author) are or are not clear to others. What kinds of questions are unclear to others?
   - *Field Experiment.* If you are daring, go into a library or eating place that is relatively unoccupied and sit directly next to someone. What happens? You might have a friend do this so you can observe. Does the person move when the friend sits down? If so, how long does it take? Do people leave their seats faster when sat next to than if not sat next to?
   - *Laboratory Experiment.* Set up an in-class experiment. Using a stop watch, or one with a sweep second hand, have people judge duration of time under some different conditions. For example, judge time duration when the room is completely silent, when someone is reading some dull mate-

rial, when someone is reading interesting material, and so on. Are there differences in average judgments of time duration? Do your subjects tend to overestimate or underestimate elapsed time under particular conditions? Could you develop an hypothesis about the conditions under which time would seem to pass faster or slower than it really does? What kinds of control conditions would you be concerned with (such as equating conditions for sex differences of subjects) so that something besides the experimental variable is not producing the observed outcome?

6. *ESP Demonstration.* Someone takes the jack, queen, king, and ace from each suit in the deck, a total of sixteen cards, and shuffles them. He or she then looks intently at each card, one at a time, and thinks about its name for five seconds. During this time each member of the class writes down the name of the card (ignore the suit, just put J, Q, K, or A). The experimenter then puts the card face down and looks at the next one for five seconds, and so on. At the end of the sixteen cards the experimenter tells the class what each card was and each person scores himself or herself for number of correct guesses. There is a 25 percent chance of guessing correctly by accident, or four out of sixteen. The experimenter writes each person's score on the blackboard. What is the average "hit rate" (number correct)? Is it very different from four? Do you think the difference from four is large enough to show ESP ability? Are there individuals in the group who scored much higher than four? Do they have "the ability"? Repeat the whole demonstration. Do the people who scored high or low the first time also score high or low the second time? If they do not, what does this suggest to you?

7. *Physiognomy.* Clip some magazine or newspaper pictures of people who are eminent and some of people who are notorious (criminals, for example). Do not use pictures of people so well-known they can readily be identified. If possible, get five of each kind and mount each on a piece of cardboard. Now have the other members of the class (or other group) classify them by their faces into "eminent" and "criminal" groups. Make sure there are no other cues as to who or what they are, such as distinctive dress or location. How accurate are your subjects at classifying?

As an alternative procedure, prepare brief descriptions of each person pictured. Have the subjects match the pictures to the descriptions and count the percentage of correct matches. How accurate are your subjects at this?

8. *Biorhythms.* Locate a biorhythm chart or calculator. Have all the members of the class say whether yesterday was a "good," "bad," or "indifferent" day for them, without any prior knowledge of their biorhythm chart. Then calculate their biorhythms. How well do these match?

If you can obtain the birthdays of the players of the most recent world series teams, plot their biorhythms for each day of the series and compare this with their batting or pitching performance on those days. Can you tell from the biorhythm charts which players actually had good, bad, or indifferent days in the series?

2

Learning and Remembering

Humans learn so much that it is virtually impossible to talk about any aspect of behavior without looking at the influence of learning. Psychologists have identified several different kinds of learning which we shall explore: classical conditioning, instrumental (operant) conditioning, imitation, verbal learning, and memory.

Classical Conditioning

Classical conditioning is commonly called Pavlovian conditioning, after Ivan Pavlov. Pavlov won a Nobel prize for his study of digestion, and many of the principles of classical conditioning were developed in his laboratory. We shall look at five principles of conditioning: acquisition, generalization, extinction, partial reinforcement, discrimination; and the role of awareness in conditioning.

acquisition

Acquisition is learning the relationship between a *neutral* stimulus and a meaningful stimulus, usually emotion-arousing, as diagrammed in Figure 2–1. A musical tone precedes the presentation of food to a dog and we measure the dog's salivation. The tone is called the *conditioned stimulus* (CS). Food is the *unconditioned stimulus* (UCS). Salivation to the food is the *unconditioned response* (UCR). And salivation to the tone after its association with food is the *conditioned response* (CR). This is appetitive conditioning, involving food and hunger. It is critical that the UCS be able to *elicit* salivation (or another response to be conditioned), because the CS cannot be associated with the response otherwise.

Classical conditioning may also involve aversive (unpleasant or painful) stimuli. This is called classical aversive conditioning. A tone might precede electric shock to the forearm, with the *Galvanic Skin Response* (GSR) (a change in electrical resistance of the skin) being measured. This is diagrammed in Figure 2–2. As we can see, it is in principle the same as the procedure for

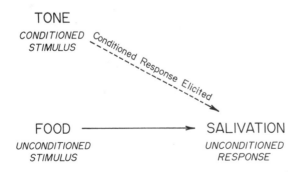

TONE
CONDITIONED STIMULUS   Conditioned Response Elicited

FOOD ⟶ SALIVATION
UNCONDITIONED STIMULUS   UNCONDITIONED RESPONSE

figure 2–1. Basic procedure and symbolism to describe classical conditioning. At first the tone is "neutral" and only the food produces salivation. After associating the tone closely in time with food, however, the tone is "conditioned" and can arouse salivation by itself.

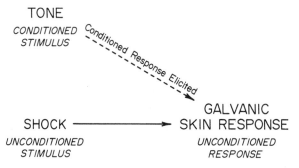

TONE
CONDITIONED
STIMULUS

Conditioned Response Elicited

SHOCK ⟶ SKIN RESPONSE

GALVANIC

UNCONDITIONED
STIMULUS

UNCONDITIONED
RESPONSE

figure 2–2. Classical conditioning with aversive stimuli. The same basic procedure as with appetitive conditioning is used, except that an unpleasant stimulus (shock) is used instead of a pleasant one (food). The galvanic skin response (an index of emotion) is a more appropriate measure of conditioning here.

establishing appetitive conditioning. We simply use different stimuli and responses.

CS-UCS Interval. In general, the association between CS and UCS is best learned if the CS occurs just shortly before the UCS. The best interval depends on the particular stimuli and responses. For simple reflexes, about a half-second interval between CS and UCS is best, but it is possible for aversive conditioning to occur with an interval of hours. Most people have sometime learned to avoid particular foods because they became sick several hours after eating the food.

stimulus generalization

Primary Stimulus Generalization. A conditioned response may be elicited by stimuli which are physically similar to the CS. This is called primary stimulus generalization. The CR is progressively smaller as the new stimulus is less like the CS. Figure 2–3 illustrates this, with a curve called a *stimulus generalization gradient.* Stimuli can vary along such dimensions as size, color, shape, brightness, loudness, or more complex stimuli. For example, if you were painfully bitten by a large dog, you might also become somewhat afraid of smaller dogs.

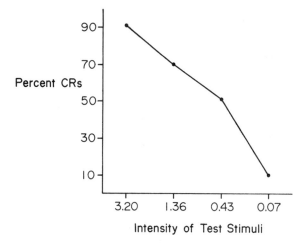

Percent CRs

Intensity of Test Stimuli

figure 2–3. Stimulus generalization gradient. Human subjects were first conditioned to blink an eye to a light of 3.2 footcandles, which was followed by a puff of air to the eye. They were then tested with stimuli of lower intensities. The percent of trials on which eyeblinks (conditioned responses) occurred when only the CS (light) occurred dropped from about 90% to about 10%. (From Vandament & Price, 1964, Fig. 1. Used with permission.)

Secondary Stimulus Generalization. Generalization may occur to stimuli with *meaning* similar to the CS. Suppose we use the word NATION as the CS and electric shock as the UCS, recording the galvanic skin response. There is considerable generalization to the word STATE, which is physically unlike NATION but has similar meaning. The complex meanings learned by humans allow for many possibilities for this kind of generalization. For example, we may be afraid in situations physically new to us, but having other associations.

extinction

If the UCS (such as shock or food) is omitted when the CS is presented, the conditioned response declines. This process is called *extinction,* and we say the response has extinguished when it no longer occurs to the CS. The shepherd cried "Wolf" for the fun of seeing the villagers run to help. But when a wolf actually did attack the flock the villagers were no longer alarmed by the cry and did not come to his aid. Their response had extinguished. Extinction is not the same thing as forgetting. The villagers still remembered what "Wolf" meant, but they had learned not to respond. An extinguished response can be quickly revived by a few more pairings of CS and UCS.

partial reinforcement

Reinforcement is the pairing of CS and UCS. If the CS is paired with the UCS only part of the time the CS is presented, then learning is slower. But it also takes longer to extinguish a response after such partial pairings than after 100 percent pairings of CS and UCS. It is harder to tell if the UCS (such as shock) has stopped coming if it has always been irregular anyway.

discrimination

We also learn to *discriminate* between the CS and other stimuli if other stimuli are explicitly *not* associated with the UCS. We may learn to be afraid of a particular dog, but learn not to be afraid of other dogs which do not attack us.

classical conditioning and awareness

Sometimes people are afraid that they might be conditioned to do things against their will. Conditioning may be caricatured as people slobbering at the sound of a bell, like Pavlov's dogs were thought to do. A number of facts are reassuring in this regard.

1. Since even Pavlov's dogs did not salivate unless they were hungry, motivation is important in classical conditioning.
2. Laboratory experiments clarify the nature of conditioning, but they *intentionally ignore* (keep constant for experimental control) other factors which may be important for behavior, such as reward and punishment.
3. For classical conditioning to occur with humans it appears that a person has to *be aware* of the relationship between the CS and the UCS. People who do not detect this relationship condition very poorly, if at all. Classical conditioning, then, is not some insidious procedure to gain control of people. It is just one kind of learning that affects us.

Instrumental (Operant) Conditioning

Classical conditioning depends on behaviors elicited by a UCS. Instrumental conditioning depends on the "voluntary" occurrence of behaviors which are then rewarded, punished, or ignored.

some historical perspective

Research on reward and punishment was spurred by Darwin's theory of evolution. "Survival of the fittest" depends partly on the ability to learn what behaviors are useful (rewarded) and which are harmful (punished). E. L. Thorndike (1913) expressed the *law of effect,* which says that organisms are more likely to repeat actions that have *satisfying* effects (reward) and stop doing things that have *annoying* effects (punishment). The greatest practical development of instrumental conditioning has been at the hands of B. F. Skinner (for example, 1953) and his followers. The technology of using reward and punishment has been highly refined, with applications to child rearing, education, and psychiatric problems.

nature of rewards and punishers

A hungry person rewarded by a good meal is more likely to return to the same restaurant. A person with a bad toothache which is relieved by a dentist is more likely to go back to the dentist with future toothaches. The nature of these rewarding events is different, however: Getting good food is not the same thing as getting rid of a toothache.

Skinnerian Terminology. Skinner defined the following:

1. *Positive Reinforcer*—a stimulus *presented* after a response which increases the likelihood of that response's occurring in the future. Examples are money, praise, and candy.

2. *Negative Reinforcer*—a stimulus which when *removed* following a response *increases* the probability of that response. Examples are removal of pain, loud noise, or annoying people.

3. *Punisher$_1$*—a stimulus (negative reinforcer) *presented following* a response which *decreases* the probability of that response. For example, verbal reprimands or spankings might be punishers.

4. *Punisher$_2$*—a stimulus (positive reinforcer) which when *removed* following a response *decreases* the probability of that response. Examples are taking away TV-viewing privileges from a child or money from an adult.

Positive and negative reinforcers are essentially the same as rewards and punishments, pleasant and unpleasant events. Reinforcers and punishers are defined by their effects on behavior, however. We know that some things are generally reinforcing: attention, praise, affection, money, privileges, or power, for instance. But attention may be punishing for someone who wants to be left alone. Common punishers are ridicule, pain, lack of attention, or losing money. For some people, though, physical pain is reinforcing. For a specific person at a specific time we may have to search out effective reinforcers or punishers.

Discriminative Stimuli. A discriminative stimulus is a cue which signals that reward or punishment will follow a response. You call your dog, and if he comes you feed him. Calling is the discriminative stimulus which tells the dog that *if* he comes he will get food. Analysis of behavior involves studying discriminative stimuli as well as reinforcers and punishers.

Secondary Reinforcers. Many stimuli are reinforcing because they signal other reinforcers, much as a Pavlovian CS signals food. Words of praise may be secondary reinforcers because they signal something of value, called primary reinforcers. This signaling is learned through association of the secondary reinforcers and the primary ones.

The trophy is valuable only as a symbolic reward, a secondary reinforcer.

reward and punishment by brain stimulation

Specific areas of the brain are related to reward and punishment. If needle-fine electrodes are permanently inserted into precise locations in the brain, a very reliable effect occurs. Dogs, cats, rats, or monkeys will press a lever for hours on end for the sole reward of a few thousandths of a volt of electrical current passed through the electrode tip into the brain. This electric thrill is the most powerful form of reward known for some animals. The same amount of stimulation is punishing if applied to other parts of the brain. There may then be general reward and punishment systems in the brain and many stimuli are effective motivators because they tap into these systems.

With humans it is not so clear that things work the same. Humans will ask that such stimulation be repeated, but they seem to do this more for curiosity than for pleasure. This may correspond to the fact that many powerful human rewards are curiosity-satisfying events.

determinants of reward effectiveness

Amount of Reward. In general, the larger the reward, the greater the effort to get it. When we want the best person for a job we pay the most we can.

Quality of Reward. Food, praise, and companionship are rewards which are different in *kind*. To attract good employees we offer a variety of benefits, not just a high salary. Table 2–1 shows a list of what employees have considered important in a job in many previous surveys. These are rewards.

table 2–1

a compilation based on 150 studies of job satisfaction and the factors that influence it ranked the factors in the following order.

1) security	8) supervision
2) interest in the job itself	9) social aspects of the job
3) opportunity for advancement	10) working conditions
4) appreciation from supervisor	11) communication
5) company and management	12) hours
6) qualities of the job itself	13) ease of the work
7) wages	14) benefits

(Guilford and Gray, *Motivation and Modern Management.* London: Addison-Wesley Publishing Co., 1970, p. 173.)

Delay of Reward. As a rule, rewards are most effective if given immediately after a response. The longer the delay the more difficult to associate response and reward. Secondary reinforcers (such as praise) are often given immediately after a response if there is going to be a long delay until the "real" reinforcer. People paid by the month, for example, need something in their jobs to reinforce them between paychecks.

stimulus generalization and discrimination

Rewarded behavior is generalized beyond the immediate situation in which it is learned. We teach children to be polite at home and hope their behavior will generalize outside the home. Such generalization may or may not occur, because different sets of rewards may operate away from home. Actually, children may be better behaved away from home.

Discrimination is learned. If a school child learns that working hard in Mr. Jones' class is rewarded the child may generalize this to Mr. Brown's class. But if Mr. Brown does not provide rewards, the child learns to discriminate and may work hard for Jones but not for Brown.

Building and Maintaining Rewarded Behaviors

shaping

It is Alice's first day in the shop and we have to teach her how to operate "Old No. 6" machine. Initially, we may talk her through it, along with a demonstration. She then goes through the steps. First, she turns on the machine. The whirring of the motor gives instant feedback that she has done it right and we say "good."

The next step might require feeding a piece of wood into the machine. Alice might hold the wood dangerously, making an accident likely. We immediately give feedback about this, then have her do it again. When the wood is fed correctly we immediately say so. It might not be fed *exactly* right, but we would accept the *approximation*. Over successive practice runs, we require closer and closer approximations to the correct method before saying "Okay." Such selective reinforcement of successive approximations to the desired behavior is what we mean by *shaping* of behavior. Shaping is particularly important when instructions alone are not adequate, as with motor skills or with people who cannot use language well. The instructor dispensing reinforcers must know

Training elephants is an ancient use of operant conditioning procedures. (Photo by Bill Henry)

in advance what behavior is finally wanted and the approximations necessary to get it.

behavior chaining

A complicated job may involve many small steps which have to be learned one at a time, then chained together. Manufacture of electronic equipment may require many different components to be assembled and soldered. Each step is learned, then all are put together in proper sequence. Breaking down a complicated task into part-tasks is often an important aspect of training.

maintaining behavior: schedules of reinforcement

A schedule of reinforcement is some rule for presenting reinforcers. We may initially reward a child with praise every time she says "please," but we can progressively reduce the reinforcement and still maintain the behavior. Animals and people learn to perform different ways on different schedules, but to see the uniformities of behavior on different schedules we may have to keep records over a period of hours or days. This led Skinner to devise the *cumulative recording* system.

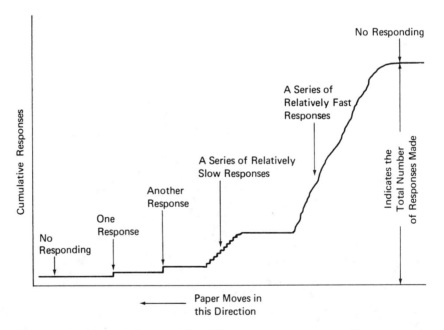

figure 2–4. A cumulative recording. The pen moves a step up the paper each time a response is made. The steeper the line, the faster is the rate of responding. A line parallel to the baseline indicates no responding at all. (From Hergenhahn, 1976. Used with permission of Prentice-Hall, Inc. Englewood Cliffs, N.J.)

Cumulative Recording. The frequency of a given response over time is measured on a cumulative recorder as illustrated in Figure 2–4. A pen makes a small step across continuously unrolling paper every time a response occurs. Rapid responding, pressing a lever for example, produces a steep line across the paper. No responding just leaves a horizontal line. A "blip mark" shows when a reinforcer is given. Responses and reinforcers are often counted automatically.

For human research in natural settings, an observer may simply make a check mark to indicate that a response occurred in some particular time interval measured by stopwatch or clock. For example, the total number of a particular response made in a day may be counted and the cumulative curve extended over days. Figure 2–5 illustrates a simple hand-check system. There are many different schedules of reinforcement, but four basic ones are illustrative.

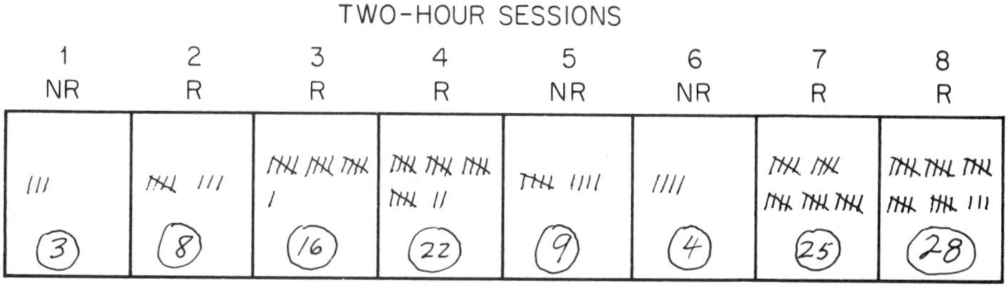

TWO-HOUR SESSIONS

1 NR	2 R	3 R	4 R	5 NR	6 NR	7 R	8 R
///	ᵀᕼᕼ ///	ᵀᕼᕼ ᵀᕼᕼ ᵀᕼᕼ /	ᵀᕼᕼ ᵀᕼᕼ ᵀᕼᕼ ᵀᕼᕼ //	ᵀᕼᕼ ////	////	ᵀᕼᕼ ᵀᕼᕼ ᵀᕼᕼ ᵀᕼᕼ ᵀᕼᕼ	ᵀᕼᕼ ᵀᕼᕼ ᵀᕼᕼ ᵀᕼᕼ ᵀᕼᕼ ///
③	⑧	⑯	㉒	⑨	④	㉕	㉘

figure 2–5. Hypothetical hand-check recording of behavior during times when the behavior is rewarded and not rewarded. The tallies refer to the frequency of times a person initiates conversation in a 2-hour period when attention is paid and when the person is ignored. (R = reinforced NR = nonreinforced.) The effects of reward on acquisition and extinction are clear.

Fixed Ratio (FR) Schedule. Here, behavior is reinforced every so-many times it occurs. A reward may be given after every fifth response, or tenth, or twentieth. Large ratios are built up gradually so that the person does not extinguish while waiting for the next reinforcer. A shop worker paid for every twenty widgets assembled would be working on a fixed ratio schedule. The FR schedule generates a highly reliable behavior pattern. The person (or animal) makes a fast run of responses to get a reinforcer, then pauses before beginning the next run. This response pattern might develop with a door-to-door salesperson who, knowing that every twentieth stop would be a sale, would make twenty fast calls, then take a break before the next twenty. Figure 2–6 shows this pattern of behavior, along with those for the other basic schedules.

Variable Ratio (VR) Schedule. This schedule delivers reinforcers unpredictably. Our salesperson would more likely learn that a sale is made after an *average* of twenty calls, but the actual number of calls between sales may range from one to thirty. This schedule produces a high response rate with little pause between reinforcement and the next response. (The very next

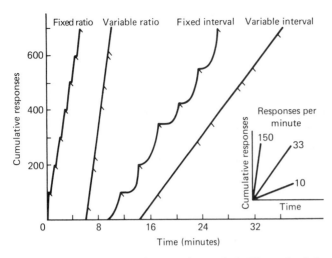

figure 2–6. Stylized cumulative response records for each of the four basic schedules of reinforcement discussed in the text. Each has its characteristic pattern and relative rate of responding compared to the others. The inset figure to the lower right is used to estimate overall response rates for the curves. (Adapted from Williams, 1973. Used with permission.)

call might be another sale.) The schedule is demanding, however, and may often be considered unpleasant.

Fixed Interval (FI) Schedule. Ratio schedules are built on the number of responses made, but interval schedules depend on elapsed time since the last reinforcement. The first response made at the end of a set time, such as five minutes, is reinforced. No further response is reinforced until another five minutes has passed. The characteristic response pattern is a slow rate of response during the early part of each interval, gradually increasing until the end of the interval. This is called a *scallop* on the record. People often put things off to the last minute, then work hard to meet a reinforcing deadline. A teacher who only checked work at the end of the hour would have students on this schedule.

Variable Interval (VI) Schedule. Here, the time between reinforced responses is unpredictable. Behavior is steady but slower than with the VR schedule. An example might be a department store clerk waiting for customers to appear; the time between sales is unpredictable.

Other Schedules. We could arbitrarily set up any schedule we wished. Two schedules of special interest, however, involve selective reinforcement for either very fast responding or for very slow responding. The 100-yard dash illustrates the former, and bomb-defusing illustrates the latter.

partial reinforcement and extinction

The partial reinforcement procedures used with schedules lead to more prolonged responding during extinction. Generally, the larger the ratio of responses to reinforcers, the more responses given during extinction.

This partial reinforcement effect is one of psychology's more venerable generalizations, but research with humans has challenged its generality. In gambling-type experiments, people sometimes continue to respond longer after 100 percent reinforcement than after partial reinforcement. Julian Rotter (1966) has suggested that individuals who believe a situation is under their *personal control* respond longer after 100 percent than partial reinforcement. People who believe that an event is due more to luck than skill show the regular extinction effect (more responses following partial reinforcement).

arranging the environment to change behavior

We can partly control behavior by rewards or punishment but we can also arrange the environment to make behavior more or less likely. In large lecture rooms the seats are usually attached permanently to the floor and face the front. This encourages watching the instructor. In a small class we may sit in a circle, to encourage discussion among the participants. The author was in a particular room recently where work was being done on the venting system and there were two holes about one-foot square in the floor. Everybody was told to watch out for the holes. It would have been a simpler safety procedure to control behavior by moving a table over the holes so no one could step into them.

token economies

Operant conditioning has been applied to entire institutions like schools and correctional institutions by setting up token economies, which are miniature economic systems. Tokens are earned for specific behaviors according to some

system. These can be periodically traded for something else, such as candy, magazines, or privileges.

To set up a token economy one must do the following:

1. Determine what the people in the system are doing *now,* before setting up the system.
2. Determine what the present rewards and punishers are.
3. Specify which behaviors are to be rewarded or punished in the future.
4. Consistently reward or punish the specified behaviors.

A problem for any such system is that there may be *unprogrammed* reinforcers, provided unintentionally by staff or other members of the group. Gelfland, Gelfland and Dobson (1967) compared nurses, nursing assistants, and other patients in a psychiatric hospital for how often they rewarded or ignored desirable and undesirable patient behaviors. The results are summarized in Table 2–2. The patients were actually better behavioral engineers than the nursing assistants. Overall, inappropriate behaviors were reinforced by the staff about 25 to 30 percent of the time and appropriate behaviors were reinforced about two-thirds of the time. The problem with these unprogrammed reinforcers was pointed out and a more consistent reinforcement program was instituted. Token economies are certainly not cure-alls, but they can reduce many day-to-day problems.

the hidden costs of reward

Though bigger and better rewards often lead to more reliable and persistent behavior, there is also increasing evidence to the contrary. Specifically,

table 2-2

frequency with which appropriate and inappropriate behaviors were rewarded in a psychiatric hospital. The nurses rewarded both kinds of behavior relatively frequently, and other patients showed the greatest discrimination in what kinds of behaviors to reward.

source of reward	behaviors	
	Inappropriate	Appropriate
Nurses	39%	68%
Nursing Assistants	30%	44%
Other Patients	12%	56%

(Adapted from Gelfland, Gelfland, and Dobson, Unprogrammed reinforcement of patients' behavior in a mental hospital. *Behaviour Research and Therapy*, 1967, 5, 201–7.)

if a person is already interested in an activity for its own sake, like a hobby, external reward may reduce this activity. This is called the effect of extrinsic reward on intrinsic motivation.

Deci (1978) makes these conclusions:

1. External rewards *facilitate* behavior when (a) they primarily convey information that a person is competent and the rewards are not perceived as controlling behavior, and (b) they are given for routine, well-learned activities.
2. External rewards tend to *impair* performance when (a) they are obvious and given for activities already of high interest, and (b) they are related to such "open-ended" activities as problem solving.

In industry there are some jobs where external rewards will facilitate behavior. These jobs are well-learned, routine, and perhaps boring. They are not of high intrinsic interest. In jobs where the work itself is more interesting and variable, as well as permitting more freedom of activity, external rewards

YEAH, HE USED TO BE REALLY ENTHUSIASTIC ABOUT RUNNING, AND THEN HE STARTED GETTING PAID FOR IT.

may not be as beneficial. Opportunity to set up one's own job and to get involved in challenging projects may be relatively more important.

People are often not striving for predetermined rewards, but they *discover* rewards as they go along. Highly creative artists, for example, do not have preset notions about what a picture should look like before they start. Rather, they change their ideas as the picture progresses. Similarly, small children may pile blocks on top of each other with no idea of what they are trying to build, but they are "reinforced" at various steps by characteristics of the block tower that appeal to them. The motivation is not only intrinsic, but is also discovered moment by moment (Csikszentmihalyi, 1978).

Jerry M. Burger (1980) reported an experiment emphasizing the relationship between perceived control and external reward. He argued that "overjustification" (payment) for doing an intrinsically interesting task would be more detrimental for people with a high desire for control over the environment than for those with low desire. The reasoning is that pay would indicate they were not themselves in control. His results are shown in Figure 2–7: Those with high desire for control showed less interest in the task when paid $2 for doing it than when not paid at all.

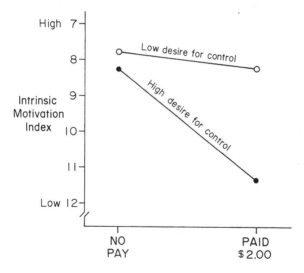

figure 2–7. Effect of paying subjects with high and low desire for control on intrinsic interest in the task. (From Burger, 1980, doctoral dissertation.)

Punishment

definition

One view of punishment is that it is the delivery of an aversive (unpleasant) stimulus following a response. The stimulus might be a physical blow or a verbal reprimand. But what *we* think is aversive for someone else may not in fact be so. The second view, then, is that a punisher is any stimulus that reduces the frequency of a response. This is the view that Skinner, for example, holds. Stimuli which are reinforcing to some people (such as loud rock music for a teenager) may be punishing to someone else (the parents). We will generally assume this second view.

finding something better to do: the alternative response hypothesis

Punishment does not actually seem to *eliminate* undesirable behaviors. Rather, a person (or animal) stops the punished activity as a means of escaping the punishment or avoiding it in the future. This inhibition is reinforced by termination of the punisher. To be most effective, punishment should be followed by the reinforcement of some *other* behavior. A child who is punished for fighting, but taught no other ways to settle arguments, may continue fighting. Training and reinforcing for nonaggressive behaviors would be more productive.

stimulus factors in punishment

Intensity. Generally, the stronger the punishing stimulus, the more suppressive the punishment. We usually assume that large court fines are more punishing than small ones.

Delay. Punishment is more effective if delivered *immediately* after a response. With a long delay the punishment may become associated with the wrong behavior or only with the punishing agent. If a parent spanks a child hours after the misbehavior, the child may learn that getting caught is bad, not the misdeed, and may just become hostile toward the parent rather than stop the behavior.

Adaptation. Punishment should be consistent, but not so frequent that a person gets used to it and the punishment only generates hostility.

Punishment as a Cue for Reward. If punishment is closely followed by reward it may become a secondary reinforcer, a cue for reward. Azrin and Holz (1966) found that if pigeons were rewarded for pecking at a disk only when being shocked, they also pecked more during extinction if they were shocked than if not shocked. The shock had become a cue for food reward.

Punishment as Reward. Remember Brer Rabbit's plea to Brer Fox: "Please don't throw me in the briar patch." Brer Rabbit convinced his adversary that the briar patch was punishing, but it actually was just where he wanted to be. A child who is sent to his or her room for punishment might happily watch television there. At best, in such a situation we are mixing reward and punishment and nullifying the punishment.

response factors in punishment

If a hyperactive child were punished for being disruptive, the punishment might increase activity even more and therefore be self-defeating. Punishment should lead to behavior distinctly different from the punished behavior. The hyperactive child might be forced to sit quietly for a brief period, then rewarded for this.

further punishment phenomena

Self-punitive Behavior: Masochism in Rats and People. Some people persist in behaving against their own apparent self-interest. Why are some people so cruel to others that they themselves are ignored, despised, and insulted? Why do some people obtain sexual pleasure from pain? We cannot answer these questions completely, but we can get some perspective on them.

We might assume that such behavior is abnormal and that the individual has no control over it. There are disordered brains which do not seem to follow reasonable patterns of thought and action. (See chapter twelve, Aggression.)

It is also possible that there are rewards for the punished behavior which are not obvious to others. Suppose Johnny is anxious in school because he is a poor student. To improve his own status he belittles better students. This may briefly reduce his own feeling of inadequacy but is not permanent. His obnoxious behavior is chided, and he becomes all the more anxious and belittles others even more.

To interrupt this cycle, there are two methods which might be effective separately, or used together. First, reduce the causes of anxiety, feelings of inferiority in this example. Second, provide an alternative by teaching Johnny more acceptable behaviors. Perhaps he has particular artistic or athletic skills which can be developed. If his self-concept can be bolstered by being rewarded for other activities, he may be less anxious about his academic situation.

This anxiety interpretation is also apparent in some religious practices. If a person feels guilty for some transgression, self-induced punishment may reduce the feelings of guilt. The guilt may be more unpleasant than the punishment, so the individual comes out ahead, psychologically speaking. Just how a person would deal with such situations would depend heavily on his or her religious training.

Learned Helplessness. A person who feels that any activity will end in failure may feel helpless and not do anything. A worker may feel so inadequate that he or she will not tackle any new job, even where success might objectively seem almost certain. This is *learned helplessness* (Seligman, 1975).

In the first experiments on this problem, dogs experienced unavoidable and inescapable electric shocks. Then they were put into a new situation where shock could be escaped and avoided by a simple movement. But about 90 percent of the animals did not even try to get away from shock, much less learn to respond before it occurred. Control animals with no prior experience of inescapable shock readily learned the response. The experimental animals were obviously fearful but apparently so resigned to their fate that they did not attempt anything but cowering.

In analogous experiments, people work on such problems as impossible anagrams. After this experience of failure a person is given a different problem, such as putting colored blocks together to make a particular design. Subjects with the prior failure do more poorly on the second task than do subjects without the failure experience.

It is tempting to extend these results to entire social groups. In the case of American blacks, systematically excluded from good jobs, education, and housing, what kind of behavior might be expected at school or on the job? The most strident advocates of social change are often not the "downtrodden masses," but the well-educated and relatively affluent people who have experienced considerable success.

What about employees who seem unwilling to tackle anything new because success seems hopeless? We might begin by rewarding the individual for doing whatever he or she can already do, then shape behavior for more complicated activities by reinforcing successive approximations to what we want. Rewarding successful behavior is more likely to be the key here, rather than just telling somebody "Go ahead, you can do it."

Verbal Learning and Memory

nature of learning and memory

To determine what a person has learned we must find out how much he or she remembers. If you explain your office filing system to a new secretary,

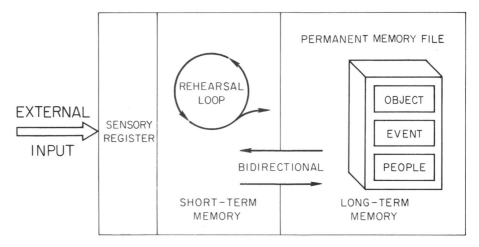

figure 2–8. Basic information processing system: Sensory information store, short-term memory with rehearsal loop, and long-term memory. External information enters the sensory information store where it is selected and passed on to the short-term store. In the short-term store, it is processed for immediate use and/or permanent storage in long-term memory. Note the bidirectionality of information flow between the short-term and the long-term storage areas. (From Meyer, 1979, p. 331. Used with permission of publisher.)

how do you know if the new employee has learned your office filing system? The person has to do something which indicates memory, such as using the system properly. Psychologists usually think about verbal learning and memory in terms of information processing, with a model like that in Figure 2–8. The model emphasizes storage and retrieval of information, with problems coming at either place.

The Tip of the Tongue Phenomenon. Suppose you are asked who starred in a familiar movie, say *The Godfather.* You may be confident you know the answer, but cannot actually give it. It is "on the tip of your tongue," and you immediately recognize the names when you hear them. There are some things, however, that we never knew and *know* that we never knew. For example, who was the American League batting champion in 1928? In the first example, there is a memory which we cannot quite retrieve. In the second example, there never was a memory. We have given the examples as if we always know what we have previously learned, but this is not the case. Sometimes we cannot retrieve things and think we never knew them either, but they "come back." We can have failure to *demonstrate* learning for three reasons, then: (1) something was actually not learned, (2) we have the memory but cannot retrieve it immediately, or (3) there is an actual loss of a particular memory.

three kinds of memory: sensory, short term, and long term

Sensory Memory. An event may occur suddenly and we think we have grasped it, but the memory fades very quickly. Many demonstrations have shown that witnesses to a prearranged "crime" do not accurately recall details of the events that happened or of the people involved. We may sometimes be rightly suspicious of someone whose memory seems "too good."

In the laboratory, subjects are briefly shown (0.1 second) a matrix of numbers and letters similar to those in Figure 2–9. They are then immediately asked to write all the numbers and letters they can from the matrix. About four of the twelve are done accurately. If the subjects are immediately asked to write down some particular row which is designated *after* they have seen the matrix, they can accurately recall any row. They must have very briefly remembered all twelve items, but only four can be written down because the rest are lost while the person is writing down those four. Such sensory memory lasts about a second. It seems to be a kind of afterimage of the stimuli which lingers in the sensory receptor (for example, the eye or ear) itself.

Short Term Memory. When you look up a telephone number for the first time you can probably remember it just about long enough to dial it. This kind of short term memory seems to involve some temporary activity in the brain, not just the receptors. Peterson and Peterson (1959) had subjects look at a nonsense syllable (a meaningless conglomerate of letters, such as XEC), say the letters, then count backwards by threes from an assigned three-digit number after the syllable was removed from sight. The counting was to prevent the subjects from rehearsing the syllable. After eighteen seconds the subjects could remember only about 20 percent of the syllables, using multiple repetitions of the experimental task with different syllables. Figure 2–10 shows the curve of retention (memory) for time intervals between zero and eighteen seconds. Without rehearsal the syllables were not getting into memory very well.

There apparently is a kind of temporary storage before memory is

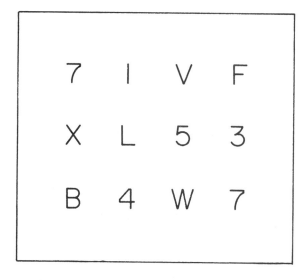

figure *2–9.* Number/letter matrix typical of those used in the study of sensory memory (see text for discussion).

If the secretary is interrupted for a few seconds she is likely to forget the number before dialing it.

"transferred" into permanent storage. Following accidental brain damage, people can often accurately recall events from years past but forget things that happened only a few moments earlier. This is called *retrograde amnesia*. The accident apparently impaired some mechanism for making memories permanent. A similar phenomenon occurs with senility and has been studied considerably in animal laboratories.

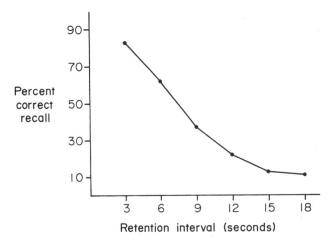

figure 2–10. Short term memory as a function of time interval between stimulus presentation and request for recall. Subjects are kept from rehearsing during the time interval. (Adapted from Peterson and Peterson, 1959. Used with permission.)

Long Term Memory. Long term memory is relatively permanent, although forgetting does occur. How memories are stored for years is not well understood (perhaps it involves a protein change in the brain), but the amount of information stored is great. Answer this question as quickly as possible: What is your mother's *middle* name? You probably answered this almost instantly even though you may not have thought about it for years. It has been estimated that we can store about one quadrillion items in memory (that's a 1 with twelve zeros following; Fry, 1972), yet we can almost instantly pull a correct memory from storage if we have the right cues.

Tulving (1972) has distinguished *episodic* and *semantic* memories. Episodic memories are for specific events or episodes, such as particular names or places. Some people are good at this (as shown in trivia quizzes) while others have difficulty with specific memories. Semantic memory is more abstract, involving such things as *rules* for grammar or mathematics. For example, a brain damaged patient was lightly stuck with a pin upon shaking hands with her doctor. A few minutes later the patient refused to shake hands again, explaining that "Somebody might stick you with a pin." "Did this ever happen to you?" "No, but it *might.*" The patient forgot the event (episodic memory) but remembered the "rule" (semantic memory).[1] Normal people show considerable variation in their capacities for episodic and semantic memories.

intent to remember

Memory is better when we *try* to remember something. This may partly be due to *attention.* We may hear people's names when we are introduced and immediately forget them because we were not paying attention. Of course, we do learn things without specifically trying to, but we generally remember better if we are trying to.

context and memory

The more cues we have for a particular memory, the easier to retrieve it. The game "twenty questions" involves obtaining retrieval cues, starting with very general questions, and becoming more specific. We can get considerable information from the yes-no answers permitted in the game. For example:

Entertainer?	Yes
Male?	Yes
Living?	Yes
Movies?	Yes
Handsome?	Yes
Blond?	Yes
Answer?	_____

A "no" answer is often as informative as a "yes" answer. If a person is not a female, then it must be a male, and so on.

A practical application of context is in studying for an exam. If you study in the same place you are going to take the exam you have a good set of context stimuli to help you during the exam. You might associate a bulletin

---

[1] I am indebted to Frank B. Wood for this example.

board with one fact, a table with another, and so on. It might be helpful to wear the same clothes to study and to take the test.

State Dependent Learning. A task learned while a person is in one internal state (hunger, for example) is better recalled if we are in the same state at recall time. Information acquired while under the influence of a drug may be better recalled under the influence of the same drug. Alcoholics may forget the location of liquor bottles when sober but recall their hiding place when intoxicated.

Training programs, then, should resemble as closely as possible the situation in which the knowledge is to be used. We sometimes distinguish learning "in theory" and "practical" learning. The difference is whether or not the same behaviors are learned in the class as are needed in the practical situation and whether the same cues are present in the two situations. Cues would be both external (context) and internal (including feelings of "pressure" from a situation). There is a theatre story about the actor whose only line in the play was, "Hark, I hear the cannon roar." He practiced his line faithfully, but not on the stage. The night of the show, the cannon *did* roar and the actor cried out, "What the hell was *that?*"

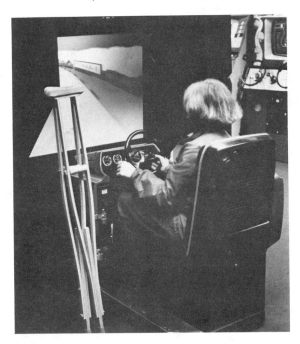

This arcade game is much like training devices which simulate natural driving conditions as closely as possible.
(Photo by Bill Henry)

transfer of training

Does previous learning help or hinder our learning and memory for new events? The answer depends on what we previously learned and what we are to learn later. We can have positive, negative, or zero transfer of training.

Positive Transfer. This occurs best when a previously-learned behavior is required in a situation similar to the situation in which the behavior was learned. Positive transfer is demonstrated if the new learning occurs faster than the previous learning. Put a tennis racket in the hands of a good baseball player and you are likely to have an excellent net player in doubles even though the person may be incapable of hitting a ground stroke.

Negative Transfer. The harmful effects of transfer are strongest when a familiar situation calls for a new response. In World War II there were many aircraft training accidents due to "pilot error." The pilot error turned out to be due to changing aircraft designs so that men in the familiar environment of a cockpit had to make different responses to perform some function. They would automatically pull a lever to adjust the flaps, and, say, the wheels might come up. The controls had been moved around.

In verbal learning, negative transfer is evident in language study. Different languages may have *cognates* (words with very similar spelling or pronunciation which mean the same thing in both languages) and *false cognates* (words that look the same but have different meanings). There is strong positive transfer with cognates and negative transfer with false cognates. For example the German word *Hund* is readily learned as meaning *dog* because of its similarity to the English word *hound.* On the other hand, the German word *bei* is a preposition pronounced like the English word *by* but it never has the same meaning as *by.* Nevertheless, there is a strong tendency for students to incorrectly translate *bei* as *by.*

Zero Transfer. This occurs when neither stimuli or responses are related to specific preceding events. Hitting a tennis ball is unrelated to learning arithmetic.

forgetting

Decay of the Memory Trace. A memory trace is some change in the nervous system following a learning situation. Forgetting apparently occurs with short term memory because the memory trace never became permanent, or never got "shifted" into long term storage. Long term memories seem to involve some growth process involving cells in the brain. An analogy would be loosely twisting two wires together to make a temporary electrical connection (short term) as opposed to soldering them together for a long term connection. As mentioned previously, it is suspected that the nervous system "solder" is some protein. Some forgetting apparently can occur because the "connection" becomes bad, that is, the "permanent" memory trace simply "decays" in some way.

Motivated Forgetting. We sometimes do not remember things because we are motivated *not* to remember them. It may be unpleasant to remember that we owe somebody money, so we forget it. Amnesia can occur after a psychologically very painful event (such as the death of a loved one) as well as after physically traumatic events (such as a blow on the head). Freud's concept of repression, related to anxiety (see Chapter Six) concerns such motivated forgetting.

Interference. The bulk of our forgetting of long term memories is due to interference from other things we have learned. When earlier-learned things interfere with recall of later-learned things, it is called *proactive interference.* Conversely, later-learned things can also interfere with the memory of earlier-learned things, and this is called *retroactive interference.* The greater the similarity of the learned items the greater the interference. This leads to the very practical suggestion that if you are studying several different subjects, you should study the most *dissimilar* ones close together in time, not the similar ones. This reduces interference due to similarity.

The Serial Position Effect. If we learn a list of things by rote memory (without any particular organization) we do not recall the middle of the list as well as either the beginning or the end. It is advantageous therefore, if feasible, to learn a list in different sequences to overcome the serial position effect. There are also other memory "tricks" to be discussed shortly.

some other learning phenomena

Sleep Learning. There are periodic revivals of the notion of learning during sleep, mostly generated by people who want to sell such apparatus as tape recorders. Laboratory studies fail to find such sleep learning if a person is in a clearly-defined state of sleep (as shown by brain waves). The only "sleep learning" seems to occur when a person is *not* really quite asleep. It is probably much more efficient to learn while *fully* awake and then sleep at night without disturbance from a tape recorder.

Massed versus Distributed Practice. Practice, spaced with rest intervals, in either motor skills or verbal learning, is more *efficient* than massed trials (going over something many times in a brief time period, like cramming for an exam). It is more efficient to study, allow some time for it to "sink in," and then go over the material again. In a crisis, however, the rule is clear: Cramming is better than not studying at all. Forgetting is more rapid after cramming, however; much of the material probably never makes it to long term storage.

Active versus Passive Learning. Many students do poorly on exams, then say "But I understood it when I read it." Several of the factors already discussed might be involved, but an additional one is *active participation*. It is helpful to read a small amount of material (passive learning), then rephrase the material *in your own words* to make sure you understand it (active participation).

The SQ3R Method of Learning. SQ3R means:

- *Survey.* Skim the material for an overview, a general framework on which to hang specific bits of information. Look at chapter titles and major headings, for example.
- *Question.* Ask questions about the material, such as "What are the main points of this chapter?"
- *Read.* Go through the material for details which you can now relate to your prior survey and questions.
- *Recite.* This is active participation again. It helps you understand the material and gives practice in *retrieving* the material from memory, invaluable for later quizzes.
- *Review.* Go back and look over the important points you have found in the previous steps. This rehearses you on what you already know and brings to your attention that which you do not know.

memory tricks (mnemonic devices)

A memory "trick" is a strategy by which you can remember things better. It does not involve "faking it" as the word *trick* might imply. Philippe Falkenberg (1981) has a good review of many practical approaches to better memory. We shall discuss four here: chunking, sequencing, "Galton's Walk," and memory categories.

Chunking. About seven unrelated items of information is the limit of what we can momentarily grasp. For example, if we are briefly shown a random dot pattern, such as:

we can instantly count the number of dots up to about seven, plus or minus two. Beyond this number we lose count. Or, if we are asked to remember a string of numbers, like a telephone number, about seven is also what we can reliably handle.

However, there are methods of *organization* of material which help us. For example, if we saw

```
  .   .          .   .   .
  .   .   .  or  .   .   .
  .   .          .   .   .   .
                 .   .   .   .
```

we could readily recognize nine or sixteen dots because we could also identify the nature of the organization. When we put things together by some system we are doing what George Miller (1956) called chunking. Suppose we are to memorize the following sequence of numbers:

149217761941

Upon a single hearing we would probably have trouble remembering the twelve numbers. If we could get them organized (chunked) properly we could memorize them instantly: Thus

1492   /   1776   /   1941

But even without such auspicious numbers as these three historical dates, chunking still makes the task easier. The random number sequence

219347619245

is more easily remembered if we break it up into

219   /   347   /   619   /   245

Sequencing Items: Thirty days hath September. . . . The trouble with memorizing a typical list is that the items are unrelated. It is very easy to remember the following ten words:

THE LITTLE BOY WENT TO THE STORE FOR ICE CREAM.

It is much more difficult to remember these ten:

paper phone stove horse film bread file tree lid coat.

If we could make a story of the second list, it would also be easier to remember. If the list is read to you slowly (about five seconds between words) you can do this. For example:

I was reading the PAPER when the PHONE by the STOVE rang, a call about my HORSE. I got some FILM and BREAD from the FILE by the TREE, removed the LID and got my COAT.

The more vivid the visual imagery you can get into your story the better the memory. If you were studying at home and had time to make up a story or sentence it might be much more interesting than this example.

It is also common to use the first letters of words to form a sentence or story. Virtually every engineer knows the color coding of electrical resistors by this sentence: Bad boys rape our young girls but Violet gives willingly. The sequence refers to the color bands around resistors which identify the values of the resistors. The colors are black, brown, red, orange, yellow, green, blue, violet, gold, and silver (white), and there is a logical sequence of numbers corresponding to these. Medical students make up similar sentences to remember zones in the body which, like the resistor color code, have no inherent organization among them, nor, as is obvious from this example, do they necessarily have to be in good taste.

Galton's Walk. Francis Galton was a pioneer psychologist primarily interested in differences among people. His work was a forerunner of psychological testing. He was also, however, very interested in memory and devised a "trick" which has since become known as "Galton's Walk." Galton would memorize things by associating them with places. He would memorize the locations of businesses in a town, for example, so he had their names and locations down pat. Then he would memorize a list of items by associating each item with a spatial location. This would be like learning the store locations in a shopping mall and then sticking an item into each store in the mall. Many "memory experts" use Galton's approach.

A variation on Galton's trick is to learn a numbered set of visual images, such as the following:

One-Bun
Two-Shoe
Three-Tree
Four-Door
Five-Hive
Six-Sticks
Seven-Heaven
Eight-Gate

Nine-Wine
Ten-Hen

Because of the rhymes, this can be learned by most people in a single presentation. With a particular *list* of items to be learned, then, the trick is to form visual images related to each of the ten rhymes. The numbers help us remember the rhymes (bun, shoe, etc.) and then bun, shoe, etc. help us remember the new list of items. Suppose we use the list from the previous section, but follow the One-Bun system. We would have

One-Bun PAPER   (We might visualize a piece of paper in a hamburger bun, or even better, eating a paper hamburger)
Two-Shoe PHONE   (We might think of a phone in a shoe)
Three-Tree STOVE   (stove holding wood from the tree)

Fill in your own images for the rest of the list.

Four-Door HORSE
Five-Hive FILM
Six-Sticks BREAD
Seven-Heaven FILE
Eight-Gate TREE
Nine-Wine LID
Ten-Hen COAT

As with sequencing, it is necessary to take a few seconds to establish each association, but the method is usually pretty effective. If you use the One-Bun, Two-Shoe set of association repeatedly you will eventually run into problems of interference because each of these cues will be for several memories. Galton therefore looked for new parts of towns to memorize, and you probably know several shopping centers as well as your home, or school, or workplace. You can also make up new rhymes besides One-Bun and Two-Shoe, such as One-Sun, Two-Blue, and so on.

Memory Categories. One final notion. In many of these memory tips we have assumed it necessary to remember items *in their original sequence.* Often this is *not* necessary. Consider the following set of words to be memorized:

HORSE TYPEWRITER COW DESK PENCIL GIRAFFE CHAIR KANGAROO

The nature of the list is such that we can see two major categories of things within the list, animals and office equipment. It is much easier to remember all the items by breaking the list, then, into two parts.

Animals	*Equipment*
Horse	Typewriter
Cow	Desk
Giraffe	Pencil
Kangaroo	Chair

Much of what we try to remember can be facilitated by sorting into categories. In language vocabulary we sort into nouns, verbs, adjectives, and other parts of speech. In biology we sort into plants and animals, then subcategories of these. Most textbooks have chapter headings, and the things in the chapters can be learned under these headings.

Imitation (Vicarious Learning, Observational Learning)

Much of our learning about rewards and punishments is indirect, or vicarious. We learn by observing others that certain behaviors are approved or disapproved. We then imitate the rewarded behaviors or suppress the punished ones. Imitation occurs with the higher primates (people and chimpanzees) and may occur with other intelligent mammals such as dogs. Only in the last twenty years have psychologists begun to study this phenomenon in depth, led largely by Albert Bandura (for example, 1977).

Bandura and his colleagues have shown, for example, that if children simply see a *model* (someone to be imitated) being rewarded for acting aggressively, the children are more aggressive in their own play. The models may be live people, films of people, or films of cartoon characters. The children often say and do the specific things they have seen in the models.

Once a behavior has been copied (imitated) its *persistence* depends on whether it is now rewarded or punished. The child who smokes or drinks in imitation of parents may be punished directly (by getting sick) as well as more indirectly (by getting caught and disciplined). The child would be less likely to smoke or drink very readily again unless there were other rewards such as peer approval which more than compensated for unpleasant potential consequences. On balance, we respond to net gains and losses (rewards and punishments) rather than just isolated rewards and punishments.

SUMMARY

1. *Learning* is involved in almost all behavior and is shown in a number of specific kinds of learning processes: classical conditioning, instrumental (operant) conditioning, human verbal learning and memory, and imitation.

2. *Classical conditioning* (also called Pavlovian after Ivan Pavlov) is learning based on the association of a neutral stimulus with an already meaningful stimulus.

3. *Acquisition* is learning the relationship between an unconditioned stimulus (UCS) and a conditioned stimulus (CS). A conditioned response (CR) to the CS replaces the original unconditioned response (UCR). *Stimulus generalization* occurs when a CR is elicited by a stimulus *similar* to the CS. *Extinction* is a decline in the conditioned response when the UCS is no longer paired with the CS. Following partial pairings of the CS and UCS, extinction is slower. *Discrimination* is learning to respond to the CS but not to other stimuli.

4. *Instrumental (operant) conditioning* is based on rewarding, punishing, or ignoring "voluntary" responses.

5. *Shaping* of behavior is done by selectively reinforcing (rewarding) *successive approximations* to the desired behavior.

6. *Schedules of reinforcement* are rules for presenting reinforcers. Four basic schedules are *fixed ratio, variable ratio, fixed interval,* and *variable interval.* Each schedule produces a particular pattern of behavior over time.

7. *Token economies* involve the application of operant conditioning techniques to *institutional* settings. They are miniature economic systems in which tokens are earned for specific behaviors and can be traded for commodities or privileges.

8. *Punishment* is the delivery of any stimulus after a response which reduces the occurrence of that response. To be most effective some *alternative* behavior should be positively reinforced after the undesirable behavior is punished. It is important not to accidentally reinforce some behavior that is to be punished.

9. *Learned helplessness* is the failure to act in situations where behavior could be rewarded, because of a past history of non-reward for behavior. This occurs with both animals and humans.

10. Learning and memory involve the *input, storage,* and *retrieval* of information. Failure of memory may be the result of not learning or of not being able to properly retrieve a memory.

11. There are three kinds of memory. *Sensory memory* is a rapidly fading after-image of a stimulus in the sense receptor itself. *Short term memory* is a temporary storage of memory in the brain, without *transfer* (on the presumed basis of neurochemical change) to permanent memory. *Long term memory* is relatively permanent and may be for specific events *(episodic memory)* or general rules and principles *(semantic memory).*

12. Previously learned material may aid, hinder, or have no effect on subsequent learning. This is called *transfer of training,* which may be positive, negative, or zero.

13. *Forgetting* of material that has been well learned may be due to a kind of "decay of the memory trace," motivation to forget unpleasant events, or interference from other things we have learned. Interference is the main reason for forgetting and involves ineffective retrieval cues.

14. Intent to learn, distribution of practice over time, active participation by the learner (such as reciting the material or writing it in one's own words), and multiple retrieval cues are important variables for learning.

15. *Mnemonic devices* are strategies to help remember. *Chunking, sequencing* of items, *Galton's Walk,* and *categorization* are all methods of organization that aid memory.

16. *Imitation* is a direct form of learning in which the behavior of a model is copied. The behavior is more likely to be copied if the imitator observes that the model is rewarded. If he or she sees that the model is punished, the observed behavior is less likely to be copied. In either case, learning takes place.

EXERCISES

1. How are classical conditioning and operant conditioning different? What principles do they share?

2. What would be an effective positive reinforcer for you right now? Would this always be equally as effective?

3. Praise can be a powerful reward. How do things like praise function as reinforcers?

4. Think of a particular reinforcer, either positive or negative. Discuss how variations in the amount and delay of receipt of this reinforcer would change its effectiveness. Examples might be coated candies and removal of TV privileges.

5. Develop a brief plan for shaping some specific behavior. What factors must you consider?

6. What are some of the schedules of reinforcement which influence your behavior? There are probably a number of these, for different behaviors. For example, you may be on one schedule of reinforcement for a particular class (such as this one), another schedule for work, and a third for entertainment. Describe how the various schedules affect your behavior in relation to the particular reinforcers involved.

7. What effect does partial reinforcement have on extinction?

8. Look around your classroom. What physical features of the setting encourage attentiveness and which are distracting? What about the place where you typically study?

9. What are some populations and settings in which token economies might be useful methods for behavior change? Can you think of some populations or settings where a token economy would *not* work? Why would it not work?

10. What activities are intrinsically motivating to you personally? Can you think of any hidden rewards involved? Have you ever even thought about this problem before?

11. Why is punishment without alternatives often ineffective? Consider your own childhood. Were there situations in which you were punished where alternatives were or were not available?

12. What are the different types of memory? Make a list of helpful hints for remembering, using conceptions from the chapter, such as serial position and active versus passive learning.

13. Construct a short hypothetical training program for some activity using as many retrieval cues as possible to facilitate learning.

14. How is interference related to learning? If you were studying for two important exams on the same day what types of interference would affect your recall?

15. What is a memory trace?

16. Use Galton's Walk to try to memorize the following list of flowers: daisy, rose, lilac, magnolia, carnation, and pansy. Now make up a set of numbered pairs of rhyming words, as in the chapter, that might be used to memorize the same list.

The Person: Motivation, Emotion, and Behavior Problems

3

Biological Motives: Survival

We now turn to some different aspects of biologically important motivation and theories related to these. These biological motives are fundamental to our survival as organisms on earth. In the next chapter we shall look at social motives, those learned in the context of our family and society. The social motives are extremely important to us, but are much more variable than the biological motives.

Nature of Motivation

Motivation is concerned with the goals we strive for—our *needs* or *wants*. Needed goals are those necessary for survival, such as food, water, and air. Wanted goals are not necessary for survival but powerfully affect us, even influencing our biologically needed goals. Thus, we may need food but we want steak. Many of the things we work for are wants, such as a TV set, a stereo, a fancy car, or a prestigious house. But our luxuries may seem to become necessities, psychologically if not biologically. A fancy car and big house may become necessary elements of life, and their loss may be psychologically greater for someone used to a large income than the loss of a job to someone at the poverty level.

Psychologists think of motives in terms of internal conditions of the body and external objects or events which a person strives to obtain (approach) or avoid. What a person will actually do is determined by the internal and external conditions *in combination.* For example, getting food is more pleasant when we are hungry and water is more pleasant when we are thirsty. Sex is partly stimulated by external objects, but the sex drive is stronger when certain hormone levels are high. Before we explore some of the relevant theories of motivation, we shall examine some biological motives.

Motivational Concepts

instinct

"Instinct" is often used by non-professionals to explain either animal or human behavior. Unfortunately it is now used in so many ways that it has been virtually dropped by biologists. Sometimes the word refers to particular behaviors which seem to be universal characteristics of a species, such as the homing of salmon, the nest-building of birds, and the web-weaving of spiders.

At other times it is used in the motivational sense, to refer to some internal *urge* or *drive* to do certain things, such as an urge to eat, or drink, or be aggressive, or have intercourse. It is this motivational use which is most appropriate to psychology.

Sigmund Freud argued that instincts have a *source, impetus, aim, and object.* Some kind of internal arousal (source), which has some degree of intensity (impetus), directs behavior into some activities rather than others (aim), and these activities cease when a goal (object) is obtained which reduces the initial arousal. Only the source and the impetus could be conceived as universal. Thus, it is pretty universal among animals that they get hungry in different degrees, but there are many ways of satisfying the hunger, mostly learned.

The only human behaviors which appear to be universal are a small number of reflexes, such as sucking and swallowing, which are indeed necessary for early survival in mammals. Few human actions occur invariably, and both psychologists and biologists look to more complex explanations for behavior than simply "instinct."

homeostasis

Homeostasis refers to the self-regulating (homeo = self; stasis = constancy) capacity of many organisms to keep their body machinery operating within narrow tolerances. When a machine runs out of oil, it may destroy itself, and when it runs out of fuel it stops. The human body, like that of many other organisms, has the remarkable capacity to make self-adjustments so that it is not destroyed and doesn't stop. Body temperature, blood sugar level, water and mineral content, to name just a few things, are kept within remarkably small tolerances of what the body must have. Small deviations, such as fever, or change in blood sugar level, indicate that something is wrong. A variety of diseases reflect the failure of some of these mechanisms. *Diabetes mellitis,* for example, is the failure of the body to utilize sugar properly; *diabetes insipidus* is the failure to regulate water properly.

The body can automatically maintain itself within these certain ranges, however, *only* if it has the necessary raw materials. Blood sugar level cannot be automatically maintained unless there is sugar stored in the liver. The body has detectors, internal receptors in the brain and elsewhere, that sample blood passing by and tell us that our blood sugar level or our water level is too low. We must then stir ourselves to *action,* seeking food or water.

Goal-striving behavior, for things such as food or water, involves perception, problem solving, and memory, as well as movement. The kinds of goals a person strives for, and the intensity of the effort, are the subject matter of the psychology of motivation. Like any other behavior, however, the things that determine it are many and complex, as we shall see now.

hunger

As we are longer without food more things may taste better to us, or at least we may be willing to eat a greater variety of things. Under extreme

Food related activities satisfy social needs as well as biological needs. (Photo by Bill Henry)

hunger, otherwise civilized human beings have been known to eat each other. Less dramatically, people lost in the wilderness are happy to eat bugs, worms, grubs, and lizards. One pair of air crash victims carefully doled out toothpaste to each other.

Few in this country ever really starve, but we nevertheless devote much effort to food-related activities. "Junk foods" are attractive to us because of their taste, appearance, smell, and crunchiness, not because of their nutrition, and a large industry is built around them. Such foods are often eaten under conditions, such as at parties, where hunger is not the primary reason for eating. Social factors play a very large role in our eating habits: The English like mutton much better than do Americans, and within the United States, there are regional differences, such as the standard practice in Southern restaurants of serving grits with breakfast.

Obesity and Starvation. Obesity is a problem of eating, and of motivation, but it is also a social problem and a health problem. Obese individuals are generally considered less attractive than non-obese individuals, they are actually less likely to receive job promotions, and on the whole they have lower annual incomes than non-obese individuals. There are, of course, many individual exceptions. Even more seriously, obesity is related to high blood pressure, heart attacks, and miscellaneous other health problems brought on by the fact that the internal machinery of a larger body has to do more work to keep that body properly fed, watered, and at the right temperature. These reasons alone are sufficient to be concerned with obesity, and psychological research has blossomed in this area recently.

Obesity and Responsiveness to External Cues. Considerable research on obesity, largely pioneered by Stanley Schacter and Judith Rodin (1974), pointed toward the notion that obese individuals are relatively more responsive to *external* cues than to *internal* cues. For example:

1. Obese individuals are more sensitive to external *time* cues for eating and less sensitive to internal cues ("feeling hungry") than are average weight individuals. Obese people are more likely to eat when the clock says they should, regardless of when or how much they last ate.

2. Obese individuals tend to react more to *taste* or other properties of foods than do average weight people. Compared to the average, obese people show an exaggerated increase of consuming good-tasting foods and an exaggerated decrease in eating poor-tasting foods.

3. Though obese individuals eat more than their normal-sized neighbors, they are less willing to *work* for food. In one experiment, average-weight individuals were equally likely to eat shelled or unshelled almonds. Of the obese subjects, however, 95 percent ate the shelled almonds. Only one of twenty subjects ate the almonds they had to shell themselves. In another observational study, it was found that about 15 percent of average weight customers used chopsticks in New York City Chinese restaurants, but only about 5 percent of obese patrons used chopsticks, which presumably requires more effort.

Since it appears that obese people respond relatively more to external food cues (taste, texture, temperature, time, social conditions, effort), a major factor in holding down weight should be to avoid food cues. At the same time, making it more effortful to eat should also be helpful. Just keeping track of how much you eat is also a big help in controlling food intake. As with cigarette smoking, people often do not realize how frequently they eat, if food is readily available.[1]

Behavior Therapy for Obesity. A *behavioral* weight control program (as opposed to a medical one) involves gaining new stimulus control over eating. We shall briefly state some general principles. First, the obese person determines a baseline of actual eating behavior by recording each time he or she consumes food and noting the circumstances. Second, eating is restricted to certain times and places, making it readily identifiable (no accidental eating) and more effortful. For example, one might agree to eat only three meals a day and only sitting at a table set for a meal (no casual snacking). Third, a close record of weight is kept, with a particular goal for so much reduction each week. The person is reinforced partly by seeing the reduction, as well as by praise from the behavior therapist. Sometimes a contract is established so that the patient has to pay a penalty if the weight loss goal is not met. Usually, the patient puts up a certain amount of money at the beginning and some of it is donated to charity if the goal is not met. To get all of his or her money back the patient has to meet all the goals. Often, groups of patients meet

_____

[1] Rodin (1981) has recently brought the internal-external difference into serious question, however.

periodically and have the opportunity to reinforce each other. Any specific weight control program might differ somewhat from what is described here, but the general principles are the same and such programs have been found to be quite effective.

Self-Starvation. A clinical condition called *anorexia nervosa* ("nervous starvation") sometimes occurs with humans, mainly young females. This is self-induced starvation, sometimes to the point of death. Medical treatment, other than maintenance on glucose injections, is seldom of help. There are some psychological therapies which have had considerable success, however. These therapies depend primarily on the fact that the anorexic patient can often be induced to eat by rewarding her for eating. Effective rewards are attention, conversation, opportunity to interact with others, and opportunity for physical exercise. This last is especially interesting since, for obvious reasons, the anorexic patient is physically very weak. The logic of this kind of therapy is that the anorexic patient has in the past been rewarded for *not eating,* by getting attention, for example. She may not be aware that she is doing this. The treatment strategy then is to reverse the reward situation, to give attention or other reward only when the patient *does* eat.

Specific Hungers. Most animals and people show *specific hungers* for particular kinds of food substances. Some animals, indeed, have such specific hungers that they will eat *nothing but* certain foods. (For example, koala bears eat only eucalyptus leaves.) More familiar is the fact that salt begins to taste better to those on low-salt diets, and the dieter would eat more salt if not prohibited. Children with mineral deficiencies may eat chalk, plaster, or leaded paint which can be lethal to them. Specific hungers have also been reported for proteins and some vitamins.

Some specific hungers (probably salt, for example) may be due to built-in biological mechanisms. This makes reasonable biological sense because salt is necessary for such important functions as proper nerve activity and proper maintenance of body water. In other instances we may learn food preferences. It has been shown with animals, many of which have food preferences in common with those of humans, that

1. Infants prefer foods that their mothers ate during pregnancy.
2. Animals prefer foods their mother ate while nursing them; apparently because some aspect of the taste was present in the mother's milk.
3. Foods associated with illness are avoided; this is true even though the illness may occur several hours after the food was eaten.
4. Foods which are otherwise not particularly preferred may become more preferred because they are *not* associated with illness. Thus, if an animal has a deficient diet which makes it feel ill, it will tend to eat other foods which are *not* associated with the illness. It may therefore "improve" its diet, get better, and show a preference for the new foods but not for the food that made it ill. This is called "learned safety."

In summary, then, searching for food, food preferences, and eating behavior are determined by a combination of built-in biological factors, individual experiences, and cultural heritage transmitted to individuals. Part of a cultural heritage, for example, may include much exposure to garlic and onions at an early age (an Italian diet) so that a person likes these tastes very much. Someone else may be exposed to hot peppers at an early age and like these very much, but not like garlic and onions. There are, thus, national differences in food preference.

thirst

Insufficient water is far more devastating than insufficient food. We have no way of storing large amounts of water in our bodies equivalent to the way we store glucose in the liver or in body fat. In a hot, dry desert, a human can perish from thirst within hours, a painful death accompanied by hallucinations and other mental aberrations. Whether or not we drink, there is a continual loss of water in perspiration, respiration, and urination. These losses are indeed smaller when we are short of water, through the action of several different body mechanisms, but none can be completely stopped and we inevitably get thirstier.

Under normal conditions, we get water from many sources, including food. Steak is more than half water; lettuce is almost all water. Some people claim they never drink water, but observation of their diet shows a large amount of water in food. (And sometimes they fail to mention they drink a lot of beer or wine!) We often forestall thirst by drinking when we are not thirsty such things as cokes, coffee, or beer. We can thus, either by eating or by drinking when not thirsty, consume an excess of water. This is usually reduced to the appropriate body level by urination, but it may be retained in excess if, for example, we eat a great deal of salt along with the fluid intake. One reason for salt-free diets is to reduce excess accumulated body water.

some physiology of hunger and thirst

Hunger and thirst are closely related in some ways. They share many of the same general areas of the brain for their control, and stimuli that increase food intake tend to decrease water intake and vice-versa. There are many specific differences, however.

Hunger. Electrical, chemical, or thermal stimulation of specific parts of the *hypothalamus* and *limbic system* of the brain arouse the urge to eat. Stimulation of other parts of these areas stops eating. Destruction of some areas in the brain leads to self-starvation and destruction of other areas leads to grotesque obesity. By the twin techniques of stimulation and destruction we thus can locate critical motivational areas of the brain.

Considerable evidence suggests that specialized cells in the hypothalamus of the brain are sensitive to changes in glucose concentration of the blood: When blood sugar is low electrical activity in these cells increases and stimulates food-getting or eating activity. A number of events normally stop eating. On such a short term basis as within a meal, eating may be inhibited by distention of the stomach or the small intestine, or by some kind of chemical released from the intestine which signals the brain to halt eating activity. On a longer term basis, it appears that some effect of stored body fat puts a limit on overall eating so that we do not overeat to the extent that is possible.

Thirst. There appear to be two main mechanisms to *stimulate* drinking. The first is an increase in relative salt concentration in body fluids as a result of body water loss. By inserting a hypodermic needle permanently into the hypothalamus it is possible to stimulate excessive drinking with tiny injections of salt solution. Second, pressure sensitive receptors in the vascular system appear to detect a reduction in volume of body water. With severe blood loss from hemorrhaging, people become very thirsty even though the concentration of blood has not changed. Through a complex chain of events, lower volume of body water leads to the release of a chemical called *angiotensin* into the hypothalamus, and this stimulates drinking even more effectively than does salt solution.

Drinking seems to be *terminated* mainly by cues from the intestine as to the amount of water consumed, and absorption of water from the intestine and a return of the body to its pre-thirst condition. This absorption of water into the blood stream can actually begin within a few seconds after drinking.

sex

Sexual behavior, in a general sense including nesting and care for the young, as well as mating, is determined in part by a number of different hormones. Prominent among these are *estrogen* and *progesterone* for females and *testosterone* for males. Menstrual cycles, among species that have them, and sexual receptivity in most species, are determined by these hormones. *Prolactin,* another female hormone, is important both for nursing of the young and for their caretaking. Injections of these hormones produce marked changes in the various sex-related behaviors. For example, injection of a male rat with estrogens may produce infant care-taking behavior typically seen in a female. Sensory stimuli (smell, in particular) as well as learning, are also involved in sexual behavior. Interpersonal attraction and sexual behavior are discussed more fully in chapter 10.

pain

Many stimuli produce pain, their common characteristic being that they are *intense* stimuli such as strong pressure, high temperature, very bright lights, or very loud sounds. Such stimuli do some kind of damage to body tissue. There is much controversy over the nature of pain because so many factors affect the perceived painfulness of a particular stimulus.

Neural pathways from the periphery of the body to the brain are typically involved. Small diameter, rapidly conducting nerve fibers carry "bright, tingling" pain and larger diameter, slower conducting fibers carry "dull, throbbing" pain. But the brain can fool itself in this regard. A phenomenon known as *phantom pain* can occur after the amputation of a limb. The amputee may perceive strong pain in the limb that has been removed. That part of the brain which normally receives pain signals from the amputated limb is still active and tells the person wrongly that the pain is "out there" (in the limb) when it is not.

A very recent and important discovery is that morphine-like substances are manufactured in the brain itself. These are called *enkephalins* or *endorphins,* and their most important function seems to be the reduction of pain. Large amounts of them are, for example, released into the body during childbirth. Pain can be reduced by a number of drugs, including aspirin and morphine, but also by *placeboes.* Placeboes are themselves supposedly ineffectual chemicals, such as sugar pills, but there is evidence that they actually induce a release of enkephalins. We used to say that placebo effects were "all in the mind," but now it appears possible that they are in the brain in the form of morphine!

Relaxation. A major cause of headaches, as well as other body aches, is persistent tension of the muscles, particularly in the neck. Various means of reducing muscle tension, therefore, have a therapeutic effect. Because these are important clinically for the reduction of stress, we will deal with relaxation techniques in some detail in the chapter on stress.

Hypnosis and Pain. Though hypnosis is not a very well-understood phenomenon, it has been useful for a variety of painful situations, including so-called painless dentistry and childbirth. An interesting pain phenomenon studied in the laboratory has been described by Ernest Hilgard of Stanford

University (1973). Some people, under hypnosis, can converse about one topic and simultaneously write about something entirely different. This is called *automatic writing*. With such people, if strong but harmless pain (such as that produced by holding one hand in a container of ice water) is aroused, the person may *say*, following the hypnotist's prior suggestion, that he or she does *not* feel any pain. The writing hand, however, may simultaneously convey the opposite message, saying that the hand in the water *hurts*. Hilgard's explanation for this is that different parts of the brain can become "dissociated" from each other during hypnosis and carry on independent activities even though we are not *aware* of the two activities simultaneously occurring.

curiosity and exploration

Why do people risk life and limb to climb mountains, hang glide, or leap out of airplanes with nothing but a glorified bedsheet to protect them? To say that one climbed a mountain "because it was there" is not terribly informative psychologically, but it may hint at something basic in human nature: a need for novel or changing stimulation.

Exploratory behavior is so widespread, among both humans and animals, that exploration and curiosity are considered a major form (if not two forms) of motivation. Chimpanzees will work hours to solve mechanical puzzles, rats prefer to explore parts of a maze not previously traversed, and newborn human infants prefer looking at slightly complex geometric patterns rather than plain sheets of paper. The amount of money people spend for entertainment suggests a need for new experiences. It is always possible that entertainment is escapism; we may lose ourselves in diverting activities to seek distraction from our daily problems. Such escapism, however, hardly accounts for all the appeal of exploration and appeasement of curiosity among humans and other animals.

Considerable evidence suggests a biological need for novel or changing

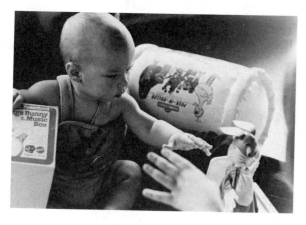

The child's attention is attracted by the novelty and surprise of the jack-in-the-box.

stimulation. Chimpanzees reared in total darkness do not even develop their visual systems; they are blind. Chimps reared in pattern-free environments (produced by keeping their eyes covered with halves of ping-pong balls) have inferior visual perception when visually released. Even humans kept only temporarily (hours or days) in a constant sensory environment are temporarily impaired in intellectual and perceptual functioning. In the human visual system, there is a continuous and rapid (about twenty-five per second) movement of the eyes, movement too small to be seen with the naked eye. This vibration is sufficient to guarantee continuously changing visual stimulation in the nervous system, however. If, by appropriate technical means in the laboratory, we arrange for visual stimuli to vibrate right along with the eye, the patterns *disappear* in a minute or so, then periodically recover and disappear. Unless constantly presented with changing stimulation, the visual system simply stops operating properly. In summary, there is apparently a real, biological need for the nervous system to have changing input and we are rewarded by the stimulation accompanying new or changing experiences.

Some Basic Motivational Theories

drive theory

The term *drive* was introduced in 1918 by Robert S. Woodworth. He wanted to distinguish an "energizing" component of behavior from a "directional" component. He likened behavior to the movement of a car, which has a steering mechanism to guide it and a motor to energize it. For living organisms, environmental stimuli are what guide them and drives (internal conditions of the body) are what energize them. Insufficient food or water were thus said to "drive" an organism to activity. Drive theory, therefore, fits in closely with the biological concept of homeostasis, on the one hand, and the Freudian use of instinct, on the other.

Hull's Theory. Clark L. Hull (1884–1952), of Yale University, was one of America's most influential psychologists. His early works were on hypnosis and aptitude testing, but in his later years he turned to a more general theory of behavior. In abbreviated form (ignoring the parts of the theory not of concern to us here), Hull (1943) made the same general argument as Woodworth. Hull's theory said

$$\text{Performance} = \text{Habit} \times \text{Drive}.$$

Put more generally, there is a learning component and a motivational component to behavior, and these multiply to affect performance. The multiplication sign means, for example, that performance of a particular behavior will not occur unless that performance has been learned and there is some level of motivation. If there is no learning *or* no motivation, there will be no performance. For Hull, habit referred to *any* strength of *association* between a stimulus and a response, so there could be weak habits or strong habits. Drive referred to a *general* internal state which could be aroused by such differing conditions as hunger, thirst, pain, or fear.

Relevant and Irrelevant Drive. Particularly important for application to humans, the theory proposes that there are relevant and irrelevant drives. A relevant drive is one which is related to a specific goal, such as thirst being related to water and hunger to food. An irrelevant drive is *not* related to the goal at hand. According to Hull, however, *irrelevant drives can facilitate performance.* Fear, for example, might facilitate performance of a hungry animal for food reward even though fear is irrelevant to hunger and food. Among humans, anxiety and "social facilitation" have been the most widely studied irrelevant drives.

Anxiety and Performance. Hull's theory predicts that (1) *when there is a single dominant response which is correct for a given situation, performance will be facilitated by high drive.* For example, if an experimental task is simply to squeeze a handgrip as hard as possible, increasing the level of an irrelevant drive such as anxiety should facilitate squeezing. We have all heard of unusual feats of strength done under the stress of emergency situations. Many simple laboratory tasks have validated this aspect of the theory. (2) *When there are several different possible responses (or a single complex response with many components), increasing the level of drive may hinder performance.* This is because the drive energizes *all* the responses or components and they interfere with each other. For example, if we are supposed to memorize a list of unfamiliar names, strong anxiety might well interfere with our doing so. A number of experiments have also supported predictions along this line, and many students have observed this phenomenon at times when taking an exam.

Educational Implications. Since the education process by its very nature involves learning many complex things, the irrelevant drive idea has profound implications. A little bit of motivation may facilitate performance, but too high a level may interfere with learning. Charles Spielberger (1962) has studied the relationship between anxiety and classroom performance of college students. Some of his results are summarized in Figure 3-1. The figure shows that where there was either very high or very low aptitude for college work, anxiety level does not make any difference. Throughout the middle range of ability, however, the low-anxiety students get better grades than do the high-anxiety students. The obvious implication is that high-anxiety students might well perform better in school if their anxiety level were reduced, or that workers on a complex job might perform better with lower levels of stress or anxiety.

Irrelevant Drive and Social Facilitation. In 1897, a psychologist named Tripplett conducted what is said to be the first social psychology experiment.

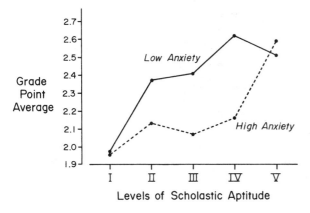

figure 3-1. Relationship between scholastic performance (Grade Point Average) and scholastic aptitude for college students with high or low levels of anxiety. The effects of anxiety are most damaging to students in the midrange of ability. (From Spielberger, 1962. Used with permission of publisher.)

It concerned the effects of "pacemaking" and "competition" on performance. He was interested in how the presence of another person affects performance, such as when runners compete against others instead of just the clock. In 1965, Robert Zajonc revived interest in the problem, interpreting "social facilitation" in terms of drive theory. He said that the presence of an audience arouses an irrelevant drive (anxiety, or perhaps just excitement) and that the helpful or hindering effect of the audience depended on the kind of task. Following Hull, he said that an audience would improve performance on a task with a single dominant response and hinder performance where a complex activity was required.

We need not detail the actual experiments here, but a "thought" experiment will clarify the point. We cheer as loudly as possible for our football team to do what it has been highly trained to do: run faster, tackle harder, and so on. These dominant responses should be facilitated by our cheers. A cheering audience might adversely affect a team of youngsters who have not yet well-learned the game, however. Imagine, also, a roaring crowd at a chess match. It would seem that the intricacies of a chess game could only be torn asunder by cheers and catcalls.

It is generally explicit in drive theory that it is *rewarding* to obtain a *reduction* in the level of drive, or tension. Some theories (including Hull's) have maintained that this drive-reduction is the basis of *all* rewards, but we have already seen with curiosity and exploratory behavior that such is probably not the case. Activation theory is a somewhat different biological approach to motivation which considers that both a *reduction* and an *increase* in internal arousal can be rewarding.

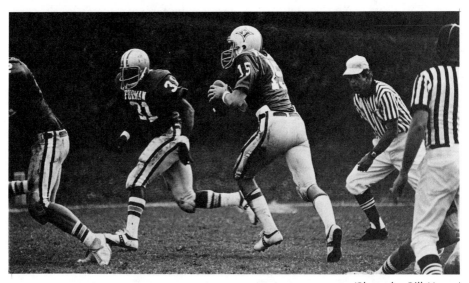

(Photo by Bill Henry)

The challenge of chess provides considerable arousal of the brain.

activation theory

Activation theory is a biologically-based theory specifically designed to account for both arousal-increasing and arousal-decreasing behaviors. In particular, Donald Hebb of McGill University (1955) argued that there is an *optimal level* of internal arousal for normal functioning. People perform best at this optimal level, and it is desirable and sought. Too low a level of arousal (as with boredom) leads to activities which increase arousal. Too high a level of arousal (as with strong fear) leads to seeking a lower level. This is generally described by an upside down U-shape figure (an inverted-U), as shown in Figure 3–2. Hebb equated this arousal with the level of activity in a part of the lower brain, the *brainstem reticular activating system.*

The reticular activating system "tones up" the rest of the brain so that we are more receptive and more responsive to environmental events. For example, we respond faster to stimuli when there is a high level of reticular activity. Conversely, if structures in this general area of the brain, or closely related

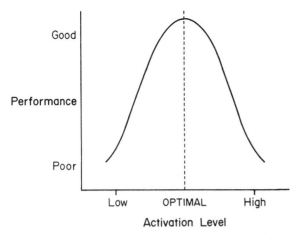

Good

Performance

Poor

Low   OPTIMAL   High

Activation Level

figure 3–2. A medium level of activation is considered optimal for performance.

structures, is destroyed, there is often coma or death. Such energizing drugs as amphetamines increase neural activity in this part of the brain and such sleep-inducing drugs as barbiturates depress activity. Mind-altering drugs like LSD and mescaline also act on this part of the brain.

The Yerkes-Dodson Law. According to the law proposed in 1908 by Yerkes and Dodson, different levels of arousal are optimal for different kinds of tasks. If the task is complex, a low level of arousal is optimal. If the task is simple, a very high level of arousal may produce the "strongest" performance, but even here there might be an impairment of function with excessive arousal. Unfortunately, we do not have any simple way to measure these optimal levels of arousal and the usefulness of the theory is therefore reduced. As mentioned in the case of drive theory, however, we can at least be aware that it is possible to become *too highly motivated* and to take this into account in our own lives or in dealing with others.

incentive theory

Whereas both drive theory and activation theory emphasize internal conditions of the body as motivational factors, incentive theory emphasizes external objects or events. Incentive refers to something which is desirable or undesirable and which we therefore strive to attain or escape. It is often said that drives "push" us and incentives "pull" us, but of course, it is the *anticipation* of the incentives which "pulls" us. *Hedonism,* one form of incentive theory, is the argument that people seek to maximize pleasure and minimize distress. The English political philosopher Jeremy Bentham (1748–1832) applied the theory to society at large as well as to individuals. The social argument is that societies seek the greatest good for the greatest number.

We can have expectancies and anticipations of goals based on the association of two situational events. For example, the sound of bells, cold weather and snow may remind us of Christmas coming. Children literally become preoccupied with thoughts of yuletide pleasures. In the spring, at a later age, another expectancy may emerge: "A young man's fancy turns lightly to thoughts of love." This may be triggered by a different set of cues, such as balmy temperatures, flowers, and moonlit nights.

Many authors have tried to combine drive theory and incentive theory. Hull simply added another variable to his equation, saying that

$$\text{Performance} = \text{Habit} \times \text{Drive} \times \text{Incentive.}$$

More commonly, however, incentive theorists have proposed that changes in internal body conditions (such as hunger or sex hormones) produce a change in the incentive *value* of external objects, such as food or a potential mate. We become more or less preoccupied with these depending on our internal state.

cognitive theory

Cognitive theories of motivation concern how our thought processes affect our goals. There are two aspects. First, many cognitive activities are inherently rewarding and are therefore goals unto themselves, such as doing puzzles or playing games. Second, the way we think about events partly determines whether those events are rewarding or punishing. For example, I am rewarded by my ferocious-looking (but gentle) dog bounding toward me when I come home; a stranger might be punished by this vision.

We can completely reverse a situation from positive to negative by how we perceive and think about it. If we get a low score on a test, we may be very unhappy until we learn that everyone else got an even lower score. The author once got an A for a math test with a score of 39 percent, thus burning this example into his memory. Similarly, if everybody is poor, as are many students, then being broke is not so unbearable. If our poverty is flaunted by a contrast with those around us, however, it is very unpleasant.

unconscious motivation

The idea of unconscious motivation is almost synonymous with the name of Sigmund Freud. There are three related ideas here.

1. Freud strongly emphasized what he called *psychic determinism;* he believed that all mental and behavioral activities had causes which could be found if one looked for them in the right way.
2. He emphasized that *early childhood experiences* are tremendously important influences on later life. Because these early experiences occur when our thought processes are not yet well-formed, however, we may not be aware of their later influence.

3. At any given time we might be motivated by forces of which we are not conscious and cannot explain. To Freud, such everyday events as slips of the tongue ("Freudian slips") implied unconscious motivation. An intended compliment which turns out bad because of a slight word change would, according to Freud, reveal our true intention, that we did not want to make a compliment. Others may often understand our motives better than we do. For example, a mother may recognize jealousy in her child when all the child recognizes is that he does not like a new person around the house.

addictions

A very powerful form of motivation is produced by drug addiction. Strictly speaking, addiction has two components. First, it takes an ever-increasing amount of the substance to produce the same effect. This is called *tolerance.* Second, when the substance is not taken, there are *withdrawal symptoms.* These are opposite whatever the effect of the substance was. The withdrawal symptoms of a depressant drug (such as a barbiturate) include extreme agitation; for an excitatory drug (an amphetamine, for example) the withdrawal symptoms include depression.

From the motivational point of view, there are two important aspects. First, a drug may have positive incentive properties because it makes someone feel good (euphoric, alert, or whatever). The drug may then be sought because of this. After addiction occurs the lack of the drug produces a very unpleasant internal state and the person may seek the drug to relieve this state rather than for the positive incentive value which was the initial attraction. There may also be a large amount of anxiety on the part of the person who does not have the drug, a fearfulness of the unpleasant withdrawal symptoms. Most people are familiar with the very strong motivation to obtain drugs and the illegal activities that people may engage in to get the money for expensive drugs.

SUMMARY

1. *Motivation* deals with the needed and wanted *goals* we strive for and the intensity of the effort. Internal conditions of the body in combination with external objects or events we approach or avoid determine our motives. Biological motives are essential for survival.

2. *Instinct* in a motivational context most appropriately refers to our *internal urges* or drives to do certain things. Since few *behaviors* appear to be universal in humans, psychologists and biologists usually look for other more complex explanations for behavior than instinct.

3. The human body, like that of many other organisms, has a remarkable ability to *automatically* regulate itself within very narrow limits so as to

function most efficiently. With the necessary raw materials, such things as blood sugar level, water and mineral content, and body temperature can be kept within small tolerances of what the body needs.

4. *Hunger* is a biological motive, and there is much effort devoted to food-related activities. Obesity is therefore a serious motivational as well as social and health problem. Obese individuals tend to respond more to *external food cues* than internal hunger cues in comparison to normal weight individuals. *Behavior therapy* has been used effectively to treat obesity by helping obese individuals gain new stimulus control with eating, such as eating only at certain times and places. *Anorexia nervosa* (self-induced starvation) has also been controlled with behavior therapy. Biological factors, individual experiences, and cultural heritage may combine to produce food preferences and hungers for *specific* foods.

5. *Thirst* is a more serious problem than hunger because water is not stored in large amounts in our bodies. It is, however, obtained from many sources, including food. This is regulated mainly by the brain, as is hunger. The hypothalamus and limbic system in the brain contain regulatory "start" and "stop" centers for eating and drinking. Other body mechanisms assist the brain in the regulation of eating and drinking.

6. *Sex* is not a motive which must be satisfied for the survival of an individual but involves important biological mechanisms. Sexual behavior is influenced by *hormones,* including estrogen and progesterone for females and testosterone for males.

7. *Pain* is produced by *intense stimuli* that damage body tissues. There are neural pathways from the periphery of the body to the brain, but the brain can generate its own pain even without these (such as with phantom limbs, sensations in arms or legs that have been amputated). Recent research has uncovered morphine-like substances called *endorphins,* which are manufactured in the brain and which seem to control pain levels to some degree. *Relaxation* and *hypnosis* have also been used as therapy for reduction of pain or stress.

8. *Curiosity* and *exploration* are also considered basic biological motives. The nervous system has its own need for changing stimulation and novel stimulation.

9. Clark Hull's *drive theory* says that behavior is determined by *"habit"* (a learning component) and *"drive"* (a motivational component). Drive refers to a general internal state and can be relevant or irrelevant to a particular goal. Performance will generally be *facilitated* by high drive if there is a *single dominant response,* but it will be *hindered* if there are *several possible responses* or a single complex response (one with many components which have to be linked together very carefully).

10. *Activation theory* says that people perform best at an *optimal level* of internal

arousal, between low and high, regulated by the *reticular activating system* at the base of the brain.

11. *Incentive theory* emphasizes external objects or events that are desirable or undesirable and which we strive to attain or escape. Incentive theory sees behavior as motivated by these incentives, which have different values to a person.

12. *Cognitive theories* of motivation deal with the effect of our thought processes on behavior. Various thought processes (such as successful problem solving) may be *rewarding in themselves* or they may *change our perception* of what is desirable or undesirable in the environment.

13. *Unconscious motivation* is very important in the Freudian psychoanalytic theory and is greatly determined by forgotten early childhood experiences. Freud believed that all behavior and mental activity have underlying causes, even though these are not all recognized by the individual.

14. *Drug addiction* can be a powerful motivating force, increasing as tolerance to the drug grows and intensity of the possible withdrawal symptoms increases.

EXERCISES

1. What is homeostasis? What is its importance to us? What types of behaviors could it motivate?

2. What controls your eating habits? What specific types of external cues influence your eating?

3. Americans are "notorious" for overeating on Thanksgiving Day. Discuss the possible motive(s) involved in this American "custom."

4. What foods do you sometimes crave? What could cause these food preferences? Pregnant women are often said to have unusual food preferences. Why might this be so?

5. When are you thirstiest? What biological reasons might cause your thirst at these particular times? Is your body telling you something?

6. Are you usually aware of the biological motives influencing your behavior? Just before your next meal try to be consciously aware of your hunger. Do you really feel hungry? How often do you actually feel hungry or thirsty prior to eating or drinking?

7. How does the need for novel stimulation affect your behavior? What do you do just for the "heck of it"? How does the need for novel (or changing) stimulation fit into our national economy? List all the products and businesses you can think of which cater to this need.

8. What is a drive? When is it relevant and when irrelevant?

9. If you are extremely nervous before a test (high test anxiety), what different ways could this influence your performance? Would you tend to do better on a multiple-choice test or a math test with long problems? Think about this answer in terms of irrelevant drive.

10. Think of situations where an audience would either hinder performance (like test-taking) or facilitate it (like a football game). How are the two types of situations different? What might happen to performance if an audience was added or removed?

11. When could high and low levels of arousal be advantageous? Give some specific examples. (Consider, for example, such illustrations as a highly-aroused brain surgeon and a soccer player with extremely low arousal.)

12. What are *incentives?* What incentives strongly influence you? How are incentives and drives different? What do we mean by the distinction between the *quality* of an incentive as opposed to the *quantity* of an incentive?

13. Have you ever done something which you simply could not explain to yourself? How might Freud explain such behavior? Have you ever seen someone behave in a way which you thought you understood but which they did not? What kind of a situation? What behavior?

14. What features of drug addiction are motivating?

4

Learned Motives
and Job Performance

The Meaning of "Learned Motives"

Hunger and thirst are the inevitable results of going without food and water; pain comes with intense stimulation. We do not need experience with these motivational events, we are born with them. As we have seen, however, learning strongly influences the manner by which we react to these events. Learned motives depend upon learning for their occurrence at all. Fear may accompany pain, but if fear is conditioned to some other stimulus and is aroused by this stimulus we speak of fear as a learned motive. This does not mean that those internal events we call fear are learned, but rather that they can be aroused by a new stimulus via learning. Because of the great human potential for learning, much of human motivation is related to learned motives.

Over forty years ago, Gordon Allport (1937) a well-known psychologist at Harvard, pointed out that people often continue to do things when the original motives are no longer present. He called this the *functional autonomy of motives,* by which he meant that behaviors can somehow become independent of their original motives. We might, for example, learn to do certain things to get food for survival but continue to engage in those activities when survival is no longer at stake. Allport identified the problem but did not provide a very satisfactory explanation. Psychologists now consider this functional autonomy an example of learned motives and ask how such motives are learned and sustained. In this chapter we shall examine just a few aspects of learned motives, but we shall come across them again in the next chapter (fear and anxiety) as well as under particular topics in subsequent chapters.

Achievement Motivation

In the late 1930s, Henry Murray of Harvard University published a book called *Explorations in Personality* in which he distinguished between *biogenic* and *psychogenic* needs. The biogenic needs were for such things as food, water, and air. The twenty psychogenic needs included needs for *achievement, affiliation, power,* and *aggression.* His complete list of these needs is summarized in Table 4–1.

definition

Murray defined need for achievement (summarized as nAch) as a desire or tendency "to overcome obstacles, to exercise power, to strive to do something difficult as well and as quickly as possible." He also devised a technique called the *Thematic Apperception Test* (TAT) as a means of roughly measuring the strength of the various needs in people. The original TAT consisted of twenty cards

table 4-1

Murray's (1938) tentative list of psychological needs. Three of the most studied have been achievement, affiliation, and aggression, but subsequent researchers have been interested in all of them.

need	brief definition
Abasement	To submit passively to external force. To accept injury, blame, criticism, punishment. To become resigned to fate.
Achievement	To accomplish something difficult. To rival and surpass others.
Affiliation	To seek out and enjoy close and cooperative relationships with other people. To adhere and remain loyal to a friend.
Aggression	To overcome opposition forcefully. To attack, injure, or punish another.
Autonomy	To get free, shake off restraint, break out of confinement. To be independent and free to act according to impulse. To defy convention.
Counteraction	To master or make up for a failure by renewed striving. To overcome weaknesses. To maintain self-respect and pride on a high level.
Defendance	To defend the self against assault, criticism, and blame. To conceal or justify a misdeed, failure, or humiliation.
Deference	To admire and support a superior. To yield readily to the influence of others. To conform to custom.
Dominance	To control one's human environment. To influence or direct the behavior of others by suggestion, seduction, persuasion, or command.
Exhibition	To make an impression. To be seen and heard. To excite, entertain, shock, or entice others.
Harm avoidance	To avoid pain, physical injury, illness, and death.
Infavoidance	To avoid humiliation. To refrain from action because of fear of failure.
Nurturance	To give sympathy to and gratify the needs of weak and helpless persons. To feed, help, support, console, protect, nurse.
Order	To put things in order. To achieve cleanliness, arrangement, balance, neatness, and precision.
Play	To act for "fun" without further purpose. To like to laugh and make jokes. To seek enjoyable relaxation of stress.
Rejection	To separate oneself from a disliked object. To exclude, abandon, or remain indifferent to an inferior person.
Sentience	To seek and enjoy sensuous impressions.
Sex	To form and further an erotic relationship. To have sexual intercourse.
Succorance	To have one's needs gratified by the sympathetic aid of another person. To be nursed, supported, protected, loved, guided, forgiven, consoled.
Understanding	To ask or answer general questions. To be interested in theory. To speculate, formulate, analyze, and generalize.

(Adapted from Murray, 1938, by Ketch, Crutchfield, Livson, 1969. Reprinted with permission.)

figure 4–1. Pictures such as this one are used in the thematic apperception tests to study achievement motivation.

of ambiguous scenes, such as that shown in Figure 4–1. The person taking the test is instructed to tell a story about each picture, the story to answer the following questions:

1. What led up to the scene being depicted?
2. What is now happening in the scene?
3. How do the characters feel?
4. What will be the outcome?

The relatively ambiguous pictures are supposed to evoke themes which will be characteristically different for different persons. The TAT is one of a number of projective tests. The defining character of such a test is that the stimuli are somewhat ambiguous and therefore the story the person tells is a *projection* from within the subject onto the picture.

Various scoring schemes applied to the stories are designed to detect particular motivational themes running through the subjects' stories. For example, one card shows a boy with a violin lying on a table in front of him as he stares into space. If the subject tells a story about a boy working hard to become a world-renowned violinist, the scoring and interpretation would be different than if the story told were about a boy who has to practice but wants to be off having a good time with his friends. The former story would be more indicative of achievement motivation and the latter of affiliation. One might think that a simpler, more objective procedure might provide better measure of need for achievement, but none has been found.

Researchers select people who have relatively high and relatively low nAch scores and compare their performances in achievement situations ranging from repetitive mathematical problems (multiplying two-digit numbers) to games involving tinker toys. People with high nAch in fact do such tasks more rapidly, but there is an even more interesting relationship between nAch and performance.

relationship between nAch and performance

High nAch people tend to select tasks which are of about *medium difficulty* for them. They seem to want tasks which are challenging enough that there is some pride in being successful. If a task is too simple, they feel they have accomplished nothing to be proud of, and if the task is too hard there is little chance of being successful. Hence, they choose medium difficulty tasks. This has been shown for such a simple situation as a ringtoss game in which the person chooses his or her own distance to stand from the peg. High nAch people (children or adults) tend to stand at a medium distance. If they initially fail, they move closer for the next round, and if it is too easy, they move farther away. McClelland therefore characterizes high nAch people as "medium risk takers."

fear of failure (ff)

Some individuals want to achieve for the "pride of accomplishment," but others want to succeed because they are *afraid of failing*. For most of us it may be a mixture of these elements. In Atkinson's extension of achievement theory (e.g., 1964), scores for nAch and fear of failure are combined. If the net result is nAch greater than fear of failure the predictions are the same as for nAch. But what if fear of failure is greater? People with high fear of failure (usually indicated by some measure of anxiety) tend *not* to be medium risk

From early childhood through adulthood people "choose up" sides which are nearly even so there is risk of losing and feeling of accomplishment for winning.

takers. In the ringtoss game they stand so close that chance of failure is very slight or so far away that failure is easily excused.

What happens when a high fear of failure person fails? We might expect that he or she would choose an easier task (such as a closer distance in the ringtoss), but in fact the person may choose a *harder* task! How can we account for this paradoxical behavior? The following explanation has received some experimental support. If the subject chose an easier task and failed, there would be even more shame for failing; therefore, the harder task (with less shame for failing) may be chosen. This may, in part at least, account for the unrealistically high goals that some people set for themselves (such as a borderline student who aspires to a medical degree).

the origins of nAch and ff

McClelland (1954) argued that individuals rewarded for achievement learn to anticipate pleasure in achievement situations. They work hard to achieve because achievement is pleasurable. Conversely, punishment for failure leads to a fear of failure. Men with high nAch tend to come from families which emphasize striving for success and young adults with high nAch often report that their parents strongly emphasized achievement and were not very "warm" individuals. In short, people with high need for achievement do what they have been rewarded for doing: They seek achievement.

the achieving society

McClelland (1961) asked whether some societies systematically emphasize achievement more than others and, if so, whether there is greater *actual* achievement in those societies. He started from the argument of Max Weber (1904), a famous sociologist, that the Protestant revolution has infused a more "vigorous spirit" into both workers and entrepreneurs (managers, promoters). What a society taught its children about independence and hard work (for example, "Idle hands are the devil's tools.") was related to social growth. McClelland correctly predicted that Protestant countries would show greater productivity than non-Protestant countries because the children were learning the Protestant ethic.

A great advantage of the nAch scoring system is that it can be applied to any written material, including old newspapers, books, or other documents. Analysis of children's books showed that Protestant families in the early eighteenth century did indeed stress independence at an earlier age than did Italian or Irish Catholic families of the same socioeconomic levels. Accordingly, Protestant children tend to have higher nAch scores, and Protestant countries tend to be more advanced economically. Over a fifty-year period in the 1800s, as achievement increased or decreased in children's stories there was a subsequent rise or fall of economic achievement about twenty-five years later. National economic activity was indexed in this study by such things as per capita use of electricity, tonnage of coal produced, and tonnage of shipping.

All high achievers do not score high on nAch measures. Nobel prize winners do not score particularly high. McClelland believes that nAch is related to the performance of what he calls the "entrepreneurial type" of person, such as independent businesspeople and managers in larger organizations and so on. These "managerial types" tend to be medium-risk takers, want immediate feedback about performance, and work harder when there is some demand for achievement. They are not happy unless they are frequently rewarded for success. Scientists, on the other hand, may wait for years with little reward or feedback on how well their research is received.

female motive to avoid success?

Thus far we have consistently referred to male subjects in achievement research, simply because the standard measures of nAch have not predicted the performance of females and the research had been limited to males. Perhaps the particular male-oriented pictures used in the tests have not been appropriate for females. Or, perhaps the definitions of achievement have been male oriented, such as not counting being a good housewife. About 1968, however, Matina Horner speculated that some females have a *motive to avoid success.* Her measurement procedure, which has become standard, is another form of projective technique: story completion. A subject is given a sentence such as, "At the end of the first term final, Anne finds herself at the top of her medical school class." A typical motive to avoid success (MAS) story would be something like "Anne decides to drop out of medical school, her fiance graduates at the head of the class, and they are married." A low MAS story might be "Anne continues to work hard, graduates at the head of her class, and becomes an eminent physician."

Various research studies have examined both performance and personality characteristics of high MAS females. High MAS females have been described as less affectionate, more critical of themselves, having low self-esteem, and being more controlled by external events than low MAS females. They also describe themselves as being more ambivalent in their professional and personal goals than do low MAS females. In laboratory tasks which are non-competitive, or described as easy, the high MAS female may do better than her low MAS counterpart. In competitive or "hard" tasks, however, the picture reverses and the high MAS females do worse.

Origin of the Motive to Avoid Success. There is no agreed upon interpretation of the female motive to avoid success, and some investigators think it is the same thing as fear of failure in men. There may well be a difference between men and women, perhaps arising from differences in

socialization, as to what constitutes success and failure. For example, low MAS females tend to have mothers in occupations which are not typically female; they may have jobs in male-oriented (or, male-dominated) environments. Their daughters then have models to emulate and encouragement for doing some things in a way that has not traditionally been considered "feminine." They would be less concerned, for example, about marriage, whereas the high MAS female might be afraid of business success because of the potential loss of an "appropriate" marriage. There has been a small explosion of research in this area which should help clarify these issues. The research may also advertise the phenomenon and thereby help reduce it.

Consistency Theories

If we are managing a company and find that sales are up but profits are down we would have an apparent inconsistency. We would be disturbed by this apparent contradiction and try to find out what was happening. The basic idea of cognitive consistency theories is that we find inconsistencies unpleasant and try to reduce them. This reduction, or return to consistency, may be achieved by changing our behaviors, beliefs, or attitudes. We shall examine two such theories: Fritz Heider's balance theory and Leon Festinger's cognitive dissonance theory.

Heider's balance theory

Fritz Heider (1958), a highly influential social psychologist, developed balance theory. If I like you and you like me, but we are in strong disagreement about the virtues of a particular politician, we are in a *state of imbalance*. If we agreed upon the merits of the candidate we would be in a *state of balance*. Since the imbalance is assumed to be aversive, we should try to do something to reduce it. We might change our minds about each other, or about the candidate, or avoid the topic. When *equilibrium* is restored, we are satisfied, or relieved. Imbalance is therefore like drive: Its presence initiates action and its reduction rewards that action. The "action" may be entirely in our heads, consisting of changing our attitudes or beliefs rather than involving overt behavior.

Large imbalances may be undesirable, but small amounts of imbalance may be desirable. If we think of imbalance as a source of activation or arousal, a low level of inconsistency may spice up our lives. We may seek some imbalance, as in friendly debates, just as we seek competition in athletic activities. If two people were always in perfect agreement with each other, they might also become very bored with each other.

Festinger's cognitive dissonance theory

Leon Festinger developed what was to become the most influential social psychological theory through the 1950s and 60s—cognitive dissonance theory. *Cognitive dissonance is said to occur when a person simultaneously holds two contradictory beliefs (cognitions) or behaves in a manner contradictory to his or her beliefs or attitudes.* Being obese and continuing to eat rich food is dissonant with knowing that obesity can be life-threatening. Or, smoking is dissonant with the knowledge that smoking may lead to lung cancer. Like imbalance, cognitive dissonance is considered an aversive state which it is rewarding to reduce.

There are a number of ways to reduce dissonance. We might add a new cognition, such as "lung cancer research is ambiguous." Or we might change our behavior to bring it in line with our beliefs, by stopping smoking. Note that it is unimportant whether the beliefs that produce the dissonance or the changes which reduce dissonance are *correct*. The important thing from the individual's point of view is that he or she *believes* them correct.

The most famous cognitive dissonance experiment was conducted by Leon Festinger and Merrill Carlsmith (1959). College students performed the boring task of repeatedly rotating rows of square pegs in a slotted board. Some subjects were then offered $1 to persuade other students to participate in the experiment; they were to say they had found the experience interesting and informative.

Other subjects were offered $20 to use this rather obvious lie to recruit new subjects. The subjects then filled out various rating scales, including one on how *interesting* the experiment had been. We might expect that the $20 subjects would report the experiment more interesting since they were rather well paid. The Festinger-Carlsmith results were just the opposite, however, with the following logic.

The $20 subjects were lying, but they had a strong *external justification* for doing so (the $20). They therefore did not perceive inconsistency between their recruiting technique and their actual belief about the experiment. The $1 subjects, however, had very little external justification for their behavior, and should therefore find their recruiting story and their real belief about the experiment inconsistent: They should experience cognitive dissonance. They could reduce the dissonance by saying, "I'm really a louse." But this should also be discomforting to the subjects. They could, however, arrive at the conclusion that they *really did* think the experiment was interesting and thereby justify their actions. And indeed the results of the study showed that the $1 subjects rated the experiment significantly more interesting than did the $20 subjects. This experiment is diagrammed in Figure 4–2.

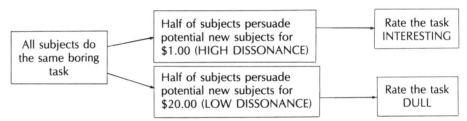

figure 4–2. The experimental plan and results of the Festinger-Carlsmith cognitive dissonance experiment. The HIGH DISSONANCE subjects seemed to convince themselves that the boring task was actually rather interesting.

There have been many experiments using the above "forced-choice insufficient justification" approach ("forced choice" because subjects virtually always agree to participate regardless of the amount of money offered). For example, subjects have written essays arguing *against* their own previously stated opinion on some issue. Those subjects who have small external justification (small reward for writing the essays) change their opinions more than do subjects who have large external justification.

In another kind of dissonance experiment, subjects rate particular objects on attractiveness (all being about equally attractive). Then they are allowed to choose one of the objects to keep (such as a toaster). They then rate the objects again. They rate the chosen object more attractive than before and the object(s) not chosen less attractive. Again, the dissonance explanation is fairly straightforward: It would be unpleasant to believe that we had chosen an object less attractive than others available (a dissonance between belief and perceived action). Therefore, the subjects reinforce the action by rating the chosen object even more attractive.

Another procedure for reducing dissonance after a choice might be to seek information to support the decision. For example, having purchased my automobile, I might keep a watchful eye on the newspaper ads for evidence that I had made a good deal. Or I might avoid reading any ads whatsoever for fear I might find I had made a very bad deal. Unfortunately, dissonance theory does not tell us which of these is more likely in a given case and is therefore of little help here. Dissonance theory has been roundly criticized on several grounds, including the difficulty of making clearcut predictions. It has survived these criticisms but has had less interest in recent years.

Competence, Mastery, and Power

Alfred Adler, an early follower of Freud, broke away from the "master" because he could not agree that sex and aggression were the source of all motives. He believed that people are more dominated by a need to have mastery over their own lives. He argued that all people have some feelings of inferiority and the overriding goal of humankind is to compensate for these feelings. As Mullahy (1948, p. 116) puts Adler's view, ". . . the fundamental law of life is that of overcoming deficiencies and inadequacies. The life process is to be regarded as a struggle aiming always at a goal of adaptation to the demands of the world." Adler's view may overemphasize one particular aspect of motivational life, but it is doubtless a very important aspect.

More recent theorists have held similar views. Robert White (1959) has argued cogently that the most fundamental motive is competence, feelings of being effective in one's day-to-day transactions. What is rewarding to a person is information that he or she is indeed being effective. The details of this reward depend strongly on social learning. The specific English words which an employee wants to hear, such as "This is a really good piece of work, Fred," obviously depend on prior learning for their effectiveness. Many expressions of approval have in common that they tell us when we are doing effectively what we want to do. If our intention is to antagonize someone, the signs of success will be different than if we are trying to please. Nevertheless, our behavior will be aimed and guided by feedback about our effectiveness.

locus of control

The phrase "locus of control" refers to whether a person perceives that he or she controls his or her own life from within (internal locus) or is controlled more by factors outside one's own control (external locus). The way a person acts, the goals one sets for oneself and the effort expended in achieving these goals are related to the locus of control. For example, people with a high

OPPORTUNITY SHOP

High achievement ↓

(Photo by Bill Henry)

Low achievement →

need for achievement tend to have more internal locus of control. People whose lives are more hopeless, such as minority groups in large cities, tend to have a more external locus of control.

Richard deCharms (1968) used the picturesque terms *origin* and *pawn* to describe the internal-external distinction. An origin is a person who perceives great personal freedom, who is in control of his or her own life. A pawn has little perceived freedom and feels buffeted about by a capricious fate. These guiding external forces are not necessarily bad: One can win the Irish Sweepstakes as well as lose a fortune in the stock market. Individuals with a higher perceived internal locus of control seem *in fact* to be in better control of their lives. This may be a kind of self-fulfilling prophecy: The person who feels in control of things may face the day's events with greater self-confidence and energy, "knowing" that he or she will do well. The classic example of a *bad* door-to-door salesperson who says "You wouldn't want to buy an encyclopedia would you?" perhaps represents the opposite (negative self-fulfilling prophecy).

The Measurement of Locus of Control. Locus of control research was spurred by Julian Rotter's (1966) publication of the Internal-External scale (the I-E scale). This consists of a series of twenty-three two-choice items in which agreement with one alternative indicates internal control and with the other shows external control. A high total value indicates a high degree of external control. Sample items are

Item 15. a. In my case, getting what I want has little or nothing to do with luck.
b. Many times we might just as well decide what to do by flipping a coin.

Item 25. a. Many times I feel I have little influence over the things that happen to me.
b. It is impossible for me to believe that chance or luck plays an important role in my life.

A person would have one point for selecting "b" in Item 15 and another point for "a" in Item 25. The I-E scale measures what Rotter called *generalized expectancies*, the extent to which an individual generally perceives that his or her own behavior determines rewards and punishments. We can summarize a large amount of research using Rotter's I-E scale (or similar scales related to it) with the following diagram adapted from Beck (1978, p 335).

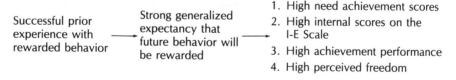

Successful prior experience with rewarded behavior → Strong generalized expectancy that future behavior will be rewarded →
1. High need achievement scores
2. High internal scores on the I-E Scale
3. High achievement performance
4. High perceived freedom

figure 4-3. People who have been rewarded for their prior behaviors develop strong expectancies that future behavior will also be rewarded and have higher motivation for achievement and feeling of independence.

Interesting examples of the attempt to maintain internal control in highly restrictive situations are given by Lefcourt (1976). For example, peacetime military enlisted men and slaves have in common that they are treated according to their position in life rather than in response to individual behaviors. In such contrived situations individuals do, however, have a great deal of control insofar as they can pace their work effort or act out a role to "fool" their supervisor (such as playing dumb or using exaggerated language) so that they can get what they want. The idea is to "play the game to the hilt," to be a "good" slave or enlisted man and thereby gain some control over an otherwise uncontrollable situation.

A general theory which incorporates locus of control is Rotter's *social learning theory*, which says that the tendency of a person to perform a particular action depends on *expectancy* of success and the perceived *value* of success. A history of success is likely to produce a strong perception of internal control (expectancy of success) and a history of failure is likely to produce perception of external control.

Various experiments [Lefcourt (1976); Phares (1976)] show that individuals with high internal locus of control are more responsive to feedback about how well they are doing than are "externals." The "internals" adjust their behavior if they are not doing well. Some experiments involved rigged games in which it was hard to tell whether skill (internal control) or chance (external control) was important to the outcome. Some subjects were *told* it was skill and other subjects were *told* it was chance, thereby experimentally manipulating the *perception* of control. When they no longer "won" in the games, the "internals" stopped betting faster than did the "externals." That is, they more realistically appraised the situation and adjusted to it. Individuals with high internal control are also more resistant to persuasion.

power

Though power is closely related to achievement and mastery, it is such a large topic that we must limit our discussion here to a small range of research. David Winter (1973) defined social power as "the ability or capacity of one person to produce some intended effect on the behavior or emotions of another person," (1973, p. 5).

Winter proposed three dimensions of power. (1) *Legitimacy* or *morality*. Power through force or exploitation is seen as immoral, whereas power gained through inspiration and leadership is moral and legitimate. (2) *Resistance* of the person over whom power is to be gained. (3) *Strength* of the individual through "moral persuasion." For example, the Indian leader Mahatma Gandhi was nonviolent and popularized the use of the hunger-strike to gain his ends.

e.g. USSR — people Don't try to even resist.

Power and Situations. A recurring historical argument is whether "great men" change the course of history or whether events shape the people who participate in them. By the latter view, whoever steps to the front at the right time in a revolution may be "leading" the inevitable. The history of science and technology lends considerable support to the situational theory. Simultaneous invention of the same product by several people is not uncommon, such as the telephone by Alexander Bell and Thomas Edison. But had neither of these giants invented the phone, most certainly somebody else would have done so shortly. It is much more difficult to answer this question at the level of, say, national politics, since politicians are happy to accept credit for leadership when advantageous, even on issues which they had opposed. Gerald Ford's presidency was clearly a situational event, without any power struggle required to attain it. Jimmy Carter, on the other hand, had to fight all the way to the top, but even in this example one could say the country may have just been ready for a change.

Measurement of Power. Winter measures power in a manner similar to the way need for achievement is measured, through the use of stories about pictures. He is specifically concerned with themes involving (1) strong vigorous actions that express power, (2) actions that arouse strong emotion in others, and (3) concern about reputation. There are subcategories of these.

Winter also distinguishes between *hope for power* and *fear of power*, which correspond roughly to hope for success and fear of success. Research has shown that some individuals are eager for power whereas others seem to shy away from it. Winter found that officers in student organizations had higher need-for-power scores than did non-officers. Interestingly, careers selected by students with the highest power scores tended to be teaching, psychology, the ministry, business, and international diplomacy. Scores below average were associated with government and politics, medicine, law, creative arts, and architecture. The reader can speculate about the reasons for this pattern, but a hint to the answer may lie in the actual day-to-day-activities involved. What is it that teachers or psychologists do, as compared to local politicians?

YES, OLD NED
HOPES FOR POWER
MORE THAN THE
AVERAGE PERSON
DOES.

Machiavellianism. Richard Christie and his colleagues [for example, Christie and Geis (1970)] approached the measurement of power from the viewpoint of Niccolo Machiavelli, a sixteenth century Florentine diplomat and author of *The Prince and the Discourses* (1513). Today the very name Machiavelli implies deceit and opportunism, although the man himself wielded little of the power of which he talked. Christie abstracted from Machiavelli's writings four characteristics of the successful "manipulator": (1) little emotion in interpersonal relationships, (2) lack of concern with conventional morality, (3) high reality orientation, and (4) low ideological commitment. In brief, the Machiavellian is a person who very coolly does what is necessary to achieve his or her goals. *eg Hitler. Nestlé scam, J.R.(Dallas)*

Christie devised a scale of Machiavellianism (called the Mach Scale) and in a series of experiments found that the "high Mach" subjects almost invariably outdid the "low Mach" subjects in situations where they were permitted to wheel and deal. They were very task oriented and not sidetracked by emotional or interpersonal considerations. In situations where the rules were much more stringent, however, high Machs did less well. They tended to be apathetic when the rules did not permit them to use their particular talents.

Theories of Motivation and Job Behavior

From this and the preceding chapter we can see that there is no single motive which we can magically turn on to get people to do what we want. Different motives are important to different people, and even these can change over time. With this background, however, we are better prepared to understand some of the motivational theories that have become important in management theory.

Herzberg's two-factor theory

Frederick Herzberg (1968) suggested that some aspects of a job allow people to satisfy "higher level" needs which are called *satisfiers* or *motivaters*. He argued that people get and want more from their jobs than pay. They also get recognition, responsibility, feelings of achievement, prestige, pleasure from social interaction, stimulation, and challenge. Activation theory, curiosity, achievement motivation, need for affiliation, or feelings of competence and internal control might all bear on an employee's performance at a particular job. The implication is that if jobs contain elements that are interesting and challenging and if employees have some control over their work, there is likely to be better job performance. A major complaint of workers in business and industry is that they do not have the opportunity to exercise their ingenuity, to work independently, or have something to say about what they do in their job.

Some job elements are more noticeable by their absence, however, and produce dissatisfaction. One of my colleagues has a particularly cold office which bothers her and about which she grumbles considerably and justifiably. But getting the heating system working properly for her office is not going to change her work performance much. She is not working for the reward of a warm office. Such dissatisfiers tend to relate to annoying external conditions, or job context. Company policy and administration, supervision, working conditions, relations with others, status, and job security are generally within the class of dissatisfiers. Satisfaction of these kinds of needs is called *hygiene;* dissatisfaction may lower performance but hygienic measures are not going to markedly improve performance according to Herzberg.

In the total context of a worker's life, however, we should also keep in mind that not all of his or her goals are related to the job. A homemaker doubling as a secretary *may not want* a challenging job; she is challenged at home. A homemaker whose children are grown may really want a new challenge, however. Or somebody who intensely follows hobbies in every spare moment may not particularly want work to be challenging and may be working to support these other activities. Even here, however, if the job *were* more attractive some of this extracurricular energy might be channeled into the job.

McGregor's theory x and theory y

Douglas McGregor (1972) has compared two sets of assumptions about the "nature of human nature" as these apply to work motivation. DuBrin (1980, p. 39) summarizes these as follows:

- *Theory X* assumes that people dislike work and must be coerced, controlled, and directed toward organizational goals. Furthermore, most people prefer to be treated this way, so they can avoid responsibility.
- *Theory Y,* the integration of goals, emphasizes the people's intrinsic interest in their work, their desire to be self-directing and to seek responsibility, and their capacity to be creative in solving business problems.

A marketing manager who believed in Theory X might then try to motivate sales representatives as follows, again quoting DuBrin (p. 39).

We have established sales quotas for each of you. Each year that your quota is reached, the company will pay for a five-day trip for you and your spouse. This will be in addition to your normal vacation. If you meet your quota for five consecutive years, you are almost guaranteed a permanent position with our company. Sales representatives who are unable to meet their quotas for three consecutive quarters will probably not be invited back for a fourth quarter.

On the other hand, a Theory Y believer might say the following:

You and your sales managers will get together on establishing sales quotas for each year. If you achieve your quotas, you will receive extra money. High perfor-

Job security is difficult to maintain in the construction industry which is at the mercy of such outside forces as the weather and availability of money for construction.

mance in sales is one important factor in being considered for a management assignment. Another important part of your job besides selling is to keep our product-planning group informed about changes in consumer demand. Many of our new products in the past stemmed directly from the suggestions of sales representatives.

personal values and goals

As we grow up and observe those around us, there are some people we admire and try to imitate. We copy their behavior, but we also learn to *value* many of the things they value and to *believe* many of the things they believe. Things or activities that we value positively provide goals (incentives) for us to strive for. At any given time we value some things more than others, and it is often to our benefit, either as workers or employers, to find out what *our* values, our *workers'* values, or what our *organization's* values are and which are most important. This is called *values clarification.* The many ways to go about this all come down to two steps:

1. List all of the things or activities which you value, or choose from a prepared list the items you value.

2. Put all these into rank order from most important to least important. These values then guide us in future decisions and behavior. Arriving at *group* consensus about values may be a complicated process.

As an example, suppose we are setting up two new youth sport leagues for the same sport, but one league is completely local and recreational while the other is more competitive, plays in tournaments, and involves travel around the state. Given the following values, which may not cover all possible, how might they be ranked for the two different leagues? Winning, having top-flight coaching, having only the best players, having a good time, financial sponsorship, learning to play the game, learning sportsmanship, making the coach feel good, making the parents feel proud, having the best competition possible? A competition league might identify its priorities as very similar to a recreation league in some cases, such as sportsmanship, but be different in other ways (player selection, perhaps). The way the priorities were set (the order of values) might determine such subsidiary matters as amount of practice time, financial investment, number and quality of coaches, and behavior on and off the field.

A sample set of values, to be ranked in terms of importance in one's *personal* life, is the following: (DuBrin, 1980, p. 38)

_____ Having my own place to live
_____ Having a child
_____ Having an interesting job and career
_____ Owning a car
_____ Having good health
_____ Being a religious person
_____ Being able to see and hear
_____ Loving and being loved by another person
_____ Making an above average income
_____ Other _____

As an exercise, rank each of these in importance to you and compare your ranking with someone else. What implications would your ranking have with regard to everyday decisions, such as playing tennis versus going to church on Sunday morning?

managerial goal setting

Often when a student or employee does not perform as a teacher or supervisor expects, it is because *the student or employee does not really know what is expected.* A student may think that she is performing very well and then be surprised to discover that she is not doing what the teacher wants. A trick which students learn early is to ferret out what the teacher wants, by looking at old exams or asking prior students, or asking the teacher what is going to be on the exam. Admittedly, goal setting is simpler for some situations than others.

Locke's Theory of Goal Setting. Edwin Locke (for example, 1968) has proposed that effective goal setting has two parts.

1. Hard goals produce higher performance than easy goals.
2. Specific goals produce higher performance than vague goals, such as "Do the best you can."

In one study, for example, Latham and Baldes (1975) introduced specific high goals for drivers of logging trucks. The problem was that the trucks were not being loaded nearly to capacity and more runs than necessary were being made by each truck. A program was introduced whereby each driver was given the specific instruction to load his truck to 94 percent of the truck's weight,

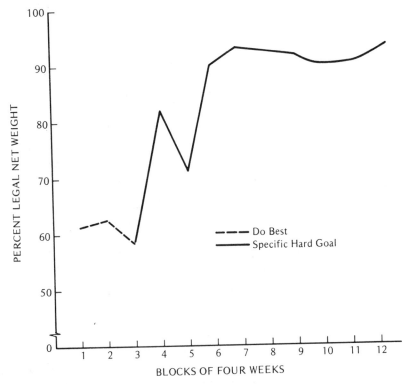

figure 4-4. When drivers were told to "do their best" loading trucks (dotted portion of curve), they only loaded them to about 60 percent of legal capacity. When given the specific instruction to load them to 94 percent, however, there was an immediate and sustained increase in load size. (From Latham & Baldes, 1975. Used with permission.)

as compared to the approximately 60 percent average the drivers had been carrying. Figure 4–4 shows the result, a marked and sustained improvement. The drivers were given verbal praise for improving their load size, but they got no other reward and there was no special training for drivers or supervisors.

Goals Should Be Attainable. Specific goals should be difficult, but not impossible. If employees are suddenly asked to double their output, they may see this as impossible and reject the goal. If the more modest goal of a 20 percent increase over a period of time is set, it is more likely to be acceptable. Research on United Fund Campaigns has supported this principle. When a goal of 20 percent increase over the previous year was set, productivity increased 25 percent, but a goal of 80 percent increase resulted in only a 12 percent rise, and performance *declined* when the goal was doubled (Dessler, 1980).

Goals Should Be Relevant. Specific goals should be relevant to the job at hand. A production supervisor should set goals for production, not sales. The goals should also be *observable* and *measurable.* Measurable factors would be quantity, quality, and time to get a job done. In sales, value of goods sold per unit of time (month, quarter), or value of goods sold per customer, is quantifiable. Percentage increase in sales is a measurable goal that both employee and supervisor can see.

Some aspects of education and training can be treated just as industrial productivity. Skills like typing or welding have specific measurable aspects. An instructor can set a typing goal, for example, at ten words per minute after a certain number of hours practice, twenty words after so many more hours and so on. In like fashion, goals can be established for learning math (being able to do progressively more complicated problems), or for reading speed and comprehension.

Goal Acceptability and Employee Participation. What a supervisor sees as an attainable goal and what an employee sees as attainable may differ sharply. Therefore, if the supervisor and employee *jointly* set a goal which is satisfactory to the supervisor and acceptable by the employee, the chances of achieving the goal appear much better. The employee who participates in the process of goal setting also becomes more *committed* to achieving the goal. Participation also produces greater job satisfaction.

management by objectives (mbo)

Management by objectives (MBO) involves employee participation, but it is typically used on a much larger scale than the simple employee participation just discussed. It might apply to an entire organization or a large section of a large corporation, whereas simple participation may be between employees and a supervisor in a small group. The MBO process can be characterized in five steps (Dessler, p. 185).

1. *Set organization's goals.* Organization-wide strategy and goals are established.
2. *Set departmental goals.* Department heads and their supervisors jointly set goals for their departments.
3. *Discuss departmental goals.* Department heads discuss the department's goals with all subordinates in the department and ask them to develop their own individual goals.
4. *Set individual goals.* Each superior and subordinate together set goals for the subordinate and assign a timetable for accomplishing them.
5. *Feedback.* There are periodic performance review meetings between supervisor and subordinate to monitor and analyze progress toward the subordinate's goals.

These principles seem to be sound, but the evidence on MBO success is contradictory (Dessler, 1980). It sometimes produces a transitory performance improvement and then there is backsliding, or there may be no improvement. Assuming that MBO is *in principle* a good technique there may be problems in implementation. Thus, the organizational commitment, clarity and acceptance of goals, and feedback about performance may look good on paper but fall short in practice. The process may be time consuming and seen by many employees as not worth doing.

Dessler (1980) puts goal setting generally into an ABC analysis of performance (Antecedents, Behavior, Consequences). Specifically, the following questions can be raised about the introduction of an MBO program, or lesser scale participation and goal setting program (p. 195).

1. *Antecedents.* Do the employees understand the new system? Are the goals they are developing specific and attainable?

2. *Behavior.* Could the employees make the plan work if they wanted to? Do they have enough time to meet and set goals? Do they have the necessary written information? Did they have the training necessary to participate in the program?

3. *Consequences.* Are the consequences for participating in the program positive or negative? Are employees who do *not* take the program seriously rewarded anyway?

SUMMARY

1. *Learned motives* refers to the arousal of motives by previously neutral cues. There are many such human motives, summarized well by Murray.

2. *Need for Achievement* (nAch) is a desire to succeed for success' sake. People high in this need tend to be *medium risk-takers;* they prefer tasks which are hard enough to be challenging but easy enough to be done.

3. The *fear of failure* also influences achievement motivation. Persons high in fear of failure tend more to choose relatively easy or relatively difficult tasks.

4. A *motive to avoid success* (MAS) in women has been suggested. Women high in MAS are less competitive than women low in MAS. Differences in socialization and sex differences in what is perceived to constitute success and failure may underlie this motive.

5. *Consistency theories* assume that we find inconsistencies unpleasant and try to reduce them by changing our beliefs, behaviors, or attitudes. The best known theory in this area is Festinger's *cognitive dissonance* theory, which has been particularly useful in understanding attitude change.

6. The need for *mastery* or *competence* in one's life is considered to be a fundamental motive by many theorists. *Locus of control* refers to the perception that one's life is controlled by oneself (internal locus) or by external events (external locus). Rotter's *social learning theory* says that a history of successful achievement produces a strong internal locus, but failure leads to the perception of external control.

7. *Power,* as a learned motive, is the "ability or capacity of one person to produce some intended effect on the behavior or emotions of another person" (Winter, 1976, p. 5). *Machiavellianism* is a particular form of *manipulative* power.

8. *Herzberg's two-factor theory* assumes that people want more than pay from their jobs; they also want rewards such as prestige and challenge. These "higher level needs" are met by what Herzberg called *satisfiers* or *motivators.*

9. *Values clarification* is a strategy which considers the relative importance of personal values, as well as organization values, in the setting of goals.

10. *Managerial goal setting* is more effective if the goals are *specific, difficult but attainable, relevant* to the job at hand, and *acceptable* to employees.

11. *Management by Objectives* (MBO) uses employee participation built on organizational commitment, clear and acceptable goals, and extensive feedback about performance. It requires a high level of participation by everyone involved and is not always effective.

EXERCISES

1. Make a list of learned motives. How might these certain motives have been learned? How are they rewarding?

2. What is the relationship between need for achievement and performance? Why are high nAch people medium risk-takers?

3. Think about a recent test you took. Would you say you were more motivated by a need for achievement or a fear of failing? Do you think this is characteristic of you? How might this characteristic have come about?

4. What types of activities would a "typical" high motive to avoid success (MAS) woman undertake? A low MAS woman? Discuss the difference between the two groups of activities.

5. What is cognitive dissonance? Why is it unpleasant? Give some specific examples from your own experience of when cognitive dissonance might have been operating. Was the condition unpleasant to you? How can cognitive dissonance be reduced?

6. Where is your main locus of control? Describe some instances where a person would act differently depending on whether he or she had a more internal or more external locus of control.

7. What are Winter's three dimensions of power? Give several modern examples relevant to each dimension. (For example, the power of the Soviet government strongly prevents resistance from the Soviet people.)

8. Discuss examples of individuals (real or fictional) who would rate high in Machiavellianism. What types of activities are they good at? In general, what types of activities are "Machiavellians" good at?

9. According to Herzberg's Two-Factor Theory of motivation, what would be an ideal working situation?

10. Do you agree more with McGregor's work motivation Theory X or Theory Y? Which one best describes you? Your class?

11. Make a list of your own personal values. Rank order these. Were you

already consciously aware of the relative order of your values before you did this? When is values clarification most useful?

12. Set some class goals using Locke's theory of goal setting. What principles did you use?

13. What are the advantages and disadvantages of Management by Objectives (MBO)?

5

Emotion, Anxiety, and Stress

(Photo by Bill Henry)

definition of emotion

We often think of emotion as *the perception or awareness of some kind of feeling, most commonly pleasant or unpleasant in some degree.* This statement is overly restrictive, however, because there may be feelings besides pleasant and unpleasant. Also, under this definition animals would be excluded from the study of emotions, because we usually cannot know much about their perceptions. Emotion is not a rigidly defined subject, but most people are confident they don't need a fancy definition, anyway. We can get a better understanding of emotion, however, by seeing *how* it is studied.

The Study of Emotion

verbal behavior

Though we cannot feel other people's feelings, we can record what they say about their emotional experiences. Freud and later therapists have used this approach in psychoanalytic treatment, as did early scientific psychologists in their laboratories. Modern researchers would also use psychological tests and scales.

Verbal behavior is subject to many biases and often has to be assessed cautiously. The research subject, the clinical patient, or the person-on-the-street may often say what he or she thinks is *expected*. A patient, thinking the clinical psychologist is judging the success of therapy by what the patient says about his emotions, may say things which make progress in therapy seem apparent.

nonverbal behavior

Nonverbal behavior is anything, besides talking, that a person or animal might do which can readily be seen by the naked eye, such as changing facial expression or making particular body movements. If I clench my fist, someone watching me could infer that I am angry. There is the possibility of error, though; I might have clenched my fist for emphasis while speaking. We have to be just as careful interpreting behaviors as we are with speech.

The study of escape and avoidance in animals is particularly useful because these are analogous to many human "neurotic" behaviors. Animals can, for example, learn to avoid electric shock and may do so for hundreds of trials. We would surely be astounded by seeing an animal compulsively moving back and forth in an experimental apparatus were we to come upon it without knowing its previous history. If we know how a behavior came to be learned, however, it makes sense and we can form ideas about how to change it. Psychologists have been long concerned with giving accounts of adult neurosis so that the "strange" behavior of humans could be as understandable as the behavior of persistently-avoiding rats.

physiology

The nervous system is divided into *central* (brain and spinal cord) and *peripheral* portions (everything else). It is also divided into *somatic* and *autonomic* portions. The somatic nervous system regulates interactions with the environment: sensory inputs and muscle movements.

The autonomic nervous system (ANS) is particularly important for emotion. It regulates internal body activities involved in maintaining and replenishing the body. It controls *heart muscle*, the *smooth muscle* of the body cavity such as stomach and intestines, and the release of hormones from *glands* such as the pituitary and adrenal glands.

The *parasympathetic* portion of the ANS is concerned with digestive activity. The *sympathetic* portion of the ANS is concerned with *emergency functions*, such as preparation of the body for *fight* or *flight* (Cannon, 1929). The intense activity we feel in our bodies when we are very active, angry, or frightened, reflects the activity of the sympathetic nervous system and the arousal of the internal organs.

In the brain, the *limbic system* and *the brain stem* are particularly important for emotion. These systems are summarized in Table 5–1 and Figure 5–1.

The parasympathetic and sympathetic systems affect every visceral organ and are generally *antagonistic* to each other. When the sympathetic system is strongly aroused, the parasympathetic system is relatively suppressed and vice-versa. We thus understand why we have indigestion when we are upset: The sympathetic system partly suppresses the parasympathetic system which controls digestion.

We commonly speak of "adrenaline flowing" during excitement. This hormone is circulated through the body via the bloodstream. Adrenaline is also released from nerve endings in the sympathetic system. This double-barrelled action produces quick and widespread arousal and preparation of the body for emergency activity, including the release of blood sugar into the

table 5–1

Divisions of the nervous system. The somatic nervous system is involved in interactions with the external environment. The autonomic system is more involved with the regulation of the internal activity and chemistry of the body.

	somatic	autonomic
central	Brain and Spinal Cord	Limbic system, hypothalamus and brain stem
peripheral	Nerves to Skeletal muscles and from sense organs	Sympathetic, Parasympathetic

body, more rapid breathing, quicker circulation of oxygen, and perspiration for cooling. Continued emotional arousal over a long time may produce the so-called *psychosomatic* or *stress diseases* discussed in chapter six.

Physiological Recording. Most of the body changes described above are impossible to observe with the naked eye but can be "observed" with the aid of electronic amplification. The following measures of "emotional responses" are typically studied.

1. *Heart rate* (measured by electrocardiogram, usually abbreviated EKG). The typical seventy-two beats per minute rate may double under extreme emotional circumstances.

2. *Blood Pressure.* This is described as two values: the amount of pressure *between* heart beats (diastolic pressure), and the amount of pressure immediately following a heart beat (systolic pressure). The pressure is in terms of millimeters of mercury supported in a column. A typical young adult's resting pressure

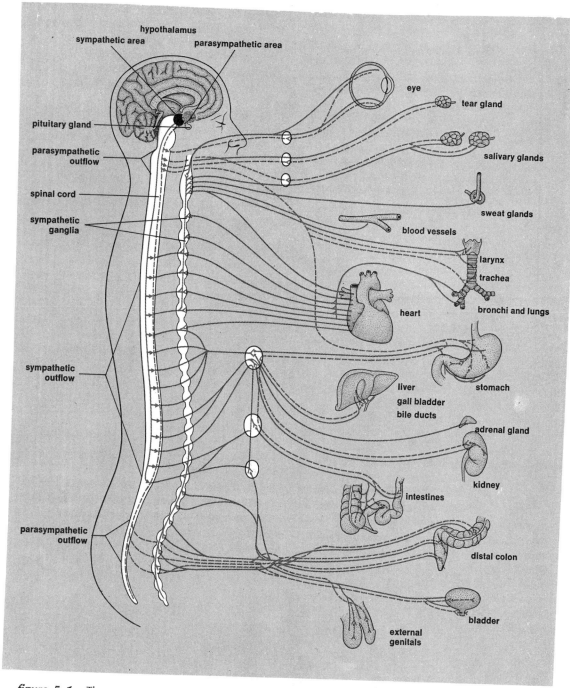

figure 5-1. The autonomic nervous system and the body organs it controls. The limbic system is a set of brain structures surrounding the hypothalamus. (From Krech, Crutchfield & Livson, 1969. Used with permission of publisher & authors.)

is about 120/70, systolic/diastolic. In time of intense emotion it might go to, say, 180/120. (Diastolic pressure might even go *down*.)

3. *Galvanic Skin Response (GSR).* This is a change in the electrical conductance of the skin related to the *activity* of the sweat glands, but not due to perspiration itself.

4. *Respiration (Breathing) Rate.*

5. *Pupil Size.* Much has been written about size change in the pupil of the eyes, but the only reliable finding appears to be that pupil size increases when a person is paying attention to something. This change is awkward to measure and is not a particularly useful index of emotion.

6. *Blood Volume Change.* When we relax or become tense, blood vessels dilate or contract and blood flow through the fingers increases or decreases. This can be easily measured by simple recording devices.

7. *Perspiration.* We can often see perspiration directly, or it can be measured chemically.

8. *Muscle Tension.* Electrodes placed on the skin over particular muscles amplify their electrical activity, which is greater during tension.

9. *Skin Temperature.* The greater the blood flow, the higher the surrounding skin temperature. A device for measuring temperature can easily be taped to the end of a finger.

Other useful measures, such as of hormone levels, can be obtained from blood or urine samples. With animals, it is possible to do surgery that cannot be done on humans for experimental purposes. Thus, much of our knowledge about the nervous system of humans comes from animals.

the lie detector (polygraph)

The so-called "lie detector" simply detects the body changes which commonly occur during emotional arousal. The polygraph typically records heart rate, GSR, respiration changes, and blood pressure. If a person does become emotional while lying, a properly conducted test can be very informative. There is presently a lively professional controversy, however, over the best methods of questioning suspects and interpreting polygraph results.

There are also problems with polygraph accuracy to the extent that results are generally not admissible as court evidence. People who do research involving these physiological measures tend to have less faith in their accuracy than do professional polygraph operators. Two problems arise. First, some people are easily aroused under many circumstances and hence may appear to be lying when they are not. They are false positives. Conversely, some individuals show very little emotional arousal under any circumstance and may appear innocent when they are in fact guilty. They are false negatives. It is difficult to tell when these errors are occuring if we are using the polygraph itself as the criterion for lying or not lying.

Employment Screening. Many corporations use the polygraph in employee selection, intending to screen out potentially dishonest employees. This is unfortunate because it is not reliably demonstrated that the polygraph can do this, and many people may be unjustly denied employment. Under federal law any psychological test (and the polygraph is a psychological test) must be demonstrated to produce scores that are actually related to job performance. The law was intended to prevent employers from using irrelevant tests to screen out minority applicants, women, and so on, but it should be equally applicable to polygraph tests.

Theories of Emotion

background

Until the late nineteenth century, emotions were generally considered "states of mind." The Roman physician Galen, in the second century, had proposed a primitive theory relating different emotions to physiological events, but William James' writings in the 1880s really stimulated modern attempts to relate physiology and emotion.

the James-Lange theory

William James and Carl Lange independently put forth similar theories, hence the dual name. James (1884) proposed that *emotion is the experience of our bodily reactions to particular situations.* These reactions could be skeletal muscular activity or visceral ("gut") activity. The internal organs became most strongly identified with the theory, however, and James thus shifted the relative emphasis in emotion from the *center* of the nervous system (the brain-mind) to a *peripheral* position (the organs controlled by the autonomic nervous system).

The James-Lange theory was important because it seemed to be readily testable. Physiologists could cut portions of the sympathetic nervous system outside the brains and spinal cords of dogs and observe the effects on emotional behavior. A great deal of this type of research was conducted.

the Cannon-Bard theory

After considerable research in this area, Walter Cannon (1927) and his associate Philip Bard concluded that the James-Lange theory was incorrect. Cannon believed the ANS reacted too slowly and too diffusely to account for the rapid occurrence and fine gradations of emotion. Furthermore, dogs could *act* fearful or angry even after the ANS was severed, as could people whose ANS had been damaged in accidents or by disease. Conversely, injections of adrenaline into normal people produced physiological symptoms of strong emotional arousal, such as heart palpitations and muscle tremor, but seldom produced the typical emotional *experiences*. Such people often reported they felt "as if" they were afraid, but not really.

Cannon concluded that emotion is basically a central nervous system phenomenon. As long as the area in and around the *thalamus* of the brain (a part of the limbic system) was not destroyed, emotion could be expressed. This was Cannon's thalamic theory of emotion.

activation theory

Elizabeth Duffy (1934) proposed that behavior could be characterized by two dimensions—direction and intensity. She attributed intensity to what she called *energy mobilization*, the mustering of body resources for activity. To her, a high level of energy mobilization *was* emotion. This view was not particularly popular until 1951 when Donald Lindsley proposed the *activation theory* of emotion. Lindsley incorporated recently published research on the *reticular activating system* of the brain. He saw emotion as the level of reticular arousal, which was in turn related to the usual autonomic functions and muscle tension.

The difficulty with activation theory is that it does not differentiate among such different emotions as happiness, sadness, fear, and anger. Subsequent investigators (for example, Donald Hebb, 1955, Daniel Berlyne, 1960; and J. McV. Hunt, 1965) elaborated on activation theory so it could account at least for pleasantness and unpleasantness. They argued that a medium level of activation (reticular system arousal) is pleasant and that either very high or very low levels are unpleasant. Boredom and terror are both aversive. The theory still does not seem to capture all the subtleties of emotion which people describe, however. Are these subtle differences possibly illusory?

cognitive-arousal theory

Stanley Schachter and Jerome Singer (1962) and George Mandler (1962) argued that there are not in fact many emotions, in the sense of unique physiological activities for each. Instead, on the basis of information available to us, we *interpret* the same kind and level of arousal in different ways and distinguish emotions by means of these interpretations. Schachter and Singer (1962) reported that different subjects given identical adrenaline injections might describe their emotional experience as *either* anger or happiness depending on the situation. If the experimenter told them that the injections would produce higher heart rate and muscle tremor, they did not report themselves emotional. In the same situations *uninformed* subjects reported themselves as happy or angry, according to what the experimental situation was.

The explanation was that the uninformed subjects interpreted their arousal as anger or happiness because they were guided only by the anger-arousing or happiness-related cues supplied by the experimenter. If they *did* know the expected symptoms, they attributed their arousal to the injections and ignored the situation in their interpretations. Cognitive-arousal theory thus says that the underlying physiology for many different emotional experiences may be the same. We experience different emotions because we interpret our arousal differently.

differential-emotions theory

Activation theory and cognitive-arousal theory both assume a small range of physiological difference in emotions. Carroll Izard (1975) postulates ten *different* emotions, as follows.

1. *Interest-excitement.* Providing much motivation for learning and creative endeavor, this is similar to the "arousal" in activation theory.

2. *Joy.* This is a state of confidence, meaningfulness, and a feeling of being loved.

3. *Surprise.* This is characterized by a sudden change in neural stimulation, said to prepare a person to respond to a changing situation.

4. *Distress-anguish.* This is commonly produced by separation from others, as well as by real or imagined failure to live up to one's own standards or those set by others.

5. *Anger-rage.* This may follow from physical or psychological restraint or from interference with goal-oriented activity. It may or may not lead to aggressive behavior.

6. *Disgust.* This is commonly produced by bad odors, tastes, or anything "spoiled." We may feel nauseated and possibly be motivated to change the conditions which disgust us.

7. *Contempt-scorn.* This may occur in conjunction with anger or disgust. It is a kind of "cold" emotion, which may lead to inhumane treatment of those we hold in contempt.

8. *Fear-terror.* Fear is related to feelings of apprehension, uncertainty, and impending disaster and helps mobilize escape from threatening situations.

9. *Shame/shyness-humiliation.* We probably learn this as a result being punished for deviating from social norms. It may lead to hostility toward the person who produced the shame or to a program of self-improvement. ("I'll never be embarrassed like that again.")

10. *Guilt.* Closely akin to both anxiety and shame, guilt occurs when a person does something known to be wrong by some standard.

These ten different emotions are also said to occur in combination, with each different emotion having a different physiological basis. Patterns of facial expression are also considered important as part of the basis for distinguishing emotion in ourselves (how our faces feel) as well as in others (how they look to us). Figure 5–2 shows some typical facial expressions of emotion.

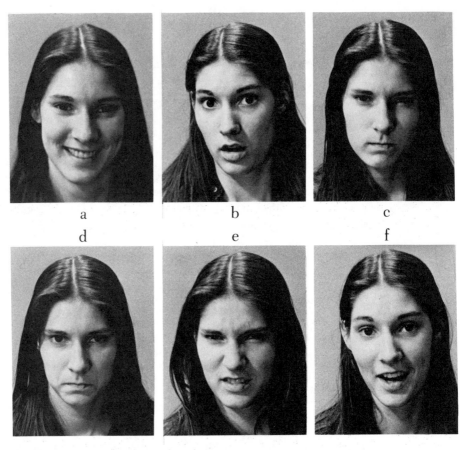

figure 5–2. Facial expressions of emotion like those used in research on emotion. These six are common around the world. Can you identify them?

a) Happy, b) fear/surprise, c) anger, d) sorrow, e) disgust, f) surprise/happy.

dimensions of emotion

Another approach is to consider just a few dimensions of emotion which vary in degree rather than a large number of separate emotions. Three of the most commonly proposed dimensions are:

1. *Pleasant-Unpleasant.* Events may be experienced as ranging from very pleasant through neutral to very unpleasant. These events are different from person to person.
2. *Tension-Relaxation.* Again, this is the dimension referred to in activation theory. A related dimension may be that of calm-excited (Thayer, 1978).
3. *Competence-Incompetence (Mastery, Power).* We saw in Chapter Four the motivational importance attributed to this dimension by Alfred Adler and Robert White.

All other emotions are considered to be combinations of the basic dimensions, along with interpretations of the situations in which the various combinations occur.

Emotional Change

learning and maturation

As we age, the conditions which produce emotional experiences change. These changes may be partly due to maturation (physical growth and development), permitting the nervous system to more finely tune in to the environment. Bridges (1934) described the first emotion of infants as variation only in the degree of generalized excitement: The baby cries when hungry or thirsty, when it has gas, or when it has diaper rash. Very young infants show some facial expressions which suggest pleasure, but do not clearly show delight or distress by smiling or frowning, for example, until about three months. The greatest emotional change appears due to learning.

classical conditioning of emotion

Watson and Raynor (1920) performed the most famous demonstration of childhood emotional conditioning. A seven-month-old infant, "Little Albert," was the subject. Watson and Raynor first showed that Albert was not afraid of a white rat, a Santa Claus mask, or a number of other stimuli. Then, over a period of days they presented the rat to Albert, followed quickly by a loud sound (a metal rod being struck with a hammer). After seven such pairings, Albert reliably became upset when shown the rat, fussing, crying, and trying to get away from it. He was also fearful of the Santa Claus mask and other fur-like objects. He had learned to be afraid of the rat, and his fear generalized to other stimuli.

Subsequently, Mary Cover Jones (1924), a student of Watson's, showed that children's pre-existing fears could be reduced by a number of methods based on learning principles. The best was *counterconditioning*, presenting a positive stimulus (such as food) at the same time as the fear-arousing stimulus. Classical conditioning techniques have now been much refined and used for therapeutic purposes.

preparedness

Some stimuli are readily conditioned and others are not. Martin Seligman (1970) has argued that organisms are "genetically wired" or *prepared* to associate some things more readily than others. Thus, Watson and Raynor were either very lucky or very shrewd in their choice of a rat as a conditioned stimulus: Fear responses are readily conditioned to furry little animals. Öhnman and Dingerg (1979) have reported that the galvanic skin response is more strongly conditioned to pictures of frowning faces associated with electric shock than to pictures of smiling faces. A major question for future research is What are the "prepared" stimuli and responses with humans, those which condition readily?

Emotional Expression and Recognition

background

In ancient Greek theatre, tragedy was symbolized by an actor holding up a mask of a frowning face and comedy by a mask with a smiling face. The Greeks established a widely recognized pair of symbols for joy and grief. Might these be *universal* expressions for these emotions?

Charles Darwin (1872) observed that many species showed similar expressions of emotion. Dogs, cats, and monkeys draw back their lips and bare their teeth when angry, much as people do. This suggests some degree of universal expression for at least some emotions in some animals.

facial expression

Only about six emotions seem to be universally recognized among humans by facial expression alone: *happiness, anger, sadness, disgust, surprise,* and *fear.* The last two are sometimes confused, perhaps because surprise often fades into fear (Ekman & Friesen, 1979). The same expressions have been found in diverse literate cultures and in isolated preliterate cultures. Deaf and blind children also show the typical facial expressions for these emotions, presumably without opportunity for learning the expressions from others. Such facial expressions may be universal because they are biologically valuable to infants. Accompanied by appropriate vocalizations, such as crying or cooing, these expressions arouse such caretaking activity as feeding by adults. In the course of evolution, those infants who could express themselves emotionally tended to survive better.

Specific cultural learning can interfere with whatever "basic" emotional expressions there might be. Japanese people watching a movie controlled their facial expression much more if they knew they were being observed. They smiled less when watched, for example. Americans, on the other hand, did not inhibit their emotional expression as much when watched. The "stoic" Britisher, the "inscrutable" Oriental, and the "excitable" Latin may represent specific cultural influences on emotional expression.

Development of Facial Expression. In newborn humans the facial muscles are fully operative, and adult-like expressions occur early. These include distress, disgust, and startle. Some imitation of adult facial expressions actually seems to occur as early as two or three weeks of age. At about three months smiling begins to occur reliably, and infants also begin to distinguish adult facial expressions and respond differently to them (Ekman & Oster, 1979). Preschool children know most of the common facial expressions and what elicits them, but this knowledge continues to increase at least until age ten.

early emotional experience

Freud's Psychosexual Theory. Freud speculated broadly about the role of early experience in later emotional life. His theory of *psychosexual development* postulated that the child goes through a set sequence of emotional stages in the first few years of life. First, there is an *oral* stage, where the infant gets emotional gratification from feeding. Second, there is an *anal* stage where the infant is more preoccupied (because of the parents' concerns) about elimination functions. Third, there is a *genital* stage where the young child is curious about his or her sexual organs and those of others. There is then a quiet, or *latent*, period until puberty when adult sexual interest begins to appear. According to the theory, if there are traumatic (highly emotional, anxiety arousing) events during any of these stages, the child may not "satisfactorily" progress from one to the other and, hence, may become a somewhat "emotionally crippled" adult. Freud's theory has been exceptionally important, not because of its accuracy in detail, but because it stimulated a great deal of research on the effects of early experience on later personality.

Harlow's Mother-Love Research. Harry Harlow (1971) studied rhesus monkeys to test the effect of lack of normal mothering. Infant monkeys were reared in an apparatus where a "wire" mother (a wire mesh arrangement with a simulated head on the top) *provided food* (a bottle in the mesh) and a warm, terrycloth fake mother provided *nothing* except "her" presence. The infant monkeys spent the great bulk of their time with the terrycloth mother, going only to the wire mother to eat. They would venture away from the terrycloth mother, but would scamper quickly back when startled. Harlow concluded that *contact comfort* was more important to the infant most of the time than was feeding. Stimuli associated with feeding (the wire mother) were less attractive than the comforting contact stimulation from the terrycloth mother. This runs contrary to theories which stress that infants become attached to those who satisfy their hunger-thirst-pain needs.

As adults, even the terrycloth-mother monkeys were emotionally unusual, however. They did not establish normal love relations with members of the opposite sex, for example, and they generally kept to themselves. If females became mothers they took care of their infants very poorly. They improved, however, if they had a second infant.

Levine's Work with Early Infantile Stimulation in Rats. Seymour Levine (1960) divided newborn rat pups into three groups during the first ten days of life. One group simply remained with their mother. The second group was taken from the mother and gently stroked by the experimenter for ten minutes daily. The third group was subjected to gentle but unpleasant electric shock for ten minutes daily. They were then all reared normally and tested for level of emotionality (fearfulness) at eighty days of age, young adulthood. The test was to put them into an "open field," a lighted arena about three feet on a side. This is normally somewhat fear-arousing for rats, as indicated by defecation, urination, and a low level of activity. It was predicted that the animals kept with their mothers would show the least fearfulness and the shocked group would show the most. The results were just the opposite. The stroked animals and the shocked animals were equally non-fearful, much below the level of fearfulness exhibited by animals kept with their mothers. Levine concluded that the important variable was *stimulation* and that supposedly pleasant and supposedly unpleasant stimulation had equal positive effect. These results have been found in many experiments.

Such research as Harlow's and Levine's is important because it relates to observational evidence with humans. Institutionalized children, if socially ignored, become apathetic and withdrawn, much like Harlow's monkeys. In many documented situations, children completely ignored for several years have been socially, emotionally, and physically immature. Fortunately, individuals besides the mother can provide the all-important stimulation. The stimulation from human (or monkey) brothers and sisters can replace the attention usually obtained from parents.

Fear and Anxiety

Henry Thoreau wrote that most people live lives of quiet desperation. Indeed, because of their everyday occurrence and clinical importance, fear and anxiety are two of the most studied emotions in psychology.

distinction between fear and anxiety

Fear and anxiety are commonly distinguished as follows: Fear has an *identifiable* cause and anxiety does not. If a snarling dog leaps toward me I *know* why I feel afraid. But if for no apparent reason my heart pounds and my palms break out in a cold sweat, I am anxious.

Fear and anxiety have also been distinguished in terms of a person's control over the situation (for example, Epstein, 1967). I may be afraid of some specific, recognized object, but *also* be anxious because I am helpless to do anything about it. If a police officer knows she is being shot at and knows where the shots are coming from, she is afraid. But if she can do nothing about it, she may also be anxious. In this view then, fear and anxiety are not only different, they can add to each other. In practice, the fear-anxiety distinction is sometimes difficult to make, but it is nevertheless important.

origins of fear and anxiety

O. H. Mowrer (1939), following some of Freud's ideas, suggested that fear and anxiety are *a conditioned form of the pain reaction*. The original pain is not recreated when a stimulus associated with that pain is presented, but the emotional response which accompanied the pain may be aroused.

John B. Watson (1924) argued that the primary sources of fear were *pain, loud noise,* and *loss of body support.* Numerous surveys of children's fears show how these change with age. Fears of animals and of the darkness decrease with age. But anticipatory fears (of things which a child can imagine might happen to him or her) *increase.* Girls seem to be somewhat more fearful than boys, but the reason is not clear.

Hebb (1946) also described *fear of the unfamiliar.* If we become accustomed to certain conditions, an unexpected change may provoke fear. Hebb described chimpanzees who were very frightened when their normal keeper wore strange clothes. Similarly, small children may become upset when a familiar person appears in a strange guise, such as a costume or fake beard.

Unreasonable fears may also result from malnutrition, disease, or fatigue. Certain illnesses may produce highly irascible patients. Maturational changes related to normal growth might produce effects in the nervous system which would be experienced as fear at one age, but not later. Many children have nightmares, but few carry them into adulthood.

state versus trait anxiety

Anxiety is often considered a personality trait, a stable characteristic of an individual. Some people might regularly be highly anxious, others low, and most somewhere between.

A different view is that anxiety levels are not stable or constant across all situations but depend on particular situations. Charles Spielberger (1966) calls this latter view *state anxiety* (A-State) as compared to the trait view of anxiety (A-Trait). Some individuals tend to be anxious in many situations (A-Trait), but there is an even greater tendency for people to have specific anxieties in specific situations (A-State). One person may be afraid of bees, but not large dogs, while the situation is reversed for someone else.

Conditioning and Instrumental Learning. A simple classical conditioning situation is to have a dim light precede an airpuff to the eye, causing the eye to blink reflexively. People high in trait anxiety condition more rapidly than people low in trait anxiety. Anxiety may generally facilitate the performance of a simple task (as in eyeblink conditioning) but be detrimental to complex learning tasks, such as school work or job performance. The relationship between anxiety and performance is often the Inverted-U we saw with activation theory in chapter three: Performance may improve with small amounts of anxiety but be impaired at high levels.

Escape and Avoidance. Since fear and anxiety are unpleasant, we should work to reduce them. Extensive research verifies that animals readily learn to escape or avoid situations in which they were previously given electric shock to the feet.

The human implications of escape and avoidance are vast because of our great learning capacity. Judson Brown (1951), for example, applied the principles of escape and avoidance to an explanation of human "miserliness." A child hears mom and dad talking about lack of money in anxious tones, and this arouses fear in the child. The child may eventually become fearful of any cue indicating lack of money. This fear is then reduced by eliminating (escaping from) the fear-arousing cue, that is, by getting money. Such a person might collect and hoard money far beyond his or her needs because money holds down the fear of lack of money. This is diagrammed in Figure 5–3. Many other compulsive behaviors might have the same general cause. For example, some people might compulsively seek out the company of others because of very high anxiety when other people are absent.

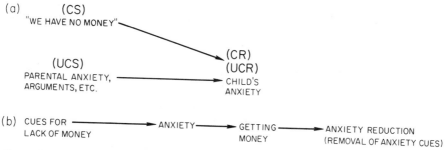

figure 5–3. Illustration of how anxiety may become a source of motivation for getting money. (a) Parents' verbalized concerns and general distress about lack of money becomes a cue for arousing anxiety in the child. (b) Cues of lack of money then arouse anxiety which is reduced by getting money. (From Beck, 1978 p. 193. Used with permission of publisher.)

test anxiety and its treatment

A *little* anxiety when taking a test may keep us alert and stimulate greater effort. Our concern here is with anxiety so strong that it *impairs* test performance.

Taking tests can be anxiety-arous-ing for many students and they may not show what they really know.

All theories of test anxiety assume that the student does something which *interferes* with giving the correct answers. A student may worry so much about not doing well that the worrying takes up time which should be spent working on the test questions. Or, anxiety may directly arouse incorrect answers. The student may put down the first thing that comes into his or her head without thinking the answer through. This may result from general "agitation" rather than worrying.

Research indicates that test anxiety is specific to test situations and not necessarily reflective of anxiety in other situations (Spielberger, 1976). A fearless soldier may be a quivering mass in a written examination.

Treatment for Test Anxiety. One way to treat test anxiety is to train the anxious student in study skills and test taking procedures. This may not reduce the anxiety much, but the student should perform better if he or she knows the material better.

A second approach deals directly with the anxiety. *Systematic desensitization* and *relaxation training* have been the most effective methods of reducing test anxiety (Spielberger, 1976). In systematic desensitization the student *imagines* a variety of situations progressively closer to test-taking, such as studying in the dormitory, walking to the classroom, entering the classroom, picking up the exam paper, and actually taking the exam. This is done under non-threatening conditions, in a relaxed atmosphere. The rationale for this kind of therapy, widely used for eliminating many different fears, is that the anxiety will be aroused, will subside, and then will extinguish to cues associated with test-taking. This should generalize to the actual test situation.

Relaxation training uses such techniques as muscle relaxation and imagining pleasant situations, which are not related to the test anxiety directly. After some practice a person can quickly relax in a tense situation. Procedures for this are described in chapter six.

Spielberger (1976) concludes that systematic desensitization is overall the most effective method of reducing test anxiety, although relaxation training is also useful. Simultaneous training in study skills also helps. On the other hand, simple counseling about test anxiety (intended to get at the cause of the anxiety) does not seem to be very helpful. It also appears that lower test anxiety *may not* immediately lead to better test performance. This may be because conditions outside the test situation are not changed. For example, if a student worries *while studying,* then learning may not be as good.

Stress

life change units

Fred just got married, Jane started a new job, John's father died, and Judy got divorced. Some of these are seemingly good events and some bad. But they all produce stress. Holmes and Rahe (1967) devised a scale for such life changes in terms of their degree of stressfulness, shown in Table 5–2. They used such indices as reported illnesses and visits to doctors as the relatively objective measures of stress. What is the nature of stress that it should lead to illness?

the general adaptation syndrome

Hans Selye and his book *The Stress of Life* (1956, 1976) are most closely associated with the study of stress. Selye has repeatedly found three disorders

Leaving for vacation at dawn may be fun, but it can also be very stressful.

table 5-2

Life change units (lcu's) and illness. A total of life change units of 300 within a short period of time is said to be something of a critical value for stress illness. There is controversy over whether it is change itself which is contributory or the total aversiveness (unpleasantness) of the changes.

	lcu values
Family:	
Death of spouse	100
Divorce	73
Marital separation	65
Death of close family member	63
Marriage	50
Marital reconciliation	45
Major change in health of family	44
Pregnancy	40
Addition of new family member	39
Major change in arguments with spouse	35
Son or daughter leaving home	29
In-law troubles	29
Spouse starting or ending work	26
Major change in family get-togethers	15
Personal:	
Detention in jail	63
Major personal injury or illness	53
Sexual difficulties	39
Death of a close friend	37
Outstanding personal achievement	28
Start or end of formal schooling	26
Major change in living conditions	25
Major revision of personal habits	24
Changing to a new school	20
Change in residence	20
Major change in recreation	19
Major change in church activities	19
Major change in sleeping habits	16
Major change in eating habits	15
Vacation	13
Christmas	12
Minor violations of the law	11
Work:	
Being fired from work	47
Retirement from work	45
Major business adjustment	39
Changing to different line of work	36
Major change in work responsibilities	29
Trouble with boss	23
Major change in working conditions	20
Financial:	
Major change in financial state	38
Mortgage or loan over $10,000	31
Mortgage foreclosure	30
Mortgage or loan less than $10,000	17

common to many causes, calling them the General Adaptation Syndrome (GAS). These are (1) enlargement of the adrenal glands, (2) shrinking of the thymus gland and lymphatic system, crucial organs for fighting disease, and (3) gastrointestinal ulcers. By such apparently unrelated circumstances as exposure to heat or cold, infection with parasites, or injection with formalin, Selye found this same triad of symptoms in experimental animals. The number of known causes has since been vastly increased in both medical and psychological research.

The Time Course of Stress. In Selye's analysis, stress responses pass through three stages if the stress is continued. This is shown in Figure 5–4.

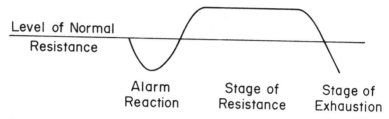

figure 5–4. The time course of stress (From Selye, 1976. Used with permission of publisher.)

1. *Alarm Reaction.* When a person is subjected to a stressful event (a *stressor*) such as fatigue, disease, injury, or extreme environmental stimulation, there is an alarm reaction. This is a shock effect, such as a sudden drop in blood sugar level, followed shortly by a compensatory rebound, such as recovery of blood sugar level.

2. *Stage of Resistance.* The body is in this stage when it uses its resources to keep its physiology to a normal course during stress. Since the body has to work harder than usual to maintain itself, or if there is additional stress for which the body is no longer prepared, the third stage may occur.

3. *The Stage of Exhaustion.* Pathological symptoms occur here, with such disorders as ulcers, stroke, or infection (due to lowered resistance) possibly occurring. If severe enough, the stress disorder may lead to death.

Psychological and biological stressors can combine. Mice living in crowded conditions (psychological stress) are less resistant to growth of injected parasites (biological stress). The concept of stress thus gives psychological and medical professionals a common framework for understanding medical-psychological problems.

stressors are not all unpleasant

Stress may occur in apparently pleasant circumstances, as indicated by the Life Change Units. An interesting job may eventually be as taxing as prolonged anxiety. Friedman and Rosenman (1974) have distinguished between Type A and Type B personalities. The former are always trying to be more efficient, stay continually busy, and are more prone to heart attacks. The latter are more relaxed, less efficient, less ambitious, and less prone to heart attacks. The type A people may be enjoying their work, however.

Solomon and Corbit (1975) have proposed a theory that says pleasurable situations produce the same internal biological events which occur in unpleasant circumstances. The pleasurable situation *masks* the unpleasant effects, so they are not immediately noticed. In the long run, however, they may "catch up with us" and produce a stress disorder.

All stress is not *bad*, however. Stress is a part of life, and a moderate amount of stress may keep us more efficient and even more healthy. It is prolonged high stress that produces psychological and medical problems.

factors influencing susceptibility to stress

Genetic, Prenatal, and Early Postnatal Influences. A pattern of results from animal research has developed which is consistent with many non-experimental observations of humans.

1. Animals can be selectively bred for either high or low emotional responsiveness to stress situations.
2. If a pregnant female is stressed, her offspring are more emotional (fearful) in stress situations than they would be otherwise. This is presumably due to body chemistry changes in the mother which are transmitted to the fetus via the bloodstream.
3. Early postnatal experiences have strong effects which appear in later adulthood, as we have already seen in the work of Harlow and Levine.
4. Some of these effects can be partially reversed by rearing the offspring with foster mothers having the opposite temperament of the real mothers. For

example, offspring of an "emotional" mother reared by a "nonemotional" mother grow up to be less emotional than otherwise expected.

Learning

1. *Classical conditioning.* Stress responses, such as higher heart rate or blood pressure can be classically conditioned and can have long-lasting effects. For example, a child that had been painfully stung by an insect at an early age became afraid of all flying insects (stimulus generalization). People who have auto accidents may be very much afraid of whatever stimuli were associated with the accidents.

2. *Instrumental conditioning of autonomic responses.* Although this is an area of controversial research results, since the work of Kimmel and Hill (1960) it has appeared that such responses as heart rate, blood pressure, and galvanic skin response are sensitive to reward and punishment. Kimmel and Hill reported that the frequency of GSR responses increased with reward. It has even been reported that blood vessels could be conditioned to constrict in one ear and not the other. The significance of such results is in the possibility that such problems as high blood pressure might be brought under control by learning techniques.

The major problems with this research have been difficulty in reproducing the results in later experiments and the possibility of non-learning explanations for the results. It is difficult to separate the effects of a general relaxation or tension from the possible effect of reward and punishment.

Frustration and Conflict

frustration

Frustration is the blocking of a goal-directed behavior. This is shown in Figure 5–5, where we have a motivated person, a goal, and a barrier which prevents the person from reaching the goal.

Barriers may be conveniently classed as *obstacles* or *deficiencies.* Obstacles may be external objects, such as locked doors, deep ravines, or great distances. Or they may be internal, such as anticipation of punishment or fear of failure.

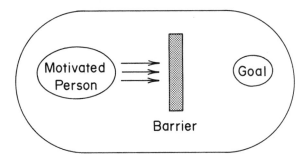

figure 5–5. A motivated person is kept from achieving her goal by some barrier and is then frustrated. Frustration may arouse many kinds of responses, including hostility and aggression. To someone else, it may simply provide a challenge.

A deficiency is some lack which prevents attaining a goal. I may want a job I am not trained for, or I may want to open a stuck door and not be strong enough. A third kind of frustration event is the reduction or absence of an anticipated reward. This is called *nonreward frustration.*

Responses to Frustration. Frustration may lead to *aggression, fixation* (rigid unchanging behavior in the face of failure), *regression* (return to more childlike ways of acting), more *vigorous* effort, *escape, avoidance,* and such *emotional* responses as crying. With such an unlimited range of possibilities, why does a *particular* response occur?

Strong frustration is unpleasant. Consequently, behaviors which reduce frustration are likely to be *learned* and *repeated.* A child may learn to throw a temper tantrum if this gets the child his or her way. As the child grows older, however, this is less effective because it does not work (especially with other children) and because the child learns better ways of achieving goals. If these new ways also fail, the older child (or even an adult) may regress to the early successful behaviors—tantrums. It is debatable whether there are any invariable responses to frustration. The great diversity suggests there are very few, if any.

conflict

Conflict is a special case of frustration: The barrier to achieving one goal is another goal. If I want to remodel my house and buy a new car, but cannot afford both, I am in a conflict frustration situation because getting one goal prevents getting the other.

Psychologists typically distinguish four kinds of conflict.

1. *Approach-Approach.* A person has two positive goals, as in the house-car example.

2. *Avoidance-Avoidance.* A person trying to escape from one unpleasant situation may be forced into another if he does so. "Out of the frying pan and into the fire" expresses this. A college student who dislikes school may have to face the wrath of a parent if he quits. Such conflicts may be resolved by picking the "lesser of two evils" or "leaving the field." A student might join the army, or a disillusioned voter might stay away from the polls.

3. *Approach-Avoidance.* A particular goal may have both good and bad features. A girl might want to go to a particular college which is so expensive that much else would have to be sacrificed to pay the tuition. Whether or not to go to this college could be a very difficult decision.

4. *Multiple Approach-Avoidance.* This involves several goals, each with good and bad features. Let's say Job A pays well and is prestigious but is in an expensive area of the country and requires commuting; Job B pays much less but is in a small city with home and recreation nearby. You have to choose and you can't have it both ways.

conflict resolution

How can we *rationally* resolve such conflicts as a choice of jobs? For each alternative there are probably a number of good and bad features, such as quality and nearness of schools, cost of living and transportation, pay, fringe benefits, job demands, and location. We could do the following.

1. For each alternative draw up a list of the good and bad features, choosing the job which has the *greatest number* of good features. This does not allow for some features being more important than others, however, so we could use a second procedure.

table 5–3

An example of how to result a conflict by summarizing the good and bad features of the alternatives and giving them different degrees of "goodness" and "badness." The example is entirely fictitious except for the names of the cities.

	job a (New York City)	job b (Boulder, Colorado)
Cost of living	−2	+2
Commuting Time	−3	+2
Salary	+4	+1
Entertainment	+5	+1
Outdoor Recreation	−3	+5
Fringe Benefits	+2	+2
Scenery	−2	+4
Schools	−1	+2
Sum +	11	19
Sum −	8	0
Net	+3	+19

Note. The numbers assigned by the hypothetical person here indicate this person values outdoor recreation and scenery very highly. Someone else might approach the problem with entirely different values.

2. Draw up the list of good and bad features and *assign each a value* from −5 to +5 in terms of importance. Adding these up, the alternative with the *highest net positive* value would be the choice. Such weighting of factors is subjective, varying from person to person. One might have to weight each factor in consultation with other members of the family.

An example is given in Table 5–3. But remember, if you arrived at a choice by this method and then said "This method does not work, it did not give me the right answer," the difficulty is with *you* and not the method. Either something important to you was left out of the list, or was weighted improperly, or you had already made up your mind and weren't even using the method.

SUMMARY

1. *Emotion,* from the point of view of an individual person, is often considered as the perception or *awareness of some kind of feeling,* most commonly pleasant or unpleasant in some degree. The study of emotion is not rigidly defined.

2. Emotion is generally *studied* from three points of view: (a) a person's *verbal self-report* about his or her feelings, (b) *nonverbal behavior,* such as facial expression and body movements, and (c) *physiology.* The *autonomic nervous system* is especially important in the physiology of emotion, along with the limbic system and reticular activating system in the brain. Common physiological measures of emotion are heart rate, galvanic skin response, blood pressure, and respiration rate.

3. *Lie detectors,* or *polygraphs,* measure some of the physiological changes which are assumed to result from emotional arousal in a "guilty" person faced with questions concerning a particular crime or other event.

4. The *James-Lange* theory of emotion proposed that emotion is the *experience of our bodily reactions* to particular situations. If we respond to a threatening situation, physiologically or behaviorally, it is the experience of the response which constitutes emotion.

5. The *Cannon-Bard* theory stressed the role of the *central nervous system* in emotion, de-emphasizing the importance given to visceral activity by the James-Lange theory.

6. *Activation theory* attributes emotion to level of arousal of the *reticular activating system* in the brain stem. Medium levels of arousal are pleasant, but either high or low levels are unpleasant.

7. The *cognitive-arousal* theory of Schachter and Singer says that emotions are a general state of bodily arousal which is interpreted by a person as emotion, depending on the information available. Cues from the situation determine what particular emotion we will experience and if it will be pleasant or unpleasant.

8. *Differential emotions* theory postulates ten different emotions as contrasted with activation or cognitive-arousal theory which recognize only "diffuse" arousal. Three of the most commonly considered *dimensions* of emotion are pleasant-unpleasant, tension-relaxation, and feelings of competence-incompetence.

9. Emotional *expression* may have a biological basis which is modified by specific experiences. Research suggests that six facial expressions of emotion may be universally recognized among humans: *happiness, anger, sadness, disgust, surprise,* and *fear.*

10. *Early experience* is important in later emotional life. *Freud's psychosexual theory* of development stressed the importance of what he considered fixed stages of emotional development in the first few years of life.

11. *Sensory stimulation* is important for normal emotional development. This has been found in extensive laboratory research with rats and monkeys, as well as in studies of children reared in environments of low stimulation.

12. *Fear* is an unpleasant emotion with an identifiable cause; *anxiety* is similar to fear, but without a recognizable cause. These commonly have their origins in painful experiences, but may also result from lack of experience (unfamiliarity) with a situation or from such biological factors as malnutrition, disease, and fatigue.

13. *Trait anxiety* is a *stable* characteristic of an individual and *state anxiety* varies in amount from one situation to another for the same person. A low level of anxiety may facilitate performance, but high levels usually produce poorer performance, such as in test situations. *Test anxiety* has been successfully treated by a combination of systematic desensitization, relaxation training, and study skills training.

14. *Stress* can cause both emotional and physical disorders if maintained for a long period of time. The *general adaptation syndrome* divides responses to stress into three stages: alarm reaction, stage of resistance, and stage of exhaustion, which involves a variety of possible medical symptoms. All stress is not inherently, bad, however, and in small amounts it may be beneficial.

15. *Frustration* is the blocking of goal-directed behavior. Possible reactions to frustration include aggression, fixation, escape, or avoidance.

16. *Conflict* is frustration caused when *two* or more goals are *incompatible.* Obtaining one blocks getting the other. The four basic types of conflict are approach-approach, avoidance-avoidance, approach-avoidance, and multiple approach-avoidance.

17. Conflicts are *resolved* in favor of the strongest motive at the moment. Resolution can be achieved by weighing the good and bad features of possible choices and selecting the most positive alternative.

EXERCISES

1. Have you ever felt especially emotionally-enriched or emotionally-impoverished? What aspects of the situation might have caused the particular condition, and what were the results? In what other ways might the enrichment or impoverishment have been expressed?

2. Make a list of specific things that could be done in the future to create emotional enrichment and avoid emotional impoverishment. Are there things in *jobs* that could be done to increase emotional enrichment?

3. There are some obvious things that people say when they are "emotional," such as "I feel happy" or "I am sad." In what less direct ways do people indicate their emotional state? How could these be measured?

4. Use your forefinger to feel your pulse (or hold your fingers gently against the side of your neck, under your jaw). You cannot measure blood pressure this way but you can count your heart beats. As you relax, count the beats for fifteen seconds (and multiply by four to get beats per minute). Now think of some frightening event and count again. Is there any change? Do some exercise, like jumping up and down for a minute. Count your pulse before, immediately after, and two minutes after your exercise. What is your heart rate at each time? Why is there usually an increase in heart rate with fear or anger and with exercise? What does this say about what the body is doing during emotional arousal?

5. What are the advantages and disadvantages of the "lie detector" as a measure of lies? What kinds of things other than lies might produce physiological changes indicative of emotion when a person is taking a polygraph (lie detector) test?

6. What are the main differences between the James-Lange theory and Cannon-Bard theory of emotion?

7. Can you think of some way to test the James-Lange theory without doing any surgery on the nervous system? (Hint: How can you affect the nervous system without directly operating on it?)

8. What is preparedness? Are there any possible examples from your own experience which might suggest that preparedness was involved in learning?

9. How do the results of the research of Harlow and Levine differ from the results expected from Freud's theory? What do the Harlow-Levine results suggest is important for child-rearing in relation to emotion?

10. What is the difference between fear and anxiety?

11. Compare trait and state anxiety. Give examples of each. Describe any personal experiences of test anxiety. How did you feel? What are possible treatments for test anxiety?

12. What is the course of stress according to Selye? When have you experi-

enced stress? Was it a single event or some ongoing situation? When would stress be pleasant?

13. How is frustration related to stress? Discuss some possible responses to frustration. Is one particular response more characteristic of you than other responses?

14. What are the four types of conflict? What real life situations would fall into each of these categories?

Defense Mechanisms
Defense Against What?
Kinds of Defense Mechanisms

Behavior Disorders
Neuroses
Psychoses
Organic Disorders

Traditional Psychotherapies
The Psychoanalytic Approach
Client-Centered Therapy
Rational-Emotive Therapy
Learning Theory Approaches to Therapy
Some New Approaches to Therapy

Coping
Nature of Coping
Rearranging Life Style
Drugs
Relaxation
Biofeedback
Meditation
Hypnosis

6

Behavior Problems, Therapies, and Coping

Behavior problems range from common everyday annoyances and anxieties to severely debilitating psychoses which require hospitalization. We will look at ways of dealing with anxiety as seen by Freud, then move on to neuroses, psychoses, psychotherapy, and means by which we actively cope with our problems.

Defense Mechanisms

defense against what?

Defense mechanisms are ways of thinking or behaving which *defend* or *protect* us from undue levels of anxiety. They are useful in keeping us from dwelling on our problems, freeing us to go about our business. If our defenses *dominate* us, however, and interfere with productive activities, then the defense mechanisms themselves become problems.

kinds of defense mechanisms

Repression. Generally considered the most important defense, this is a kind of "pushing" of anxiety-arousing ideas out of consciousness. A young woman may have sexually-explicit thoughts about young men, but because of her upbringing these thoughts may make her very anxious. Consequently, she represses them. To keep them repressed, though, she may have to avoid many situations which might arouse her sexual thoughts, and she therefore might even be limited in nonsexual activities. She might avoid any activities involving males.

Denial. Denial is the refusal to admit the existence of an anxiety-arousing reality. A poor student may deny that he or she does not have the ability to go on to medical school.

Projection. This is attributing one's own motives or traits to others. A person who sees everyone else as being dishonest may be projecting onto others his or her own tendency toward dishonesty.

Reaction Formation. This is doing the opposite of what one's impulses are. A highly aggressive person may be anxious about this tendency and become very passive. The self-styled censor who must read or see all the pornographic materials in order to fight pornography also fits the description. Reaction formation is notable because it is *exaggerated.*

Sublimation. This is a switch from unsocial to socially-approved activity to express an impulse. An aggressive street urchin who switches from gang fighting to prize fighting may be showing sublimation. Talking about love may replace sex. Freud believed that much of socially acceptable behavior is "energized" by the unacceptable urges of sex and aggression.

Regression. This is a return to more childish ways of behaving. The spouse who goes home to mother when there are marital difficulties is doing what he or she did as a child. An adult may stomp his or her foot and scream. A child may start wetting the bed when a new baby claims parental attention.

Compensation and Overcompensation. Alfred Adler argued that attempts to master the environment are sparked by feelings of inferiority. *Inferiority complex* refers to excessive feelings of inferiority, followed by *overcompensation,* going beyond the minimum necessary to compensate for the inferiority. Teddy Roosevelt, the sickly child, became the "roughrider." Demosthenes, the great Greek orator, had a speech impediment which he is said to have overcome by practicing speech with pebbles in his mouth.

Rationalization. In Aesop's fable, the fox could not reach the grapes, so said he did not want them anyway because they were sour. In common language, rationalization is making excuses, but the person making them also *believes* them.

Intellectualization. Emotional situations may be looked at coldly, as science-fiction scientists do. "This may hurt, but it's for your own good." Similarly, a soldier can intellectualize that the havoc wreaked with deadly weapons is just part of the job.

Behavior Disorders

neuroses

Neuroses are more extreme activities to control strong anxiety. A person may go to excessive lengths to control his or her anxiety.

Anxiety Neurosis. Here the individual *fails* to control anxiety by any defense mechanism or coping procedure. The result is frequent and long-lasting bouts of terror, without apparent reason. There is strong sympathetic arousal, including heart palpitations and sweating, and a feeling of dread. There may be continuing *chronic anxiety reactions,* with intermittent stronger attacks; *acute attacks,* which have the strong physiological and psychological symptoms described above; or *panic reactions,* stark raving terror.

Such anxieties may result from earlier experiences, as well as present situations. We saw in Chapter Five the possibility of inherited tendencies toward anxiety.

Phobic Reactions. People often have strong, unreasonable fears of particular objects, such as snakes or high places. These fears are disproportionate to the reality of the danger, but they can be handled by avoiding the feared objects or situations. Phobic reactions which completely dominate life are of clinical concern. Psychotherapists often believe that such phobic reactions are *not* due just to fear of the particular object, but are a kind of straw at which a person grasps in order to control anxiety aroused by some other source. If one *believes* that he or she is only afraid of high places, avoiding high places may control the anxiety. If the anxiety is actually due to something else, however, there may be a *spread* of objects about which the person is fearful, such as standing on a chair or short ladder.

Obsessive-Compulsive Reactions. An *obsession* is *thought* that won't go away, like a song stuck in our heads. A *compulsive reaction* is a persistent *behavior*, such as Lady Macbeth's continual handwashing. Many people have minor obsessions and compulsions which are not "abnormal." Children become obsessed with Christmas, and adults with getting a new car. The night before a trip a person may compulsively check and recheck the alarm clock to reduce anxiety about not getting up on time.

Neurotic levels of obsession or compulsion cannot be willingly stopped by a person. There is sometimes a ritualistic character to compulsions, and if the ritual is interrupted, anxiety becomes unnecessarily strong.

Hysterical Disorders. Sometimes people lose *functioning* of sensory systems, such as hearing or vision, or of motor systems (paralysis) when there is no structural damage to the affected parts of the body. Such disorders are called hysterical. (This use of the term does not apply to a frightened person who screams and cries.) People with hysterical disorders do not seem to get as excited about the dysfunction as we would expect. The individual obtains a *secondary gain,* a positive value from the disorder. Perhaps deafness keeps a person from hearing something very anxiety arousing. There have been numerous instances where front line soldiers were terribly frightened but felt guilty about attempting to leave their buddies. A functional paralysis, not a fake injury but one which seems real to the individual, gets the soldier away but without guilt.

Depression. A common problem is depression. Aaron Beck (1967) described five characteristics of depression:

1. Mood alteration, such as sadness, apathy, or loneliness;
2. Negative self-concept, including self-blame for problems;
3. Desire to escape the situation, such as running away or even suicide;
4. Changes in body activity, such as loss of appetite, sleeplessness, or loss of sex drive;
5. Increases or decreases in activity level.

Depression probably has a number of causes, but a common one may be a loss of reward. Depression may follow a severe illness, or the loss of a loved one. The more depressed one feels, the less likely one is to do anything which would help get out of the depression. Fortunately, time favors most of us and we recover. Most people feel depressed sometimes, but chronic depression may be neurotic or even psychotic.

(Photo by Bill Henry)

psychoses

The neurotic individual may have an unpleasant life, but he or she does respond to the world, even if in exaggerated ways. The psychotic person is said to have "lost contact with reality," and behaviors may be practically irrelevant to reality. Psychotic disorders are more debilitating than neuroses.

Affective Disorders. These are the *manic-depressive* psychoses, of which depression is the most common. They are called affective disorders because the person's emotional affect may be "high" (manic) or "low" (depressive). We shall focus on the manic state here. A person may be uncontrollably euphoric and exuberant, have wild flights of ideas, and be hyperactive to the extent that nothing is accomplished and he or she is a hindrance to others. Most of us get a little manic sometimes, but we are able to control it; the psychotic does not have this control.

Paranoid Disorders. Paranoid individuals are commonly characterized as having *delusions of persecution* or, less frequently *delusions of grandeur*. Paranoids often believe that others are "out to get" them, or that the television set is watching them. They are therefore defensive and secretive, and because of intense suspicion of others paranoids may be dangerous. Believing that someone is after them, they may defend themselves by a blind attack on the world.

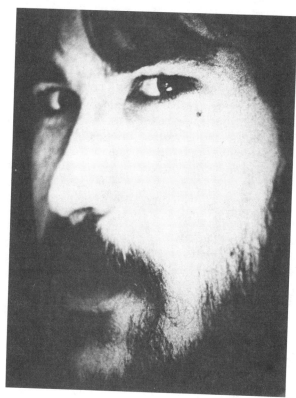

Paranoid individuals often believe they are being watched by dangerous others. (Photo by Bill Henry)

Every year or so someone runs amok and kills several people, with subsequent reports that the killer had previously been diagnosed paranoid. Paranoid individuals are hard to detect because they may not seem entirely unreasonable. Their delusions may make sense under certain conditions. People on the television screen *do* appear to look at you. The severity of the paranoid's problem may not be recognized until some dramatic event occurs.

Schizophrenic Disorders. In its literal translation, *schizophrenic* means "split mind," but another disorder called *multiple personality* more closely fits that description. *The Three Faces of Eve* (Thigpen and Cleckley, 1957) was an example of apparent multiple personalities in the same body. The cause of multiple personality is not known, and it may be more like role-playing than actually different personalities.

Schizophrenia is typically characterized by withdrawal from social contact, apathy, listlessness, possibly hallucinations, and inappropriate emotional expression. The schizophrenic may not enjoy things other people enjoy but show senseless laughter at things not amusing to anyone else. Although divided into subtypes, the diagnosis of different forms of schizophrenia is difficult. In an "experiment," normal individuals got themselves admitted to mental hospitals by a very simple statement of schizophrenic symptoms, and then were treated by hospital personnel as if they were completely schizophrenic even though they acted normally after admittance.

One important distinction, however, is between *reactive* and *process* schizophrenia. Reactive schizophrenia appears to be a temporary response to highly stressful situations and may disappear with rest or relief from the stress situation. Process schizophrenia begins in early childhood and gradually gets worse, perhaps requiring intensive treatment or hospitalization in the teens.

The origins of schizophrenia have been long debated, the pendulum swinging between learning and biological interpretations. A biological factor is indicated by the effectiveness of drugs therapies (particularly the phenothiozines) when psychotherapy is without success. Also, there is evidence for genetic transmission. Psychoses *tend* to run in families, although it certainly is not a rule that everybody in a family will become psychotic if one member does! People may have different genetic predispositions toward schizophrenia; for some it takes relatively little stress to produce the disorder, while for others it takes a tremendous amount.

organic disorders

The neuroses and psychoses have real physical causes in complex biochemistry, which we are only beginning to understand. Other disorders of thinking, emotions, and behavior have definite organic causes, however.

General Paresis. With advanced syphilitic infection, paresis occurs when the infection reaches the brain. Symptoms include a slurring of speech and shuffling walk, decreasing interest in personal hygiene, hallucinations, memory loss, and, eventually, death. Fortunately, the infection is now easily detectable by the Wasserman blood test and treatable with penicillin.

Traumatic Disorders. Blows on the head may cause permanent damage, the exact symptoms varying according to the damage. Changes of personality, as well as problems in thinking, memory, and sensory functions have been found.

Senility. With aging there may be hardening of the arteries and loss of blood supply to parts of the brain. This often produces symptoms similar to the traumatic disorders since the underlying problem is brain damage.

Psychosomatic Disorders. These are the so-called stress disorders discussed in Chapter Five. They result from continued stress, but different specific organs (heart, stomach, lungs) may be affected in different individuals. Why is one person asthmatic and another ulcer-prone? One view is that a particular organ is "weak" in one person and "strong" in another. The weakest organ "collapses." A second view is that organs are *selected* by unconscious symbolism. For example, asthma attacks may be related to anxiety about something said, or may represent a "call for help." A third view is that the disorder is related to personality. For example, the ulcer-prone person frequently has conflict between desires for independence and dependence on others, striving for the former while desiring the latter.

Traditional Psychotherapies

the psychoanalytic approach

Freud simultaneously developed his theory of personality and his method of therapy, called *psychoanalysis.* There have been many variations of psychoanalysis, differing according to what a given theorist believes about unconscious conflicts, basic motives, and so on. We will discuss only the classical approach here.

It is assumed that the neurotic individual's problems are based on conflicts which are unconscious because they have been repressed. The analyst first tries to gain insight into the patient's problems in frequent sessions where

Psychotherapy involves intense concentration on listening to and trying to understand what a client is saying and feeling.

the client *free associates*. The client says what he or she is thinking about, freely associating one idea with another. This process may follow a circuitous path as anyone is aware who has lain in bed, floating along on a stream of thoughts and then tried to retrace the route the thoughts have followed. The client's associations often return to a particular matter of concern, a problem which he or she may not recognize. The analyst recognizes a problem area when a patient *resists* further associations along a certain line, or resists the analyst's suggestions about the problem.

Dream interpretation is also used. In Freudian theory, dreams are considered to have a *latent content*, which is their *real* meaning for the individual, and a *manifest* content, which is a *symbolic distortion* of the latent content. There may be a latent sexual content but apparently non-sexual manifest content. Dream interpretation is not simple, however, and requires considerable knowledge about the individual involved.

The analyst helps the client overcome the resistance and make the underlying conflicts conscious. Once the patient understands the nature of the conflicts, it is assumed that they can be managed. The client may realize, for example, that earlier conflict over authority with a parent is no longer relevant. The analytic process may take years and many people doubt its value. It has never been very successful with psychoses.

client-centered therapy

Developed by Carl Rogers, client-centered therapy assumes the client is the person best able to understand his or her own problems, and that the client can make his or her own decisions. The therapist provides an atmosphere of understanding and acceptance in which the client is free to think and talk freely about things which might otherwise be avoided. Often, the opportunity to talk about a problem and to explore possible solutions is all the client needs.

rational-emotive therapy

This approach (for example, Ellis, 1973; Meichenbaum, 1977) assumes that the way individuals *think* about their problems is crucial and the way to help people is to *restructure* their thinking. If a person is anxious about giving a speech and then sees some people walk out during the talk, the person may say, "I knew I wouldn't be any good" and be even more upset. Another person in the same objective situation might think, "I wonder what was so important to them that they had to leave. Too bad for them." Neurotics do apparently have more irrational beliefs than non-neurotics. One faulty neurotic idea, for example, is that people ought to be perfect. The discrepancy between the perfect person one *ought* to be and the way one *really is* can be a strong source of anxiety. Changing this idea could be very therapeutic.

learning theory approaches to therapy

We can roughly divide learning approaches into *behavior therapy*, which predominantly relies on principles of aversive classical conditioning, and *behavior modification*, which relies predominantly on instrumental (operant) conditioning principles. Unlike psychoanalysis, learning approaches to therapy assume that very specific fears or behaviors should be treated rather than trying to deal with hypothesized, but unseen, motivational conflicts.

Behavior Therapy. *Systematic desensitization* eliminates strong fears by a combination of *extinction* and *counterconditioning,* as we saw in Chapter Five for treating test anxiety. Assume that a person has a strong snake phobia (a good example because about 25 percent of the population has a snake phobia). The behavior therapist would first teach the client deep relaxation techniques. Then in the safety of the office the client would think about or imagine a snake, thus arousing anxiety. The client would then do relaxation exercises which reduce autonomic arousal and are incompatible with fear. The client might then think about handling snakes. If this aroused fear, relaxation would again be induced. Finally, the client might be confronted with a real snake, again with fear followed by relaxation. At this point, the client should have overcome the fear of snakes.

The same basic techniques are used for treatment of sexual dysfunction. Impotence and frigidity often are due to anxiety about performance, or even about being with someone of the opposite sex. The treatment is to introduce relaxation, have the client think about sex, then relax, and finally engage in close physical contact with a partner, and relax. This is reported to be very effective treatment.

Aversive conditioning has been used with anti-smoking drugs, for example. A person takes the drug, then smokes. The cigarette has a terrible taste and

151

the smoker should be less inclined to smoke thereafter. (Smoking is confounded by nicotine addiction, making it more difficult to get people to stop.) Smoking and drinking have also been paired with electric shock to produce aversive conditioning.

Some modest success has been reported in modifying male homosexuality by pairing pictures of nude males with the onset of electric shock and pictures of nude females with the termination of shock. A problem for conditioning therapy, however, is that conditioning typically occurs under different conditions than the individual is facing in real life and may not generalize well to real life situations.

Behavior Modification. Behavior modification (B-mod, for short) uses reinforcement for specific behaviors and under certain conditions. B-mod techniques are not entirely separate from those of behavior therapy, but B-mod emphasizes operant conditioning more.

As an example, a college student was having problems with his work and had insomnia. Analysis of the situation showed that he lived in one room, where he ate, slept, studied, and had his girl friend in occasionally. As a result, the same environment became associated with many different reinforcers as well as anxieties. When he wanted to sleep he was reminded of all these things, and he had difficulty sleeping. The treatment was to separate these activities and their respective reinforcers into different environments: He only slept in his room, ate out, studied elsewhere, and met his girlfriend at a fourth place. His insomnia disappeared and he soon got his life back in reasonable order.

There has been some success treating psychotics with B-mod, using the following steps:

1. Determine what you want the person to do—to talk, for example.
2. Find out what is reinforcing to that person.
3. Shape the desired behavior, along the lines described in chapter two.
4. Put the behavior on a schedule of reinforcement.

The shaping may be complicated because the final behavior you want is complex. It may have to be gradually built up, starting with single words, then sentences, then conversations.

some new approaches to therapy

Some recent approaches to therapy have emphasized *growth* and emotional enrichment of normal individuals rather than recovery of severely ill ones. *Transactional Analysis* (TA) and *Gestalt Therapy* are among these. Transactional analysis is essentially a Freudian approach put into more commonsense terms. At various times we may act like a *parent* (superego), *mature adult* (ego), or *child* (id). The approach is to help people improve their dealings with others by clarifying these various ways of behaving in oneself and others.

Gestalt therapy is mainly a group approach, not unlike the various kinds of encounter groups that became popular in the 1960s. The emphasis is on "getting in touch with your feelings," another way of saying "find out what you do and don't like," and dealing with these things constructively. Many people are pleased with such approaches; others believe they tend to feed egotism without dealing constructively with problems.

Coping

nature of coping

Coping refers to any way we may voluntarily try to control stress in ourselves. The following rules were apparently very successful for coping.

1. Avoid fried meats, which angry up the blood.
2. If your stomach disputes you, lie down and pacify it with cool thoughts.
3. Keep the juices flowing by jangling around gently as you move.
4. Go very light on the vices, such as carrying on in society. The social ramble ain't restful.
5. Avoid running at all times.
6. Don't look back. Something might be gaining on you. (*Time,* June 15, 1953)

These rules were devised by Satchel Paige, the great baseball pitcher. A legend in the Negro major leagues, Paige broke into the "white" major leagues with the Cleveland Indians sometime between his forty-fifth and fifty-fifth years (he was never consistent about his birth date). In exhibition games in his prime he handled the greatest of the white major league batters with ease. The longevity of his career might be due to something besides his rules, but they are close enough to "good" psychological practice to repeat and we certainly will not find any principles more plainly stated.

Coping behaviors are *self-regulatory.* The individual *consciously* does something to deal with his or her own situation, in contrast to defense mechanisms which are said to be more or less unconscious.

rearranging life style

Satchel Paige's rules were more than a list of do's and don'ts; they represented a style and philosophy of life which guided him. Many people have to change their lifestyles to deal with stress. Following a heart or ulcer attack,

YES, I USED TO WORRY EXCESSIVELY ABOUT PAYING MY BILLS, FEEDING THE KIDS, CUTTING THE LAWN, BEING A RESPONSIBLE PERSON... THEN ONE DAY, I CHANGED MY WHOLE PHILOSOPHY. I DUMPED EVERYTHING AND RAN OUT.

a person may have to completely rearrange his or her life to reduce stress. This may call for a change in jobs, giving up some activities, and resting more. Successful coping may be relative to the individual, however. A high powered executive might drop back to being merely the president of a *small* corporation, which would be a highly stressful position for someone else.

drugs

Here we shall describe a few of the more important drugs used in relation to stress.

Minor Tranquilizers. These are commonly called anti-anxiety drugs; they reduce tension and anxiety without producing sleep. We will list generic names, with common trade names in parentheses.

- *Diazepam* (Valium) is the most widely prescribed drug in the world.
- *Chlordiazepoxide* (Librium) and *Meprobamate* (Miltown, Equanil) are also widely used. Most of the minor tranquilizers are non-addictive, but meprobamate is mildly addictive. Drugs are often given in combination for different purposes. For example, Meprobamate may be mixed with another drug to treat ulcers.

Barbiturates. *Phenobarbital* (Luminal), *pentabarbital* (Nembutal), *amobarbital* (Amytal), and *secobarbital* (Seconal), have been used for years as sedatives and sleeping pills. They are highly addictive and dangerous if abused (overused). *Addiction* (requiring increasing doses for the same sedative effects) can occur within a few days. An addict has to have the dosage reduced gradually to avert the danger of withdrawal symptoms, which can include nervousness, tension, and in extreme cases, seizures and death. There may also be a hangover effect so that a person taking one drug (such as Seconal) to get to sleep is drowsy the next day and takes another drug (caffein) to wake up and be alert.

Opiates. Opium and its derivatives *(codeine, morphine, heroin)* are readily addictive. In the United States, opium was an over-the-counter drug as late as the early twentieth century. A major therapeutic property is the reduction of intestinal upset, as well as a feeling of euphoria. It was widely used by Chinese laborers working on the railroads, and it is said that a major reason for making it illegal was to protect American workers from "unfair" Chinese competition.

Codeine is still used as a cough suppressant and morphine as a rapid-acting pain-killer in severe accidents or painful illness, such as cancer. Heroin, the strongest of the three, is not legal anywhere in the Western world and is not used therapeutically. Many problems with heroin are due to its illegality: Organized crime controls its production and distribution, there is no quality control, and infectious hepatitis from dirty hypodermic needles is a more dangerous health threat than addiction itself.

Alcohol. There are three forms of alcohol: *ethanol* (made from grain, fruits, or vegetables), which is drinkable; *methanol* (wood alcohol) which is very dangerous and may cause blindness or death if consumed; and *isopropyl* (which is not as lethal as methanol but is not to be drunk). Ethanol can be distilled from potatoes (vodka), corn, wheat, barley, or rye (whisky), or fermented from grapes (wine) or malt (beer).

A little alcohol releases inhibitions, which might promote a "good time" at a party. With greater quantities, there is a loss of judgment and body control. Long term excessive drinking may produce brain and liver damage. *Korsakoff's syndrome,* with hallucinations and loss of memory, follows damage to an area of the hypothalamus. Liver damage (cirrhosis) may cause death. These effects seem to be due to improper diet of the alcoholic as well as to the alcohol itself.

Major Tranquilizers. These include *chlorpromazine* (Compazine, Thorazine) and *reserpine* (Serpasil), and are used psychologically only in severe psychiatric cases, especially schizophrenia. Reserpine is also an effective treatment for high blood pressure, but since it is a tranquilizer the person using it for blood pressure has to be particularly careful around machinery.

Uppers. Tranquilizers and barbiturates are called "downers" because they suppress neural activity. "Uppers" increase autonomic activity and alertness. The best known are the *amphetamines* (Benzedrine, dexedrine) and *meth-amphetamines* (Desoxyn, for example, commonly called "speed"). Individuals can come to tolerate large amounts, and withdrawal symptoms include severe depression. Physicians now appear much less willing to dispense amphetamines. Other uppers include cocaine (illegal) and caffein in coffee or tea.

Hallucinogens. Hallucinogenic drugs produce strange perceptions and thoughts. These include *LSD, MDA, mescaline* (from the peyote cactus), *psilocybin* (from certain mushrooms), and many others from natural or synthetic sources.

Marijuana. A product of the hemp plant *Cannabis Sativa,* marijuana is one of the most controversial drugs. It produces a euphoric effect when smoked

Many drugs produce distorted perceptions of the environment.

or eaten in other food but does not apparently lead to addiction. The active ingredients are not known with certainty because it is not known exactly what chemicals reach the brain, nor what effects they have, when it is smoked. One synthesized component, tetrahydracannbinol (THC), is involved but in research is usually given by injection so that the comparability with smoking is uncertain. Marijuana is controversial because it is widely used and enjoys a kind of borderline legality, and there is little clear evidence of severe health threat from its use. Large scale studies of habitual marijuana users in other countries indicate little health hazard. Although *legally* classified as a narcotic, it is not a narcotic by definition. (It is not analgesic nor sleep inducing, as is morphine, for example.) Its narcotic classification, however, has led to severe penalties for possession, and in many states there are now attempts to decriminalize possession of small quantities.

relaxation

Many stress reduction techniques involve relaxation. We know it is easy to *say* "relax" but difficult to do so. Meditation, hypnosis, and biofeedback all involve relaxation, but specific relaxation exercises have also been developed. Jacobson (1939) developed the widely used set of exercises summarized below. The procedure is to produce a large amount of tension and then relaxation in major muscle groups. This helps a person learn the difference between tension and relaxation and increases blood flow. This increased blood flow, from opening up constricted blood vessels, is beneficial in itself.

The Jacobson Exercises[1]

1. *Hands.* The fists are tensed; relaxed. The fingers are extended, relaxed.
2. *Biceps and triceps.* The biceps are tensed; relaxed. The triceps are tensed; relaxed.
3. *Shoulders.* The shoulders are pulled back; relaxed. The shoulders are pushed forward; relaxed.
4. *Neck (lateral).* With shoulders straight, the head is turned slowly to the right, but to an extreme position; relaxed. With shoulders straight, the head is turned to left; relaxed.
5. *Neck (forward).* The head is brought forward until the chin digs into chest; relaxed. (Bringing the head back is *not* recommended.)
6. *Mouth.* The mouth is opened as wide as possible; relaxed. The lips are pursed as in exaggerated pout; relaxed.
7. *Tongue (extended and retracted).* With mouth open, the tongue is extended as far as possible; relaxed ("allow your tongue to come to a comfortable position in your mouth," during all relaxation phases involving the tongue). The tongue is "brought back" into the throat as far as possible; relaxed.
8. *Tongue (mouth roof and floor).* The tongue is "dug" into the roof of mouth, as hard as possible; relaxed. The tongue is "dug" into floor of mouth, as hard as possible; relaxed.
9. *Eyes.* The eyes are opened as wide as possible, until brow is visibly furrowed (this usually requires considerable encouragement, stressing tension in eyes and forehead); relaxed. (Getting the client to relax his eyes and brow following this exercise is often difficult. Gentle encouragement by the therapist to "relax the eyes and forehead just a little bit more" is recommended, especially when the therapist can discern tension about the eyes and forehead.) The eyes are closed as hard as possible until a definite squint is apparent; relaxed. (It is probably well to conclude the relaxation phase with instructions that the eyes be opened only slightly, but that concentration be such that the client does not "see" anything.)
10. *Breathing.* The client takes as deep a breath as is possible (encouragement to inhale "even more deeply" is desirable, since this is an extremely effortful response); relaxed ("resume normal, smooth, comfortable breathing"). The client exhales until "every drop of air leaves the lungs." (If instructions are followed, the client will be in considerable distress. Many individuals find it difficult to remain in this state for the full 10 seconds, and it is recommended that the tension phase be reduced to 5–7 seconds.) Relaxed ("resume normal, regular breathing").
11. *Back.* With the shoulders resting against the chair, the trunk of the body is pushed forward so as to arch the entire back; relaxed. For this exercise extreme care should be taken to prevent any injury to the back. The client should be advised to carry out the tensing phase rather slowly, and to relax immediately should he experience any pain.
12. *Midsection.* The midsection is raised slightly by tensing the buttock muscles; relaxed. The midsection is lowered slightly by digging the buttocks into the seat of the chair; relaxed.
13. *Thighs.* The legs are extended and raised approximately 6 inches above the

---

[1] Rimm and Masters. *Behavior Therapy.* Academic Press. 1974, p. 49.

floor (care should be taken that simultaneous tensing of the stomach muscles be minimal); relaxed ("allow the legs to fall to the floor"). Tensing the opposing set of muscles would normally involve bringing the forelegs back underneath the thighs. Since this would involve rather large-scale adjustments in body position that would tend to destroy rhythm and continuity, it would probably be well to omit this exercise. A reasonable alternative would be to have the client "dig" his heels or the backs of his feet into the floor.

14. *Stomach.* The stomach is pulled in as hard as possible "as if it were about to touch the backbone" (stomach exercises, like breathing exercises, are quite effortful and may require encouragement by the therapist); relaxed "until every muscle fiber in the stomach is relaxed"). The stomach is extended, "as if preparing for a punch in the abdomen"; relaxed ("until every muscle fiber is relaxed"). (For both stomach exercises, while it is possible to breathe while tensing, it is difficult. For the stomach muscles *only,* if the client is observed to catch his breath, it may be best for the therapist to ignore this.)

15. *Calves and feet.* With legs supported, the feet are bent such that the toes are pointed toward the head; relaxed. With legs supported, feet are bent in opposite direction (cramping of the calf muscles may occur during tensing, at which point the therapist immediately says "relax," suggesting that the client "shake the muscles loose"); relaxed.

16. *Toes.* With legs supported and feet relaxed, the toes are "dug" in the bottom of shoes; relaxed. With the legs supported and feet relaxed, the toes are bent in the opposite direction touching the top of toe area of the shoes; relaxed.

Following completion of the last tension-relaxation cycle, the therapist may wish to bring about even deeper relaxation by an additional series of suggestions as illustrated by the following:

Now I want you to imagine, actually experience if you can, a wave of warm, comfortable, pleasant relaxation . . . a wave of relaxation that is going to permeate and engulf your entire body: so that when this wave of relaxation reaches a part of your body, this will be a signal to relax even further, totally relax that part of your body. Feel the wave of relaxation engulf your feet and now your calves and thighs so they are completely, totally, perfectly relaxed . . . and now your buttocks and midsection . . . warm relaxation making all the muscles loose and flaccid. Now your midsection and up your back and chest, and in your hands and arms, so that if any tension was there it is now draining away . . . draining away.

biofeedback

Biofeedback is electronic amplification of such body activity as heart beats, blood pressure, muscle tension, or body temperature so they can be easily perceived. Body temperature may be displayed on a digital readout thermometer, and muscle tension by different pitch tones. Tension may not be noticed because it builds up gradually. By receiving very concrete feedback about tension it is easier to learn how to recognize and control it.

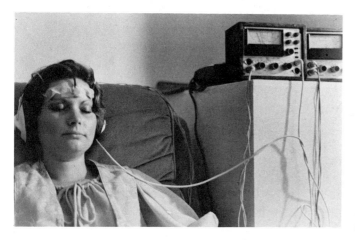

In a typical biofeedback setup, a client gets information about increasing or decreasing forehead muscle tension through the earphones.

Like any other tool, biofeedback has a certain range of usefulness. Even migraine headaches can be helped to some degree, since these commonly start with muscle tension. The results are sometimes dramatic, but not unexplainable.

A highly publicized line of research has been on brain waves. There is a widespread belief that with biofeedback one can reach some "higher level of consciousness." This is said to be done by producing in oneself very high amplitude *alpha* waves (eight to twelve cycles per second) or *theta* waves (about six to eight cycles per second). Research indicates however that (1) people in these conditions learn to relax generally and the alpha waves are part of the general relaxation, and (2) there is nothing especially mystical or important about the waves themselves except perhaps as *indicators* of overall relaxation.

meditation

Meditation is an ancient technique recently popularized in the United States. The most widely practiced form here is called Transcendental Meditation (TM), a modified form of Zen Buddhism, as taught by the Maharish Mahesh Yogi. Its main claim to uniqueness is the ease with which it is learned and the small amount of time each day (twice for twenty minutes) that it takes to do it.

In TM the person concentrates on silently repeating a particular word or syllable, called a *mantra.* The mantra is supposed to be specially selected for an individual by his or her personal instructor, and is "in tune" with the individual's personality. Since inductees are sworn to secrecy about their mantra this is hard to verify. Clearly, however, the mantra is some soft-sounding, easily repeatable syllable such as "om." By focusing attention on the mantra the individual blocks out other details of the environment.

Proponents of TM make extravagant claims for a healthier and happier life, greater creativity, improved learning ability, and more energy. A great deal of scientific evidence is said to support these claims, but close evaluation

HE'S ALL SHOOK BECAUSE HE
SLIPPED AND GAVE AWAY
HIS SECRET MANTRA TO
HIS GIRL.

shows a wide discrepancy between the advertised *implications* of the research data and the facts themselves. The actual data are often not presented, and the details of the research are seldom available. The religious fervor of the TM promoters overrides scientific caution. (In fairness to some of the researchers, they themselves do not make the same claims for their results that one finds in the TM advertising. TM, by the way, is a trademarked name.)

There are some good things to say about TM, as with most other coping techniques. The evidence suggests that TM may produce a quick relaxation, although not as dramatic as the earliest and most widely publicized research (Wallace and Benson, 1972) indicated. The ritual accompanying TM, including the very positive approach of its proponents, may foster a confidence in TM that makes it more effective. But its effectiveness, as Benson (1975) has subsequently argued, is probably in its ability to produce relaxation. Other forms of meditation, including religious, involve different details, but all are aimed at concentration in an environment with minimal distractions and the production of a calming effect on the individual.

hypnosis

From movies and stage shows we get the idea that through posthypnotic suggestion a person can be made to do anything. It is, in fact, controversial whether hypnosis is a special kind of "trance state" or whether the procedures are just done under unusual conditions so that hypnotism appears special.

There is no question that *stage* hypnotism is pure showmanship; the hypnotist often tells people what to do in order to make the performance "look good." Mark Twain describes how as a boy he got involved with a stage hypnotist. The young Samuel Clemmons quickly discovered the hypnotist would take credit for anything Samuel did. Since Clemmons was a youth of great imagination, the townsfolk of Hannibal, Missouri saw better demonstrations of "hypnosis" than most of us are ever likely to see.

A strong proponent of the view that hypnosis is *not* a special trance is Theodore X. Barber (for example, 1969). Barber's considerable research indicates that most of the things said to be unique to hypnosis can be done by normal waking people. One stage trick is the "human plank." A volunteer goes through the hypnotic induction procedure and then is instructed to hold his or her body rigid between two chairs, supported only at the heels and the back of the head. I have never had a student who could *not* do this under normal waking conditions.

The analgesic properties of hypnosis are also said to be overestimated, resulting from (1) relaxation, (2) doing things in a way that they are not painful, such as wetting the palm of the hand before applying a match to it, and (3) in the case of surgery, sometimes using a local anesthetic in conjunction with an hypnotic technique. Various methods of prepared childbirth are as "painless" with relaxation techniques as are those requiring hypnotic induction.

Ernest Hilgard (1968) believes that hypnosis *is* a special state. He believes there is some kind of "dissociation" (separation) of brain functions so that the brain quite literally acts in a different way under hypnosis than it does normally. How this happens is not clear, but Hilgard has presented rather convincing evidence. Other theories of hypnosis are that it is a kind of *role-playing* or that subjects under hypnosis are less critical and *more suggestible* than usual. There are large differences in degree of susceptibility to hypnotic induction procedures.

SUMMARY

1. *Defense mechanisms* are ways of thinking or behaving which protect us from high levels of anxiety. They are useful until they interfere with productive living. *Repression*, the most important defense mechanism, is the process of "pushing" anxiety-arousing ideas out of consciousness.

2. *Neuroses* are conditions resulting from strong anxiety. The major forms of neurosis are (1) *anxiety neurosis*, (2) *phobic reactions*, (3) *obsessive-compulsive* reactions, and (4) *hysterical* disorders. *Depression* is a common form of reaction, although not formally classified as a neurosis.

3. *Psychoses* are more severe than neuroses in that psychotic individuals are "out of touch with reality" when in their psychotic states and cannot function well in everyday living. The psychoses include the *affective* (manic-depressive) disorders, *paranoid* disorders and *schizophrenic* disorders.

4. *Organic psychoses* have clear physical causes, such as infection from syphillis which in late stages affects the brain, blows to the head, strokes, or senility related to reduced blood flow to the brain. *Psychosomatic disorders* are body malfunctions (for example, heart attack, ulcers) brought on by prolonged emotional stress.

5. *Psychoanalysis,* as a method of therapy, assumes that a neurotic individual's

problems are the expression of *unconscious conflicts* that need to be brought into consciousness and resolved. It is more effective with neuroses than with psychoses.

6. *Client-centered therapy* considers the individual capable of understanding his or her own problems and making his or her own decisions if given an atmosphere of acceptance and understanding in which to explore the problems.

7. *Rational-emotive therapy* sees the way people think about their problems as crucial. Restructuring this thinking is central to dealing with the problems, according to this view.

8. *Learning theory* approaches assume that it is actual behaviors and present fears that should be treated, not unconscious conflicts. *Behavior therapy* uses classical conditioning principles, particularly procedures involving extinction and aversive conditioning. *Behavior modification* emphasizes instrumental learning principles, changing the conditions of reinforcement for undesirable and desirable behaviors.

9. *Transactional analysis* and *Gestalt therapy* emphasize the personal growth of normal individuals rather than the recovery of severely disturbed individuals.

10. *Coping* involves the *voluntary* control of internal stress. This may be done by a rearrangement of one's life style to reduce stress (for instance, by changing jobs), or it may involve the use of drugs, relaxation techniques, biofeedback, meditation, or hypnosis.

EXERCISES

1. How would a specific personal (emotional) problem be handled by different defense mechanisms? How would a person behave differently according to whether he or she was using denial, projection, or reaction formation?

2. What are some common phobias? Can you think of any you might have to some degree? If so, do you have any idea of *why* you have a particular phobia? For example, can you date it to a particular experience?

3. What is the difference between hysterical disorders and psychosomatic disorders? How, according to different theorists, are the particular body systems involved related to personality?

4. Most people have unimportant obsessions or compulsions (like the girl whose dolls must always be in their proper places before she goes to bed). What are some common examples of obsessions and compulsions? How might these become major problems?

5. How do neuroses and psychoses differ? When is a disorder considered *functional* and when would it be considered *organic?*

6. Make up a brief description of a delusion of grandeur or persecution. Act it out and describe it. Would your delusion always be obvious to other people?

7. What physical causes can lead to psychological problems? What conditions result?

8. Choose a particular disorder (for example, a neurosis) and discuss how several different types of therapy would approach the problem. For example, how might it be approached by psychoanalysis, client-centered therapy, behavior therapy, and rational-emotive therapy?

9. How do *you* cope with stressful situations? What other methods might be more effective for you?

III

The Social Animal:
Personal Interactions

7

Attitudes:
Meaning,
Measurement,
and Modification

(Photo by Bill Henry)

Definition

The term *attitude* is used in a variety of ways. We shall define attitude here as *a positive or negative feeling toward some person, object, or event.* These feelings incline us to act positively or negatively toward certain individuals or groups. We may think of attitudes as being relatively weak emotions most of the time, ranging from mildly positive to mildly negative. Thus, typically our attitudes toward politicians may not be very strong. Sometimes, however, our attitudes erupt into strong emotion and the continuity of "attitude" and "emotion" is more obvious.

can we predict behavior from attitudes?

Surely both commonsense and psychology textbooks make it obvious that attitudes influence behavior. But consider this. Between 1930 and 1932, R. T. LaPiere (1934) travelled around the United States with a young Chinese couple. The couple was well-educated, fluent in English, well-dressed, and personable. The three stopped at 184 restaurants and 67 hotels and auto-camps (the forerunners of modern motels). There was a fairly strong prejudice against Chinese at the time, but in spite of LaPiere's fears they were readily accepted

ONE LAST QUESTION... DO YOU SERVE ALIENS?

OH, NO, M'SIEUR. NEVAIR! UNLESS...

..OF COURSE, THEY'RE WEARING A TIE AND PAYING CASH, OR ARE ESCORTED BY A GENTLEMAN.

at 250 of the 251 places they stopped. Six months after each visit LaPiere sent each establishment a questionnaire which included the question: "Will you accept members of the Chinese race as guests in your establishment?" Over 90 percent responded with a flat "No."

These results were virtually opposite the previous behavior in these establishments, and this demonstration of the apparent discrepancy between attitude and behavior has long been "ritually cited at the beginning of almost every discussion of this issue" (Brannon, 1976, p. 163). A number of other studies cited by Brannon demonstrated behaviors which bore little or no relation to stated attitudes or beliefs, though some other studies have shown very good correlations between attitudes and behavior. To reconcile these contradictory results, Brannon (1976, p. 186) lists eight conditions which seem to be necessary in order to predict behavior from attitudes. These are summarized in Table 7–1. Recognizing it is not always easy to relate attitudes and behavior, let us

table 7–1

Brannon's eight conditions for effectively predicting behavior from attitudes

1. The respondent must have an attitude reasonably congruent to the behavior to be predicted.
2. An attitude-expression (that is, the statement of the attitude) must be elicited which fairly represents that attitude.
3. The attitude must not be substantially altered by the process of measurement.
4. The attitudes must not have changed substantially by the time the behavior is performed.
5. The respondent must not be subject to overwhelmingly strong situational constraints at the time the behavior is performed.
6. There must not be conflicting attitudes which are also congruent to the behavior in question, or more realistically if there are such competing attitudes, they must be taken into consideration.
7. There must be no powerful cues in the behavioral situation which render the measured attitude irrelevant.
8. Respondents should not be aware that their attitude expressions and behavior are being compared.

(Brannon, R. Attitudes and the prediction of behavior. In Seidenberg & Snadowsky, 1976 (p. 186).

look at some of the things we know about attitudes, their measurement, and their change.

attitudes, thoughts, and actions

The importance of attitudes is in their relation to thoughts and actions, but these are two-way relations. Attitudes influence thoughts and actions, but also vice-versa.

1. *Attitudes affect actions.* If we have a positive attitude toward a presidential candidate our actions will be supportive. We may vote for him or her and try to convince others to do so. The opposite would hold for a candidate we do not like.
2. *Actions affect attitudes.* If someone acts favorably toward a candidate we could conclude that she likes the candidate, just from the action. Indeed, acting favorably toward someone can further increase our liking for that person.
3. *Attitudes affect thoughts.* If I like a person I may think that person is smarter, more reliable and nicer than I would otherwise.
4. *Thoughts affect attitudes.* Suppose you meet a total stranger, toward whom you feel neutral. Then you find he is a member of your fraternity and immediately you like him better. New knowledge has affected your attitude.

Measurement of Attitudes

We cannot directly see or hear attitudes in other people. Attitudes are inferred from what we can observe: behaviors, self-descriptions, or attitude scale scores. If we are concerned with relating attitudes to other activities, we need some understanding of how attitudes are measured.

behavioral observations

We may infer attitudes from behavior in natural settings. Under the caste system in India we would have had no difficulty telling who the "untouchables" were or in recognizing attitudes toward them. The behavior of those around the untouchables would have made this clear. The South African policy of *apartheid* (racial separation) is a current example of this phenomenon. We might also infer from listening to the kids from Block A in the Bronx screaming obscenities at the kids from Block B that they do not like each other.

We must remember, however, that we are *always* dealing with fallible inferences. That a ten-year-old boy acts nasty to a ten-year-old girl is not proof positive that he dislikes her; this may be his way of getting her attention.

verbal self-description

We can directly ask people questions, such as Do you think the President is doing a good job? and get a "yes" or "no" answer. Or we may ask "open-ended" questions, such as What do you think of the administration's foreign policy? In the first case we get less information, but the scoring is easy. In the second case, we get more information but the scoring is harder. We would therefore be likely to use yes-no (or other equally simple-answer) questions with large groups and open-ended questions with a smaller number of people.

attitude scales

Social scientists have devoted considerable effort to the development and refinement of attitude scaling procedures. Although sometimes laborious to devise, attitude scales are easy to score and analyze. Several different kinds of scales are in relatively common use.

Social Distance Scale. One of the earliest attitude scales was developed by Emory Bogardus (1925). It consists of a series of statements indicating how close a relationship you would let the "typical" member of some group (for example, nationality or race) establish with you. At one extreme is "Would not allow into my country" and at the other extreme is "Would marry into this group." It was intended as a measure of prejudice. The entire scale is shown in Table 7–2a. With such a scale we can readily compare different groups as *subjects* (how they fill out the scale in reference to others) or as *objects* (how others fill out the scale for them).

Thurstone Scales. Thurstone and Chave (1929) selected sets of attitude or opinion statements from a large pool of items, then had them judged on the degree to which they expressed positive or negative attitudes on a particular topic. The attitude score for a given person is the average of the pre-judged scale values of all the items with which he or she agrees. Table 7–2b is a sample Thurstone scale. Thurstone scales have been widely used, but they are time-consuming and expensive to construct, they have to be completely designed for each new topic, and after awhile the statements may become

PSST! NO, QUIGLEY. THAT'S NOT THE KIND OF SCALE WE ARE TALKING ABOUT!

table 7–2

Samples of four different kinds of attitude scales on the peacetime draft. In each of the marked examples, what attitudes toward the topic is expressed?

---

a. social distance scale (check as many as you agree with)

I would admit draft dodgers
1. To close kinship by marriage
2. To my club as personal friends
3. To my street as neighbors
4. To employment in my occupation
5. To citizenship in my country
(6.) As visitors only to my country
7. Would exclude from my country

b. Thurstone scale for peacetime draft. (check as many as you agree with)

1. It is the patriotic duty of every able-bodied American to serve in his country's armed services if called.
(2.) The draft serves no useful purpose.
3. I do not care whether we draft or not.

c. Likert scale (circle the alternative that expresses your opinion)

1. Every able-bodied American should be willing to be drafted.

Strongly   Agree   Neutral   (Disagree)   Strongly
Agree   Disagree

d. semantic differential

Peacetime Draft

Good	_____ : ✓ : _____ : _____ : _____ : _____ : _____	Bad
Strong	_____ : ✓ : _____ : _____ : _____ : _____ : _____	Weak
Slow	_____ : _____ : _____ : _____ : ✓ : _____ : _____	Fast

---

irrelevant, quaint, or obscure and make it necessary to construct a new scale for the same topic.

Likert Scales. Rensis Likert (1932) devised the method of using a series of strongly favorable and strongly unfavorable statements about a topic, and then having people indicate on a five-point scale how much they agreed or disagreed with each statement. The scales are scored so that high numbers on a positive statement are opposite the high numbers on a negative statement.

Table 7–2c shows a sample Likert scale. For formal research Likert scales require development and pretesting, but less than do Thurstone scales. For less formal use, statements can be rather quickly devised. Even though new sentences are devised for each topic, it is relatively simple to do so since only the extremes are used. If you were asked to make up an attitude scale, the Likert scale would be your best approach unless you had considerable training. The chances that sometime you may want to make up a scale are greater than you might suppose. Attitude scales are common in business and industry,

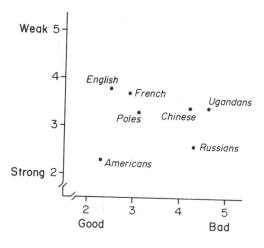

figure 7–1. Average Semantic Differential ratings for six nationalities to illustrate graphic comparisons with this testing procedure. Such ratings are subject to changing world conditions. At the time these data were collected, Idi Amin was president of Uganda, which was perceived as "worse" than Russia, but weaker.

but are also useful for church groups, civic clubs, or professional organizations which want to determine attitudes about some project.

Osgood's Semantic Differential. The name "Semantic Differential" (Osgood, Suci, and Tannenbaum, 1957) refers to differences in word meaning. The format is a set of paired adjectives which are opposites, such as good-bad, fast-slow, strong-weak. These adjectives are placed at the ends of seven-point scales, as illustrated in Table 7–2d. There are three main dimensions underlying the scales: evaluation (good-bad), potency (strong-weak), and activity (fast-slow). The respondent checks each scale at some point which represents his or her feeling toward the topic indicated at the top of the page, as shown in Table 7–2. The semantic differential has been called a generalized attitude scale because it can be applied to virtually any topic without changing the format. Topics include people, nations, political parties, or such abstract ideas as democracy. The individual scales are scored and the immediate inference is that a person has a positive attitude toward something marked as relatively "good" and a negative attitude toward something marked toward the "bad" end of the scales. The evaluative scales are virtually always found to be the most useful (averaging the scores for all the evaluative scales to obtain the evaluative score), but the other two dimensions provide some further information.

Two advantages of the semantic differential are that (1) The same set of adjectives can be used repeatedly; it is not necessary to reconstruct the entire set of scales for every new topic, and (2) It is possible to plot out in two or three dimensions a number of topics (for example, political figures, nations, ideas) on a graph and thereby make a direct comparison of them. Figure 7–1 shows such a two-dimensional plot.

Williams' Preschool Racial Attitude Measure (PRAM). John Williams of Wake Forest University, and his associates (e.g., see Williams & Morland, 1977), developed a picture-story technique for studying racial attitudes in children too young to read or understand the typical attitude scale. There are twenty-four pairs of schematic figure drawings. Each pair has the same figure side by side, but one is dark skinned and the other light. A story is told for each pair of pictures, involving either a "good" person or a "bad" person and the child is then asked, Which of these is the *good* person (or, bad person, depending on the story)? The child has only to point to one of the two figures. Other evaluative words (for example, "nice" or "not nice") are used in other stories. Solely by chance, a child should point to a figure of each color twelve times, with the figures equally often on right and left sides. However, it is found that preschool children more consistently point out the darker figures as "not nice" than they do the lighter figures. From this it is inferred that these children have already learned some negative racial attitudes. These attitudes become stronger throughout the primary school years. This type of measurement technique is adaptable for almost any situation involving very young or other non-literate individuals. Williams and a number of his colleagues have used the technique to study sex stereotypes in young children (Best, Williams, Cloud, Davis, Robertson, Edwards, Giles, and Fowles, 1977).

scale validation

Saying that an attitude scale measures "political liberalism" doesn't make it so. A scale has to be *validated* to determine if it measures what is claimed for it. A common procedure is to give the scale to *criterion groups* which represent the opposite extremes of an attitude. For example, a scale of liberalism-conservatism could be given to such known groups as the John Birch Society on the far right and the American Communist Party on the far left. If the liberalism-conservatism scale does not distinguish well between such groups it hardly does what is claimed. If, however, the scores for the two groups cluster at opposite ends of whatever scale we are studying we could then apply it with some confidence to identify attitudes of groups or individuals whom we did not know in advance.

the problem of sampling: the good apples are on the top

Whatever measure we use, we have to consider whether the particular people we get information from are representative of the group of interest. If we were buying a bushel of apples we would want to know what the whole basket was like, not just the top layer. If we are interested in a small group, like a recreational club, there is no problem: We can talk to everybody. But if our concern is a large group which cannot be studied in its entirety, the best general approach is to get a *random sample* of the members of the group. A random sample is one where every member of the group of concern (called a *population*) has an equal chance to be in the sample. If we wanted to know Illinois voters' attitudes toward national health insurance we would randomly

THE APPLES? YES, THEY'RE REALLY GOOD. I JUST TOOK ONE FROM THE TOP OF THAT A BARREL A FEW MINUTES AGO.

sample from Illinois voters, obtaining names from voter registration lists, for example. We could then reasonably *generalize* from the sample to the population.

In practice, it is difficult to get a completely random sample from a large population. A slightly modified procedure would be to work with selected geographic areas. In Illinois for example, the populous Chicago area is mainly Democratic, whereas downstate there are many small towns and more Republicans. In a statewide survey we could (1) make sure that each geographic area was represented in proportion equal to its voter registrations, and (2) sample randomly within each geographic area. The major television networks use a similar procedure to forecast the election outcomes and are quite successful at doing so with only a small fraction of the votes counted in a state.

Formation of Attitudes

Psychologists have been greatly concerned with the way attitudes develop and with how they change. These are similar topics, but since they do involve slightly different principles, we shall separate development and change of attitudes into two sections.

Development of Attitudes

reward and punishment

As small children we are praised or blamed for our actions toward others. If we are praised for acting negatively toward a certain group, we are more likely to develop negative attitudes toward that group. Similarly, if we are praised for positive actions we are likely to develop positive attitudes. If punishment is used in conjunction with reward (for example, praise for acting kindly toward a minority group and punishment for acting negatively) we would expect the positive attitude to develop even more strongly. The same would hold for prejudicial attitudes.

classical conditioning

When Adolph Hitler blamed all of Germany's post-World War I economic and social problems on the Jews, he was using a classical conditioning procedure. By continually associating the Jews with the very real ills of German society, Hitler produced strong anti-Semitic attitudes. The conditioned stimulus, like the furry rat for Little Albert, was "Jews" and the unconditioned stimulus, like the loud noise for Albert, was "German misery." At the same time, he rationalized ill treatment of the Jews by insisting on their racial inferiority compared to "true" Germans.

We may say that "It can't happen here," but in fact "it" has. In the Joe McCarthy era (early 1950s), there was unreasonable fear of communism in the U.S. "Guilt by association" (another way of describing classical conditioning) was one of Senator McCarthy's smear tactics. He would have had us believe that so-and-so must be a communist (or a pinko, communist sympathizer) because he or she has associated with communists. With virtually no documentation, McCarthy identified many groups as Communist fronts. Eleanor Roosevelt came under the harsh glare of McCarthy's indiscriminate spotlight because of her activity on behalf of the United Nations. Even supporters of UNICEF (the United Nations Children's Emergency Fund) were indirectly accused of communistic leanings. Regardless of their fairness, or lack thereof, such tactics are effective. It is generally believed that Richard Milhouse Nixon gained election to the United States Senate in 1950 by accusing his California senatorial opponent, Helen Gahagan Douglas, of being a communist supporter. The assertion was proven to be totally without evidence, but it was enough to defeat Douglas and permanently remove her from public life. The subsequent course of Nixon's political career is, of course, well documented.

Away from the glamorous world of political intrigue, similar results have been demonstrated in the laboratory. In the "real world" it is harder to interpret what we see, so it is nice to have laboratory support. Many experiments have shown the role of classical conditioning on attitude formation. For example, if emotionally-neutral words (even meaningless conglomerates of syllables like "NEV" or "ZEC") are paired with other words having bad connotations, like COMMUNIST or TOOTHACHE, the neutral words take on bad connotations. This is shown by semantic differential ratings of the "neutral" words before and after being paired with the "bad" words. Even so innocuous a stimulus as a dim light can become "bad" if it signals electric shock and "good" if it signals the end of a shock (Beck & Davis, 1974).

imitation

Perhaps the most powerful forces for developing attitudes, however, are the models that adults provide for children.

It is widely believed that such imitation accounts for more attitude development than almost anything else. If a child is then rewarded for the imitation, there is an unbeatable combination. Punishment for copying adults may or may not be terribly effective as a means of keeping children from imitating. We've all been told "Do as I say, not as I do." And it never worked, did it? Research on imitation (Bandura, 1973) even shows that simply seeing a "model" rewarded or punished for a particular behavior increases or decreases the likelihood that the child will imitate that behavior. This is true of aggression, for example.

(Photo by Bill Henry)

strangeness and familiarity

Either direct or indirect experience with the object of an attitude can influence the strength and direction (positive or negative) of that attitude. Curiously, however, *lack of experience* may also produce negative attitudes. A precondition for this, however, is that *a person must already be familiar with something else.* Novel events can be interesting, as well as surprising. But if a very unexpected event occurs there may be a strong negative response. A child may be frightened by a familiar person in strange garb, such as a Halloween costume. Or, the Vermont farmer and the California urbanite, each used to a particular

way of doing things, may eye each other distrustfully. The phrase *fear of the unfamiliar* sums up the idea.

Fear of the unfamiliar does not apply equally to all individuals. Many people actively seek out and enjoy unfamiliar situations. How much we enjoy these, however, depends partly on how well we can *cope* with new situations. Foreign travel is a pleasant prospect to some people and dreaded by others.

We may be particularly upset if new situations are thrust upon us. George has been doing a good steady job in the factory for ten years, but this particular job is all he really knows. Suddenly one day it is announced that there are going to be drastic changes in production procedures which will make George's job obsolete. George is not fired, but he must learn to do a different job. We can well understand any resistance he might have to the change. He does not know whether he can make it in the new job and is anxious about it. He might do very well, be happy, and in retrospect wonder why he had been anxious. But his fear of the unfamiliar would not be unusual.

the "mere exposure" effect

Suppose that every day for an hour you had to sit in a room full of unfamiliar modern paintings and listen to equally unfamiliar modern symphonic music. Would you be more or less likely to enjoy these paintings and music after a few days or weeks? Robert Zajonc (e.g., 1968) has demonstrated rather convincingly that merely being exposed to new material makes it more pleasant. So our tentative answer is that you probably would like the paintings and music more. This assumes that there is *only* exposure and no associated pleasant or unpleasant experiences. (An experiment conducted many years ago showed that paintings associated with food became more pleasant; and we would hardly develop an affinity for a stranger who beat us up every time we saw him. But these are not what Zajonc is talking about.) In the laboratory, unusual paintings, geometric patterns, and music have all become more pleasant after repeated exposure.

We can illustrate the phenomenon outside the laboratory. A few years ago, a multinational corporation in Winston-Salem, N.C. built a new World Headquarters building and decorated it with art selected in juried contests conducted within the state, but independently of the company. Within a year, a local art gallery began to show a marked upswing in sales of modern art, as opposed to the more familiar paintings of rustic barns and dead ducks. Talking to his customers, some of whom he had known for years, the owner of the gallery found that they had been walking by these abstract paintings every day at work and had "kind of gotten to like them," to the extent that they were actually willing to buy some for their own homes. This is a clear example of people's willingness to put their money where their "mere exposure" effect is.

There are, naturally, limits on the mere exposure effect; most of us can take only so much of the top twenty tunes before becoming irritated by them. The importance of the mere exposure effect for attitude change, however, is in showing that attitudes can change with experience, even if this experience is not associated with good or bad events. The mere exposure effect is different from classical or instrumental conditioning.

Attitude Change

Everybody wants to change somebody's attitudes. Politicians want to change voters' attitudes. The Surgeon General wants to change smokers' attitudes. The Environmental Protection Agency and the Sierra Club campaign against pollution and dentists talk against sugar. Let us see how we can study attitude change, then look at some of the ways we might change attitudes.

how we study attitude change

Suppose we want to find out if an advertising campaign for a political candidate changed voter attitudes. *Change* implies that we knew the attitudes of the "target group" we are trying to change *before* our promotion and can measure that group again *after* the promotion. This is called a before and after, or pre-post, design and could use any of the attitude measures we discussed earlier. This is illustrated as follows:

Pretest————Attitude Change Campaign————Posttest
(Attitude   (Attitude Measure
Measure)   Repeated)

If the attitudes of our target group changed in the desired direction we might conclude that our campaign had been effective. But is this a fair conclusion?

Consider the case with Jimmy Carter. By November, 1979, his popularity had reached a dismal low. Then suddenly there was the Iranian crisis with the hostages, followed shortly by the Soviet invasion of Afghanistan. The President's popularity leaped upward. Had we mounted an attitude change campaign to bolster Carter's candidacy just before these world-shaking events and measured its effect after they occurred, we might have been fooled into believing that our promotion bordered on magic. We can all see that this example is too obvious; any politically-sensitive person would realize other factors were involved. But what about other, less world-shaking events and their influences on attitudes that might sneak in unbeknownst to us?

To be confident of our promotion campaign we need data from people who have *not* been exposed to our alleged attitude-change techniques. This more complete approach is diagrammed as follows:

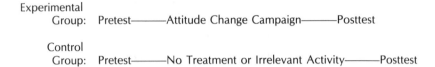

Experimental
Group: Pretest———Attitude Change Campaign———Posttest

Control
Group: Pretest———No Treatment or Irrelevant Activity———Posttest

Only if the attitude change is significantly greater in the experimental group than in the control group (as determined by statistical analysis) could we conclude that our campaign did anything. *The control group accounts for those things that might produce a change in attitude scores for the experimental group other than the attitude change treatment itself.* It does not identify those things for us, however. In the case of our hypothetical pro-Carter campaign we might be able to tease out from the data that our campaign did have some effect, as illustrated in Figure 7–2.

One common reason for change, which the control group may show, is inherent in the very procedure: *Taking the attitude measure the first time may influence how we take it the second time.* The procedure itself can influence the results. There are additional, more complex, approaches to attitude-change research, but the two-group design makes the point: A simple pretest-posttest procedure is not even adequate to show the actual occurrence of attitude change, much less pinpoint a reason for it. With this behind us, let us turn to some attitude change techniques and factors influencing their effectiveness.

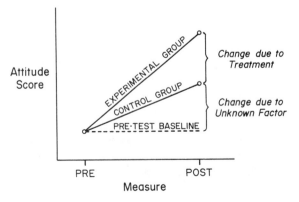

figure 7–2. Hypothetical results for attitude change study, showing a pre-post change due to unknown causes in the control group and additional change between the control group and experimental group due to the attitude-change treatment. The experimental group might not have changed more than the control group and neither group might not have gone above the baseline established by the pretest.

making logical versus emotional appeals

Is it better to "give them the facts" or "give them hell" if you want to change attitudes? This question has been studied on issues ranging from smoking (arousing fear of lung cancer), to taking care of teeth (arousing fear of cavities), to getting tetanus shots (arousing fear of lockjaw). At various times data have suggested that fear arousal produces greater attitude change, no attitude change, or less attitude change than no fear arousal at all.

The question is not quite as simple as it appears, however, because of the difficulty in separating logical (informational) and emotional appeal. If your physician calmly informs you that you have terminal cancer, you will undoubtedly become very upset. In fact, in one attitude change study the subjects were not able to distinguish what the researcher thought was a very clear distinction between logical and emotional appeal. If this is true in research situations, it must be even more confusing in real life situations.

At present, the best thinking on the subject seems to be that fear arousal evokes different reactions depending on how the fear-arousing communication is presented (Secord & Backman, 1974). When fear is aroused a person can try to control either the *fear itself*, or the *situation* which aroused the fear. In the first case, the person may try to withdraw from the situation, stop thinking about the danger, and so on. The latter approach, coping behavior, would involve facing the danger and following the recommendation of the attitude change message.

Five rules relating fear arousal and attitude change are

1. If there is *strong* fear arousal and an immediate response is necessary, the communication is less effective. The recipient may be too busy trying to reduce his or her immediate fear to follow any other "rational" suggestion contained in the message.

2. If it is possible for the recipient to delay responding until some time *after* receiving the strong-fear message, the rational part of the message may be more effective. There is time for the recipient to calm down and be less defensive.

3. "Action instructions" (what to do) are not very effective without *any* fear arousal, but a small amount of arousal is about as effective as a large amount.

4. Fear-arousal is more effective if the action proposed is something that will reduce the fear. Thus, "If you have the following symptoms of VD . . . do this. . . ."

5. People with high self-esteem are more likely to accept the instructions accompanying high fear messages than are people with low self-esteem.

No set of rules will be applicable to everybody in any situation because there are personality differences in the audience. One study divided the subjects into "copers" and "avoiders" by means of a prior test. The copers responded equally well to low- and high-fear messages, but the avoiders responded better to low-fear messages (Goldstein, 1959). If we don't know who is "out there" we cannot gear a persuasive communication terribly accurately to receive it.

Positive Emotional Arousal. Fear is not the only way to arouse emotion for attitude change. The ability to arouse strong positive emotions by campaign promises is the stuff of politics. Probably no one has won a national election by promising higher taxes and fewer government services. The promise of better things to come, however stated, is used to raise hope and then associate that hope with a particular candidate or party.

Ego Involvement. When people get personally and actively involved in a project, attitude change is greater and more effective. During World War II, Kurt Lewin (1952) compared a lecture-only with a lecture-discussion procedure for changing attitudes toward such cheap (and available) meats as kidneys. Since the best meat was going to the armed services, this was a timely and practical problem. Just telling consumers about the virtues of kidneys was less effective than following such a lecture with audience participation discussions in which members of the audience "sold themselves." Only this second group showed any significant change in subsequent meat purchases. Ego-involvement and self-persuasion have been considered important for attitude change ever since this pioneering study.

BUT, IF I'M GOING TO CHANGE THEIR ATTITUDE ABOUT OUR SHOES, I'VE **GOT** TO GET THEM ACTIVELY INVOLVED IN THINKING ABOUT THEIR FEET.

role playing

A commonly used ego-involving procedure is to have individuals act out various roles in a miniature improvised "play." In industrial relations and management training, for example, there is great emphasis on seeing things from the other person's point of view. A management person might play the role of an employee. The manager is then forced to look at situations the way an employee might under the circumstances. With this different perspective, it is expected that the manager might develop a somewhat more tolerant attitude and better understanding of the workers. Such role playing also gives opportunity to practice managing skills under supervision. Research shows that role play is effective in attitude change.

cognitive dissonance

Insufficient Justification. The discrepancy between contradictory beliefs, or between beliefs and actions, is considered a major motivational process (Chapter Four), but it is also a major factor in attitude change. Recall that contradictory ideas produce dissonance, which is unpleasant, and we reduce dissonance by various means. One of these is to change our attitude.

Suppose I know that you, a student, believe that liquor *should* be allowed on campus, or that intervisitation between men's and women's living quarters *should* be unrestricted or liberalized. Now I ask you to write an essay *against* having liquor on campus or *against* intervisitation. I offer you a generous five dollars for writing this essay which is opposed to your own attitude. How much are you likely to change your attitude? Probably not much. But suppose I offer you a piddling fifty cents to write the essay. How much are you likely to change your attitude? *You are likely to become more favorable toward the position you were previously opposed to.* This experiment has been done many times, with many variations, and the results are pretty consistent. People who write essays against their own attitudes with *small* justification change much more than those who do so for *large* justification. The cognitive dissonance explanation is that the five-dollar subjects find no conflict between what they were writing and what they believe; they are arguing against themselves for the five dollars payment. The fifty-cent subjects, on the other hand, have a large dissonance because they are getting so little for writing something they don't believe. Their way of reducing the dissonance is to come to believe that they must like the opposite side of the argument better than they had previously thought. Attitude change, therefore, is considered an important dissonance-reducing strategem.

Post-Decisional Dissonance. Suppose we have bought a new car, after much agonizing over many models and prices. After we make the purchase, does our attitude toward our new car change? Does our attitude toward those we rejected change? Research suggests that we will in fact like our choice more and the rejected alternatives less. This reduces any dissonance we might have about having made the wrong choice. Similarly, suppose we voted for a candidate who turns out to be a poor public official. Do we immediately reject the creep? Probably not. We may actively seek to find his or her good points, defend them, and have an even more positive attitude toward the officeholder—all this in order to reduce the dissonance between our own self-concept as a good decision-maker (voter) and the bad decision we made.

Disparaging Others. An unusual twist on cognitive dissonance is the effect of disparaging someone unjustly. Suppose you acted nasty to an innocent stranger? Would you change your attitude toward this person? And if so, in what direction? Research indicates you might actually develop a *more negative* attitude. Dissonance theory accounts for this as follows: Disparaging someone for no good reason is dissonant with most people's self-concept of being nice. In order to reduce the dissonance, we lower our view of the disparaged person to justify our behavior.

And, just as curious, the *nicer we think we are, the greater the dissonance* and therefore, presumably, the greater the demand for a negative attitude toward the disparaged person. On the brighter side, this effect seems only to work under conditions where we believe we have *voluntarily* chosen to be nasty, but not if we feel we have been coerced into doing so (by an experimenter). Furthermore, the effect is alleviated if we know in advance that we can later set things straight with the "innocent party." In the research, for example, the experimenter might tell the subject: "You read this bad personality evaluation to this person you don't know, but later you can tell him you only did it as an experimental requirement." The negative attitude doesn't develop here.

self-perception

Daryl Bem (for example, 1972) argued that people often change their attitudes because *they watch their own behavior.* Suppose someone spends a lot of time working on mechanical things around the house. She may reach the conclusion that since she spends so much time at this, she must really enjoy it. Similarly, a political campaign worker discovering the number of hours he is working in an election might decide he likes the candidate even more than he initially thought.

modeling and imitation

We have already noted that children and adults emulate their elders or others of high esteem. In the process of this imitation they may come to change their attitudes in a more or less favorable direction, depending on what they are imitating. Imitation might have this effect, in part, because the person doing the imitating might perceive his or her own actions, as just discussed for Bem's theory.

changes in attribution

How often do we see somebody do something, such as fumble an easy grounder in a baseball game, and ask ourselves, "Now why did he do that?" Or, how often do we wonder out loud to ourselves when we've pulled a boner, "Why did I do that?" And we often come up with some kind of reason. Attribution theory deals with exactly this question: *What kinds of causes do people give for their own or other people's behavior?* The theory is *not* concerned with what *professional* psychologists think are the causes but with what the average person (a "naive" psychologist) sees as causes.

Causes can be *personal, environmental,* or a combination of the two. Personal causes are such things as ability and energy; environmental causes are such things as the difficulty of a task and the characteristics of the work situation. We shall mention only some of the more important findings. These are causes *as perceived by the person searching for them,* not necessarily the "real" causes.

1. Many authors believe there is an overall greater tendency to attribute behavior to *personal* causes than to environmental causes. This may be because we generally like to think of ourselves as controlling our own lives.

2. We may attribute *our own behavior* relatively more to *external* causes (circumstances) when we do something poorly but to *personal* causes when we do well. The amateur playing the stock market may blame world conditions if a favorite stock goes down but credit personal astuteness if it goes up.

3. There is an even greater tendency to attribute the causes of *other* people's behavior to personal characteristics, such as intelligence, stupidity, or laziness. For example, "Joe couldn't get that job done because he's not smart enough." But, relatively speaking, we tend more to attribute our own behaviors to both internal *and* external factors. This may be because we have more realistic knowledge of situational factors related to us, than we do about others. However, there is also a psychological economy in thinking about others in a simplistic way. It is *easier* for us to say that Joe is "dumb" than to figure out other possible reasons his job is not done right.

Attribute Change and Attitude Change. How does a change in attribution produce a change in attitudes? Suppose one of our employees, Fred, has not been doing a good job recently. He used to be a ball of fire, but now he's not showing any initiative; he misses work too often and is getting careless. We might attribute this to Fred's not taking the job seriously, getting lazy, or playing around too much at night. All of these attributions would lead us to have an unfavorable attitude toward Fred. Then someone tells us, "By the way, did you know that Fred's wife is very ill in the hospital, he has real financial problems, and he is taking care of his five kids all by himself. I really don't know how the man keeps going and still manages to get to work." Abruptly, our attitude may change from disapproval to admiration, a complete reversal, and we are willing to help Fred during his time of need. Fred has not changed his job behavior, but our attitude has done an about face because we now perceive the cause of his behavior in a different light.

Attitude Change Theories

As we looked at processes and procedures we saw most of the theoretical ideas about attitude change. We shall therefore review theories briefly to put them into context.

learning theories

Principles from theories of classical conditioning, instrumental conditioning, and social learning (imitation) have all been applied as partial accounts of attitude development and change. All seem to make some contribution to the total picture.

consistency theories

Cognitive dissonance theory is one of a group of theories collectively called consistency theories. The basic premises of all these is that (1) a person *perceives* some kind of inconsistency in himself, in the environment, or between himself and the environment; (2) this arouses an unpleasant tension in the person; and (3) the person does something to reduce the tension. Changing one's attitude is one way of reducing tension. For example, if you and your best friend strongly disagree about the merits of a movie you might modify your attitude to reduce the tension between you and your friend.

attribution theory

Attribution involves the assignment of causes to events, as we have seen. Attitude change can occur very quickly if new causes for behaviors are perceived. For example, an employee may be unhappy with her salary and then find that the company is going broke and having to borrow money to pay her. Her attitude toward the company might change quickly.

adaptation level (contrast) theory

A theory we have not yet seen is adaptation level theory. This simply says that in time we get used to something, whether good or bad, and that events or people get judged against this background. If we have been used to a rascally bunch of politicians, an otherwise unremarkable entry into the field might look good. Indeed, following the Nixon administration Gerald Ford looked pretty good although he had hardly been considered an outstanding national figure before. Just about anybody would have looked good against the immediate contrast of Spiro Agnew and the motley cast of Watergate characters. As the contrast became less marked over time, however, and Ford did nothing spectacular for eighteen months (except pardon Nixon), Ford looked less good and could not win against Carter. In brief, then, we might develop a fairly strong positive or negative attitude toward something, at least temporarily, just because it stands in strong contrast to what we have become used to. As an example of the negative side, no one was eager to follow in John Wooden's shoes as basketball coach at UCLA. Fans tend to turn nasty toward coaches who lose, especially if the fans have become used to a long winning streak like Wooden's.

SUMMARY

1. An attitude is a positive or negative feeling toward some person, object or event. Attitudes influence thoughts and behavior, but thoughts and behavior also influence attitudes.

2. Behavioral observations, verbal self-report, and attitude scales are used to measure attitudes indirectly; the attitudes are inferred from these various sources.

3. Attitudes are developed through rewarded and punished behaviors, classical conditioning and imitation. Models are particularly powerful influences in the development of attitudes. Unexpected (unfamiliar) events can arouse fear, but "mere exposure" to new situations can increase positive feelings.

4. Attitude change is typically studied with a pretest-treatment-posttest procedure for an experimental group and a no-treatment control group. A control group is necessary to ascertain whether any observed change in attitude is due to the "attitude change" treatment or to something else.

5. Persuasive messages can give either logical or emotional appeals. Which approach is better depends on a number of conditions specific to a particular situation, such as the knowledgeability of the audience about the topic at hand.

6. Active participation, such as discussion of an issue, is more effective in producing attitude change than is just hearing an attitude-change message. Role-playing can also be an effective attitude change mechanism.

7. Cognitive dissonance, considered an aversive condition, may frequently be reduced by a change in attitude. A person working hard for a political candidate for no pay may reconcile this discrepancy between effort and benefit by having a more positive attitude toward the candidate.

8. Bem's self-perception theory suggests that people often establish or change their attitudes by watching their own behavior. A person watching someone else play tennis every day would conclude that the other person really likes tennis. Similarly, a person "watching himself or herself" do something frequently might conclude that he really does like that activity.

9. Attribution theory is concerned with assigning causes to behaviors, either the behavior of oneself or of others. Attitude change can be powerfully influenced by a change in attribution. Though we might have a negative attitude toward someone we believe initiated an aggressive attack, we might change this attitude rapidly if we find that person was attacked first and acted in self-defense.

10. Adaptation level theory says that we become used to situations after some exposure to them and then judge new situations in contrast to the familiar one. A person used to very bad politicians might find an average politician very appealing in contrast.

EXERCISES

1. How do you infer the attitudes of others?

2. What are some of the difficulties of attitude measurement?

3. Complete the Social Distance Scale and Semantic Differential (according to whatever group you wish). Now compare the two scales. Which do *you* think is a better measure of your actual attitudes toward that group? Why?

4. When is a scale *valid?* How do we demonstrate this?

5. Choose a random sample from people in your class. In a random sample everyone has an equal chance of being in the sample. What method did you use to obtain the random sample? What makes it a random sample? What population does your sample represent?

6. How can "mere exposure" affect attitudes? Can you think of specific instances of this effect from your own experience?

7. Ego involvement is considered important in attitude change. Choose an attitude you want to change. How could you get the target persons (those you want to change) involved in order to facilitate attitude change?

8. Almost everyone has made at least one rotten decision at sometime or other. After one of these, how might original attitudes change? What particular type cognitive dissonance is involved?

9. How could *perception* of self or others influence attitudes?

10. According to attribution theory, if you were playing golf and made a hole in one, would you most likely attribute this to external or personal causes? What relevant information would be involved in this determination? Suppose you narrowly missed a putt? How would you attribute this?

8

Social Norms, Roles, Stereotypes, and Prejudice

Norms and Roles

definitions

Frank is sitting in class when the instructor makes a mistake. Ellen, another student, leaps up, points out the error and proceeds to the front of the class to take over for the rest of the hour. Frank thinks something has gone wrong. But what?

An army squad snakes its way through the jungle, led by Private Smith. Sergeant Jones follows, obviously taking orders from Smith. Does this seem out of place?

In these examples there seem to be violations of our expectations about what *should* have been happening. The teacher should have been teaching and the sergeant should have been leading. These people were not filling their *roles* properly.

Groups, whether large or small, have norms and roles. A *norm* is a *prescribed* way of behaving established by a group with regard to particular activities. The group expects its members to follow the norms or be sanctioned. We have legal norms and sanctions, such as stopping at red lights or paying fines for not stopping. But we also have informal norms and sanctions. Business executives are "expected" to dress one way (in a tailored suit), male office workers another (white collar), and laborers a third (blue collar). People who depart from the code may be ridiculed or called down by their superiors or even their peers. In recent years, the norms have been considerably relaxed, but dress codes (norms) do exist. Swimming attire is almost always out of place except at the beach or pool.

The role of law enforcement officer is sharpely defined by uniforms and other symbols. *(Photo by Bill Henry)*

social roles and norms

A social role is a whole set of norms and expectations about how a person should act if he or she is in that role. A role is defined by a group and has its place in the group. Most organizations have organizational charts with particular functions (activities) assigned to particular positions, such as President, Vice-President, Secretary, Treasurer, and Sergeant-at-Arms. Whoever fills any of these positions is expected to play the role of that position in a prescribed manner. Such organizational roles are interlocking; they relate to each other in particular ways in order to achieve particular goals effectively. In general, social roles are established to help oil the wheels of society.

Some roles are defined *reciprocally;* one cannot exist without the other, such as leader-follower, father-son, teacher-student, and husband-wife. In our opening examples, what was really out of place was the reversal of the roles involved: Student became teacher and follower became leader.

Experimentation with husband-wife role-reversal is a much-discussed phenomenon. The husband's role had traditionally been defined as breadwinner, the wife staying home to care for house and family. Though it is hard for many husbands to accept any other possibility, more flexible roles work well for many others. The strength of our social expectations for these roles is indicated by the fact that "role reversal" is newsworthy at all.

Multiple Roles. Most of us play more than one role. A woman may rise early in the morning to get her children fed and off to school (*mother* and *cook* roles). She counsels her husband on a family matter *(wife)*. Then she goes to her own office where she is a *business executive,* giving orders, making plans, consulting, and deciding. At noon she meets her own mother for lunch and is *daughter* for an hour. In the evening she may again be mother, wife, and cook, as well as *lover.* Men have similar role shifts during the day. Small wonder there is sometimes confusion about how we should behave when we are switching roles so fast. The business executive role may not fare so well if the situation at hand calls for husband or father.

Role Conflicts. Different roles can make incompatible demands. A purchasing agent may have to order a product manufactured by her son's company. As a *mother* she would want to help her son, but as *purchasing agent* she is bound to get the best competitive price. Such conflicts are often anticipated by prohibitions against doing business with relatives. Role conflicts, fortunately, are often minimized because the conflicting roles are played at different times, and seldom would such a purchasing agent-mother conflict arise.

Role Incompatibility. The roles defined by a group may not be filled by people who are compatible in temperament, experience or training, with the demands of the role. A first-rate engineer may be promoted to management on the basis of his engineering feats. But these very engineering skills may be detrimental in his managerial position. He may try to manipulate people like objects and expect they will respond gracefully. Of course, they don't.

Selection and Training for Roles. Role compatibility may be enhanced by proper selection and training. Selection procedures are intended to take into account individual differences in people in order to provide a good match between persons and roles. A potential employee may be given a number of aptitude tests for certain general skills (such as finger coordination) and then given specific training for a particular job (such as assembling delicate parts). Our engineer-manager might have been sent to school for management training to improve his skills in dealing with people. Of course, if he applies these techniques mechanically, as in an engineering problem, he is not much advanced over where he started. Good *selection* would uncover people who would be properly adaptable for their new roles. In general, the selection procedure should enhance the compatibility between people as they are and their roles, and training should refine the compatibility.

For some very important social roles, there is little or no training. Parenthood is a prime example. A high school student might have a course in home economics or family relations, but it seems that most of us are expected to either learn on the job or by imitation. Fortunately, there is now greater concern in this area and there are courses in "parenting," such as the Parent

Effectiveness Training course, developed by Thomas Gordon. There appears to be no selection for parents, however, other than that practiced by males and females in their relations with each other.

The social definition of a role is no guarantee that the role can be filled satisfactorily. There is a growing suspicion that nobody can successfully perform the role of the President of the United States. In an adaptive society we might expect that failure to find people to fill roles adequately would lead to role redefinitions, new roles, new combinations of old roles, and new role expectations.

Role Diffusion. Erik Erikson, a psychoanalyst who has studied adolescent behavior extensively, developed the concept of *role diffusion* (Erikson, 1963). As a young person enters adolescence, he or she begins to consider the future. The adolescent may consciously "try on" different roles before finding a "proper" identity, a way of behaving, and a place in society that feels comfortable. During this tryout period there may be a mixing up, a confusion of roles. This is role diffusion. Some young people readily "find themselves" and make a smooth transition from childhood to mature adulthood, but most have some difficult times. An important function of education should be to help people find *what is available* in life that one can find satisfaction in doing and being.

Stereotyping

a class demonstration

Table 8–1 contains fifty adjectives. Go down the list and check each adjective in the appropriate column according to whether you consider it relatively more characteristic of males or of females. Each adjective should be marked, but only in one column. Even if you think a particular adjective applies equally to males and females, put it in one column or the other. Do this before reading further.

Now, count the number of times you marked odd-numbered adjectives (1, 3, 5, etc.) as being *male* and even-numbered adjectives (2, 4, 6, etc.) as *female*. The maximum per column by this scoring is twenty-five. The chances are good that whether you are a man or a woman you checked twenty or more of the odd-numbered as male and twenty or more of the even-numbered as female. Compare your scoring with somebody else's. Why did you check the adjectives this way? Probably because there are very consistent *stereotypes* about males and females. *A stereotype is the assignment of the same personality or behavioral characteristics to an entire group of people with little regard for individual differences.* The above example illustrates *sex-trait stereotyping.*

table 8–1

for each of the following adjectives, indicate whether you think they are more characteristic of males (by checking the appropriate column) or characteristic of females (by the same procedure.)

		male	female				male	female
1	Active				26	Mild		
2	Affectionate				27	Forceful		
3	Adventurous				28	Nagging		
4	Appreciative				29	Handsome		
5	Aggressive				30	Poised		
6	Attractive				31	Humorous		
7	Assertive				32	Sensitive		
8	Changeable				33	Inventive		
9	Autocratic				34	Sentimental		
10	Dreamy				35	Lazy		
11	Boastful				36	Soft-hearted		
12	Emotional				37	Logical		
13	Coarse				38	Sophisticated		
14	Excitable				39	Masculine		
15	Confident				40	Submissive		
16	Feminine				41	Rational		
17	Courageous				42	Sympathetic		
18	Frivolous				43	Reckless		
19	Cruel				44	Talkative		
20	Fussy				45	Robust		
21	Daring				46	Timid		
22	Gentle				47	Rude		
23	Dominant				48	Warm		
24	High-strung				49	Severe		
25	Enterprising				50	Weak		

This woman enjoys . . .

the woods . . .

the sunshine . . .

parties . . .

playing tennis . . .

But her occupation is . . .

college professor. She

teaches

does research . . .

and counsels students.

So don't be fooled by stereotypes.

the Williams research

The list of adjectives in Table 8–1 comes from research by John Williams and his associates (Williams, Giles, Edwards, Best, and Daws, 1977). Initially, a large group of subjects was given the Adjective Check List, and instructed to check those adjectives in the total list of 300 which were characteristic of males. This was done *for* both males and females *by* both males and females. The result was two lists of adjectives, 30 describing males and 27 describing females, which at least 75 percent of subjects of both sexes agreed upon. Males and females have very similar stereotypes of each other's sex traits.

Furthermore, data from many different countries and cultures are highly similar. Figure 8–1 summarizes data according to a standard scoring system

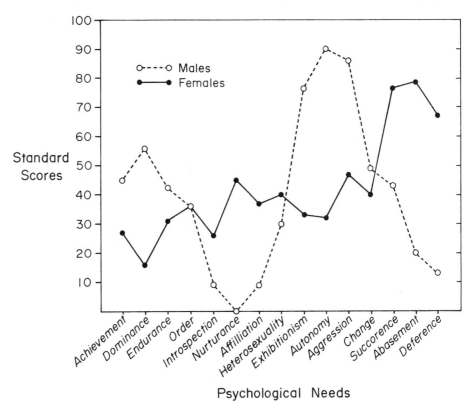

Psychological Needs

figure 8–1. Need profiles obtained by treating male and female stereotypes on the Adjective Checklist as hypothetical individual male and female (Williams et al, 1977). The scoring scheme is for needs from Murray's list of psychological needs summarized in Table 4–1. These data are combined from the United States, Ireland, and England. Data from around the world, representing many cultures, show almost identical results (Williams & Best, in press. Used with permission.)

for the Adjective Check List (Gough & Heilbrun, 1965). This scheme is based on Murray's list of psychological needs (see Chapter Four). Figure 8–1 is a kind of "personality profile" which is normally applied to individuals but in this case has been applied to the average results for males and females in three countries. There are distinctively different male and female profiles common to many countries. Males, for example, are consistently described as more achievement oriented and more domineering than are females.

The stereotype character of the adjectives in Tables 8–1 and the graph in Figure 8–1 is indicated by the fact that if you ask a large number of males and females to describe *themselves* on the Adjective Check List, the results do not look at all like Figure 8–1. Self-report averages are almost straight lines across the graph.

If the stereotype profiles actually had been obtained from one man and from one woman describing themselves, those two people would each be considered atypical. One clinical psychologist gave the following personality description of "Mr. Stereotype" and "Ms. Stereotype," as if the profiles were from two individuals:

The hypothetical female student was described as follows:

Exaggeration in negative direction—*passive dependent personality pattern:* gives impression of being lazy, scatterbrained to cover profound self doubts; alternates between complaining and self blame with self blame prevailing; may attempt to manipulate via martyrdom; weepy, clinging vine, rattles easily in emergency, may avoid by fainting, trouble with own hostility; has some nurturant, mothering kinds of instincts, i.e., might gush over a puppy or baby but would plead inadequacy or try to transfer responsibility for cleaning up messes or delivering discipline.

The hypothetical male student was described as follows:

Exaggeration in negative direction, particularly in denial of anything positive—*passive–aggressive–personality pattern:* false cockiness, bravado, fearful, impulsive defense of imagined slights to ego and potency, immature, depressed, juvenile delinquent-black leather jacket—either "Lord of the Flies" fascination with violence and brutality (pulls wings off of all flies—goes out of way to step on any small, defenseless creature) *or* the cruel, vicious, frightened striking out of the cornered rat. Most fearful of show of affection or relationships involving meeting human needs. Compulsively cruel but in a fundamentally inept, weak, cowardly way. Grotesque characterization of "high school Harry" in way over his head.

Cecilia Solano (1977) has described the differences between reports about oneself and reports about others as "the variable self and the constant other." When people assign causes to their own behavior they tend to take the specific situation into account and hence give variable reports from one situation to another. But when they assign causes to the behavior of other people they tend to use fixed personality characteristics more, with much less accounting for behavior in terms of specific situations. This tendency is greater the less familiar one is with the person to whom behavioral causes are being given.

JONES LIKES TO BELIEVE THAT HE IS A LIVING EMBODIMENT OF THE MASCULINE STEREOTYPE.

What this and similar research suggest is that the less well we know a person the more likely we are to use some kind of stereotype as an explanation or description of that person's behavior.

Over the years psychologists have studied stereotypes in relation to many different ethnic and racial groups. Katz and Braly (1933) had college students assign personality traits to a dozen different nationalities. There emerged such stereotypes as that the English are "sportsmanlike, intelligent, and conventional" whereas Italians are "artistic, impulsive, and passionate."

Stereotypes are not even limited to such natural groups as nationalities. Wells, Goi, and Seader (1958) had subjects characterize the owners of Cadillacs, Buicks, Chevrolets, Fords, and Plymouths. Buick owners were judged to be middle class, brave, masculine, strong, modern, and pleasant whereas Plymouth owners were quiet, careful, slow, moral, fat, gentle, calm, sad, thinking, patient, and honest. Such divergent personality characteristics were divined solely on the basis of car ownership! These results have fascinating implications for marketing, and they were in fact obtained in marketing research. Though more recent research reveals less stereotyping along some lines (for example, nationalities), we have seen that sex-stereotyping is still very prevalent.

functions of stereotypes

Stereotypes are usually considered "bad," related to prejudice. Stereotypes of blacks as "lazy" or of Jews as "moneygrubbers" clearly have bad connotations. But what about the stereotype of the English as "sportsmanlike" or the Italians as "artistic"? Are these also bad? If so, in what sense?

One apparent function of stereotyping is a kind of psychological economy: By applying a stereotype to a group, we have less to remember about individuals. And, if there is a kernel of truth to the stereotype, we have some advantage in dealing with individuals in that group. The tendency to categorize and form concepts about objects (including people) seems to be universal, and the ability to do it well is a highly-prized human trait. As Roger Brown (1965) points out, it would be wrong-headed *not* to categorize people in some way, simply because it is realistic to categorize people. If we took the argument that no two people are ever exactly alike to its extreme, we would never have *any* idea of how to deal with strangers, as individuals or as groups.

The more serious problems arise in how we use the stereotypes. Williams speculates that though sex-trait stereotypes may be well-nigh universal, differences which may be taken casually or playfully in one country form major social policy in another. Women are treated as inherently inferior in many cultures, including parts of our own.

In Brown's view, the two major ill effects of stereotyping lie in *ethnocentrism* and in the implication that stereotype traits are *inborn*. Ethnocentrism means that members of a group *evaluate* other people on the basis of their own group norms. For example, Americans might consider the relatively less frequent bathing by inhabitants of some European countries as negative. But hot water is an expensive commodity in Europe, and Europeans are more likely to consider Americans wasteful than to believe that Europeans do not bathe often enough.

The second perverse characteristic of stereotypes, considering them inborn, is clearly unwarranted. A television documentary once showed a southern congressman explaining to a constituent why Negroes had inferior intelligence compared to whites: The Negroes had limited brain development. It is certainly controversial whether there are any racial differences in intelligence, and there is absolutely no evidence of brain differences among any identifiable racial groups. In fact, there aren't even any known "pure" races. Still, towering social policies are constructed on such quicksand, as when the United States Immigration Department excluded Orientals, Africans, and Southern Europeans in favor of Northern Europeans. Another example was slavery. A third was the German attempt at genocide.

the self-fulfilling prophecy

If we believe a stereotype we may treat members of a group in such a way that they will themselves fulfill the stereotype. If you treat people as if you expected them to be lazy or stupid, they may well act that way. This self-fulfilling prophecy seems to work in schools and industry, as well as in society at large. With the stereotype we may be *defining a role* for someone. The TV situation comedy *All in the Family* had many episodes where a member of some minority group (black, Jewish, Polish) acted out in exaggerated form the stereotype of his or her group simply because it was easier to get along with Archie Bunker that way. This tended to support Archie's stereotypes, while at the same time mocking for the audience the stereotype and Archie's prejudice. If a stereotype is played often enough in real life it may become believed by the person playing it.

the origin and maintenance of stereotypes

Origins. Some stereotypes contain at least a kernel of truth. There is much evidence, for example, that males of various species are more aggressive in their play at an early age than are females. On the average, human males are bigger and stronger than females.

Most stereotypes, like attitudes generally, however, probably grow out of group influences rather than personal experience. We hear people say that "Arabs are such and such" or that "Jews are so-and-so." This topic grows livelier by the year (if not the day) as OPEC increases oil prices, the Palestinian problem persists, and Western European and other nations are fearful of an oil cutoff. What we learn from our parents, peers, or culture at large is a prime source of our stereotypes.

Maintenance. Stereotypes can be maintained in several ways.

1. We get *repeated exposure to stereotype statements,* on television, in newspapers, or in our conversation with others. The sources of our stereotypes continue to function.

2. We may see *examples of the stereotype* in action in limited cases and thus have our stereotype of a whole group supported. There may be *false examples* of a stereotype in action. If a woman acts weak and indecisive, even though she actually is not, she will nevertheless support a stereotype. The pre-Civil War "Southern Belle" is a model for this.

3. We may hold onto the stereotype in the face of negative examples by *discounting the negative examples* as exceptions. The efficient, hard-headed businesswoman may still be considered an exception.

changing stereotypes

Changing stereotypes, like changing attitudes, is a matter of re-education. Many groups have initiated such re-education: blacks, women, and gay rights activists have all worked hard to change their image. In the case of the gay community, it has been enlightening for "straights" to discover that the bulk of male or female homosexuals are not overtly anything like the stereotypes. The only great similarity among homosexuals is their sexual preference. The stereotype of the hip-swishing male has to be rapidly re-evaluated when respected athletes, professional people, and business leaders identify themselves as homosexual. Similarly, the "butch" lesbian is a minority figure even in lesbian culture.

For blacks, especially, one of the major breakthroughs has been the shift in portrayal of Negroes in movies and TV from the shufflin' Stepinfetchit and Amos and Andy characters to police captains, detectives, macho private eyes, and business executives. The sharp edge of TV's *All in the Family* has cut through the facade of many a stereotype, as has the series *Soap*. It does not necessarily follow that all this will change deeply held stereotypes, but it may make it harder to hold to the old stereotypes and perhaps more difficult for a younger generation to learn them. What we must be wary of is letting *new stereotypes and prejudices replace the old ones.* If indeed it is human to categorize, then we cannot expect that stereotypes will totally disappear.

Prejudice and Discrimination

definitions

Prejudice refers to a *negative attitude* toward the members of some group based solely on the basis of their membership in that group. Such groups are typically racial, ethnic, or religious but are not limited to these categories. Prejudice is not necessarily limited to negative attitudes (there are positive prejudices) but in this context we shall use the word prejudice in its negative meaning unless otherwise stated.

Discrimination refers to *negative actions* against the members of a group toward which there is prejudice. A restaurant owner who does not like blacks, but allows them equal service, is showing only prejudice. If the restaurant owner literally beats them away with an ax handle, as did Lester Maddox, a restaurateur who went on to become governor of Georgia in the 1960s, that would be discrimination. Discrimination is usually shown a *little* more subtly than this, in the form of differential job opportunities, pay, educational opportunities, and housing.

We are usually concerned with prejudice and discrimination against *minority* groups. The WASP (White Anglo-Saxon Protestant) sits in the catbird seat in the United States and has actively discriminated against the numerically fewer Catholics, Jews, blacks, Orientals, Puerto Ricans, and Chicanos, to name the obvious.

Prejudice and discrimination can be directed at *numerical majorities,* however. In Africa, white minorities have discriminated effectively against black majorities for many years. Similarly, there are more women than men, but women are more discriminated against. To save the definition of minority, then, the concept of *psychological minority* was invented. A psychological minority may have more people but has little *social power* and little influence in major social decisions (such as about school policy, city-county budgets, and so on). The South African apartheid policy has kept the blacks there powerless. Blacks must have passes to come into the capital, Johannesburg. It is illegal for blacks and whites to fraternize at all, much less intermarry. Whites from South Africa will tell you in all seriousness that it is for the blacks' own good (the author has been told this by South Africans). Not all South African whites believe in apartheid, but the more outspoken ones who don't are under "house arrest," literally being restricted to their homes most of the time and only permitted one visitor at a time.

A quick glance at any statistics for women in major administrative positions in large organizations or as elected public officials shows they are not "queenpins" in social decision-making. Two facts will make the point: In 1981 there were only two women in the 100-member United States Senate and there were no female governors in fifty states.

It is, of course, easier for most minority groups to hold negative attitudes than to practice discrimination. Blacks may be as prejudiced against whites (Honkies) as the other way around, but it is not as easy for blacks to discriminate meaningfully. Economic boycott of white businesses by blacks is rare, though potentially effective.

reverse discrimination and tokenism

Reverse discrimination refers to "bending over backward" so far not to discriminate against one group that another group is discriminated against. Many white males believe this has happened to them in the national rush to comply with federal affirmative action (equal opportunity) legislation. It is a popular "truism," if not really accurate, that black females have the best chance for jobs because an employer can right two wrongs simultaneously in the minority employment statistics. The shortage of qualified black applicants in some fields *has* led to considerable competition for their services. This is true, for example, in positions where doctoral degrees are required.

Tokenism refers to non-discrimination or reverse discrimination in trivial matters only. There is the "token black" invited to a party, or a "token woman" on an executive board. An individual or group can thereby give the appearance of no prejudice or discrimination while at the same time actively engaging in both where it counts.

An interesting research example of such apparent tokenism is found in an experiment by Dutton and Lennox (1974). They had white subjects participate in an "experiment," then go elsewhere to collect their participant's pay. On the way they were panhandled by either a black or a white person. The average amount of money given to the blacks was almost twice that given to whites (sixty-nine cents versus thirty-six cents). Two days later all the subjects were approached about volunteering for activities which involved actually working with blacks. Those who had previously been approached by the black panhandler were much more reluctant than those approached by the white panhandler. The tokenism interpretation is that by being relatively generous in small matters (a few cents to a beggar), one can justify to oneself not becoming involved with blacks in more important situations.

attitudes, stereotypes, and prejudice/discrimination

We can now relate several of the previous topics.

First, since we defined prejudice as a particular kind of attitude, whatever is true about attitudes in general applies with equal force to prejudice. Information about attitude development and change is especially useful in dealing with prejudice. Attitude scales are commonly used to measure prejudice.

Second, stereotypes provide support for prejudice and discrimination. If blacks are stereotyped as "lazy, dirty, and stupid" there is built-in justification for prejudice and discrimination. Who would *not* have negative attitudes toward *any* group with these characteristics? The fact that the stereotype is wrong and that there are whites with the same characteristics is ignored.

where does prejudice come from?

Baron and Byrne (1977, p. 164) categorize the origins of prejudice and discrimination into (1) intergroup conflict, (2) personality dynamics, and (3) social-learning experiences. All three may be involved in any particular real-life example.

Intergroup Conflict. The argument here is that when a minority group attempts to improve its status, the majority group is threatened and reacts with hostility. The Irish who migrated to the United States during the potato famine in the mid 1800s were extremely poor. As they settled into the East Coast of the United States, they worked hard to improve themselves, and there was much hostility toward them. The Irish gradually became respectable and were replaced on the bottom of society's totem-pole by upwardly mobile blacks, largely migrating from the South in hope of better opportunities. Then came the Puerto Ricans. And now come the Cubans.

Experimental support for the intergroup conflict interpretation is found in the elegant field experiments of Muzafir Sherif (1966) and his associates (see also Sherif et al., 1961). Middle class eleven- and twelve-year-old boys in summer camps especially established for this research were divided (within camp) into two carefully matched groups. Enjoying many camp activities together, each group developed a strong feeling of group solidarity.

The groups were put into conflict by having competitions at various camp activities. One group could get a prize in the competition, to be shared by all the members of the winning group. At this point considerable verbal and non-verbal hostility began to develop between the two groups. Fights almost broke out; there was much name-calling, raids on each others' cabins, and food fights in the mess hall.

Conditions were then arranged so the two groups had to act *cooperatively* to obtain a series of goals, such as getting a stalled truck moving. Of several attempted procedures, these cooperative activities were the only ones which actively reduced the competition-induced hostilities. In a recent description of the research, one of the original researchers (Carolyn Sherif, 1976) notes how the results seem so obvious in retrospect, but were surprising at the time.

Personality Factors. During and after World War II a group of social psychologists at the University of California put to research a most important question: What kind of person does it take to be a Nazi and engage in Nazi-like practices? Many of the researchers were themselves European Jews who managed to escape Hitler. The question can be generalized to ask what kind of person is actively anti-Semitic (or anti-any other group).

The result was a book called *The Authoritarian Personality* (Adorno, et al., 1950). The most important finding was that the strongly-prejudiced person does not carry his or her prejudice in splendid isolation. Rather, a whole set of attitudes and beliefs go together. Several thousand subjects were administered attitude measures, personality tests, and clinical interviews. What seemed to go together were anti-Semitism, political and economic conservatism, ethnocentrism, and authoritarianism. As personality research goes, there were fairly high correlations among the four measures for these characteristics.

Briefly summarized, the Authoritarian Personality was said to hold conventional middle-class values, to be unduly submissive to authority, to strongly condemn others who violate conventional norms, to oppose things that are imaginative (for example, daydreaming, reading fiction), to be superstitious, to be overly concerned with power, to have a generalized hostility toward people, and to project one's own hostilities onto the outer world and therefore be very suspicious. Most of us probably do know somebody who can be described by several, if not all, of the above.

There has been considerable controversy, however, over the methods used to arrive at the above description, and hence its accuracy, and whether there is an authoritarianism of the left (for example, communism) like that of the right (for example, Naziism). Also, as Brown (1965) points out, no such description *could* apply to *all* communists or Nazis because in either case a much greater diversity of personalities was necessary for the kind of success these two parties enjoyed. Both required visionaries, both violated the conventional norms of their groups when they started out, and so on.

What produces an Authoritarian Personality? It was believed that very authoritarian individuals were "reared by harsh, punitive parents who created in their offspring a pattern of submissive obedience to authority, and punitive rejection of groups other than their own. Largely as a result of such characteristics, high-authoritarian individuals were held to view the world in rigid black-and-white categories: Either you are a member of their own group and are for them, or you are a member of some other rejected group and must be against them." (Baron & Bryne, p. 166) In any event, one does see clusters of beliefs and personality characteristics in individuals, and these often seem to be related to prejudice.

Social Learning. This approach emphasizes the learning of prejudice and discrimination as part of the socialization process in early childhood. Parents, peers, teachers, and mass media all contribute. As is the case with attitude formation, other learning processes such as modeling and imitation are involved. Harding, Proshansky, Kutner, and Chein, (1969) divided the development of prejudice into three stages. First, there is *awareness* of group differences, which may come quite early. Williams and his associates have detected racial awareness in children barely over two years of age. Second, there is *negative orientation* toward other groups, including unflattering names and descriptions. Third, there is an *integration* of beliefs and feelings into very specific negative attitudes toward a particular group or groups.

An unintended effect of *All in the Family* may be to *increase* prejudice by having it modeled by the sympathetic lead character, Archie Bunker. This was certainly not what the producer, Norman Lear, had in mind. He intended to make fun of the prejudices shown. But a research study, conducted with both American and Canadian subjects, showed that (1) already-prejudiced subjects admired Archie and thought they would like to be like him, and (2) the already-prejudiced subjects had a greater tendency to watch the program than did the non-prejudiced. This suggests they were selectively watching the program because it supported their beliefs! As with other possible effects of television (for example, whether TV violence promotes or inhibits viewer violence), the last word is far from in. It does seem a little discouraging, however, to have an apparent backfire like the one suggested (Vidmar & Rokeach, 1974).

changing prejudice

Socialization Practices. If parents want to prevent their children from becoming prejudiced against members of another group, there are several things they can do.

1. When questions come up about the group, emphasize the similarities of the outgroup to the child's own group, and in a positive manner. "Being 'black' just happens to be a skin color. White people have different color skins, too. Sometimes your skin may get very dark in the summer."

2. If a child has learned something derogatory from a peer and says it to some outgroup member, such as calling a name, the parent can try to get the child to see how it might feel to be called a name. "You made that child feel bad. Wouldn't you feel bad if somebody called you 'stupid' or 'stinky'? You wouldn't want to make someone else feel bad."

3. It may be possible to demonstrate the arbitrariness of racial or ethnic distinctions. "Suppose that we said all blue-eyed children were not as good as brown-

eyed children. You have blue eyes? How would that make you feel? Would you believe it?"

4. The parent can be a model of how he or she wants the child to act.
5. Don't reward discriminatory actions.

Teachers are in a good position to bring home morals since they have groups to work with. One teacher, Jane Elliot (Baron & Byrne, 1977) actually divided her class into eye color groups for a few days, then reversed the group roles. The "superior" group had many more privileges than did the "inferior" group, who were ridiculed and had to wear special collars. The effect was demoralizing to the "inferiors." Weiner and Wright (1975) did a controlled experiment along similar lines. They found that afterwards the children were more willing to go on a picnic with black children than were control groups. Apparently, their own experiences as the recipients of prejudice and discrimination made them less willing to act in a discriminatory manner.

Direct Contact. If, as we generally believe, prejudice is mostly learned by imitation, through the media, and from parents and peers, we might expect that direct contact with the target group would reduce prejudice. This assumes that stereotypes will break down with greater familiarity. The quality and emotional characteristics of the contact situations are important, however. Baron and Byrne point out some special conditions that may need to prevail.

- The contact had best be between people of equal social and economic status. Otherwise, communication is difficult and suspicion and mistrust may *increase*.
- The two groups should be equal in *social power*. If one group has much more control over events than the other group, the less powerful group may feel patronized and hence hostile.
- The groups should share common goals, as was the case in the summer camp experiment.

SUMMARY

1. A *norm* is a prescribed way of behaving established by a group. Norms refer to specific behaviors. Members who do not follow norms receive disapproval.

2. A *social role* is a set of norms and expectations about how a person should act in a particular role, which the group defines.

3. Most people have multiple roles, such as father, husband, son. Sometimes there is *role conflict,* when roles make conflicting demands on the individual. *Role incompatibility* occurs when a person's personality, training, or abilities do not fit the requirements of the role.

4. *Role diffusion* is a confusion or mixing up of roles. This commonly occurs during adolescence when there is a search for identity and various roles may be "tried on."

5. A *stereotype* is a set of personality or behavioral characteristics which are assigned to an *entire group* of people with little regard for individual differences. Problems with stereotypes arise from *ethnocentrism* and the belief that stereotypes are inborn. Such stereotypes may form a basis for self-fulfilling prophecies.

6. Stereotypes are most commonly learned by means of *group communication* rather than individual experience and are maintained by repeated exposure to stereotype statements and selective perception of examples which support the stereotype.

7. *Prejudice* is a *negative attitude* toward members of some group solely on the basis of their membership in that group. *Discrimination* refers to *negative actions* against a group.

8. *Reverse discrimination* is "bending over backward" *not* to discriminate against a group so that as a result another group becomes discriminated against. *Tokenism* is the attempt to appear non-discriminating (typically in relatively unimportant situations) while engaging in discrimination and prejudice in important matters.

9. The *origins* of prejudice and discrimination are intergroup conflict, personality factors, and social learning in early childhood.

EXERCISES

1. What is the difference between a *norm* and a *role?*

2. What happens when social norms are violated? How much does this depend on the kind of norm? What examples of norm violations and sanctions have you seen or been involved with?

3. Is there a dress code of any kind where you work or go to school? Is this code formal (defined by the institution) or informal? What happens if you or anyone else violates the dress code? What changes in dress code have there been for men and for women in, say, the last ten years? Make up a list of situations and dress codes which are normally appropriate for different people and various situations.

4. What are some other organizations with well-defined roles for officers and members? These may be social, business, educational, and so on. Do you know of any organizations with very unusual roles for officers or members? In what ways are the roles unusual? What functions do they serve? Are there any with unusual *names* for officers?

5. What are some reciprocal roles other than the ones mentioned?

6. Roles are sometimes identified, such as by military uniform and insignia. Do you know of any other distinctive role identifications? Any that are particularly interesting or unusual?

7. Of course we would want to do some role-playing for a chapter discussing roles. If there are both males and females in class, have them reverse sexes for husband and wife, and have them improvise a domestic situation—for example, the "husband" coming home from a hard day's construction work and the "wife" having taken care of troublesome children all day, with various things going wrong. The husband arrives home and wants to know why dinner is not ready. What can you learn from this kind of exercise? What other role situations would be useful to examine?

8. What are some role conflict situations other than those described in the text? How are they dealt with? Have you ever been in such a conflict situation? What did you do?

9. Sometimes we inadvertently have the wrong idea about somebody's role at the moment. Have two people play out the following situation. A person comes into an office for a job interview. The interviewer, however, has misunderstood and thinks the appointment is with a salesperson, but the interviewer doesn't know the product.

10. What selection or training procedures have you ever been through for either educational or employment purposes?

9

Communication:
Words, Actions, and Listening

The Communication Model

introduction

Communication is literally everywhere. We are surrounded by invisible radio and television transmissions which we can pick up easily with a little equipment. My radio plays softly, then a voice tries to sell me something. A student knocks at the door and wants to know about a class assignment. Another student wants help with a computer program. The phone rings and the treasurer's office wants a report. A parent calls and wants to know what time to get her child to soccer practice. I call the service station to find out when my car will be ready. All these examples illustrate our definition of communication: *Communication is the transmission of an idea from one person to another person by means of symbols.* Figure 9–1 shows the elements of a communication model: It must involve at least two people. From this simple definition we can derive many questions and see where communication problems are lurking.

a detailed example

Suppose that Marian, the chief of a bank collection department, finds that Leonard is consistently making some mistakes. She wants to communicate to him that something needs to be corrected. She will in some way face all the following problems and act.

1. *What ideas* does Marian want to communicate to Leonard? Does she just want to correct a minor problem in calculations, or does she want Leonard to know his job is on the line?

2. How is Marian going to *encode her ideas into a symbolic form* that Leonard can understand? Until she does so, they are just ideas, not communications. She will probably choose the English language as her code. But does Leonard understand English well? Is his vocabulary level considerably lower than Marian's so that she has to pick her words very carefully? Will she need to use non-linguistic codes, *showing* what she wants as well as saying? Even under the best of circumstances, it is sometimes difficult to use only words. Try to explain to someone what a spiral staircase looks like *without* using your

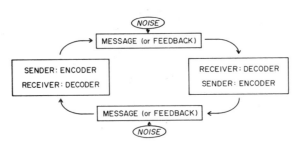

figure 9–1. Dynamic communication model for two people. Each person is a sender and a receiver and each message can (but does not necessarily) include feedback about the previous message. Noise may be introduced into the process at any point, not only in the message transmission.

hands. In some countries, Italy for example, hand signals are used much more as an aid to spoken language than they are in the United States.

The importance of similar past experiences between sender and receiver can hardly be overemphasized. Look at the following message and try to interpret it before going on:

No wist hetim eforall go odme ntoc omet otheaido fthe irco un try.

Make sense? Hardly. In fact, however, all the letters are in the correct order and the punctuation is all there. The problem is in the *spacing* of the letters. We learn words as units, separated from each other, and these must be encoded and decoded in a manner understandable by the sender and the receiver. The above sentence is the familiar: "Now is the time for all good men to come to the aid of their country."

3. Marian has to *transmit* her message. How shall this take place? Will she call Leonard on the phone? Speak to him face-to-face? Send a memo? Can Marian speak well, easily saying just what she wants to say? Does she write clearly? Even such simple problems as handwriting legibility can produce transmission problems. Two useful ideas here are *signal* and *noise*. Signal is the message that you want received. Noise is any unwanted interference with the message reception. Noise may be introduced by the sender of the message, by something as simple as a misspelled or misused word. Or, noise may be introduced by the transmission system. For example, we sometimes have trouble hearing radio transmissions because of static. To see the deterioration of a communication due to noise introduction, get a Xerox copy of a Xerox copy of a Xerox copy. With each successive copy of a copy the reproduction is not quite so good; there is relatively less signal and more noise.

4. Leonard has to *receive* whatever message is transmitted. He has to hear or see what Marian has to say or show him about the job. If he does not hear well, if he cannot read well, or if a note to him gets lost in the interoffice mail, he will receive no message. Or, he may receive an incorrect message.

5. Having received the message, Leonard has to *decode* it, to translate what he sees or hears into the ideas that *he perceives* in the message. His perception of the message is influenced not only by its content, but also by all the other things that influence perception, such as his previous experience and motivational or emotional state at the moment (as discussed in Chapter One). He might read an ominous sounding note from Marian, say to himself "Marian's at it again," and ignore the message. Another person reading a much milder message might think "She's really angry; I might get fired!" The decoding and interpreting process is subjective, just as the original encoding process was.

An unusual communication medium. (Photo by Bill Henry)

A message may be decoded wrong because sender and receiver are not using the same code. In the United States we code months, days and years in that order: 1/10/82 means January 10, 1982. But in Europe the code puts the day first, then the month, so that 1/10/82 means October 1, 1982. Someone who misunderstood the code could show up nine months early or late for an appointment!

Another source of decoding error is the *ambiguous* message. Thus, Marian might say: "I want you to pay more attention to the market for older men and women in your campaign." What does *older* refer to here? Both men and women, or only men? The encoding and decoding can both be technically correct, but the message be received wrong.

6. Leonard's *response* to Marian's message gives her *feedback* about his interpretation of the message. If he does just the opposite of what she *thought* she said, she would have good reason to wonder what she actually did say (a not uncommon experience for teachers reading the answers to test questions). Without some kind of feedback it is very difficult to know if your message has gotten across the way you intended.

In real life communication, messages fly back and forth among people with great rapidity and complexity. Consequently there are many possibilities for communication breakdown (messages not being received as intended). This going back and forth is also useful, however, because it allows for adjustments to be made if it appears that the receiver is not getting the message correctly. Each person (or group) can adjust the communication to clarify meaning on the basis of feedback.

repetitive one-way communication: rumor transmission

An example of what happens when there is *not* adequate feedback is rumor transmission. Larry wins a $5 betting pool. Some impoverished student thinks this is a lot and passes the word that Larry won a big betting pool. Someone else thinks that this must mean he won at least $100. This escalates until poor Larry is beseiged with salespeople, relatives, and the Internal Revenue Service, all trying to get a piece of his non-existent half-million-dollar sweepstakes winnings.

Three general processes have been described to account for the distortions in rumor transmission: *sharpening, leveling,* and *assimilation.*

1. *Sharpening* is a process whereby some things get *accentuated* in retelling. Larry's dramatic increase in wealth is an example of sharpening. The degree and kind of sharpening depend on what the receiver is paying attention to and his or her interests, motives, emotions, and knowledge at the time the message is received. If an employee is laid off, for any reason, during hard times, other workers may get the message via the *grapevine* that the plant is closing down and there will be massive layoffs or salary cuts. Workers are very sensitive to such information, even though the grapevine is generally the least accurate information channel.

2. *Leveling* is de-emphasizing or dropping certain parts of the original message. Parts may be dropped because they are *not received* (simply not heard), *not understood* properly, not of *interest* at the time, or simply *not remembered.*

3. *Assimilation* is altering the message so that it fits into the receiver's own understanding of things. In an early experiment Allport and Postman (1947) used the picture shown in Figure 1–1, in which a black man is facing a white man who is holding a razor. The last in a chain of verbal descriptions about the picture content consistently had a razor in the hands of the black man, not the white. As the story is told and retold somebody decides that it doesn't make sense and changes this detail. One reason why it would not make sense in 1947 was the *stereotype* held at that time: A white man with a razor did not fit the stereotypes of either blacks or whites.

Sharpening, leveling, and assimilation accomplish specific purposes for the recipient of a message: They *simplify a complex situation* which is otherwise not easily understood or recalled, and they *fit the story into the individual's own scheme of things* so that it fills his or her own needs, values, prejudices, fears, hopes, or expectations.

Comparison of Different Kinds of One-way Communications. Dahle (1954) compared five different communication procedures for accuracy of recall of the message. These were used in five different departments of the Spiegel mail-order firm. The procedures were (1) a letter to the employees' homes and a supervisor making an oral presentation about company benefit plans; (2) only the supervisor's presentation; (3) only the letter; (4) information put only on the bulletin board, and (5) only grapevine information from the other

table 9–1

effects of media of communication on accuracy of answers to a test of recall

medium	number of employees	mean accuracy on a test of recall
Combined letter to home and supervisory presentation	102	7.70
Supervisor presents only	94	6.17
Letter to home only	109	4.91
Bulletin board	115	3.72
Grapevine	108	3.56

(From Dahl, 1954, p. 245.)

four departments. Table 9–1 shows the accuracy of recall of the information by these various means, with a decline in accuracy from the first to the fifth method.

communication networks

Communication networks within small groups have received considerable study. A network is any system for getting the message to all the group. Figure 9–2 shows a number of different kinds of networks. One such form is linear: The supervisor tells George, George tells Helen, Helen tells Eileen, and she tells Frank. From a leadership point of view there are two problems here. First, it is liable to the inaccuracies we saw with rumor transmission. Second, it diffuses the leadership because only one person deals directly with the leader.

Leavitt (1951) has noted that the *circle* (called All-channel in Figure 9–2) is active, but leaderless, unorganized and erratic. However, it is *enjoyed* by its members. At the other extreme, the *wheel* with its pivotal person (Figure 9–2) is less active and has a distinct leader by virtue of his or her position of *centrality*. The communication net is stable but not very satisfying to most of its members because they are peripheral, away from the center of the action. In the wheel, the central person is *perceived* by others as being the leader because they must communicate through him or her. If this person can manage to stay in the central communication position, the leadership role can be maintained. The central person does tend to be satisfied. Secord and Backman (1974) point out two advantages of the wheel. First, there is maximum information transfer, with minimum loss due to additional transmission and hence less chance for error. Second, it is an efficient organizational structure for a small group. In general, the more interaction there is among group members, the greater the satisfaction, but not necessarily the greatest effectiveness. One must be hesitant in generalizing the results of this line of research to large organizations where there are enough communication channels so that a person is not limited in sources of information.

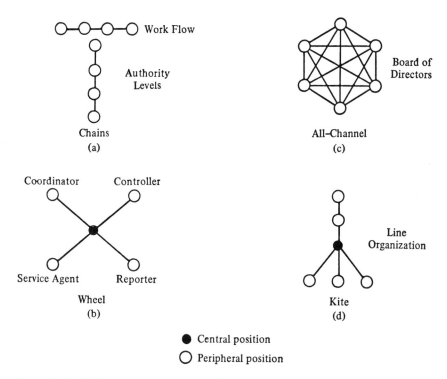

figure 9–2. Linkages in a company analogous to experimental communication networks. (Adapted from Dubin, 1959, 1962. Used with permission of publisher.)

Non-Verbal Communication

The communication model in Figure 9–1 is not restricted to formal languages, although the bulk of research is linguistic. Recent years have brought a heightened interest in non-verbal communication. We saw some of this in the Chapter Five discussion of expression of emotion. Much of the present section comes from the excellent book by Weitz (1979) who analyzes non-verbal communication along five lines: (1) facial expression and visual interaction, (2) body movement and gesture, (3) paralanguage, (4) proximity behavior, and (5) multichannel communication.

Beyond its faddish exploitation in the popular press (e.g., Fast, 1970, *Body Language*) the reason for interest in nonverbal communication is that we may get different information from linguistic and nonlinguistic cues. Some authors consider nonverbal communication the royal road to the inner self, believing it a more reliable source than verbal information. From Freud on, psychologists have tried to find more reliable cues to the nature of the psyche than what people say about themselves. Other authors consider nonverbal communication interesting and important, but not any more important than linguistic information. All agree that nonverbal communication is fertile terri-

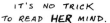

tory, ripe for intensive study. The reader is warned, however, that there is no more "magic" in nonverbal communication than in verbal.

facial expression and visual interaction

Emotion. We need say little here since this was covered in Chapter Five. We might note again that there seem to be a few universal facial expressions for emotions, such as happiness, sadness, anger, fear, disgust, and surprise.

Visual Interaction. Facial activity is not all emotional, however, and a number of specific findings about visual communication can be stated.

1. Eye contact can be used to *elicit either approach or avoidance* on the part of someone else. Argyle and Dean (1965) have suggested that, in conjunction with other movements, eye contact helps maintain an optimal level of interpersonal intimacy. We may look away from someone we want to keep at a distance, or we may stare at someone who intrudes too closely on us. Certain other kinds of prolonged looks and facial expressions obviously invite approach.

2. During relatively long verbal interactions eye contact is used to *encourage* interruptions, and avoidance of eye contact serves to *discourage* interruptions. Visual contact may be a signal to initiate talking with someone, such as a stranger at a street corner.

3. Visual contact is related to *power* and *aggression*. With non-human primates, a direct gaze is a challenge to a fight and often evokes a violent response. An animal that wants to avoid a fight looks away. The dominant monkey in a group can stare with impunity at all the other members of the group, but not vice-versa. In humans, staring has been shown to produce "escape" behaviors (e.g., Ellsworth, Carlsmith and Henson, 1972). For example, staring at people when the light turns green at an intersection tends to get them to move out faster than otherwise.

4. There are *cultural myths* about visual contact which, though not true, have an impact on social relations. At the extreme, there is the "evil eye," a person who can cast spells on people, animals, or crops. Since being stared at is often unsettling, it is not surprising that the notion of the evil eye developed.

    Other, less dramatic beliefs are also important to know about, such as the notion that people who "look you in the eye" are more honest than people who do not, and people who avoid looking others in the eye lack self-confidence. There is little verification for either of these beliefs, but they are important if they are held by a personnel manager interviewing candidates. Looking at people frequently in conversation, then, may be an important social skill just because other people think it means something.

body movement and gestures

Like dieting, sex, and how to get rich quick, body language has become a hot literary topic. How easy it would be if what the popularizers said were

Such nonverbal behaviors as facial expressions and hand gestures provide emphasis and sometimes substitute for words.

true! We could carry little "body language dictionaries" and quickly flip to the interpretation of what other people were saying with their bodies. There are indeed body movements which, in context, are clear in their meaning. If I talk to the salesperson who has come to my office door while holding my hands poised over my running electric typewriter, it is fairly obvious that I don't want to extend the conversation. But every little movement, gesture, or posture does *not* have a single meaning all its own, and this dictionary theory of body language should be avoided. What are some of the things we do know, however?

Courtship Behavior. Many animals, especially birds, have complex courtship rituals which involve strutting, preening, calling, and so on. Some human behavior may also have this element, perhaps a biological carryover from an earlier evolutionary age. Humans "preen" by adjusting their clothes, combing their hair, or checking their appearance in the mirror.

The *major* signal for *courtship readiness*, however, is thought to be *heightened muscle tension*. Men pull in their stomachs, straighten their backs, and generally try to look more athletic. Women do the same things, but in addition wear high heels which tighten up their leg muscles (tension) and make them more

attractive. Courtship partners face each other, lean toward one another, gaze at each other, and generally tend to block out would-be intruders or distractions (Schlefen, 1965.)

Signals for *invitation* to courtship include softly spoken words, adjustment of vocal quality and loudness, as well as possible words of invitation and flirtatious glances or body movements. Such signals can be *misread*, however. Some females, for example, may not realize such movements are considered invitations. American women traveling overseas are often misunderstood because of their "openness." Some people know how to *qualify* such flirtatious behavior so that it is perceived simply as playful or friendly rather than as serious courtship, but others do not. The message received in such cases is often not the message intended to be sent.

paralanguage

Paralanguage concerns such non-linguistic aspects of language as the loudness, pitch and tremor of the voice. Recent interest has focused on the relation between paralanguage and emotion. Most people can recognize when other people "sound" emotional, especially if they know them very well. It is this emphasis on *how* things are said as well as on *what* is said, that characterizes paralanguage.

There are various procedures for separating linguistic from paralinguistic meaning in research. For example, if a tape recording is cut up and spliced back together randomly the linguistic meaning (sentences and words) is lost but people can still identify the emotional meaning. Completely artificial sounds, generated electronically by a MOOG synthesizer, can also have recognizable emotional qualities. To illustrate the point for yourself, recite the alphabet as if you were happy, or sad, or angry. The sequence of letters has no inherent meaning, but you can get across your emotion pretty well. In natural speech, anger is characterized by high pitch, fast pace, and loudness, but sadness or depression are characterized just the opposite.

There is evidence that voice pitch rises when a person is lying. A device called the Psychological Stress Evaluator has been promoted as a form of lie detector, recording small tremors in vocalization. The evidence does not support the use of this device for this purpose, however (Weitz, 1979). The stress evaluator is subject to at least as many problems as the other form of lie detector we discussed in Chapter Five.

proximity behaviors

The terms *proxemics* and *personal space* have about the same meaning, both referring to distances between people which those people consider to be appropriate for certain activities. Hall (1966) distinguished among four different "per-

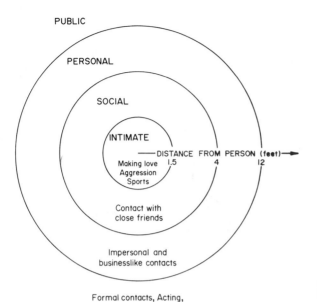

PUBLIC

PERSONAL

SOCIAL

INTIMATE

——DISTANCE FROM PERSON (feet)——

Making love 1.5   4   12
Aggression
Sports

Contact with
close friends

Impersonal and
businesslike contacts

Formal contacts, Acting,
Public speaking

figure 9–3. Personal space and the types of interpersonal body contact allowed by the various distances.

sonal distances," which we can imagine as invisible bubbles of different size surrounding a person. (1) *Intimate* space is from about zero to eighteen inches; (2) *personal* space, such as for conversations, is about three feet; (3) *social* space is several feet, such as for business interactions, and (4) *public* space is ten to twenty feet and beyond. Figure 9–3 shows some of these distances and the types of activities they might encourage.

As an anthropologist, Hall was also interested in cultural differences in the spaces. Among other procedures he showed subjects pictures of people at different interpersonal distances and asked what might be going on in the pictures and why. He found, for example, that *personal* distance for Arabs is within the range of *intimate* distance for Americans. Personal transactions at intimate distances tend to make Americans uncomfortable; they feel their intimate space is being "violated." There are individual differences even among

Americans, however. It is amusing to see one person back another person across a room and up against a wall by staying at an intimate distance for a non-intimate conversation.

Politics of Touch. Touching has many meanings. It can be aggressive or tender. It can be just a signal of awareness of another person or merely attention getting. We sometimes describe a person as being "touchy-feely" because he or she frequently touches others innocently during the course of non-intimate conversation. In Italy, young men walk down the street with arms slung over each other, but without the connotation of homosexuality this would have in the United States. Touching may also be a sign of *dominance,* however, hence the expression "the politics of touch." Males may try to show dominance over females by touching them. Or a person of higher social status or business position may feel free to touch a person of lower status, but not the other way around. Presidents of companies may put their arms on the shoulders of employees, but the reverse is very unlikely. One way we can identify status, then, is by who is touching whom.

multichannel communication

Communication is a continuously changing process of interaction between people with many kinds of messages and channels. You will have recognized the artificiality of imagining that communication could be restricted to a single *channel,* whether written words, spoken words, paralanguage, or body movement. Though the research is correspondingly more difficult, researchers have looked at different channels individually and collectively (such as facial expression alone as compared to facial expression plus voice). Rosenthal and his colleagues (1978) have used a test called the *Profile of Nonverbal Sensitivity* (PONS) as a measure of accuracy in perceiving the meaning of many different social situations presented with audiovisual film clips, using single channels and combinations of channels. We summarize here just a bit of their research on over 7,000 people.

1. With very short exposures, subjects judge body positions and gestures more accurately, but with longer exposures they judge facial expressions more accurately.

2. In 133 different samples with about 2600 subjects total, females were more accurate judges than males in about 80 percent of the samples.

3. With children in grades three through six there was increasing accuracy of judgment. Younger children were relatively more accurate at judging *vocal tone* as compared to *visual* cues. Most parents realize that even very young children recognize anger in the parents' voices.

4. Accuracy of judgments was not correlated with intelligence test scores.

5. Psychiatric and alcoholic patients were not as accurate as "normal" groups, but these patients were not totally lacking in their ability to "read" various kinds of cues.

6. Actors and visual arts students scored the highest and were significantly higher than clinical psychologists, who did about the same as average college students. Teachers and business executives scored lower than any of the above, about the same as high school students.

7. There were positive correlations between scores on the PONS test and supervisor's ratings of teachers' and clinicians' skills. But there was a negative correlation between PONS scores and teacher *advancement*. We leave it to the reader to speculate as to why people with low nonverbal sensitivity are relatively more likely to get promoted.

8. People can be trained to use nonverbal cues more accurately.

Improving Communication

Improving communication involves consideration of all the steps in the communication process.

make sure the message is encoded clearly so it can be decoded properly

Speak or write *clearly*. A rule of thumb is to write messages "so your grandmother can understand them." This means

- Use simple, concise sentences.
- Use good spelling and punctuation.
- *Write legibly* or *enunciate clearly*.
- Do not use unnecessary *jargon*. Jargon is the shorthand language used within

a particuar group (such as initials for government agencies) but which is not typically understood outside the group.

- *Do not send conflicting information over different channels.* This may be a problem, for example, between verbal and nonverbal communication. Words of invitation may be spoken in such a way as to invite rejection. If a supervisor says to an employee, "Tell me what the problem is" and then proceeds to look here, there, and everywhere except toward the employee, the employee gets the message that the supervisor is not really interested. This may or may not be correct, but it would be unfortunate if the supervisor really *did* want to hear and accidentally "turned off" the employee.

make sure you have your receiver's attention

A message sent is not always a message received. In the weekly flood of junk mail we usually toss some things into the trash. It is not a good idea to send out bills in envelopes that look like fourth class mail; they may suffer the same fate as the magazine ads. Important communications should be readily identifiable as such. Special styles of envelope, paper, typing, or wording might be used to call a message to someone's attention. Envelopes might be color coded to indicate degree of importance. In face-to-face communication, wait until the other person is looking at you, or otherwise signals he or she is paying attention, before you start the important part of your communication.

avoid excessive "noise" in your messages

The message you want to send (signal) should be clearly distinguishable from other miscellany (noise). For example, most schools and businesses have bulletin boards set aside for messages. These eventually become so cluttered

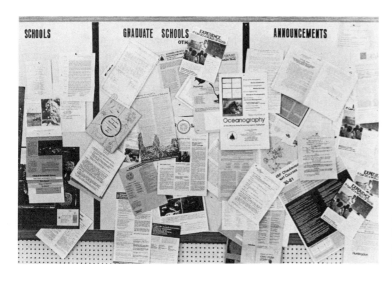

Many bulletin boards have more "noise" than "signal" and therefore convey little useful information.

that someone walking by can hardly find the messages of importance. Further-more, if we get used to seeing "junk announcements" on the bulletin board or in the mail, we may tend to ignore *all* announcements. In learning terms we *extinguish* on reading the announcements because we are not rewarded by anything of interest when we do read them. In like manner, filling a memo with trivia may obscure what you really want to say.

avoid information overload

The story goes that a little girl came home from school one day saying she had just learned more about hippopotamuses than she cared to know. There was an *information overload.* A business executive who has to read daily reports from ten people wants them as short and to the point as possible. If more information is needed, the executive can always ask. Say what you *need* to say (the "bottom line") in as few words as possible. People have a limit on how much information they can handle in a given period of time.

be redundant if possible

A redundant message is one sent more than one time or by more than one channel. Such redundancy helps make sure a message is accurately received. You might meet Bill in the hallway and tell him there is an important meeting Tuesday at 3:00. You then follow this with a written memo. Any method of gaining redundancy is useful if it makes important communications more accurate.

get feedback if you can

You have no guarantee that anyone has received your message unless you get feedback. If Frieda does not appear for a meeting, it might be because she never got the notice of it. A request for verification, or a follow-up phone call, could help. Face-to-face communication usually gives the best feedback, although even here people will happily nod "yes" when they really do not understand the message. When important, it is often a good idea to have the other person repeat the message to assure its correctness. We typically have people repeat phone numbers. If you make it a practice to give feedback, other people may be more likely to return the favor.

be open and honest in your communications

If you have a reputation for *not* being open and honest in your communication with others you may be ignored or disbelieved even when you are being totally honest. I have many times talked with employees who were "down" on a particular manager who had promised raises and promotions which never came through. These managers lost their credibility, were distrusted, and hence were presumably less effective as managers than they might have been.

consider the emotional impact of your message

Messages may be emotionally loaded, even when that is not the sender's intention. Most people are sensitive about being told they are at fault, are wrong, are stupid, or anything else damaging to their self esteem. They may react with anxiety, embarrassment, or hostility which carries over into future situations. Criticism should be as positive as possible. Particularly when dealing with subordinates over whom we have some control of salary, promotion, and working conditions, we should be cautious about what (or how) we communicate and avoid unnecessary emotional arousal.

be a good listener

It is especially important to realize that good communication involves being a good "receiver" (listener) as well as a good sender.

Listening

hearing is not listening

Hearing refers to the process of sound waves acting upon the ear to produce nerve impulses to the brain. If this system is intact we can say that a person is *hearing.* We hear a car go by, we hear a voice. Listening is the more complex act of *attending* to and *processing* what we hear. Consider this:

Wife: George, I'm not very happy with the way things have been going.
Husband (reading newspaper): Yes, dear.
Wife: I think I need a change.
Husband: That's nice.
Wife: I'm leaving. I'm going away.
Husband: Good. While you're out would you pick up some cigarettes for me.
Wife: Good bye, George.
Husband: Please hurry.

George is hearing what his wife is saying, but he is not listening. He is not paying attention, he is not understanding, and he is not remembering. In essence, then, all that is being communicated to him is that his wife is in the room. We can imagine the same kind of conversation in business.

Worker: Boss, things are not going too well right now.
Boss (looking over reports): Too bad.
Worker: I think we need some help pretty quick.
Boss: You're probably right.
Worker: We've got some people out and a machine isn't working right and its going to be tough to meet production.
Boss: Well, just tell those people to get with it. Good talking to you. Say hello to the family.

The boss heard the worker, but the worker's message simply was not getting through.

eight rules for effective listening

1. *Pay attention to the other person.* When introduced to someone, we often forget the name quickly because we never really learned it. We often don't pay attention when we hear the name, because we don't consider it important. Good salespeople remember and use the names of their customers almost instantly. They pay close attention and use the name quickly to rehearse it. In Chapter Two we saw the importance of intent to learn as a factor in later recall.

   Besides facilitating memory, paying attention to other people is *rewarding* to them. Because they are rewarded, they are more likely to feel comfortable and to "open up" more. If we don't pay attention people are less likely to talk to us. When the boss turns away and starts reading, it is a sure sign he or she doesn't want to listen to us anymore, and we stop talking. If we want to get information, we need to pay attention.

2. *Do not interrupt needlessly.* Many times we are more interested in hearing ourselves talk than finding out what the other person has to say. We may pick up on a key word, perhaps not important, and turn the conversation that direction. For example:

Worker: Last night during the ball game. . .
Boss: Say wasn't that some game. Now I think that. . .

What *was* the worker trying to say? She may have been using the ball game only as a time reference and never gets to what she really wanted to communicate because of the interruption.

Many people find silence hard to tolerate and will not wait for someone to speak. In psychotherapy there are often long silences while the client is pondering his or her situation, perhaps reluctant to say something important. If the therapist were to leap in and start talking the client might never speak out. On the job we might have the following:

Worker: Boss . . . . I kind of wanted . . . . to talk . . . . with you . . . . about something . . . . . . which has been bothering me.

Boss: Yes. What is it?
Worker: Well ....
Boss: Spit it out man!
Worker: It's not really very important. Never mind.
Boss: Good. Well, see you later. Nice to talk to you.

Again, the boss may have missed something critical by not waiting out the silences. The conversation might have gone like this:

Worker: Boss . . . . I kind of wanted . . . . to talk . . . . with you . . . . about something . . . . . . which has been bothering me.
Boss: . . . . Yes what is it?
Worker: Well ....
Boss: This seems to be important. Take your time.
Worker: It's about the . . . . . . second shift, there are some real problems there . . . .
Boss: (Silent, but attentive)
Worker: . . . . that I have to spend an hour every day straightening out when I come in.
Boss: Tell me about them.

Though the worker may have been reluctant to put the blame on someone for a bad situation, there is nevertheless a real problem. The boss who did not let the worker talk might not find out about it until it was too late.

3. *Observe nonverbal as well as verbal cues.*
    (a). *Listen to paralanguage.* What is the tone of voice of the other person? Does she say that everything is fine, but in a voice so low that you can hardly hear it? Is there a "crack" in the voice which indicates strong emotion? Is the speaker really very angry and trying to suppress it? Is the speaker raising her voice to a shout or higher pitch, even though saying she is not upset? Is the speaker stuttering when he normally does not do so, possibly indicating some disturbance? Does the speaker sigh a lot? The psychiatrist Theodore Reik called attending to such cues "listening with the third ear."
    (b). *Watch body language.* Does the speaker look as if he is carrying the world on his shoulders? Does he walk with a light step or heavy? Does she slump down when sitting as if exhausted (as compared to sitting back and relaxing)? Does the speaker clench her fist, as if angry? Is she frowning, or blushing or pale?
        These paralinguistic and body language cues help us understand the speaker's "frame of mind," particularly if the speaker is not behaving in his or her typical manner.

4. *Be empathic.* Empathy means putting yourself into the other person's shoes, intellectually and emotionally. If we correctly understand all the verbal and non-verbal cues we can better understand how the other person sees a situation. Remember that the goal of communication is to accurately transmit and receive ideas (or emotions). When we can empathize we better understand another person's ideas and emotions. One good procedure is to verbally *reflect* the ideas and feelings of the other person. This requires an *active* attempt to understand the other person and provides *feedback* to the other person. If you are not correctly "reading" the situation this will show up in your "reflections"

and can be corrected. Oftimes just a sincere *attempt* to understand the other person is helpful. It may be that what the other person needs is a "sounding board" to bounce ideas off.

5. *Do not be too much of an expert.* In the client-centered approach to counseling (Chapter Six) the counselor is not considered a fountain of wisdom from which spring the solutions to all problems. Rather, the counselor tries to understand, and to help the client understand for him or herself, what the situation is. If we are "too ready" to give "expert opinions" we may be giving solutions to the wrong problems. Sometimes we really are expert: An employee says her computer program has a "bug" in it and this can be fixed by an expert. But if an employee has a problem with an interpersonal relationship or in setting up a complex new job, some careful listening and some suggestions may better fit the bill.

6. *Be patient.* Don't jump too quickly to conclusions. Don't act too hastily. You may not really understand the situation. When you have heard a person out, and have given the person sufficient feedback to make sure that you understand him or her, then it is more appropriate to get excited (if necessary). If someone comes in shouting "There's a fire down the hall" it might be appropriate to find out if it involves the whole hallway or a wastepaper basket before calling out the fire trucks. Don't make mountains out of molehills by inventing crises where they don't exist, but do make sure you have the right information so you can respond correctly to a real emergency.

7. *Ask opening up questions.* An "opening up" question is open-ended, such as, Would you tell me more about that? What do you think of this proposal? What would you do in this situation? A question in the form, You wouldn't do it this way would you, George? is certainly asking for a "no" answer. In general, if a superior asks a question in a leading way, the subordinate is likely to take that lead. People tend to give *socially desirable* responses, answers that they *think* somebody wants to hear, and this tendency is accentuated in the superior-subordinate situation unless the superior makes honest attempts to get information. A department chief might make a proposal, and then say to the staff, "Now tell me, what's wrong with this?" If the staff believes the chief sincerely wants feedback, they are likely to open up. But if the chief says, "Okay, now who thinks they want to disagree?" the chances are pretty slim that there will be any disagreement.

8. *Use self-disclosure.* Many writers believe that a useful technique to get someone else to open up is to lead the way with some *self*-disclosure. If a superior shares some doubts and concerns with subordinates, they may be more likely to share their concerns with him or her. If the superior seems a little more vulnerable, then perhaps the subordinate will not be so defensive about his or her problems.

transactional analysis (ta)

Transactional analysis is an approach to communication based on Freudian ideas put into more commonsense terms. The heart of TA (Berne, 1964; Harris, 1967) is to think of people as operating predominantly in one of three *ego states* at any given time. These are the *parent*, the *adult*, and the *child*. Each state has the characteristic behaviors and motions which we commonly associate with these names. The parent is protective, gives orders, expects to be obeyed, and puts great emphasis on rules. The adult is a rational, thoughtful, relatively non-emotional problem-solver. The child is emotional, sometimes thoughtless and impulsive, expects support and guidance from others, and is very self-oriented.

A *transaction* is a verbal or nonverbal interaction between two people. The nature of the interaction is dictated by the kinds of ego states the individuals are in at the time. Given the following statements and actions, what ego state would you say the primary actor is in and how would *you* respond if you were the other person?

1. A major league baseball manager runs out on the field screaming, stomping his feet, jumping up and down, and kicking dirt on the shoes of the umpire who has made a call against his team.

2. When an employee asks the boss the reason for doing something a particular way, the boss replies, "That's the way we do things around here. Get to it."

3. An employee comes running to her supervisor, very upset about some unexpected problem. The supervisor (primary actor here) says: "Well now, Margaret, let's sit down and take a look at this. I think we can work out something."

4. In an episode of All in the Family, Archie Bunker gets into an argument with his son-in-law because his son-in-law puts on a sock and a shoe, then the second sock and shoe rather than both socks and then both shoes.

5. A husband feels very guilty about getting home a little late after stopping on the way to have a drink with an old friend he has not seen for a long time.

The foregoing situations illustrate child, parent, adult, parent, and child in order.

The interactions between two people are said to be *complementary* if the two people are in the ego state they *expect* each other to be in and if they get the expected responses. The interactions are *crossed* if the two individuals are *not* in the states they expect each other to be in and hence do not respond to each other "appropriately." The interaction is *ulterior* if a person pretends to be in one state when actually in another. For example:

1. *Complementary.* In a real parent-child relation the situation is complementary if the father acts like "parent" and the child acts like "child." If a supervisor is in the parent state, expecting an employee to be in a child state (take orders without question, for example), the situation is complementary if the employee acts like a child. The employee is fulfilling the supervisor's expectations and the supervisor is reinforced. Such reinforcement is called a *stroke* in TA terminology. Such parent-child interactions are particularly

common in the military and in penal institutions between guards and prisoners.

2. *Crossed.* If someone in the parent ego state interacts with a younger person who is operating in the adult rather than the child ego state, there may be friction. An intelligent son or daughter (or employee) who wants explanations or expects his or her opinions to be heard and respected will not interact well with an individual in the parent ego state, but would interact well with someone else who is also in the adult ego state. If the older person (or employer) recognizes the need to shift from parent to adult ego states, communication should be better.

3. *Ulterior.* Not infrequently a manager may act *as if* he or she wants to interact with a subordinate (or even someone of equal status) on an adult-to-adult ego state basis but actually may want a parent-child relation. The manager may go through the motions of problem-solving when he or she already plans to give certain orders and have them followed. The subordinate's input is irrelevant since there is no intention to use it. The interaction is artificial, perhaps strained, and employees eventually get the message that they are expected to act in the child ego state and accept what they are given.

Most people shift from one state to another as the situation requires. The adult is occasionally playful like a child. Or, a child may play the parent for an even younger child. It would be inappropriate to always rigidly act like either parent, adult, or child. Sometimes adults *need* to be in the child ego state, to be directed and encouraged, or supported, or just to have fun. It is appropriate for a person in the adult ego state to shift to the parent ego state for awhile.

Transactional analysis is not a cure-all for communication problems, but

it can be useful to be aware that *we* and the person we are communicating with are in particular states at a given time so we can adjust our communications accordingly.

SUMMARY

1. *Communication is the transmission of an idea* from one person to another person by means of symbols. The steps involved are encoding, transmission, receiving, decoding, and feedback. The signal or message the sender wants the receiver to get may be affected by unwanted interference (noise).

2. *Rumor* transmission may occur when there is inadequate feedback in communication. Message distortion may be caused by *sharpening, leveling,* or *assimilation,* which are three general processes which simplify complex situations and fit the story into the receiver's own scheme of things.

3. A communication *network* is any system for getting messages to an entire group. Some of the possible forms are linear, circular, or wheel-shaped.

4. Most research with the communication model is related to language, but *non-verbal* communication is of increasing interest. Facial expression, visual interaction, body gestures, and paralanguage are forms of nonverbal communication. Eye contact, for instance, can be used to elicit approach and avoidance behavior, as well as to encourage or discourage interruptions. Paralanguage comprises the nonlinguistic aspects of language, such as loudness, pitch, and tremor.

5. *Proxemics,* or proximity behavior, deals with the distance between people *(personal space)* which is considered appropriate for particular activities.

6. *Multi-channel* communication is the usual situation in which several different types of communication go on at once.

7. Ways to *improve* communication include encoding the message clearly and avoiding excessive noise; avoiding information overload; sending the message several times; getting feedback from an attentive listener; and being open, honest, and sensitive in the communication.

8. *Effective listening* is more than simply hearing. It involves paying attention to the speaker without frequent interruptions; being sensitive to nonverbal cues; and being empathic, patient, and interested. Open-ended questions and self-disclosure are often effective ways of getting others to open-up in conversation.

9. *Transactional analysis* (TA) is an approach to communication which views people as operating predominantly from one of three *ego states* (parent, child, or adult) at any given time. A transaction consists of a verbal or nonverbal interaction between two people, and its nature is determined

by the ego states of the two participants. Interactions can be complementary, crossed, or ulterior.

EXERCISES

1. What are the steps in communication? Think of any idea and use the different steps to discuss how your idea would be communicated to someone else.

2. The sender and receiver of a message must have shared some similar past experience for the message to be meaningful. Construct several hypothetical situations in which communication would not be meaningful due to the participants' unfamiliarity with necessary information. (An obvious example would be an American in a foreign country not moving out of the way of a falling object because he cannot understand the yelled warning.)

3. Find a partner and say to him or her: "Do you want to dance?" Which word was emphasized the most? Now repeat the question three times putting exaggerated emphasis on *you* the first time, *want* the second time, and *dance* the third time. After each sentence have your partner tell you exactly what he or she thought you were asking. For example: to dance, rather than to sit, *you* rather than just anyone . . .

4. Demonstrate how each of the three processes of rumor transmission would occur (sharpening, leveling, and assimilation) as some piece of information is passed from person to person in small groups. A sample starter sentence: Bob got a new job so he and Sarah bought a new house and are moving to another street in their neighborhood.

5. Compare linear, circle, and wheel communication networks from the viewpoint of a leader, and then group members.

6. In what kinds of situations does a lot of visual contact facilitate communication, and when would it be disruptive? What are the underlying reasons?

7. Look at your classmates now. Is anyone sending out a loud nonverbal message? For instance Joe's asleep (he's bored); Sue's biting her fingernail's (she's nervous); Fred's staring out the window (he wishes he were somewhere else).

8. How many nonverbal ways can you think of to express happiness? How effective would each one be, and in what situations would they be particularly appropriate or inappropriate?

9. Keep in mind the different aspects of paralanguage and use them to convey different meanings of some simple statement like "I'm hungry." What aspects are you varying?

10. Get into pairs and hold simple conversations at the four different personal

distances described in the text. Which would be most appropriate for this particular interaction? Did the other three feel uncomfortable or inappropriate?

11. Describe the ideal listener, and then a poor listener. In what ways would the two differ?

12. What are some useful opening-up questions? Which, if any, do you use regularly in conversation?

10

Persuasion and Propaganda

Sudsing the Mind: Brainwashing

During the Korean War, reports filtered back to the United Nations member states about brainwashing. The Chinese, it seemed, had mysterious oriental techniques for turning patriotic American soldiers against their own country. They could even be induced to propagandize against the U.S. in public utterances. This led to a splurge of interest and investigation. The conclusions from extensive interviews with released captives showed a set pattern on the part of the Chinese toward the prisoners of war (POW's).

Now let us leap forward about twenty-five years. A wealthy young woman, Patty Hearst, was kidnapped, became a soldier in the Symbionese Liberation Army (SLA) with the new name Tania, voluntarily participated in a bank robbery, and repudiated her family and background. Zimbardo, Ebbeson, and Maslach (1977) summarize the factors in the Hearst case, which are essentially identical to those found with the so-called brainwashing.

1. *Initial Position.* Hearst's political beliefs were not well formed, as perhaps those of many young American soldiers were not. The lack of an established belief makes it easier to produce a belief you want.

2. *Fear and Anxiety.* Patty Hearst was very much afraid, having been kidnapped by a group of strange people. However, they were at least reasonably kind to her, arousing some feeling of gratitude as well as reducing her fear. Similarly, American POW's were afraid for their lives, as well as being nearly starved. An extra piece of bread was received with gratitude, the POW's tending to forget why they were starved in the first place. The Chinese woke the POW's at all times of day and night, so that there was always anticipation of being taken from their cells for interrogation, as well as fatigue from missing sleep.

3. *Guilt Arousal.* Guilt may have been aroused in Hearst because of the discrepancy between her wealth and the poverty of so many others in America. Certainly this theme was played upon by her captors. In the case of the POW's, guilt was aroused by convincing them that they were involved in inhumane acts of aggression and destruction. They could reduce their guilt by repudiating their acts and their government. Patty could reduce her guilt by repudiating her parents and helping the poor people of America (by becoming a member of the SLA).

4. *Isolation form social support.* None of the people or things that supported Hearst's beliefs and lifestyle in the past were available from her captors. She was kept isolated from any kind of social reinforcement except what the SLA members were ready to give. The POW's were isolated for long periods of time so their comrades could not reinforce whatever beliefs they had.

5. *Persuasive Communications.* The only information Hearst received was from the members of the SLA. There was no one to rebut them, and her own ideas were insufficiently developed to resist them. The POW's were continuously bombarded with communist propaganda with no one to help resist.

6. *Cohesive Peer Group.* The small SLA group (eight people) lived together, were very close, and were the dispensers of social rewards. Isolation from other Americans and the company of Communist Chinese captors was a major part of the Chinese strategy.

7. *Communicator Characteristics.* The SLA members were dedicated to their cause and were not apparently out for personal gain. They were probably seen by their captive as trustworthy, expert, dynamic, altruistic, and attractive. The Chinese, of course, proclaimed themselves as liberators.

8. *Illusion of Free Choice.* One of the major factors in persuasion is that the person being persuaded should believe that he or she has a choice in the matter. People generally resist coercion. Hearst was induced to believe she could have a choice, and the POW's were "urged" to "freely" sign documents.

As Zimbardo, Ebbesen, and Maslach (1977) point out, nothing is mysterious about any of these elements except the pure amount of time and energy devoted to them. In the more usual persuasive situations, there is a much more limited time. A TV commercial may have thirty or sixty seconds to convince us. A car salesperson has fifteen minutes. A teacher has a few hours a day. A soul-searching question is whether any of us, subjected to POW circumstances for a long enough time, could actually resist such persuasion.

A more widespread application of the above principles is in the conversion of typical, everyday young people into "Moonies," followers of Sun Myung Moon, founder of the Unification Church. Anyone who has crossed an airline terminal more than once, or who frequents shopping centers, has probably encountered Moonies and knows their persistence (which can change in an instant from sweetness and light to a biting sarcasm if you fail to make a contribution).

According to Zimbardo, Ebbeson, and Maslach, in 1976 there were 120 Unification Church "awareness training centers" (indoctrination centers) in the United States and some 10,000 young people a year going to them. One author quoted by Zimbardo et al. likened the magnitude of the effort to make conversions to the Unification Church with that of the intensity of the Hitler Youth Movement in the 1930s. It is a sobering comparison. These young people are not the misfits of society, either, just as Patty Hearst or the American POW's were not misfits. Their parents are understandably upset, and there has been considerable publicity about parents literally "kidnapping" their own children and hiring professional "deprogrammers" to get their children "back to normal."

education, persuasion, propaganda, and brainwashing

"Persuasion" and "education" have relatively good connotations. Society supports both enterprises on a large scale. "Propaganda" and "brainwashing" have bad connotations, especially if they are directed at us. But what are the real differences except for the question of who is doing what to whom? Much of our educational effort is aimed at teaching values and ideals, not just readin', 'ritin', and 'rithmetic. When we try to convince our own children of the many positive aspects of the "American System" we don't usually *call* it propaganda, but is there really any difference?

In each case, we are trying to form or change someone's ideas, attitudes, or behavior by means of persuasive techniques. Some of these techniques are more subtle than others. Some techniques we would have strong ethical prohibitions against using (such as keeping children isolated and afraid). It is enlightening, however, to discover how quickly change can be produced by such groups as the Moonies or the SLA.

Persuasion and Attitude Change: Principles and Techniques

Persuasion and attitude change are closely related topics. Our reason for separating them is that persuasion may be concerned only with *overt* behaviors which may or may not involve attitude change. I might try to persuade someone to go to the movies or have a beer. There may be some temporary inhibition on that person's part ("I really ought to be cutting the grass") but not actually a *negative attitude* toward either the movies or beer.

Research on persuasion and propaganda has been guided by the communication model described in Chapter Nine. The *source* of the communication *encodes* an idea into a *message* which is *transmitted* to a *receiver* who *decodes* the message. Researchers have systematically studied characteristics of the source, the message, and the receiver (audience) to determine what makes persuasive communications effective. Much of this work was initiated by the late Carl Hovland and his students (e.g., 1953).

A carnival barker uses all the persuasive techniques he can to entice people into his show. (Photo by Bill Henry)

the source: communicator credibility

The credibility (believability) of the person presenting the message is of utmost importance. If the audience just does not believe the speaker, the effect of the message is nullified. If a known drug peddler says that marijuana is good for your health you are less likely to take the claim seriously than if the American Medical Association were to make the claim. Similarly, we seldom give the *National Enquirer* the same credence as we do the *New York Times*. Some people, however, even believe the *National Enquirer*, perhaps on the grounds that anything in print has to be true. Two factors are especially important in establishing credibility, *trustworthiness* and *expertness*.

Trustworthiness. The drug pusher is not too believable because he or she is not very trustworthy; there is a product to be sold and the seller is probably not very scrupulous. Curiously, oil company executives have managed to get themselves into the same situation; we have become leery of what they tell us.

Hovland and Weiss (1951) studied trustworthiness in a carefully executed experiment typical of the way much research in this area has been conducted. Classroom students were given an opinion questionnaire on a variety of topics, including those related to the subsequent experiment. One of the experimenters, a stranger to the class, came in about a week later as a guest "communications" lecturer. Among his various activities he asked the students to read articles on four topics. There were two *favorable* and two *unfavorable* arguments with one of each being attributed to a high and a low credibility source. The general topics and the source are summarized in Table 10–1. Immediately after reading the four messages, the students filled out a questionnaire which was different from the one a week earlier, but which contained the same items relevant to the research.

The opinion changes for the two groups are summarized in Table 10–2. With the trustworthy source the changes were about twice as great as with the untrustworthy source, for three of the four messages. The exception was Topic D, about TV viewing and theatres. Perhaps on these relatively frivolous topics an otherwise untrustworthy source is considered believable. Additional questioning revealed that the subjects *remembered* the same amount of material from trustworthy and untrustworthy sources. Therefore, they *accepted* what they read from the trustworthy source; they did not just remember it better.

A communicator's trustworthiness is increased if he or she argues against his or her own apparent self-interest. A burglar arguing in favor of stiffer penalties for breaking and entering would be more persuasive on the subject than a politician up for reelection. The burglar would apparently be arguing against his or her own self-interest. The term *apparent* is important, however. Bootleggers might support restrictive liquor laws in order to keep up their own trade.

A communicator's trustworthiness is increased if he or she does not seem to be trying

table 10–1

attitude change topics and high and low credibility sources used

topic	high credibility source	low credibility source
A. *Antihistamine Drugs:* Should the antihistamine drugs continue to be sold without a doctor's prescription?	*New England Journal of Biology and Medicine*	Magazine A (A mass circulation monthly pictorial magazine)
B. *Atomic Submarines:* Can a practicable atomic-powered submarine be built at the present time?	Robert J. Oppenheimer	*Pravda*
C. *The Steel Shortage:* Is the steel industry to blame for the current shortage of steel?	*Bulletin of National Resources Planning Board*	Writer A (An antilabor, anti-New Deal, "rightist" newspaper columnist)
D. *The Future of Movie Theaters:* As a result of TV, will there be a decrease in the number of movie theaters in operation by 1955?	*Fortune* magazine	Writer B (A movie gossip columnist)

(From Hovland and Weiss, 1951. Reprinted by permission.)

to influence us. People are often more persuaded when they think the speaker is not trying to persuade them. If people believe they are being coerced or manipulated, they may react against the persuader's arguments. In one experiment, subjects were more influenced by what they "accidentally" overheard from a hallway while waiting in an experimental room than they were by a persuasive speaker.

Communicator Expertise. If a speaker is identified as "Doctor X" as compared to "John Doe," the message is more persuasive. One interpretation for this is that audiences are rational recipients seeking truth. A less idealistic interpretation (Jellison, 1974) is that a highly expert source causes people to

table 10–2

net changes in opinion in the direction of a persuasive communication for high and low credibility sources

topic	percent of subjects changing	
	High Credibility	Low Credibility
Antihistamines	23%	13%
Atomic Submarines	36	0
Steel Shortage	23	−4*
Future of Movies	13	17
Average Change	23	7

* Negative number means in direction opposite the message.
(Adapted from Hovland and Weiss, 1951, Table 2. Reprinted by permission.)

lose confidence in their own judgments. They are then more vulnerable to the persuasive message.

There are at least three disclaimers on the role of the expert, however.

- The communicator who acts so overconfident as to appear "cocky" may be rejected.
- If the audience considers itself expert, the competence of the source is not very critical since the audience does not need the source.
- If the assertions made are blatantly ridiculous, the source may not be believed. In one study, a "highly expert" source could convince more people they only needed *one hour's* sleep a night than could a low expert source, but the audience could not be convinced by anybody that they could get along with *no* sleep.

An apparent exception to this last disclaimer is the so-called Big Lie. The idea here is that almost anything, no matter how ridiculous, may be believed if said often enough and loud enough. Much of the experimental research on persuasion is short term because of the difficulties in maintaining experimental control over a long period (or even keeping track of the subjects). With control of the newspapers, radio, and television, it has been possible (as in the Soviet Union or Nazi Germany) to get people to believe almost anything. The first thing new dictators do is get control of the media.

the source: communicator likability

Sources who are attractive or likable are more effective than those who are unattractive or unlikeable. It is not accidental that semi-nude females, dogs, babies, and popular movie and TV stars appear so often in advertising. Likability is probably more influential in relatively minor issues, however. We can go along with Joe Namath's pantyhose or snack food, but even Joe Willie is unlikely to be a strong influence in our choice of a $9,000 car.

Sometimes, however, *unpopular* sources may also be persuasive. Cognitive dissonance theory accounts for this rather nicely. "If I bothered to listen to this obnoxious character," we might say, "he must have something worthwhile to say." It is also possible that obnoxious communicators get our attention so that we notice what they are saying and then we later forget who said it. It has long been an axiom in selling soap that the audience doesn't have to *like* the commercial, just make sure they remember the name of the soap.

the message: presentation characteristics

The message is what gets transmitted, or presented, to the recipient. We can distinguish the characteristics of the *presentation* from those of the *content*.

Media. The technical aspects of presentation are the medium in which it appears: person-to-person, newspaper, magazine, radio, or television. Face-to-face presentations are superior to written messages or other mechanical forms (McGuire, 1969), because we pay greater attention to a live person. A live person is more sensitive to the recipient's activities and can adjust the presentation accordingly, and the communicator can use gestures and special inflections of words.

Order of Presentation. Suppose you are going to argue *for* an issue and someone else is arguing *against*. Is it better for you to go first or second? The answer is complicated because there are both *primacy* and *recency* effects. With primacy, the first message is more effective and with recency, the second message is. The question then is When is primacy or recency stronger? The following rules seem to hold.

- If the audience is supposed to react immediately (as by voting in a meeting) try to go second; the more recent argument is better.
- If there is some delay (as with an election several days later) better to go first because the first argument is more effective over the long run.
- If the second argument *immediately* follows the first (one speaker right after the other), go first.

(Photo by Bill Henry)

Advertisers have a rule of thumb that when all else fails you can use a picture of a pretty girl, an animal or a baby to sell your product.

NOW, HERE ARE SOME PEOPLE WHO REALLY KNOW HOW TO STAGE A BIG PRIMACY EFFECT!

- If there is a fairly long delay, go second.

    If you do go second, remember that the audience may already be a little tired from the first presentation. So do something to give the audience a chance to relax before you start.

Distraction. Distracting a person while he or she is listening to a persuasive message affects opinion change, but sometimes in favor of the persuader and sometimes against. If the person being persuaded is munching pretzels and drinking something cool he or she may be more receptive. Even neutral or unpleasant distractions may enhance persuasion. One way to reconcile the various favorable and unfavorable effects of distraction is this (Regan & Cheng, 1973): If the message is *simple,* distraction may *help* the persuader, especially if it is pleasant distraction. But if the message is complicated, distraction works *against* the persuader because the message is not completely received.

the message: content characteristics

Logical versus Emotional Appeal. A general rule is that a *combination* of logical appeal and emotional arousal provides the most persuasive impact. In advertising, we are promised wondrous rewards for using the right brands of toothpaste, shampoo, aftershave lotion, bathsoap, and deodorant, as well as dire consequences if we do not.

There has been more research on negative emotional arousal, however. The trick is to get the "correct" amount of fearfulness into the message. If the fear-arousal is too low, you may not get the recipient's attention; if it is too high, the recipient may "tune you out." This is easier said than done, however, because it also depends on the recipient's fear level in the first place. The same message may be too arousing for already fearful recipients and not arousing enough for non-fearful recipients. There are some useful facts, however, which might apply to an audience over all.

- To the extent that the audience is *already familiar with the arguments,* such as the danger of not getting cancer checkups, they may have adapted to the fearfulness of the situation and higher levels of fear arousal can be built into the message.
- If the persuasion involves some *long-term* recommendation, such as giving up smoking, medium fear seems to be best.
- But, *if immediate action can be taken,* higher fear may be more effective—perhaps because this high fear can be reduced quickly.

One-sided versus Two-sided arguments.

- If the members of your audience are *naive* (uninformed) about the issue in question, don't confuse them by presenting the other side of the argument. Just hit them with your side.
- If the audience is *already on your side,* as at a political rally, don't plant any doubt by presenting the opposition's side. Common practice in such situations is not to deal with information at all, only emotional appeal.
- If the audience is initially *against* you, or is *sophisticated* about the issues, present *something* of the opposing side of the issue. If you present only one side, your credibility may be suspect; the audience may believe that you don't really know the issue or are trying to hide something.

Discrepancy between Message and Audience Opinion. Exaggerated statements are more acceptable from a high credibility source than from a low credibility source. A speaker of only modest credibility had best make statements which are only mildly discrepant from the audience's beliefs.

audience characteristics

It is important to know your audience. According to an old story, a famous hell-raising preacher was invited to deliver the Sunday sermon at a certain church, but he was astonished when his most stirring routine left the audience unmoved. He then learned the audience was entirely deaf. Most of us would never encounter such an unusual situation, but we might well run into a group or an individual with a different background, interest, or motivation than we are prepared to deal with.

Differences in Persuasibility. Some people are easily persuaded and others are almost impossible to change. Is there a general personality trait of persuasibility? William McGuire (1969) a foremost researcher in attitudes, has suggested that personality factors influence persuasibility in two ways. They influence the recipient's *comprehension* of a message and *willingness to comply* with the message. Let us think of intelligence as a personality characteristic for a moment. Low intelligence people might be more persuaded by a simple message than high intelligence people. High intelligence people on the other hand might be more persuaded by a complicated message which the low intelligence people just would not follow.

People with low and high self-esteem perform as we just described the case might be for those with low and high intelligence (Zellner, 1970). It is not clear just why they do so, but it may be that people with low and high self-esteem differ in their ability to cope with simple and complex information. That is, people with low self-esteem may do better with simple information and people with high self-esteem may handle complex information better.

Audience Mood. In a good "old timey" political rally you warm up the audience with food, drink, and music before bringing on the speaker. Salespeople use the same gimmick, which is a tax deductible expense. And lovers have long capitalized on this phenomenon, even with such refinements as "Candy's dandy but liquor's quicker." Suffice it to say that laboratory studies support the observation that people in a good mood are more easily persuaded than those in a bad mood.

resistance to persuasion

Most of us are more interested in persuading than in being persuaded. When does persuasion fail and how can we protect ourselves from unwanted persuasion?

Psychological Reactance. The importance of perceived freedom of action has been noted several times previously. If this freedom is threatened, a person may react negatively. One such threat is when another person or group is obviously trying to get you to do something you don't want to do. There may then be a "boomerang" effect; the persuasion backfires and the audience works hard *not* to do what is being promoted. How many of us have sworn we would never buy a particular product because of the "hard sell" approach being used in its advertising? This boomerang effect is called *psychological reactance* and occurs when a message "orders" us to do something. When a well-known beer commercial almost said "Buy beer X if you know what's good for you," sales actually went down. It has also been found that simply knowing someone *intends* to be forcefully persuasive will produce reactance (Heller, Pallak and Picek, 1973).

Innoculation against Persuasion. In the Korean and Vietnamese wars the actual number of captured American soldiers who seemed to embrace the enemy party line was small, although highly publicized. It was suggested in Congress that we should introduce more courses on American ideology into our schools to combat *any* such ideological defections. McGuire (1969) suggested this was the wrong way to approach the problem. He proposed the problem was that our soldiers did not know enough about the *enemy's* ideology to have any counterarguments. McGuire proposed that we would do better to teach our soldiers something about the Communist Party line, along with the arguments against the line. Such knowledge is what McGuire meant by innoculation. Few Americans actually recognize the Communist Party line when they hear it, being unable to separate it from excerpts of, say, the Constitution of the United States.

group influences on individual persuasion

One of the more important factors in "brainwashing" is isolating the individual from his or her usual group and replacing them with a new group that has different norms. There are a number of well-researched phenomena in this area.

Group Norms. There is a strong tendency for individuals to conform to whatever standards are set by their group. A person is rewarded for conformity and sanctioned for nonconformity. For most people this pressure is so powerful that they may conform to groups they have never seen before, such as the Moonies or SLA. There are several classic studies of this kind of conformity.

In the 1930s, Muzafir Sherif (1935) hit upon the *autokinetic phenomenon* as a way of studying group pressure. The phenomenon is that if a person sits in a room completely dark except for a stationary spot of light on the wall, pretty soon the light seems to move by itself (auto = self, kinetic = movement). Individuals judge what they think is the range of movement (so many inches) and groups arrive at a consensus. But if one person thinks a group is establishing a norm which is different from what he or she believes is the range, that person readjusts his or her own judgment to match the group more closely.

Solomon Asch (e.g., 1951) carried this line of research further, using social and perception judgments. He would, for example, have several "subjects" (all but one were confederates of the experimenter) judge which of a set of lines matched the length of a standard line. The confederates all made incorrect judgments before the real subject was allowed to judge. The real subjects frequently went along with what they thought were the judgments of other people.

If subjects had to say *out loud* which they thought was the matching line they conformed more than subjects who were permitted to write their answers. *Public* compliance and *private* compliance were thus distinguished. The group persuades the individual to say one thing publicly even though he or she may perceive (or believe) something different. Not surprisingly, the more ambiguous the situation, the more powerful the group influence on the individual.

Social Support. In the small group situation if even a single supporter backs the real subject, that subject is much more resistant to group pressure. And three supporters make the subject practically invulnerable. These same numeric results might not apply to a group of thousands, but there are individuals who have gone against the masses with just a very small number of followers. The number twelve comes to mind.

SUMMARY

1. *Brainwashing* involves a radical change of thinking, particularly with regard to political or social events. The success of brainwashing depends on the initial beliefs of the victims, fear and anxiety, guilt arousal, isolation from social support, persuasive communication, a cohesive group of "persuaders," and communicator characteristics.

2. Research on persuasive communication has followed the communication model, systematically studying characteristics of the *source* of communication, *message* characteristics and *audience* characteristics.

3. The source, or communicator, of a message must be credible (believable) to be effective. Two important factors in establishing credibility are *trustworthiness* and *expertness*. Trustworthiness can be increased if the source argues against his or her own apparent self-interest or does not seem to be trying

to exert influence. Attractiveness and likeability also increase the effectiveness of a source.

4. The *message* (what gets transmitted) can be presented through different media, but face-to-face contact is most effective. There is considerable variation for specific situations with regard to the order of presentation of opposing messages and effectiveness. (Sometimes going first is better, sometimes going second is better.) Depending on the nature of the distraction, *distraction* may either help or hinder the persuader.

5. The *content* of a message can vary in its *type of appeal* (logical versus emotional), whether the message presents one or both sides of an argument, and how much it differs from the previous opinion of the audience.

6. The persuasibility of an *audience* depends on the audience mood (more easily persuaded when in a "good" mood) and the characteristics of the members of the audience. Personality differences (such as in level of anxiety) affect the recipients' comprehension of the message and willingness to comply with the message.

7. *Psychological reactance* is a boomerang effect, when persuasion fails because there is a negative reaction toward someone who is obviously trying to persuade you to do something you don't want to do.

8. *Innoculation against persuasion* is the idea that if we know counterarguments against a persuasive message we are less likely to be persuaded.

9. The effectiveness of persuasion is influenced by the tendency to *conform to group norms* and whether or not there is *social support* for compliance with a persuasive message.

EXERCISES

1. Can you think of any recent cases of "brainwashing"? How might they fit into the factors that control persuasion (e.g., uninformed initial position or fear and anxiety)? What do the different situations you have thought of have in common? What might be possible ways to resist brainwashing?

2. What is propaganda? Have you been the target of propaganda? How did you respond to it? Did it change your attitudes? Your behavior? In what ways were you changed, if any?

3. Who are some sources of persuasive messages in popular television commercials (e.g., sports figures, actresses, models)? Are they credible? Consider their trustworthiness and expertness? Why should you believe their message?

4. What aspects of the source and message are most effective in persuasion? What attracts attention?

5. What are some particular examples of persuasion that use fear arousal? Are they effective in general? What about in TV ads?

6. Make up a persuasive message using principles discussed in the chapter. Read it to your classmates and see if they detect what principles you used and why you used them. Discuss with the class.

7. What are some different audience characteristics that would require different specific persuasive techniques?

8. When would an individual be most open to a persuasive message (that is, under what particular life circumstances)? What techniques might be used to persuade him or her to do something he or she did not want to do.

IV

The Three A's:
Attraction,
Aggression,
and Altruism

11

Interpersonal Attraction and Human Sexuality

Walster and Walster (1976) put the matter bluntly: "A person who is liked by his comrades will amass enormous benefits; a person who is hated is in trouble" (p. 279). Although sometimes overemphasized, as by Willie Loman in *Death of a Salesman* who kept repeating to his sons, "You've got to be well-liked," interpersonal attraction is important.

We can distinguish several aspects of attraction, however: *affiliation, liking,* and *loving.* People may *affiliate* for many reasons other than liking each other. The *Sunshine Boys* kept their stage act together for forty years, but hated each other. We may choose to be with someone we *like,* even without romantic involvement. Many friendships within and between the sexes persist for years without romantic love. Finally, there is *romantic love,* with real or potential sexual involvement. Romantic love involves all kinds of feelings and ideas, many of which are recognized but not well understood. Long a matter of poetic speculation, love only recently has become a "proper" subject for *experimental* inquiry. We have not put sex into the context of biological motives (Chapter Three) because there are powerful social forces related to sex drive, and sex is not necessary for survival of the *individual,* as are food, water, or air.

affiliation

The need for affiliation has been measured in a manner similar to that of achievement motivation. People tell stories about pictures involving people (the TAT, Thematic Apperception Test), and the themes of the stories are scored to produce an overall need for affiliation score. To test the validity of this approach, the researchers first using it attempted to show that it was possible to *arouse* a need for affiliation (nAff), as measured by TAT scoring. Then they showed that people with high and low scores performed predictably different in certain situations.

Shipley and Veroff (1952) aroused nAff by having a group of fraternity members rate each other on fifteen different adjectives. A control group rated food preferences. The two groups then wrote TAT stories which were compared on various characteristics thought to be related to nAff. The experimental group gave more affiliative statements, thus indicating affiliation is a motive which could be aroused. An important question is whether there may be two kinds of need for affiliation: *Hope of Affiliation* and *Fear of Rejection.* This is somewhat like Hope of Success and Fear of Failure in achievement motivation. At present, however, there is no clear measurement procedure for making this distinction for affiliation.

Affiliation Motive and Performance. We can summarize some of the evidence relating nAff and other performances as follows.

- High nAff subjects are more accurate at picking out faces from a number of very rapidly exposed stimuli than are low nAff subjects (Atkinson & Walker, 1956).
- High nAff people are more accurate at describing other people than are low nAff people (Berlew, 1961).
- High nAff students got better grades in courses taught by teachers judged to be warm and considerate than did low nAff students (McKeachie, Lin, Milholland, & Issacson, 1966).
- High nAff subjects performed better in cooperatively structured groups than in competitively structured groups (de Charms, 1957).
- Persons with *moderate* levels of nAff are better *managers* than either those very low or very high (Boyatzis, 1973). Individuals low in nAff are apparently unconcerned with interpersonal relationships, but those at the high end are overly concerned, to the detriment of actually getting a job done effectively.

determinants of affiliation

Fear and Anxiety. When people are fearful they tend to prefer to be with others. Apparently, other people lower the level of fearfulness. Epley (1974) suggests three possible reasons for this. (1) The "other" person may serve as a "calm" model for the anxious person to imitate. (2) The companion may *distract* the anxious person from what is bothering him or her. (3) The mere physical presence of another person might be anxiety reducing, even without modeling or distracting. A number of experiments have arranged conditions to arouse low or high anxiety and then observed whether the subjects preferred to be alone or with someone else. The results show preference for being with someone else, and the subjects report lower anxiety if someone else is present (Wrightsman, 1960).

Others as Sources of Assistance, Stimulation, Information, or Self-evaluation. There are many reasons we seek the company of others.

Mutual assistance.

- *Assistance.* We can frequently achieve our goals only with the assistance of others. As the joke goes, "If I'm stranded on a desert island, I want a good shipbuilder with me."
- *Stimulation.* In Chapter Three, we discussed the need for stimulus variation. What is more variable, more full of suprises, more stimulating than other people? "Interesting" people attract friends and followers more readily than "dull" people. There does appear to be an optimal level of stimulation here also. A particular person may be *too* stimulating for some people, too dull for others, and "just right" for somebody else.
- *Information.* We may seek others because they have information we need about how to fix our car, how to do our job, and so on.
- *Self-evaluation.* We all need to evaluate ourselves, our opinions, our abilities, and our work from time to time. One way to do this is by *social comparison.* According to social comparison theory (Festinger, 1954), we tend to make such social comparisons when we are uncertain about ourselves. It is easy to tell if you are a good runner just with a watch. But tennis or gymnastics requires a social comparison, judging your performance against other individuals. We tend to seek information for judging ourselves from people who are similar to ourselves in age, background, interests, and experience.

Freedom from Internal Constraints. Groups often restrain their members, but they may also "release" the individual. Nude encounter groups and lynch mobs both support behaviors not often socially acceptable elsewhere. In a group, at a party for instance, one can temporarily lose one's self-control and feel free to behave in ways that are not typical of one's usual behavior.

attraction (liking)

Why is one person particularly attracted to another specific person? As compared to affiliation, where liking is not necessarily involved, we now consider some determinants of liking. Liking other people is a major reason for grouping together.

determinants of attraction

- *Proximity.* We are more likely to be attracted to people physically close to us (e.g., the boy or girl next door). In dormitories, people who live next to each other are more likely to become friends even though they are initially thrown together randomly or alphabetically.
- *Familiarity.* The effects of proximity are partly explained by the fact that closer individuals become more familiar with each other. Zajonc (e.g., 1968) has demonstrated what he calls the *mere exposure* effect. Even with such unlikely stimuli as fake Chinese characters, "goodness" (as rated by subjects) increases with more frequent exposure.
- *Similarity.* Similar people are more likely to get together than dissimilar people. Similarity involves attitudes, personality, and physical characteristics. For example, the greater the percentage of attitude statements that different people agree upon, the greater their attraction to each other. Both dominant and submissive personality "types" tend to prefer dominant types, and both introverted and extroverted individuals tend to prefer extroverted others. This does not exactly support the similarity notion, but it does not support the "opposites attract" idea either. The *matching principle* says people *tend* to choose others of similar height, weight, and degree of attractiveness. This does not always hold true, but the principle is so widely accepted that we usually make special notice of discrepancies. (If an exceptionally attractive woman is seen with an unattractive man it is notable; or, if a 5'1", 90-pound man dates a 5'11", 170-pound woman we notice.)

Theories of Interpersonal Attraction

social comparison and self-evaluation

Festinger (1954) argued not just that people engage in social comparison but further, that there is a "drive" for self-evaluation which leads to social comparison. If objective means of evaluation are not available, people will use "social yardsticks." There are differences in the extent to which people seem to want their opinions and attitudes *publicly* evaluated by others, however.

cognitive dissonance

Cognitive dissonance theory predicts that how we treat someone should affect our liking of them, just as dissonance affects our liking of boring tasks. If we behave in a cruel way toward a neutral stranger, for example, this should be at odds with our self perception. There should be dissonance. We should, therefore, change our attitude, probably toward the stranger rather than toward ourselves. A number of experiments show that we develop negative attitudes toward people we have "done wrong." Glass (1964) added the curious twist that individuals with *high* self-esteem should become more negative in such a situation (usually, giving bad written evaluations to "strangers"—actually experimenter cohorts) because people with a high self-evaluation should have greater dissonance. His results supported the prediction.

The research is fairly consistent in showing that people will try to justify "harmdoing" by becoming more negative toward the "victim," but there is little evidence for the analogous positive prediction. If someone acts especially kindly toward a stranger, the research does not reliably show that the experimental subject develops a more positive evaluation of the neutral stranger. There is a ray of hope for humankind, however. "Harmdoers" in experimental situations will try to "compensate" their "victims" if the experimental situation allows.

social-exchange theory

Social-exchange theory is a kind of marketing theory. Associating with others involves *benefits* and *costs.* Positive attraction occurs when the benefits outweigh the costs, and avoidance of another person occurs when the costs are greater than the benefits. Whether a person is approached or avoided, liked or disliked, depends on whether the sum of all the benefits is greater or less than the costs.

Exchange theory deals with *mutually* rewarding behaviors between people. For example, a male and a female may each have socially desirable qualities they can "trade off" to each other. In our society it has been true that a male seen with a very attractive female is judged highly by others. Attractive females have been more likely to date or marry men of higher social status than they themselves are. Money, status, and power are particularly strong attractive qualities of men (not to speak of charm, grace, intelligence, and wit). Political power seems to be a universal bargaining commodity, but the "groupies" who follow rock musicians and professional athletes attest to other kinds of stature that can be traded for an attractive companion and sexual favors. At some point, however, the cost of maintaining a particular interpersonal relationship may be too high, in terms of emotional stress, money, effort, or time, and we may determine that the costs outrun the benefits.

Since it is a form of reinforcement theory (benefits = rewards; costs = punishment), exchange theory can make predictions based on basic motivational principles. For example, social approval should be a more effective reward for someone who has been deprived of approval. Or, approval should be a more durable reward if doled out on a partial reinforcement schedule. Research does support such deprivation and scheduling effects of approval (Rubin, 1973). Approval for *every* act may lose its value because it is indiscriminate, or it may even be perceived as insincere and ingratiating.

A problem for exchange theory is how to deal with altruistic behavior, that "selfless" giving of one's time and energy to others. There are two ways out of the dilemma. One is to say that exchange theory is wrong, and that some people really do things with no thought of gain for themselves. The other is to say that the rewards are there, but not obvious. The *guilt* we might feel for *not* behaving "altruistically" may also be important. We may be altruistic sometimes because we have learned to feel guilty if we do *not* give more than we received. For those who hold to other views of moral behavior, this approach may seem empty, but is nevertheless something to think about. Doubtless all of us have at one time looked at someone who seemed "too good" and asked what he or she was *really* getting out of it. A *little* cynicism is healthy in everyday life.

equity theory

Equity theory (e.g., Walster & Walster, 1976) also assumes that individuals try to maximize the good things in life. Equity theory differs, however, in assuming that *society rewards people for being equitable in their relations with others.* That is, people are encouraged and rewarded for giving about the same as they receive. If a person gets involved in an inequitable relationship, he becomes *distressed* (anxious, upset) and tries to restore equity. A special twist of the theory is that there is distress when one is *either* giving too much *or* getting too much. If you do an outrageous number of expensive favors for me and I do nothing in return, we may *both* be distressed because of the inequity and do something to *restore* equity.

Will people voluntarily behave equitably? People might well monopolize resources and behave inequitably *if* they thought they could get by with it. Equity operates in a *social climate*, however, and there usually are social rewards for treating others fairly and sanctions against treating them unfairly.

Applications of Equity Theory. The following brief accounts indicate the breadth of equity theory.

- *Exploitation: The Exploiter.* If one person does another harm, he or she can try to restore *real* equity or *psychological* equity. The harmdoer might minimize the victim's suffering, deny being responsible for the suffering, or say that the victim *deserved* what he or she got.

- *Exploitation: The Exploited.* A rational victim would, if possible, try to induce the exploiter to restore equity and make restitution. If this does not work, the victim might just acknowledge the exploitation, along with powerlessness to do anything about it. Or, the *victim might justify his or her own exploitation,* and come to believe by distorting reality that the exploitation was justified. This plays right into the hands of the exploiter. Karl Marx said that religion is the opiate of the masses, a way of keeping them in line so they could be exploited. We do not argue the truth or falsity of this claim, but it would seem to find some justification in religions which teach that everything is God's will and therefore good.

- *Altruism.* Sometimes philanthropy is only a thinly disguised way of helping oneself by helping others. The mill owner might provide cheap rent in company housing but more than get it back by paying low wages. But consider the case where there is no obvious advantage to be gained by altruism. The recipient of altruism (including social welfare) might have negative reactions in this inequitable situation for three reasons (Walster & Walster, 1976). First, it is an inequitable relation and the theory postulates that this produces distress. Second, the altruism is *potentially* exploitative: If I save your life, I might ask you to return the favor forever. Third, the recipient may feel humiliated because the altruistic favor established the superiority of the benefactor over the recipient.

- *Intimate Relations.* Are intimate relations between two individuals special and not self-serving? Walster and Walster (p. 299) suggest that ". . . even in the most intimate of relations, equity considerations determine both how viable and how pleasant a relationship will be." One clear prediction is the so-called *matching relationship,* that partners of similar characteristics will tend to get together because they are most likely to provide equity. Romantic choices are somewhat, but certainly not completely, determined by "equity considerations."

Love and Sexuality

measuring love

Rubin (1973) distinguished between liking and loving as follows: Liking is based on *affection* and *respect;* loving is based on *attachment, caring,* and *intimacy.* He incorporated these distinctions into two measurement scales. Each of thirteen items on a scale is rated from 1 to 9—"Not at all true" (1) to "Definitely True" (9). The "liking scale" has such items as "I think that _____ is usually well adjusted" and "I have great confidence in _____'s good judgment." The "love scale" has such items as "I feel that I can confide in _____ about virtually anything" and "If I were lonely, my first thought would be to seek _____ out." The importance of these scales is that they were among the first *attempts* to measure liking and loving. In every field of research, large advances are made when there are new measuring techniques. Research on anxiety got its greatest impetus when scales for measuring anxiety were developed; the same could be expected in the area of love.

(Photo by Bill Henry)

determinants of choice of a romantic partner

Physical Attraction. Physical appearance has always been assumed to be important in attracting others but actual research is relatively new. Walster, Aronson, Abrahams, and Rottman (1966) arranged a "computer dance" for freshmen at the University of Minnesota. The actual pair assignment was random (except that the cultural norm of the males being taller than the females was followed). At the time of the original sign-up, four experimenters rated the participants on attractiveness and at intermission time during the dance, partners rated each other. Several months later the experimenters checked to see if there had been further dates. About a third of the most attractive females (judged by their partners) were later asked for dates but only about 10 percent of the least attractive were. The differences were not overwhelming, but attractiveness predicted subsequent dating better than any other variable of many that were studied. The judges' ratings did not predict this, however, only the partner's ratings during intermission did. Attractiveness is a complex variable (e.g., facial characteristics, body characteristics), so it is not surprising that the judgment made by the person who is later going to ask (or not ask) for a date is the most important.

There are a number of possible reasons for the relationship between attractiveness and liking:

- Simple sexual arousal may be involved. Attractiveness does, however, seem to be more important for dating than for marrying.
- Males with attractive dates believe they will be judged more positively by others, and in fact they are.

265

- Attractive individuals are not only liked more; they are also *perceived* more positively on other characteristics and are more positively treated by others.
- Since they are treated more positively by others, attractive people may tend to be more self-confident and more socially adept. They may, in fact, *be* somewhat better adjusted people.

Because of its immediate obviousness, physical attraction may be relatively more important for first impressions than for long-term contact. The physically attractive person may use his or her attraction more effectively in situations where there is relatively brief interpersonal contact (such as in sales or advertising). Attractiveness may become relatively less important in such long-term associations as marriage or occupations requiring prolonged interpersonal contact (Berscheid & Walster, 1974b).

Playing Hard to Get. Young girls are still probably told they should "play hard to get" because they will be more desirable. There are several reasons why this might be true.

- According to cognitive dissonance theory, "We come to love what we have to suffer (or work) for." If this person is this hard to get, I must really like him or her.
- It is readily inferred that if someone is hard to get, there must be more there than meets the eye.
- There is frustration and arousal. This may in itself have a certain amount of attraction value (the "excitement of the chase") as well as relating to a cognitive arousal theory of romantic love, which we shall discuss shortly.

Social Influences. Proximity, familiarity, and similarity are individual determinants of attraction, which are in turn affected by social factors. There is a so-called social filter, established by cultural groups, parents, and peers through which a prospective partner has to pass before serious involvement is considered. Love may blind us to all but our beloved, but society goes a long way in determining who our beloved will be. People tend to marry others of the same race, religion, social class, and education. Proximity, familiarity, and similarity are facilitated by such social variables.

Some social structures are almost exclusively designed for such filtering. The debutante ball and campus fraternities and sororities are generally designed for the "right people" to get together. Parents generally believe they know what is best for their children and may try to influence romance and marriage, including sending their children to the "right" school, and so on. This may backfire, however (an example of the "boomerang" effect with persuasion) and produce the "Romeo and Juliet effect." The more the parents try to separate the couple, the more the couple gets involved. Explanations that account for the "hard to get" phenomenon may be applied here, also.

a theory of passionate love: the cognitive-arousal model

Research on romantic love has been historically hindered by social prohibitions. One of these is the argument that romantic love cannot be studied, that it is beyond science. We have now overcome that barrier, but there is little scientific theory to provide a framework for studying romance. Romantic novels, poems, or individuals may tell you what there is to know about love, but these do not quite constitute scientific theory.

Rubin (1973) describes what he calls the "Ovid-Horwicz" phenomenon. In his *Ars Amatoria (The Art of Love),* a first-century how-to-do-it manual for romantic conquest, the Roman poet Ovid gave all sorts of helpful hints, involving grooming and behavior. Our interest here, however, is the suggestion that a good time to arouse passion in a woman was while watching gladiators fight in the arena. Nowadays, a boxing match or football game might suffice nicely. Adolph Horwicz, a nineteenth-century German psychologist, suggested that any strong emotional arousal could facilitate love. Until recently this effect

HEY, FELLAH... YOU'RE **NOT** IN LOVE... YOU ARE IN PAIN!

was limited to empirical observation; it seemed to work. But we now have a theory to account for it: Schachter's cognitive-arousal theory.

The theory, you may recall from Chapter Five, says that emotional arousal is diffuse until *labeled* by the individual. The label given to the arousal depends on the circumstances, and on what the person involved *thinks* is happening. Any number of events might then produce arousal, but the presence of an attentive member of the opposite sex could cause a young person to interpret arousal as love.

The theory would also explain the sometimes rapid alternation between love and hate: The arousal process is the same, but the labeling may change quickly because of circumstances. The theory suggests why frustration may heighten attraction: Frustration produces arousal which is interpreted as love. The hard-to-get lover produces frustration. Even *rejection* by someone, or discovering that the object of one's affection has another partner, may produce stronger emotional arousal which may be interpreted as even stronger love. Some people are "turned on" by a certain amount of danger in love making, such as doing it in situations where there is a chance of being seen or caught. The cognitive arousal theory would seem to account for this.

person perception

George, an experimental subject, is read a list of personality traits and then asked to write a brief personality sketch of the person described. The traits are "intelligent, skillful, industrious, warm, determined, practical, and cautious." He writes the following:

> "A person who believes certain things to be right, wants others to see his point, would be sincere in an argument, and would like to see his point won."

Frank, another subject, is given the same task with the following list of traits: "intelligent, skillful, industrious, *cold,* determined, practical, and cautious. He writes

> "A rather snobbish person who feels that his success and intelligence set him apart from the run-of-the-mill individual. Calculating and unsympathetic."

The above examples come from a classic study by Solomon Asch (1946, p. 263). They are notable by two particulars. First, the descriptions are very different, even though the only difference in the list of traits was the substitution of the word *cold* for the word *warm* in the second list. Second, both descriptions go far beyond what is called for by the traits. The subjects are "fleshing out" the descriptions rather dramatically.

Asch went on to have his subjects indicate which of eighteen adjectives were applicable to the two hypothetical persons described by the above traits.

table 11–1

percentage of subjects who judged the following adjectives as being characteristic of persons who were described only as being *intelligent, skillful, industrious, warm* (or *cold*), *determined, practical* and *courtious.*

		"warm"	"cold"
1.	generous	91	8
2.	wise	65	25
3.	happy	90	34
4.	good-natured	94	17
5.	humorous	77	13
6.	sociable	91	38
7.	popular	84	28
8.	reliable	94	99
9.	important	88	99
10.	humane	86	31
11.	good-looking	77	69
12.	persistent	100	97
13.	serious	100	99
14.	restrained	77	89
15.	altruistic	69	18
16.	imaginative	51	19
17.	strong	98	95
18.	honest	98	94

(Adapted from Asch, 1946, Table 2.)

This more objective procedure corroborated the more subjective character descriptions. Table 11–1 summarizes the results from one of Asch's experiments. The substitution of "cold" for "warm" changed the personality evaluations from generous to ungenerous, wise to shrewd, happy to unhappy, and so on. There were also many traits, however, where it did not make any difference whether the person being judged was warm or cold (for example, reliability, persistence, and seriousness). We conclude from this and subsequent research that an entire constellation of characteristics is quickly judged on limited information.

A trait may be considered more "central" or important in some situations than others. Asch called warm or cold *central qualities.* Characteristics which did not make much difference were called *peripheral qualities.* What would be central qualities for a professional football player would be more peripheral for, say, a college professor. The most striking fact from such research is that people make judgments of each other very, very quickly and with little evidence. Such judgments are important for attraction between people as well as a variety of other reasons.

Person Perception Algebra. We don't literally add up the separate qualities of someone to arrive at an overall impression, but, there must be some kind of "algebra" that quickly comes into play at a less conscious level. There have been two major approaches to account for the way people put together characteristics of others to form impressions of them. These are the *additive model* and the *averaging model*. Suppose that you know *three* good things about Janet, which you can assign values of +3, +4, and +5. For Mary you know five good things which you can assign values of +2, +3, +4, +5, and +6.

If we *add* the numbers for each, we get Janet = 12 and Mary = 20. By this calculation, Mary should be much more positive than Janet. Suppose, however, we take the *average* of the values for each: Janet = 12 ÷ 3 = 4 and Mary = 20 ÷ 5 = 4. They are both the same. Which procedure more closely approximates what we actually do? The answer from many experiments is that we *average* in making judgments, or forming impressions, of others. A *large* number of good (or bad) qualities of a person does not necessarily average to anything different than just a few good (or bad) qualities. Additional qualities have to be very high or low to change the average much.

In the above example it is implied that some things are more important than others. What determines the different *values* of personal qualities which go into averaging? We will speak about several: primacy, situational factors, negativity bias, set, and individual differences.

Primacy. First Impressions are important, even if Incorrect. Some people may initially seem very brusque and rude. It may take a long time to discover (perhaps because you avoid them) that they are really not this way. Since first impressions tend to be weighted more heavily than later impressions, it requires considerable effort to modify first impressions. To have a strong positive effect when presenting oneself to others, say in a job interview, the first impression should be as good as possible (grooming, clothes, manners). Any later defects will be weighted less.

As another example of order effects, Asch (1952) asked subjects to form impressions from two lists of characteristics: (A) intelligent, industrious, impulsive and (B) critical, stubborn, envious. Each subject characterized two *different* individuals easily, one from List A and one from List B. When Asch then requested the same subjects to characterize a *single* person with all six characteristics, they had much more trouble doing so than did subjects who had initially used all six to characterize one person. If we initially have incomplete information about a person we may develop incorrect ideas which are then very difficult to change.

Situational Factors. The importance of a given personal characteristic depends on the situation. Playboy bunnies are not selected by the same criteria as welders. Actually, construction work is an interesting example because, by its nature, jobs tend to be short-lived, always rushing, and moving from one place to another. Consequently, the most heavily weighted characteristics are experience, speed, and reliability. Beyond this, not many questions are asked, and nobody much cares what a first-rate welder looks like.

Negativity Bias. Negative qualities tend to be weighted more strongly than positive ones. President Carter's budget advisor, Burt Lance, was forced from his government position because of apparent improprieties in his banking procedures in Georgia. In fact, it appears that what he was doing (such as being a little lax on dealing with overdrafts, or being slow to call in loans) were quite regular practices in his community. He was highly regarded as a progressive businessman who tried to help people by not applying pressure too rigidly. Nevertheless, his departures from what were "normal" practices elsewhere were considered very negative and outweighted all his good qualities in Washington. Politicians do live in a fishbowl and the very appearance of wrongdoing has to be dealt with strongly. Carter succumbed to the pressure and removed Lance.

Set. By "set" we mean a temporary readiness to respond in a certain way. In one of the classic studies of person perception (Kelly, 1950) subjects were given prior thumbnail sketches of a visiting lecturer. The sketches were identical except that some subjects were told that the visitor-to-come was "warm" and others were told he was "cold." The subjects then proceeded to hear the lecturer for a few minutes, following which they judged him on various characteristics. The results were essentially the same as those found in the earlier Asch (1946) experiment. In this instance, however, the subjects were *set* to perceive the lecturer in a certain way by the differentiating words *warm* and *cold*.

Individual Differences in Person-Perception Accuracy. It should be important for anybody involved in personnel selection to perceive other people accurately. Some individuals are better at this than others, but it is not so simple as "some can" and "some cannot." Also, there are two kinds of accuracy, called *stereotype accuracy* and *differential accuracy*.

Stereotype accuracy is the ability to detect social stereotypes. Differential accuracy is the ability to make accurate perceptual distinctions among different persons. Some people are good at one of these tasks, but not the other. The stereotype vs. differential distinction went unnoticed for a long time and many people who were considered "good judges of other people" were actually only describing people in terms of cultural stereotypes. For example, I might give a description of a particular male and a particular female which *seem* to be good differential descriptions. I might, however, be giving only descriptions of male and female stereotypes. We can at least be aware that there is a problem here to guard against.

Human Sexuality

historical background of research

Much of the early psychology of motivation, beginning with the work of Freud, dealt with sex and anxiety. Anxiety research has since raced far ahead of that devoted to sex. Only in the last thirty-five years has there been serious *research* devoted to sex, asking such pertinent questions as How *often* do people engage in sex? What *kinds* of sex do they engage in? What *differences* in sexual interests and practice are there between men and women besides those demanded by anatomy? How have sexual *standards* changed in the last generation? How and when should we *educate* our children about sex? What is the effect of explicit sexual material ("pornography") on sexual activity, including sex crimes?

The Kinsey reports of sexual behavior in the human male (Kinsey, Pomeroy & Martin, 1948) and female (Kinsey, Pomeroy, Martin & Gebhard, 1953) provided the first good data. Based on interviews with thousands of people of all ages, these reports publicly documented things that were "known all along" by some people but not believed at all by others. The high incidence of oral-genital sex and homosexual encounters was particularly surprising to many. Many skeptics believed the Kinsey reports were based on nonrepresentative samples (for example, "only those women that would consent to be interviewed"). Subsequent surveys (for example, Hunt, 1974) have verified the Kinsey findings much better than the critics would have preferred.

The most dramatic breakthrough in human sexual research, however, was made by Masters and Johnson (1966). Using direct observation and color cinematography of both autosexual (masturbation) and heterosexual behavior, as well as extensive physiological recordings, they arrived at some general characteristics of both male and female sexual responses. In the process, they laid to rest such myths as there being an "immature" kind of female orgasm (from stimulation of the clitoris) and a more "mature" kind (from stimulation of the vagina). In fact, all female orgasms are the same and depend on clitoral stimulation. To anticipate some of the discussion to follow, it has subsequently been found that (1) repeated exposure to sexually explicit material actually reduces sexual arousal to the material and facilitates only a person's normal sexual behavior for a brief period of time, and (2) women are generally aroused by the same kinds of explicit sexual materials as men. Any differences between the sexes in this regard appear to result from different socialization (and guilt) about sexual interest and behavior.

an approach to studying sex

It is difficult to organize, much less implement, a systematic research program on human sexuality because of prevailing morals and laws. Much of what we know experimentally comes from research with animals; we often extrapolate from detailed animal experiments and less precise human observations to attempt to arrive at generalizations about humans. The difficulty in implementing a complete program of sexual research is illustrated in a scenario in Baron and Byrne (1977) where the social norms for food and sex are reversed. Children are taught from early on how to have sex right, what to do, and where to do it. There are sex supermarkets and fast-sex shops. Food, however, is discussed only in hushed tones except by vulgar people. Eating is done in darkened rooms, usually only by married couples, and some perverted adults. You can fill out the story as well as we can retell it. There are obstacles that face researchers in one area of biological research which do not confront those in another.

Baron and Byrne outline a general approach to the study of sexual behavior, however, summarized in Table 11–2. The approach is to divide the phases of sexual behavior into stimulation, behavior, and orgasm. Cutting across all three of these are three different levels of development: *reproduction, learning,* and *emotions.* By systematically raising questions from each of the nine cells in Table 11–2, we can get some idea of where we stand in our knowledge about human sexual behavior.

reproduction: species survival

Stimulation. Sexual arousal is determined both by *internal* events (hormones, etc.) and *external* cues. In many species, sexual arousal can only occur at certain times of the year for relatively brief periods because hormonal activity is controlled by seasonal changes in temperature and amount of light. Humans, male or female, are about the only species ready to mate at any time of year, day or night, year in and year out. There is no strong correlation between hormone levels and sexual readiness or arousal in humans.

The external cues for arousal can be through any of the senses. The stimulation phase can be brief or prolonged. In some species, it is one or the other, but in humans it may vary for the same individual (ranging from encoun-

table 11–2

a framework for conceptualizing human sexual behavior in terms of stimulation, behavior, and orgasm at three levels of development: reproduction, learning, and emotions

	phases of human sexual behavior		
Levels of Development	*Stimulation Phase*	*Behavioral Phase*	*Orgasm Phase*
Reproduction	Sexual excitement is elicited by a sexual partner.	The sexual act involves contact with the partner which leads to intercourse.	Semen is ejaculated into vagina.
Learning	Through conditioning, other stimuli acquire the power to arouse the individual; imagination and fantasy become powerful cues that elicit arousal.	Individuals learn a wide variety of possible sexual behaviors.	Orgasm for either sex can be brought about in many different ways.
Emotions	Internal and external sexual cues can evoke positive and/or negative feelings.	Any sexual act can evoke positive and/or negative feelings.	Orgasm can evoke positive and/or negative feelings.

Byrne, *Introduction to Personality*, 1974, p. 450.

ters lasting a few minutes to several hours). Though for many animals, odors are particularly strong sexual attractants, this is less obviously so with humans, advertising claims to the contrary.

Behavioral Phase. At the reproductive level, once two members of the opposite sex get together the only mammalian necessity is that the penis enter the vagina to the extent that sperm can be deposited deep enough to eventually reach an egg. Other behaviors are incidental, although such activities as touching and mouthing may be used to maintain the arousal level of the participants.

Orgasmic Phase. It is biologically necessary for sperm to reach the egg for conception, but it also appears that orgasms are *pleasurable* for mammalian species. This is generally true with males and appears to be potentially true for *almost all* human females. The physiology and behavior specific to human males and females during orgasm have been described in detail by Masters and Johnson (e.g., 1966). One finding disconcerting to some male egos is that human females can have many orgasms in the same time a male can have only one or two.

learning: cortical complications for sex

As Baron and Byrne suggest, primitive humans probably approached both food and sex in the simplest manner possible. But we have grown more intelligent and gained the ability to complicate simple things.

Stimulation. Through the process of conditioning, virtually any stimulus can become associated with sex and therefore can be sexually arousing. Rachman (1966) showed that males could become sexually aroused by pictures of footwear if footwear was associated with pictures of nude females. There are a variety of *fetishes,* sexual arousal stimulated by nonsexual objects, and it is generally assumed that these develop through association with sexual arousal.

Probably an even more important result of human brain complexity is the use of *imagination.* With mammals lower than primates, there is a fairly abrupt decline of sexual activity after castration. Human males can remain sexually active for *years after* being castrated, so it is apparent that male sexual hormones from the testes are not absolutely crucial for sex. Males may normally provide self-arousal by fantasizing various sexual activities and partners.

It is well known from survey information that both males and females can be aroused by sexual fantasies and that both sexes often fantasize during intercourse itself. It may be that differences in "sex drive" are really differences in self-arousal through fantasy. This may also account for some of the differences in sexual activity in later years.

Behavior. It is physically *possible* for most mammals to engage in sex in a variety of ways but only humans *do* show much variation. It is still an irony of society, however, that imagination and creativity are considered the apex of human development, except when applied to sexual behavior. Sexual creativity is often considered immoral and illegal.

Orgasm. Orgasms can be delayed or hurried, intensified or weakened, by various means, including imagination or learned self-control. Furthermore, whereas at the reproductive level, it is necessary (and normally occurs among other species) to deposit sperm in the female genital tract, orgasms are arrived at in a variety of other ways by humans. The Marquis de Sade, writing in the eighteenth century, probably described in about as many ways as anybody ever has the number of possibilities for orgasms *without* any possibility of pregnancy (de Sade, *Philosophy in the Bedroom*).

emotions and sex

Stimulation. Positive emotion is obviously related to sex, but sometimes there are negative emotions, particularly anxiety and guilt. At some point in the history of mankind, it was apparently considered necessary to make certain sexual activities taboo, perhaps so that sex would be limited to reproduction which was necessary for social survival, and perhaps to have offspring to take care of the parents in their old age. Strong moral codes prohibiting such activities as masturbation, homosexuality, and artificial contraception developed. These are still major issues in the Roman Catholic Church. The problems raised by this (Baron & Byrne, 1977) are that situations may change (such as over-population) but old rules are retained, and each generation has to teach the next

generation what is good or bad about sex. Unfortunately, the "teaching" generation often does not hold up its end of the bargain very well. In its attempt
to regulate sexual activities, it may pass on completely *false* information (such
as that masturbation leads to insanity).

Even well-educated people are often ill-informed about sex. It is usually
expected by the public that physicians will be "experts" in sexual matters, but
in fact the average physician is neither well trained nor emotionally prepared
to cope with a patient's sexual problems. Surveys of senior medical students
and of practicing physicians, even in recent years, show that large percentages
of them subscribe to long outdated myths about sex. Medical education in
this area is improving, but it is still relatively neglected.

Because of the differences in background and experience with sex, different people develop completely different attitudes about any given sexual activity. In one study, for example, it was found that people who were "sexually
liberal" and people who were "sexually conservative" were *all* aroused by
sexually explicit pictures of varying kinds. But, whereas the former group
considered the pictures entertaining, the latter considered them disgusting (Wallace & Wehmer, 1972).

We might think that a given person would fall at some specific point
along a line ranging from strong positive emotion to neutrality to strong negative
emotion about sex. But Byrne, Fisher, Lamberth, and Mitchell (1974) found
that positive *and* negative aspects could occur in virtually any combination
for a particular person. The *positive* aspects of sexually explicit materials they
identified were *excited, entertained, sexually aroused, anxious, curious,* and *bored.* (*Anxious*
correlated positively with *entertained,* so *anxious* in this instance apparently was
not a negative emotion.) The *negative* emotional responses were *disgusted, nauseated,*
angry, and *depressed.*

Byrne et al. then had their subjects, married couples, judge nineteen explicit pictures according to whether they considered the pictures pornographic
or not. Figure 11–1 summarizes the results. We see that male subjects low in
positive affect (emotion) and high in negative affect considered many more

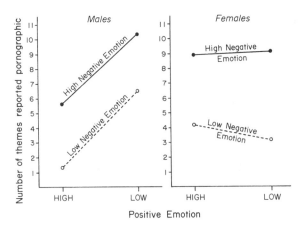

figure 11–1. Number of 19 photographic themes judged to be pornographic in relation to the subjects' own self-reported positive and negative emotional responses. The males were affected by their own positive emotional responses whereas the females were not. (Adapted from Byrne, et al., Table 2. Used with permission.)

of the pictures pornographic. For females who were high in negative affect, the degree of positive affect did not make any difference, however. It was also found that people high in authoritarianism considered more of the pictures pornographic. The authors suggest that "what is taught about anatomical structures, physiological processes, and techniques of the sexual act may not be as important as what is intentionally or unintentionally conveyed *affectively*" (p. 115).

Behavior. Individuals who are more negative in their emotions regarding sex are also more restrictive in what they consider "permissible" sexual acts. This also carries over to their actual behaviors. The emotion of guilt seems to be particularly important insofar as the evidence indicates that the greater the guilt associated with sex, the smaller the range of sexual activities a person is likely to engage in.

Orgasm. People with strong negative emotions toward sex are more likely to have difficulty in achieving successful orgasm. This is called *frigidity* in females and *impotence* in males. Since these problems are more commonly emotional or psychological problems rather than medical problems, we can see why medical treatment is often ineffective or why physicians often don't know what to do with such problems. It is not reasonable to treat a lifelong-development of negative attitudes toward sex by a prescription the way one would treat a sinus infection.

Obscenity and the Law

What we regard as "pornographic" or "obscene," depends on our attitudes about sex. Our sexual attitudes, in turn, are learned by all the same processes (conditioning, imitation, etc.) that determine attitudes generally. In the case of sex, however, there is much more "institutional" support (legal and church) to reinforce many negative attitudes. The words "pornographic" and "obscene" carry strong negative meanings, whereas "sexually explicit material" does not. The national commission to study "the problem," however, was called The Commission on Obscenity and Pornography, *not* The Commission on Sexually Explicit Materials. This suggests a certain attitudinal bias in the initial establishment of the Commission, although its final report (1970) contained rather modest recommendations.

Attempting to answer the question of whether sexually explicit materials directly contribute to sex crimes, the Commission had to contract new research as well as examine past research. This was an important spur to research in this field. These are some of the relevant findings.

- Repeated exposure to erotica (words, sounds, or pictures) leads to a progressively smaller sexual response. Apparently there is a degree of boredom after awhile.

The evidence strongly indicates that sexually-explicit reading materials simply move a person to do what she or he would otherwise do anyway.

- Sex offenders apparently have *less* contact with erotic materials during adolescence than do non-offenders. Those who commit sex crimes have heard, seen, read, and talked less about sex than nonoffenders.

- A large scale "social experiment" was the legal decision in Denmark to allow all forms of explicit sexual material (including books, movies, and sexual contraptions) to be sold freely. If it were true that such materials lead to sex crimes, even in a small percentage of the population, there should have been a large increase in Denmark. Just the opposite occurred. Sex crimes *decreased* rather than increased. In particular, reported cases of child molestation decreased by about 60 percent.

- Sexually explicit material *is* sexually arousing. But does this necessarily lead to any overall increase in sexual activity, particularly types of which much of society would condemn (such as group sex, unusual positions, unusual partners)? According to Baron and Byrne (p. 499), at least a dozen experiments led to the conclusion that "in general, exposure to erotica is found to have very little effect on overt behavior, and any increases in sexual activity seem to involve only behavior that was already part of the individual's sexual pattern."

SUMMARY

1. *Interpersonal attraction* is a blanket term which covers *affiliation, liking,* and *loving.*

2. *Need for affiliation* involves joining in pairs or larger groups for numerous reasons and does not necessarily involve liking. People affiliate with each other to reduce anxiety or fearfulness, as well as to receive assistance, stimulation, or to compare themselves with others in terms of abilities, beliefs, or attitudes.

3.   Some of the *determinants* of *liking,* which involves a positive attraction, are *proximity* (physical closeness), *familiarity,* and *similarity.*

4.   There are several theories to explain interpersonal attraction. *Social Comparison Theory* proposes that there is a "drive" for self-evaluation, which is done in a social context. *Cognitive Dissonance Theory* suggests that our liking of others partly depends on how we treat them. *Social Exchange Theory* says that we apply informal cost/benefit analyses to interpersonal relations and we are attracted to individuals where the benefits of interaction outweigh the costs (in time, money, effort). *Equity Theory* is somewhat like social exchange theory, but it also argues that society rewards people who are equitable in their relations with others (give and receive benefits equally).

5.   Rubin developed a pair of scales for measuring *liking* and *loving.* By his definition, liking is based on *affection and respect* whereas love is based on *attachment, caring,* and *intimacy.*

6.   The *choice of a romantic partner* is determined by such factors as physical attractiveness, "playing hard to get," and various social influences (family, culture), as well as proximity, familiarity, and similarity.

7.   *Cognitive-Arousal theory* explains passionate love as the *labeling* of a *general* state of arousal as love under the appropriate circumstances, such as in the presence of another person.

8.   In *person perception* we emphasize some *central* qualities as more important than other *peripheral* qualities. We tend to average very quickly the good and bad qualities we perceive in others and then judge them with regard to various characteristics. Three important determinants of perception are *primacy,* or first impressions which are hard to change: *negative qualities,* which we count for more than positive qualities; and *set,* or a readiness to see some things rather than others.

9.   There are large *individual differences* in how accurately people perceive others. *Stereotype accuracy* is the ability to detect social stereotypes. *Differential accuracy* is the ability to make accurate distinctions among persons, separately from the social stereotype. Some people are good at recognizing stereotypes, but not at differential accuracy.

10. Research on *human sexuality* has been inhibited both by custom (morals) and by law. Major breakthroughs were the *Kinsey survey reports* on the sexual behavior of human males and females, published about 1950, and the subsequent work of *Masters and Johnson* on direct observation and measurement of sexual activity in the 1960s.

11. Human sexuality includes *stimulation, behavior,* and *orgasm,* which develop on three levels: *reproduction, learning,* and *emotions.* Reproduction is necessary for species survival, but learning and emotions are important components of sexual activity in mammals.

12. By *classical conditioning*, almost any stimulus can become associated with sexual pleasure. This explains *fetishes*, sexual arousal without usual sexual objects.

13. *Sexual creativity* in humans can be expressed through *fantasy* as well as a variety of sexual techniques. However, whereas society values creative activity in other endeavors, it discourages creativity in sexual conduct.

14. Emotions strongly affect sexual behavior and attitudes toward sex, especially anxiety and guilt resulting from strong moral codes and beliefs in myths about sexuality. Such negative attitudes can produce difficulty in achieving orgasms in either females (frigidity) or males (impotence).

15. Social views about *pornography* (sexually explicit material) are based on our attitudes about sex. Research on exposure to erotica generally indicates, however, that erotica changes behavior very little. The main effect is a temporary increase in whatever the viewer or reader was previously doing sexually.

EXERCISES

1. What are the differences among affiliation, liking, and loving?

2. What factors would make you want to affiliate with a particular person (perhaps even someone you don't like)? Are some more important than others?

3. Think of someone you *like*. What attracted you to that person? Which of the theories of interpersonal attraction would best explain your relationship with that person?

4. Describe what your *ideal* partner would be like, based on determinants of choice of a romantic partner.

5. List ten positive personality traits of someone you like. Substitute a negative word for one of them. Does this drastically alter the total description?

6. By the time you have reached this chapter, you may know your classmates fairly well. What were your first impressions of some of them? Have these first impressions changed? Have the changes been positive or negative? How important were those first impressions in governing your actions toward particular people?

7. Review the *matching principle* of attraction. Think of couples you know. Are they alike in personality or appearance (height, hair color . . .)?

8. What social factors affect your choice of a romantic partner? What social institutions and programs help or hinder your choice? (An example of a hindrance would be separate high schools or colleges for males and females.)

9. What are some internal and external influences on sexual arousal?

10. Discuss the relative importance of biological factors and learning in sexual behavior. Are they of the same importance in animals and humans? Where do animals and humans get their information about sex?

11. How are emotions related to sexuality?

12

Hurting and Helping: Aggression and Altruism

Aggression

what do we mean by aggression?

Many times we are immediately sure that a particular behavior is aggressive, as when one person hits another. But it is not always so clearcut. Behaviors *called* aggressive range from attack and killing to fantasy stories told about pictures. In Table 12-1 (Beck, 1978) is a set of situations where aggression might or might not be involved. Check the list for those which you think are aggressive. Why do you think so? Do other people agree with you completely? There is almost certain disagreement on some.

If we define aggression to include *all actual harm* we would have to include Item 1 (Boy Scout) and Item 3 (Flower Pot) as well as Item 21 (Hired Killer). If both actual harm and *intent to harm* are considered necessary to define aggression, we eliminate Items 1 and 3, among others. If *just* intent to harm is considered sufficient, even though the act may have failed (Item 2, Assassin Misses Target), another set emerges as aggressive. If we *exclude food-getting* (Item 4) or an act committed under someone else's orders (Item 6) the set changes again. No single circumstance seems to satisfactorily characterize everything that might be considered aggressive. This is in part because what is considered aggressive also depends on some very arbitrary social standards that fluctuate from time to time and place to place.

For lower animals, several kinds of aggressive behaviors (such as predatory, between-male, fear-induced, pain-induced, territorial defense, maternal, sex-related, and for reward) have been distinguished, and may possibly have different brain circuits. For humans, however, it is doubtful that such neat categories can be distinguished biologically. The human capacities for learning and reasoning may override simpler, more direct responses.

Intent and Aggression. A common definition of aggression for humans is *aggressive behaviors are those intended to do physical or psychological harm to someone.* Intent is the crux of many court proceedings. Did the defendant, with malice aforethought, intend to kill the victim? What, however, do we mean by intent? We may say that intent is strongly indicated, if not completely proven, when a person has several options and *chooses* that one which leads to someone's harm. We may physically harm someone by hitting them or psychologically harm them by damaging their self-esteem. We may, for example, make "cutting" remarks. Lest we bog down in problems of definition we shall go on to look at what people have actually been studying under the heading of aggression.

stimulus-aroused aggression

The Frustration-Aggression Hypothesis. Though Freud made the first modern statement that frustration leads to aggression, a group of Yale psycholo-

table 12–1

aggressive behaviors. Different behaviors in the following list might or might not be considered aggressive depending on how you define aggression. Which ones do you think are aggressive and why?

1. A Boy Scout helping an old lady across the street accidentally trips her and she sprains her ankle.
2. An assassin attempts to kill a presidential candidate but his shot misses.
3. A housewife knocks a flower pot off a fifth story window ledge and it hits a passerby.
4. A farmer kills a chicken for dinner.
5. In a debate, one person belittles another's qualifications.
6. A soldier presses a button that fires a nuclear missile and kills thousands of people he cannot even see.
7. A policeman trying to break up a riot hits a rioter in the head with a club and knocks him unconscious.
8. A cat stalks, catches, tosses around, and eventually kills a mouse.
9. A wife accuses her husband of having an affair and he retorts that after living with her anyone would have an affair.
10. A frightened boy, caught in the act of stealing and trying to escape, shoots his discoverer.
11. One child takes a toy away from another, making him cry.
12. A man unable to get into his locked car kicks in the side of the door.
13. A man pays 25¢ to beat an old car with an iron bar, which he does vigorously.
14. A football player blocks another player from behind (clipping) and breaks his leg.
15. A businessman hires a professional killer to "take care of" a business rival.
16. A woman carefully plots how she will kill her husband, then does so.
17. Two students get into a drunken brawl and one hits the other with a beer bottle.
18. A businessman works vigorously to improve his business and drive out the competition.
19. On the Rorschach inkblot test, a hospitalized mental patient is scored as being highly aggressive, although he has never actually harmed anyone.
20. A young boy talks a lot about how he is going to beat up others, but never does it.
21. A hired killer successfully completes his job.

(From Beck, 1978, p. 286. Reprinted with permission of publisher.)

gists (Dollard et al., 1939) developed the statement into a more testable theory. Many of their ideas are still widely used. Among practicing clinical psychologists it is considered a good hunch to look for prior frustration when an individual appears overly aggressive. It is recognized, however, that frustration is not the sole cause of aggression nor is aggression the sole result of frustration.

Dollard et al. used the following example. Four-year-old James hears

OH, I'M NOT INTENDING TO DO ANY HARM. I'M JUST PROVIDING A LITTLE UNEXPECTED EXCITEMENT!

A broken vending machine sets up a frustration-aggression situation familiar to almost everyone.

the ice-cream truck bell and says he wants ice cream. Building around this situation we have the following concepts basic to the theory.

1. *Instigation.* The bell is an *instigator* for the response of trying to get ice cream. Instigators can be external (bell) or internal (such as hunger).

2. *Goal Response.* A goal response is any act which *reduces the instigation* to make the instigated response. If James eats the ice cream he is less likely to ask for ice cream again immediately.

3. *Interference. Prevention* of the goal response is interference. If we bought James an ice cream cone and then did not let him eat it this would be interference.

4. *Frustration.* This is an *internal state* produced by interference with a goal-directed response. If we interfered with James' getting the ice cream this would produce frustration.

5. *Aggression.* A response to frustration, aggression is behavior *intended to hurt* someone. *Frustration is thus an instigation to an aggressive response, and aggression reduces the instigation to be aggressive.* Note that if the aggressive behavior itself is frustrated, this is further instigation to be aggressive. The strength of instigation to aggression depends on how much the goal is wanted, the degree of frustration, and the number of prior frustrations (as suggested by the saying "the straw that broke the camel's back").

6. *Inhibition.* Not all instigations lead to aggression. We aren't as aggressive if we expect to be *punished* for it. Few arrested motorists jeer at police officers, and few students rail at their professors in the classroom. Instigation to aggression and anticipation of punishment are in conflict, and as with other conflicts, the strongest tendency (to act or not to act) wins out.

7. *Direct versus Indirect Aggression.* Because of the threat of punishment our aggression may not be aimed at the actual source of frustration (direct). Instead, it may

be *indirect* or *displaced.* Such displaced aggression may be a change in the *object* of the aggression or in the *form* of the aggressive behavior. The person who comes home from a frustrating day at the office, yells at the children, and kicks the cat exemplifies a change in object. Verbal aggression may be a change in form. In highly totalitarian states, indirect aggression is often shown by making jokes about the government, but only very privately! If *any* form of aggression directed toward others is *too* threatening, a person might aggress against himself, such as hitting his head against a wall.

8. *Catharsis.* Aggressive acts are assumed to reduce further instigation to aggression. This is called *catharsis* (after a Greek word for cleansing, or purging). Bobo dolls and sponge rubber bats are sold with the express claim that it is good for the child (or adult) to release his or her aggression harmlessly via these objects. They provide a form of catharsis. It is assumed that releasing aggression this way will reduce the instigation to more serious kinds of aggression. We shall return to the catharsis idea later, because it comes up in several contexts.

Impulsive Aggression (Berkowitz). Leonard Berkowitz (e.g., 1974) has maintained that environmental situations provoke attack behaviors that occur "impulsively." Most homicides, for example, are not premeditated, but are spontaneous and passionate, often arising from disagreements about relatively trivial matters. The threat of capital punishment has little deterrent effect in these cases because in the rage of the moment the consequences of killing simply are not anticipated. Impulsive aggression may be aroused by internal or external stimuli. "Internal stimuli" would include a variety of things, including, for example, pain or passion-raising thoughts.

The Weapons Effect. Suppose you were asked to serve in an experiment studying physiological reactions to the stress produced by mild electric shocks. You and another subject are suppposed to evaluate each other's performance on the task of listing in five minutes the ideas a publicity agent might use to increase product sales. You are to evaluate each other by giving each other electric shocks. You go into separate rooms and you get evaluated first. You get seven shocks of the maximum possible eight. Not very good. In your experi-

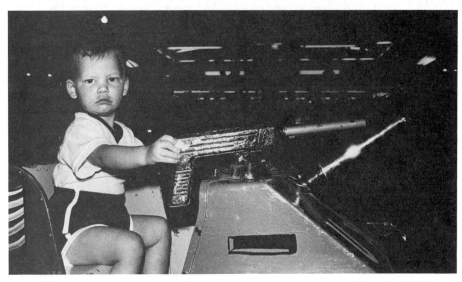

(Photo by Bill Henry)

mental room there is a telegraph key for delivering shocks to your partner, along with a rifle and pistol left by a previous experimenter from an unrelated experiment. You deliver six shocks to your partner as evaluation of his performance.

You, of course, were in just one of a number of experimental conditions and your "partner" was really the experimenter's assistant. Your experimental condition (one of seven different ones) was intended to (1) anger you by giving you a large number of shocks, and (2) provide aggression-arousing cues (the guns). Both of these are expected to make you more aggressive so that you would give more shocks than if you were less angry or did not have cues for aggressive behavior. Table 12–2 summarizes the results of this experiment

table 12–2

The joint effects of being shocked and seeing weapons on aggressive responses. Average number of shocks given in return for one or seven shocks received under various experimental conditions.

condition	number of shocks received by the subject	
	1	7
Associated Weapons	2.60	6.07
Unassociated Weapons	2.20	5.67
No object	3.07	4.67
Badminton Rackets[a]	—	4.60

[a] There was no one-shock group with badminton rackets.
(Berkowitz & LePage, 1967. Reprinted with permission of publisher.)

by Berkowitz and Le Page (1967). Subjects *getting* seven shocks gave back more shocks than did those getting only one shock. This supports the anger-arousal part of the hypothesis. Those subjects seeing the guns gave back more shocks than those not seeing the guns, supporting the cue-arousal part of the hypothesis.

Berkowitz and his associates have varied many conditions with this general procedure, and some of their results are as follows:

- If the "other subject" is associated with violence, he or she gets shocked more often.
- If the "other subject" is perceived as an unsympathetic character, that person gets more shocks.
- Subjects frustrated by working a difficult jigsaw puzzle gave more shocks to the "other subject."
- Presentation of loud noise (unrelated arousal) stimulates more shocks.
- A brief sex film prior to the experiment led to more shocks to an antagonistic partner.
- Justification for violence in a movie shown prior to the experiment led to more shocks.

Not all experimenters have been able to reproduce these effects, and there have been other interpretations than those of Berkowitz. Nevertheless, the evidence has been compelling enough to warrant attention because of the implications of this research for the control of aggression.

Victims May Provoke Attack. The victim of an attack may actually provoke the attack upon him or herself. Wolfgang (1957) found that a fourth of almost 600 homicides he studied were provoked by the victim. Most murders are committed by people who know the victim well, the victim is often a relative, and the homicide is likely to have been preceded by an argument

which escalated into the killing. One of the best ways to avoid being attacked is not to do anything to provoke it. One argument for gun control is that even a robbery victim is less likely to get shot if he or she does not have a gun to provoke attack by an intruder. An acquaintance of this author was killed by a robber because after the small store where he was manager had been robbed, *he followed the robber outside into the darkness carrying a gun.* The robber thereupon shot and killed him.

instrumental aggression

Instrumental aggression is harmful behavior rewarded by something not inherently related to the aggression. The prize fighter may fight for money, not because he wants to hurt somebody. Instrumental aggression may therefore be quite different from the more emotional impulsive aggression. We can look at intent again. If I intend to make five dollars and have to hit somebody to get it, this is different than if I intend to hit somebody because I want to hurt them. Johnson (1972) noted that in 1969 there were 6.5 times as many property crimes as crimes against persons, and many of the latter were incidental to obtaining money. In a number of laboratory experiments both adults or children have acted more aggressively if rewarded for doing so.

Obedient Aggression. In this century alone, many major atrocities have been committed around the world. These include the Nazi attempts to exterminate the Jews; the terror of the Stalinist regime in Russia; Japanese atrocities in World War II; civil strife in Ireland, Israel, Pakistan, Chile, and various African countries; and the My Lai massacre by Americans in Viet Nam. There is no discrimination according to race, creed, or national origin among those who commit such crimes. The question is, Who is responsible? After World War II it was very difficult to find anybody guilty of the murder of millions of Jews. It is usually said that the "little guys" who pull the triggers are the scapegoats for the "big guys" who give the orders.

Stanley Milgram (1974) made this into a laboratory experiment. How far, he asked, will a normal person go in following repugnant orders? By advertising in newspapers for people to be subjects he obtained a much better cross section of subjects than in the typical college student experiment. The subjects were supposed to give a "learner" electric shocks of increasing intensity every time the learner made a mistake in memorizing a list of words. The "learner" was the experimenter's assistant, a middle-age friendly person whom the subjects met prior to the experiment. The fake shock apparatus was clearly marked in thirty levels, ranging from 15 to 450 volts, and such written labels as "Slight Shock" (15 to 60 volts), "Danger: Severe Shock" (375 to 420 volts), and "XXX" (435 to 450 volts). The learner followed a set routine: He was wrong about 75 percent of the time and complained how painful the ever-increasing "shocks" were. The learner was in a different room than the subject. The subjects looked to the experimenter for guidance, but were told to continue and even to treat failure to respond as an error and to give another shock.

Before he began these experiments Milgram asked his students and colleagues what percent of subjects they thought might continue shocking the learner right up to the highest level. The estimates averaged only three percent, but in the very first experiment *no subject stopped below 300 volts* and twenty-six of forty subjects went the limit to 450 volts. Various checks indicated the subjects really did believe they were giving highly painful shocks. These results are astonishing in their suggestion of how easy it is to get one human to hurt another, especially since the subjects were not just jaded college students who did not believe anyone would really get hurt in an experiment.

Subsequent experiments generally found the same results under the same conditions. Other factors are important, however. For example, the closer the contact between a subject and the learner (for instance, in separate rooms without any contact, hearing the learner's voice, being in the same room, or touching) the *less* likely the subject is to give the strongest shock.

There has been a wide range of public reaction to this research, which was dramatized on prime-time TV. Some people considered the experiments dehumanizing to the subjects and said that the results were therefore not worth the experiments. Milgram's research turned out after the fact to be highly controversial and to raise questions which Milgram certainly never fully anticipated. We cannot dismiss the importance of the topic which Milgram addressed, however, nor the dramatic effects he reported.

SHAME ON YOU PSYCHOLOGISTS FOR TRYING TO SHOW IT IS EASY TO GET PEOPLE TO ACT MEAN! PEOPLE ARE **NOT** MEAN. WE ARE NICE... AND I'LL SOCK YOU IN THE NOSE IF YOU WON'T AGREE WITH ME!

Social Learning and the Modeling of Aggression. Modeling and imitation are particularly important problems when we consider the time spent viewing television. The role of TV as an instigator or reducer of aggression is a lively and controversial topic. The TV industry itself seems to be of two minds, selling advertising on the basis of TV's effectiveness in changing one behavior (purchasing) but denying influence on another (aggression).

In particular instances, TV plots have been closely imitated. A hoax following the story line of a TV program was perpetrated on an airline. A bomb was said to be planted on an airliner and set to go off at an altitude less than 5,000 feet. The airliner was then rerouted to Denver, Colorado which has an airport above 5,000 feet. Even more violent instances, including throwing gasoline on a woman and setting her on fire, have been reported to be copied from a television plot.

Bandura, Ross, & Ross (1963b) compared aggressive behaviors of nursery school children after observing aggressive behavior by live adults, a film of adults, or a film of cartoon characters (adults dressed in cat costumes). A control group was not shown the aggressive sequence. The groups were further subdivided according to whether the models were of the same or of a different sex from the child. The main aggressive behavior was hitting a three-foot tall vinyl "Bobo" doll. The model sat on the doll, hit it with his or her fist, or a mallet, or threw it up in the air and kicked it about the room. The model also said things like "Sock him in the nose" or "Hit him down." Such very specific things said or done by the model were intended to be ones that could clearly be identified as imitative on the part of the child. The children were then (individually) mildly frustrated by being allowed to play a little while with an attractive toy, then told they could not play with it any more but could instead play with some toys in a different room. These included the Bobo doll, as well as a toy gun. The children were scored for the occurrence and kind of aggressive activities they were doing every five seconds for twenty minutes. The results are shown in Figure 12–1.

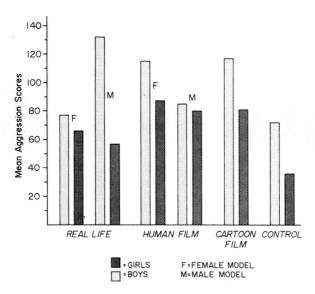

figure 12–1. Average aggression scores for boys and girls who had seen aggressive behavior by live models, film with human models, or film with cartoon models. The control group had not seen any of these. All experimental groups were more aggressive in the test situation than was the control group, and boys were generally more aggressive than girls. (Adapted from Bandura, Ross & Ross, 1963, p. 6. Used with permission of publisher.)

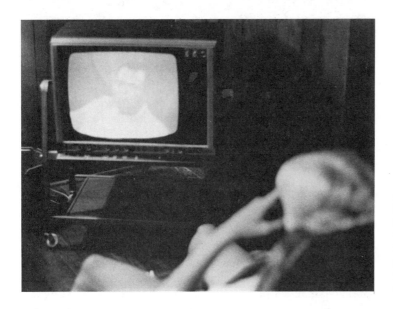

Does watching violence on television increase or decrease violent actions by viewers? The "cathartic" view says it decreases violence, but the "social learning" view says that it increases violence.

We see in Figure 12–1 that (1) all the aggressive-model groups were more aggressive than the control group; (2) boys were generally more aggressive than girls; (3) sex of the model was important, (4) girls were more aggressive following observation of female aggressive models and boys were more aggressive with male models, and (5) it did not make a significant difference whether the models were live, film, or cartoon characters. In another experiment, the same authors (Bandura, Ross & Ross, 1963a) showed that children were more aggressive if they saw the model rewarded and less if the model were punished. Though the children correctly identified the character as "good" or "bad," they nevertheless *preferred the aggressive model if the model succeeded* but not if the model failed. The children were very frank in their reasoning. They preferred the successful aggressive model because it was the one who got what he or she wanted. The children in these experiments came from the Stanford University Nursery School and could hardly be considered deprived or "sick" prior to the experiment.

A major study conducted over a ten-year period (Eron, Lefkowitz, Huesmann, & Walder, 1972) compared amount of aggression and amount of violent television viewing of several hundred children in the third grade with their violence and television viewing just out of high school ten years later. The conclusion was that preference for watching violent TV in the third grade was a significant factor in aggressive behavior ten years later. We assume, of course, there was TV viewing of a similar nature in the intervening ten years.

Other researchers have disputed findings like those in the experiments described above, but there does seem to be a developing consensus that

- Modeling of violence increases the occurrence of violence in laboratory experiments and there is some imitation of television.

- Television programs show a tremendous amount of violence.
- Watching violent television is related to subsequent aggressive behaviors.

This seems to be a sufficiently strong chain of evidence to warrant consideration of control over children's TV viewing. This is a matter for parents to control, however, not the government or the industry itself. The industry is sensitive to public viewing habits and if these change, programming will change.

control of aggression

Biological-Frustration versus Social Learning Views. Konrad Lorenz (1966) considered aggression to be instinctive and to "well up" inside the individual and then erupt into aggressive behavior. This is very similar to the frustration-anger point of view previously discussed in this chapter. Some animals, Lorenz argued, have developed inhibitions to aggression, so that fighting within a species does not lead a species to destroy itself. For various reasons, people do not have these inhibitions, but they do have aggressive energy building up and will therefore aggress against each other on a massive scale, says Lorenz. His solution is to provide alternative outlets (catharsis via displaced aggressive activities) so that the aggressive energy does not build up too much. Such displacement activities as athletic contests should then be cathartic.

The alternative view, held by social learning theorists, is that aggressive behavior is frequently rewarded and that aggression is more likely to increase because it is rewarded than decrease because it is cathartic. If either of these opposing views were entirely correct, to act on the wrong one could be disastrous. There is the possibility that both views may be partly correct, depending on circumstances. One does question the cathartic effect of observing sports, however, when 300 fans were killed in a riot at a championship soccer game in Peru in 1964.

Reducing Internal Arousal by Nonaggressive Behaviors. If a person is moved to anger, is aggressive behavior the only means of reducing this anger?

Hokanson (e.g., 1970) used blood pressure as a measure of arousal and drop in blood pressure as a measure of "catharsis." He found that aggressive responses in males were followed by rapid drops in blood pressure to normal levels. Females, however, showed a more rapid blood pressure drop when they made *friendly* responses to antagonistic behavior on the part of the experimenter. Further studies indicated this was not necessarily specific to females, but is (or can be) learned. Hokanson says (1970, p. 80), "Any response which serves to terminate, reduce, or avoid noxious stimulation from others will acquire cathartic-like properties." In a nutshell, we can effectively cope with a threatening (aggression-arousing) situation by virtually any behavior we have learned is effective. Modeling and imitation can thus be very important for learning non-aggressive responses to threat.

biological factors in the control of aggression

Brain Mechanisms. The limbic system and the hypothalamus are particularly important for the arousal or modulation of aggressive behavior. It is possible to increase or decrease aggressive behavior in animals by destruction or direct electrical stimulation of the relevant brain areas. Areas involved in perception and memory are also important, as well as the limbic areas more intimately related to emotional arousal.

Psychosurgery. Psychosurgery refers to brain operations intended to change a person's feelings or behavior. Frontal lobotomy, an operation appropriately scorned in Ken Kesey's book *One Flew Over The Cuckoo's Nest* (1962) is the separation of the frontal lobes of the brain from the rest of the brain. In spite of the rather widespread use of this operation between 1936 and 1951 (on about 20,000 patients worldwide), there never was a sound basis for performing the operation. Early reports of its effectiveness in reducing irrational fears, obsessional behavior, and so on were overstated and the side effects (loss of memory, apathy) were devastating. The use of drugs has now ended any demand for such gross surgery, and where psychosurgery is performed at all it is restricted to very limited parts of the brain.

There is an important ethical question involved here: Do we know enough about the causes of aggressive behavior to do brain damage that cannot be repaired and which may have severe side effects (such as problems with learning, memory, and emotion)? We have already seen that such factors as learning, frustration, and pain also influence aggression and these are *not* neatly pinpointed in the brain. This is not to say an identifiable brain problem never exists. Sometimes a tumor, or scar tissue from injury, may be found. These can be removed by very finely localized lesions without wholesale destruction of other parts of the brain. It is also possible to implant electrodes permanently into the brain so that a patient who feels an "uncontrollable" aggressive urge coming on can stimulate his or her own brain and reduce the potential aggressive behavior. This is far removed from the crude surgery of the prefontal lobotomy.

Mark and Ervin (1970) and Valenstein (1973) have booklength discussions of the problems here.

Genetics. In one sense aggression is obviously related to genetics: Predatory animals are more aggressive than prey animals, and we can selectively breed either vicious watchdogs or children's pets. More recent concern has been expressed over a particular chromosome abnormality, however. Humans normally have either a pair of X (female) chromosomes or one X and one Y (male) chromosome. The XX individual becomes female and the XY becomes male. Sometimes a baby gets an extra Y chromosome and is XYY. Some initial reports suggested an unusually high percentage of XYY men in prison and the theory quickly developed that this "supermale" was genetically more aggressive. Two extensive reviews of the literature, however, reached the following conclusions: (1) "No consistent personality or behavior constellation has been successfully predicted from the XYY complement" (Owen, 1972), and (2) "No evidence has been found that men with [the XYY] chromosome complement are especially aggressive" (Witken et. al., 1976). Present evidence, then, does not appear to warrant any special consideration of XYY individuals (whom it is possible to identify), and arbitrary labeling of the XYY child as *potentially* antisocial is inconsistent with any principle of being innocent until proven guilty.

Sex Differences, Hormones, and Aggression. In many species males are more aggressive than females. The hormonal basis for this is indicated by such facts as that males are more aggressive during the mating season when male sex hormones are at their highest level and that castration (as with a gelding steer or horse) produces a less aggressive animal.

There is also reported to be a disproportionate incidence of irritability and antisocial behavior of human females during premenstrual and menstrual periods. Possible reasons for this are (1) lower progesterone levels, (2) an increase of the adrenal hormone *aldosterone,* (3) low blood sugar level, and (4) social learning; women may learn they are supposed to be irritable before or during their periods. We thus see a host of individual, social, and biological factors related to aggressive behavior in either males or females and not any simple cause-effect relation.

when punishment backfires: the punishment-aggression cycle

Punishment is intended to reduce or eliminate some behavior and if administered along with the opportunity to do something else, it can be very effective (see Chapter Two). However, punishment *may* directly arouse aggressive behavior. The Catch 22 is this: If you are trying to get rid of aggressive behavior by punishing it, you may in fact increase it instead. For example, restrained monkeys will bite a rubber ball dangling in front of their face if shocked. Shocking them as punishment for biting the ball simply induces them to bite the ball more.[1] Human children given excessive physical punishment also tend to be more aggressive in their activities. Similarly, prison punishment for aggression may increase the very behavior the punishment is supposed to inhibit.

Altruism Behavior: Helping Each Other

We now turn from harmful behavior to helping. *Helping, altruism,* and *prosocial behavior* are essentially equivalent terms referring to behavior intended to benefit others without obvious return benefit. The question is, Under what conditions are people more or less likely to help someone else?

bystander apathy

In 1964 a young woman named Kitty Genovese was returning from work at about 3:00 A.M. to her home in Queens (New York City) when she was attacked by a man with a knife. Over a half-hour period she was stabbed again and again and screamed repeatedly. At least thirty-eight neighbors watched from their windows without so much as calling the police even as they saw someone being killed before their very eyes.

The horror of this scene is described in virtually every discussion of prosocial behavior because of the dramatic *failure* of anyone to help. An immediate interpretation was that "big city people" had become callous and indifferent to the plight of anyone else. This may be part of the story, but not the whole explanation. There appear to be several factors at work.

The Presence of Other Bystanders. Latane and Darley (1970), two of the foremost researchers in this field, argue that it is the presence of other bystanders that makes it less likely that any one person will help. They staged elaborate "emergencies," in laboratories and in public places, and observed bystander behavior. For example, they had smoke pour into a room where students were working, arranged for subjects to hear an apparent accident over an intercom, staged an epileptic seizure, and pulled a fake robbery in a liquor store (with the manager's permission). In general, their results were

---

[1] This research received considerable notoriety when awarded one of Sen. William Proxmire's famous "Golden Fleece" awards. Senator Proxmire makes political hay by picking strange sounding titles of research projects (without bothering to find out what the projects are about) and ridiculing the projects and the government for supporting them. In this instance, Ronald Hutchison, the researcher, sued Senator Proxmire and won his case in the United States Supreme Court. The case hinged largely on whether a researcher is a public figure just because he or she publishes research results. The court ruled that, unlike a politician, a researcher is not automatically a public figure open to ridicule.

consistent in showing that bystanders were more likely to help if alone than if someone else were present. They proposed three complementary explanations.

1. *Audience Inhibition.* If others are present we are slower to act because we are concerned about their evaluation of our behavior. Perhaps that smoke is not really an emergency and we would look foolish if we treated it as such.
2. *Social Influence.* We watch others to see how they are acting. If *everyone* is trying to be "cool" and nonchalant, then a whole group may fool itself into believing there is no emergency.
3. *Diffusion of Responsibility.* Psychologically, we may feel that if there is a single person present at an emergency there is 100 percent necessity for that person to do something; if there are two people it drops to 50 percent, 33 percent for three and so on. When more people are present there is less pressure for any single individual to act. Hence, nobody may act.

In an experiment varying several of the above factors, Latane and Darley found that if a person was alone, there was a 95 percent chance that person would help. This dropped to 84 percent if there was someone else present. The percentage dropped to 50 if the subjects could see another person present who failed to respond to the emergency and if they believed the other person (a research assistant) could also see them. There is, fortunately, also evidence that people *will* help in the presence of others. Piliavin, Rodin, and Piliavin (1969) faked a collapse on a subway train and found that 70 percent of the time bystanders immediately helped. The authors believed that the reason for the difference between this and some of the previous research was that the people on the train could clearly see there *was* an emergency. Also, it was not possible for them to believe that some unseen person might be going for help.

Costs and Benefits of Helping. As we have seen, people weigh the relative costs and benefits of getting involved with any particular activity. Intervening in situations involving others carries the potential costs of inconvenience, unpleasantness and actual danger. The costs of *not* helping may be feelings of guilt and possible scorn from others. Benefits of helping may be a feeling of greater self-esteem, praise from others, or thanks. We should not lose sight of the observational fact that sometimes people will jump in and help somebody without thinking at all.

Researchers studying some of the costs and benefits have found, for example, that

- Bystanders are *more* likely to help someone neat and well-dressed (low cost as compared to helping an apparent derelict or drunk or trouble-maker).
- Bystanders are *more* likely to help someone with a cane rather than an apparent drunk carrying what appears to be a bottle in a brown bag.
- Bystanders are *less* likely to help if there is apparently some person more capable present (a person in a white hospital uniform).

characteristics of the helper

When we ask *who* is likely to help in emergency situations we find personality variables important. Schwartz (1968) has developed an *Ascription of Responsibility Scale* (the AR Scale). High scorers tend to ascribe responsibility to themselves whereas low scorers tend to put responsibility onto others. It is found that high scorers are more likely to take action in the typical fake-emergency experiment and are less inhibited in the presence of others than are low scorers (Schwartz & Clausen, 1970). People who feel *competent* are also more likely to help, even if this feeling has just previously been engendered in an experimental situation (by success at an experimental task, for instance). It has also been suggested, however, that people who have *low* self-esteem may be more likely to help if they can thereby raise their self-esteem.

Finally, it doesn't hurt to be in a good mood. Christmas music and decorations help foster Christmas charity, and experiments show that feeding people or letting them find money increases the chance they will subsequently help somebody.

characteristics of the victim

A reputable appearing victim generally has a better chance of getting helped than a disreputable victim, but people are also more likely to help others who are like themselves. Enswiller, Deaux, and Willits (1971) had a "hippie-looking" person and a more conservative looking person solicit money from "hippies" and "straights" on the street. The person-on-the-street was more likely to help the solicitor who was more like him or herself.

There is also the so-called *just world hypothesis*. Some people believe that others bring their problems on themselves; the world is fair and people get what they deserve. Not everyone believes this, of course, so we are dealing with both the characteristics of the helper (whether he or she believes the just-world hypothesis) and of the victim (whether he or she is dirty, poorly dressed, etc.). Some people are then unwilling to help others because they believe that people in trouble are getting what they deserve. This attitude is frequently expressed with regard to welfare: People on welfare are poor because they are lazy and won't work; if they would just go out and get jobs we wouldn't need welfare. This runs contrary to fact. Welfare is very largely to the elderly, the disabled, and to mothers with small children. The "loafers on welfare" view is nevertheless a widely shared "just world" belief with strong political and social implications.

Victims clearly *dependent* on the helper also get more help. An obvious case is a baby in distress. Or, if a boat capsized and you were the only person in a position to help those in the water (they are dependent on you) you would be more likely to help than if a coast guard cutter were rapidly approaching (Harrison, 1976, p. 326).

Finally, the *norm of reciprocity* comes into play. This says that if a person has *given* help to others in the past, then this "helping person" is more likely to *get* help in the future (reciprocation). Goranson and Berkowitz (1966) gave experimental subjects the opportunity to help a laboratory supervisor. They found that (1) if the supervisor had previously refused to help the subjects, the subjects were less likely to help her; and (2) subjects were more likely to reciprocate if they believed the supervisor's earlier help had been voluntary rather than mandatory. We are more likely to return freely given favors.

situational influences

Severity. If the severity of the situation were an overriding influence, Kitty Genovese might have gotten some help. The costs associated with helping seem particularly important here. For example, in one study a bloodied victim was less likely than a nonbloodied victim to receive direct help. The bloodied victim did get more help indirectly, however, such as by a phone call.

Modeling. Bryan and Test (1967) had two disabled cars along the side of a busy street. Under one condition someone was helping the first woman driver, but under another condition not. Fifty-eight motorists stopped to help the second driver when they saw the first being aided, as compared to thirty-five when the first driver was not being aided. Similar results were obtained with people who saw another person donate to Salvation Army solicitors. If the model is *too* generous, however, it may scare off potential donors who might be embarrassed about their own small contributions.

Number of Bystanders. As we saw in the earlier discussion of this point, the more bystanders there are, the less likely it is that any one of them will help.

The Setting. Being a Good Samaritan may be discouraged for many reasons. Physicians and nurses may refrain from spontaneously helping accident victims for fear of malpractice suits. Within large cities there is also an element of trying to keep a certain amount of social distance between oneself and others, as a reaction to the amount of sheer physical crowding. In urban areas like New York or Boston people tend to scurry about their business, to be somewhat mistrustful, to lock their doors, and to be careful for whom they open the door. These precautions may be realistic, since these urban dwellers may stand a good chance of getting robbed.

The great amount of activity in a city may also make it more difficult to attract anyone's attention and therefore more difficult to solicit help. Darley and Bateson (1973) found that if subjects were told to be someplace in a hurry they were less likely to stop and help someone in apparent difficulty. The subjects were theology students told to go to a lecture on Good Samaritanism!

theories of prosocial behavior

Freud's Psychoanalytic Theory. Freud divided personality into three parts—*id, ego,* and *superego.* The id refers to such "basic" drives as hunger, thirst, sex, and aggression. Superego is equivalent to "conscience." Ego is the rational part of the personality that tries to "referee" between the demands of the id for immediate gratification and the hesitancy on the part of the superego. These are not separately identifiable parts of the brain but are Freud's metaphorical way of looking at the mind. Our interest here is in superego, or conscience.

According to Freud, the superego develops as a child learns values (what is good and bad) from his or her parents and culture. These values are "internalized" and become part of the individual, serving as ideals and internal sources of reward and punishment. In a sense, the child develops a set of imaginary parents who, like Jiminy Cricket in *Pinnochio,* direct the child's behavior. If we do something we have learned is "wrong," we may be punished by feeling guilt and anxiety. If we do something that is "right" we are rewarded by feeling good. If certain ideals are strongly internalized we may, for example, do almost anything rather than lie or cheat. Martyrs appear to be people who would give up their lives rather than their ideals.

Reinforcement Theory. Reinforcement theory is similar to psychoanalytic theory, but reinforcement theorists would tend to emphasize reward and punishment for *specific* behaviors. Altruistic behavior would in this view occur only if it had been rewarded in the past. The anticipation of future rewards and punishments for helping (or not helping) are of course also important. Anticipations of punishment (inconvenience, possible danger) are weighted against possible rewards (being thanked, getting money, or intangible reward in the hereafter).

Moss and Page (1972) studied the effect of reward for helping on future helping. They approached passersby on the street and asked directions to a particular department store. The strangers were either rewarded with a smile and a thank you, were punished by being rudely told the directions did not make sense, or were left neutral (with just an "okay"). Farther down the street a female confederate dropped a small bag as the same passerby approached. Only 40 percent of the just-punished individuals picked up the bag for her, but 82 percent of the neutral subjects and 85 percent of the rewarded subjects did so. The rude response clearly had a detrimental effect, but the neutral subjects were about as helpful as the rewarded. Perhaps the simple acknowledgement of their previous help was sufficient reward to carry over.

Kohlberg's Theory of Moral Judgment. Kohlberg (e.g., 1964) has proposed a theory of the development of moral judgment which depends on the increasing ability of the child to understand complex situations. **There are six stages** of development, summarized in Table 12–3. The progression is from the very young child who obeys adults because the adults mete out punishment, through concern with the feelings and thoughts of others, through a very mature level of conscience which actually is more influential than society's laws. The last stage, which some individuals never reach, is important for any change in a system of justice. It does not represent a flagrant disregard for all of society's rules, but it is concerned with the basis of these rules and their moral correctness. For example, someone may intentionally break a law in order to test its constitutionality in court. This is common practice.

Less common, but of the same level of morality, are those who burned their draft cards during the Vietnam era on the grounds that we were engaged

table 12–3

Kohlberg's (1967) theory of stages of moral development

preconventional level	
	Stage One The child obeys because adults are powerful and can punish those who misbehave.
A young child is primarily influenced by the consequences of what he or she does.	Stage Two The child attempts to obtain need satisfaction in a way that will lead to rewards.
conventional level	
	Stage Three There is a desire to be a good boy or girl so that others will offer approval.
An older child becomes aware of and concerned about what others expect and tries to behave in a conventional way to meet these expectations.	Stage Four There is a developing notion of doing one's duty, respecting authority, and preserving the social order because such things are accepted as right and proper
postconventional level	
	Stage Five The person begins to think about the rights of others, the general welfare, and the laws adopted by the majority.
As maturity approaches, an individual becomes oriented toward abstract moral values and toward what he or she personally believes to be right.	Stage Six One's self-chosen standards of justice and one's own conscience have more effect on behavior than society's actual rules and laws.

(From Kohlberg, in Sizer, 1967. Reprinted with permission of publisher.)

in an illegal and immoral war. Many of these people fully expected to be prosecuted for burning their cards but did so anyway as a matter of conscience. There are many historical examples of this kind, including the 1960s "sit ins" which started in Greensboro, North Carolina as a protest against the refusal of a department store to serve blacks at its lunch counter. Such nonviolent methods of breaking the law as a matter of principle have been effective around the world.

Latane and Darley's Cognitive Analysis. Latane and Darley (1970) approached the problem of helping behavior from a perception-cognition point of view. They suggest that the potential helper has to go through five steps.

1. You must *perceive* that something noteworthy is happening. If you do not hear gunshots, you are not going to rush to help someone who might be shot.

2. You must *interpret* what you have perceived. Having heard several loud sharp sounds, you might interpret them as gunshots or as a car backfiring. Only if you interpret your perception as a real danger are you likely to help someone, otherwise you might appear foolish.

3. If you correctly interpret that someone needs help you must *decide* that it is *your responsibility* to help. If you think it is someone else's responsibility you may do nothing.

4. You must decide *what* to do. Should you call the police or fire department, take things into your own hands, or what?

5. You must actually *do* what you have decided is the best action.

Each of these five steps is influenced by many factors we have already discussed.

increasing prosocial behavior

If prosocial behavior is "good," then increasing its occurrence should also be good. The following suggestions are made by Baron and Byrne (1977).

1. *Rearing children with prosocial values.* Studies have shown that altruistic children also have at least one altruistic parent. This suggests the importance of *modeling* on the part of the parent, as well as *rewarding* the child for prosocial behaviors.

2. *Type of behavior control.* Children whose parents depend mainly on physical punishment for discipline learn to follow the rules, whatever the rules are. If the rules change from day to day, the behavior will switch correspondingly, even if the rules become completely reversed. Children reared in a less punitive atmosphere are more likely to develop strong *internal* standards of right and wrong.

3. *Teaching responsible behavior.* People may refrain from helping simply because they do not know what to do. We actually train people how to act in emergency situations in very few ways, such as fire drills. We teach a few other

things (such as first aid) on a relatively small scale. What *should* you do if you saw somebody in distress? Baron and Byrne suggest the possibility of teaching by use of simulated emergencies, role playing, or having films or television programs illustrating prosocial behaviors. In the past, children's textbooks have been important sources of moral learning, and there is no reason why Buster Bear could not do cardiopulmonary resuscitation in a children's book.

SUMMARY

1. Aggression is *defined* as behavior intended to do physical or psychological harm to someone.

2. The *frustration-aggression hypothesis* says that interference with goal-directed behavior causes frustration, an internal state which may instigate aggression. These instigations, however, may be inhibited by threat of punishment, or displaced onto objects or persons who are not the source of frustration. Aggressive behavior is said to produce *catharsis,* a lessening of the frustration.

3. *Impulsive aggression* may be aroused by internal or environmental events and is emotional, with little consideration of possible consequences of acting aggressively.

4. The *weapons effect* suggests that stimuli which are cues for aggression (such as guns) may increase aggressive behavior.

5. *Instrumental aggression* is harmful behavior (such as prize fighting) where there is a reward for the aggression other than the aggression itself. *Obedient aggression* is aggressive behavior carried out under orders from someone else, such as in the military.

6. *Modeling of violence* in laboratory experiments increases the subsequent amount of violent behavior on the part of children who imitate what they have seen modeled. Similar findings seem to occur with television viewing, although there are strongly opposing views on this subject.

7. *Social learning theories* say that aggression which is encouraged or rewarded leads to further aggression, not to catharsis or a lessening of aggression.

8. In the *brain,* the *limbic system* and *hypothalamus* are important in the regulation of aggressive behavior. Very extreme aggressive behavior is now more effectively controlled by drugs than by surgical procedures. Any psychosurgical procedures still performed are limited to very small parts of the brain.

9. *Genetic inheritance* is one factor determining level of aggression in an individual, including sex differences. There is no genetic "supermale" (XYY sex chromosomes—an extra male chromosome) phenomenon related to overly aggressive behavior. The only difference between XY and XYY males that is certain is that the latter are a little taller.

10. *Altruism* (prosocial behavior, helping) is behavior intended to benefit another without *obvious* return benefit.

11. *Bystander apathy* refers to the lack of helping behavior by people observing an emergency. This may be due to *audience inhibition* (concern over a negative evaluation by others), *social influence* (what others are doing), and *diffusion of responsibility* (the more observers, the less likely one will do something). Bystanders are more likely to help others if the bystanders are alone and if they perceive that the benefits from helping (for example, a "thank you") outweigh the costs (inconvenience, possible danger).

12. *Characteristics* of both the *helper* and the *victim* affect helping behavior. One helper characteristic is belief in the "just world hypothesis" which says that people get what they deserve, so why help them?

13. *Situational factors* which influence helping are severity and setting of the emergency, number of bystanders, and modeling of helping by others in the situation.

14. *Freud's psychoanalytic theory* sees altruism as the result of *internalized* values which the individual has learned from parents and culture. This is called the "superego" or conscience.

15. *Reinforcement theory* interprets altruism in terms of specific helping behaviors which have been rewarded in the past and for which future reward is anticipated.

16. *Kohlberg's theory of moral judgment* interprets developing moral judgment in terms of the increasing ability of the child and adult to understand complex situations. At the highest level the individual perceives the reasoning and spirit behind codes of conduct and acts on these as compared to following the strict letter of a code of conduct.

17. *Darley and Latane* have proposed a *cognitive analysis* of helping behavior which involves a series of steps, from perceiving that there is an emergency to knowing what to do about it.

18. It is suggested that *modeling* and *teaching* of very specific helping behaviors for various kinds of emergency situations would increase the incidence of responsible altruistic behavior.

EXERCISES

1. What is aggression? How is intention involved?

2. Consider a particular aggressive act. Describe it in terms of instigation, goal response, interference, frustration, and other appropriate concepts (depending on the example).

3. Do you participate in activities which are cathartic for you? List some

of these (from your own experience, or from the experiences of others, which are familiar to you).

4. What is the weapons effect? What are its implications for society?

5. How are impulsive, instrumental, and obedient aggression different? Give specific examples of these, preferably not from the text.

6. What are the effects of modeling of violence on the behavior of observers, as found in experimental studies? Discuss how watching violence on TV might affect society. Would you want your children exposed to this type of influence?

7. After you act aggressively, are you personally more or less likely to do so again? Consider this in terms of the two opposing views about the effects of aggressive behavior on further aggression.

8. What biological factors influence aggression?

9. Bystanders have been shown to help more readily in an emergency when alone than when in a crowd? Why? Would you have guessed this? Why?

10. Write a description of two victims, one who would probably not be helped and one who would more likely be helped. On what characteristics do they differ?

11. What situational factors are involved with helping? Again, set up two situations, one in which helping would not be likely and another in which there would be a good chance of someone helping the victim(s).

12. Use the Cognitive Analysis theory of prosocial behavior to work through a specific emergency situation (like a car accident) as if you were a bystander.

13. How would you work to promote prosocial behavior on the part of your children? If you were a teacher, how would you do this for your students?

14. Who do you think should say what prosocial behaviors are the ones to be taught in the schools?

Groups and Environments

Groups and Decisions
Definition of Group
Advantages and Disadvantages of Groups
Audience Effects of Individual Performance: Social Facilitation

Group Decision Making
The Risky Shift Effect
Groupthink
Why Should People Become More Extreme in Groups?

Conformity
Static versus Dynamic Conformity
When and Why Do We Conform?
Conformity and Productivity
Increasing Group Productivity

Small Group Processes
Bales Interaction Process Analysis

Encounter Groups
Nature of Encounter Groups
Criticisms of Encounter Groups
Potential Good and Bad Effects of Participation
Advice on Joining Encounter Groups

13

Small-Group Behavior

Groups and Decisions

definition of group

We are concerned here with relatively small groups—between two and fifty people—not the masses of people one might find at a college football game. What, however, distinguishes a *collection* of people from a *group?* A collection of people milling around in a shopping center does not necessarily constitute a group. Two criteria are commonly used.

1. *The members of a group themselves recognize some kind of affiliation or connection with each other, if only temporarily.* A pick-up basketball game consists of two groups briefly formed; a professional team is a longer-term formation. A department in a business could be a relatively permanent group, but businesspeople meeting at a convention might be a temporary group.

2. *The fates of the members are somehow related to each other.* This is often phrased in terms of the common goals which group members share. The milling crowd does not necessarily constitute a group, because its constituents are not doing anything in particular relation to each other. A family, a church organization, or a civic club each has members with common goals whose interests and successes (or failures) are related.

advantages and disadvantages of groups

People form into groups because there seems to be some advantage to doing so; they can do something collectively (including having a good time) in a way they could not do alone. On the other hand, there may be disadvantages as well. We list some of the advantages and disadvantages in Table 13–1. Groups are not necessarily an unmixed blessing.

We can see from Table 13–1 that there are valid arguments for and against groups. The question is, When is a group better or worse than individuals, either in its effects on individuals or in its ability to get things done? In some cases the answer is trivially obvious. It takes a group to build a bridge or

table 13–1

advantages and disadvantages of group membership in relation to decision making and getting a job done.

advantages	disadvantages
1. Pooling of skills and resources 2. Division of labor 3. Group members can stimulate one another 4. Members may be more thoughtful about others' concerns and not rush into foolish action. 5. Members can provide encouragement and support for one another.	1. The group has to be organized with reference to its goal, conflicts among members resolved, rules established, and so on. 2. Groups are often formed because novel ideas are needed, but established communication patterns, social norms and conformity may prevent this. 3. Negative motivational factors often are operative; people may be reluctant to say or do things because they fear negative evaluations of other members. 4. People in groups may spend time either bickering or having fun and stay less with the task at hand than would a collection of individuals working separately.

From *Individuals and Groups: Understanding Social Behavior*, by A. A. Harrison. Copyright © 1976 by Wadsworth, Inc. Reprinted by permission of the publisher, Brooks/Cole Publishing Company, Monterey, California.

run a ship; by definition it takes a group to have a team. We are concerned with less obvious situations than this.

audience effects on individual performance: social facilitation

We have already encountered social facilitation effects in Chapter Three, in the discussion of drive theory. Recall that it seems the following pattern holds: If there is a simple, dominant response to be made, the presence of observers facilitates performance; but if the dominant response is incorrect, or if there are many or complex behaviors involved, observers tend to worsen performance.

There is an important question, however. Is it simply the presence of other bodies which is facilitative, or is something else involved? Recent evidence suggests that social facilitation effects occur when others are actually observing *and evaluating* our behavior. The observers may not be formally evaluating us

in the way an athletic coach or theatre director would do in making player selections. But we may *think* we are being evaluated and have some *evaluation apprehension* anytime there is an audience. Evaluation apprehension is a fancy phrase for being nervous or anxious about being judged by others.

Experiments summarized by Baron and Byrne (1977, p. 565) indicate that concern over being evaluated by observers was crucial to the facilitation effect. We can think of the adolescent boy who wants to make a good impression on a girl but is nervous in her presence. As a result, rather than being the smooth and sophisticated person he envisions himself, he trips clumsily over his own feet. A real difficulty for the evaluation apprehension interpretation is that the social facilitation effect has also been shown with non-human animals. It stretches credulity to argue that cockroaches or ants would get apprehensive because other cockroaches or ants are evaluating them. It is possible that the drive (generalized arousal) interpretation is correct and that concern over evaluation happens to be a very reliable way to produce a high level of arousal in humans.

Group Decision Making

We often want decisions made by groups so that more thought can go into the necessary considerations. At the same time, we have seen that groups can arrive at atrocious decisions. ("A camel is a horse designed by a committee.") The ill-fated Bay of Pigs invasion of Cuba in 1961 was one such camel, and Vietnam seems to have been a whole herd. There are clearly some situations where groups arrive at more valuable decisions than do individuals. But how is it they can get so far off in other situations?

314

the risky shift effect

An MIT graduate student, James Stoner, studied decision-making of a large number of groups. He started with the generally-believed assumption that groups tend to be more *conservative* in their decisions and recommendations than do individuals. But to his surprise Stoner repeatedly found that groups made *more risky* recommendations than did individuals. This was ascertained by having standard situations studied by *individuals,* who then made a recommendation (for instance, about a change in jobs from one with an adequate but stable income to another high risk, high gain job.) Several individuals would then be formed into a group and discuss the situation, with the result that the group consensus was less conservative than the prior individual recommendations.

The social implications of these results are staggering, and many social psychologists immediately did further research and were able to consistently repeat Stoner's findings. As the research over the years became more sophisticated, however, it became apparent that some groups *do* become more conservative than their individual members previously had been. So, sometimes it's one way and sometimes another. Why? It now appears that members of groups tend to *become more extreme in whatever view they held before the group discussion.* If the collective views of a group prior to discussion are somewhat risky, they become more so during discussion. Conversely, if the individuals are somewhat conservative, group discussion enhances this.

groupthink

Irving Janis (1972) has described some extreme conditions where groups may become so enthralled with an idea, no matter how divorced from reality it may be, that they may act on it. He calls this *groupthink.* Three conditions which especially foster groupthink are strong group cohesiveness, isolation from other views, and endorsement of the policy decision by the group leader. There are then eight characteristics which Janis has described for such group situations.

1. There is an illusion of *invulnerability,* leading to excessive optimism and taking extreme risks.
2. *Rationalization* of the group's actions so that the group discounts evidence contrary to its decision.
3. *Unquestioning belief* in the morality of the group so that moral considerations are not even taken up. ("God is on our side.")
4. *Stereotyped views* that the enemy (in military or other adversary situations) is weak, evil, or stupid.
5. *Strong pressure* on group members to conform and not dissent.
6. *Self-censorship* of deviant ideas by members of the group themselves.

7. An *illusion of unanimity,* partly coming from the pressure to conform.

8. The emergence of self-appointed *mind-guards,* members of the group who "protect" the others from inconsistent information and suppress views deviating from the consensus.

The Bay of Pigs was a prime example of groupthink before Janis' book was published in 1972. But just as the book was coming out a more dramatic example unfolded—The Watergate Affair. The three prime conditions for the occurrence of groupthink were readily met at the Nixon Whitehouse. (1) There was a tight little group surrounding Nixon (cohesiveness). (2) There was isolation from other views. Virtually no one could get to Nixon from the outside and almost all his top staff were involved in one way or another. (3) The policy decisions were endorsed by Nixon. The delaying tactics, called "stonewalling it," became the strategy until one of the conspirators, John Dean, came forth with his encyclopedic memory and blew the whistle. The eight characteristics of groupthink were also all apparent.

why should people become more extreme in groups?

Two speculations about why group discussion leads to more extreme views are that the processes of social comparison and self-supporting arguments are involved.

Social Comparison. Roger Brown (1974) suggested that since most people strive for a positive self-image they tend to view themselves as having "good" values and not as being "just average." This is something of an illusion, however, because most of us are not really very extreme in either our virtues or our vices. But we only discover this when we actually get into a group and compare ourselves with others. When we suddenly discover that we are not particularly unusual, in order to maintain our positive self-image we must become *more extreme* in the direction we think is good. Virtue cannot be just average.

Self-supporting Arguments. Two things may happen here. First, we argue for our own views and hence become more convinced. Second, we may selectively pick up on favoring arguments presented by others. A number of experiments (Baron & Byrne, 1977) support this general view.

Conformity

Situations such as groupthink involve extreme conformity. Not all behavior-in-common is conformity: If we all put up our umbrellas when it rains we are doing the same thing, but not in response to *social pressure.* But when teenag-

ers, for example, go through clothing fads or new uses of slang phrases, they *are* responding to social pressure and this *is* conformity. The Milgram research on aggression, where the subjects conformed to the experimenter requirement that they shock the hapless "learner," was an extreme experimental example, as were the original situations on which the Milgram research was modeled. (See Chapter Twelve.)

What people will agree to under group pressure is sometimes extraordinary. Subjects in experiments have been induced to agree with such absurdities as "The United States is largely populated by old people, 60 to 70 percent being over sixty-five years of age." And 58 percent of a sample of college students agreed that "Free speech being a privilege rather than a right, it is proper for a society to suspend free speech when it feels itself threatened" (Brown, 1965, p. 672).

static versus dynamic conformity

We can distinguish two kinds of conformity. *Static conformity* refers to how close a person comes to matching an *unchanging* (static) norm for behavior. In a classic study, Floyd Allport (1934) developed what he called the J-curve for conformity, illustrated in Figure 13–1. This applies particularly well to something like stopping at a stop sign, where everybody is supposed to follow the norm. Most drivers come to a complete halt, a few come to a "rolling stop," and occasionally someone barrels right on through. Such static norms may be established by *law* (as with stop signs) or by *tradition* (as with dress codes). Traditional norms may carry almost the force of law, however.

Dynamic conformity refers to conformity behavior which *changes* with changing situations. A driver who comes to a rolling stop when not observed, but to a complete stop with a squad car nearby, is showing dynamic conformity. A person who shifts political allegiance rapidly because of group pressure illustrates dynamic conformity. It is sometimes difficult to *identify* dynamic confor-

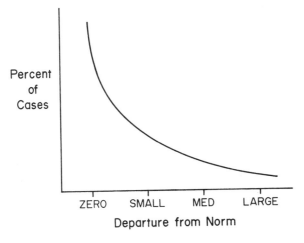

figure 13–1. Idealized J-curve for conformity. Actual data described by this curve have been found for such activities as number of motorists stopping at stop signs, percentage of people punching time clocks at the designated time, and time of arrival for church services.

mity just because of its changing nature. Without knowing what norms an individual is following it is difficult to say whether a person *is* conforming. Seidenberg and Snadowsky (1976) suggest that dynamic conformity applies more to short term situations and static to longer term socialization processes such as the development of morality.

when and why do we conform?

Conformity, in contrast to individualism, is often a dirty word. But any society has to have a large amount of conformity just to survive as a society. Driving is a good example of such needs: If traffic were completely unregulated the results would be predictably disastrous. The same is true (although the limits are debatable) for taxation and other laws. On the other hand, conformity may stifle innovation and reduce a group's competitive advantage as well as the satisfaction of its members. A major complaint against large businesses is that conformity is emphasized to the point of leaving people little freedom to do anything original which might be an improvement.

Motivation. A group, like an individual, has goals, whether to maintain production, win a game, or build a house. The group pressure for cooperation helps attain these goals. Indeed, the phrase "team player" specifically means someone who subordinates his or her own interests to the greater goals of the group. The group, or its leader, provides rewards and punishments to individuals for "going along." Schacter (1951) found that individuals who consistently differed from a group in their attitudes were rejected by other group members. This can be severe punishment. Imagine the college freshman who dearly wants to be a member of a particular fraternity; he is unlikely to deviate much from the norms for that group, lest he not be asked to join. Groups also provide such positive incentives as praise, prestige, or pay.

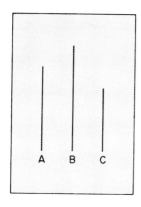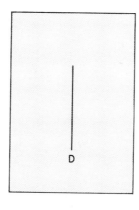

figure 13–2. Asch line judging task. The subject is supposed to say whether line D is the same length as line A, B or C.

The Asch Conformity Research. In research briefly mentioned previously Solomon Asch (1956) would have one real subject in a group of experimenter confederates. Asch presented the whole group a series of very simple visual discrimination tasks of the kind illustrated in Figure 13–2. All the subject had to do was say which of three lines was the same length as the isolated fourth line. The situation was rigged so that the confederates would give their answers before the real subject did. At first the confederates gave the obviously correct answers, but then they began to give blatantly wrong answers. This provided a confusing dilemma for the real subject. Everybody else was "obviously" wrong, but they seemed to believe what they were saying. When as few as three confederates gave the same wrong answer, the real subjects conformed about one-third of the time.

Strongly-conforming subjects (those who went along with the fake group judgment at least half the time) were mostly people who were not sure of their own judgment. They did not actually *perceive* the incorrect line as the same length as the standard, but they somehow felt their judgment was bad and therefore went along with the group. If conditions were changed so the real subjects could reasonably doubt the group, the amount of conformity dropped to almost nothing. This occurred, for example, if the subject were led to believe that the other members of the group had some possible eye problems.

Conformity did not increase if the number of confederates was increased much above three. But conformity dropped dramatically if there was at least one confederate who gave the correct answer, or if the subject were isolated so he or she did not have to disagree *publicly* with the false answers. Some of the subjects who maintained their independence against the group nevertheless reported feeling tense about the situation.

There are two main reasons conformity drops if someone agrees with the real subject. First, the deviant confederate simply breaks up the unanimity of the group in the subject's eyes. Second, the deviant confederate may provide social support for the subject. Evidence has been found for both of these explanations. If a confederate disagrees with both the subject and the group (breaking up unanimity) there is less conformity. But if the confederate also agrees with the subject (social support) there is less conformity still (Allen & Levine, 1969). There is evidence that conformity reduces *anxiety* about non-conformity. Anything which might reduce this anxiety (such as social support) would reduce the need for conforming.

Conformity and Personality. To a small extent there is some relation between conformity and personality. People high in feelings of personal competence are *less* conforming than typical, and people high in authoritarianism are *more* conforming. But, in general, conformity is determined more by situational circumstances than by personality type. We can specify the *conditions* under which conformity will occur better than we can say *who* will conform.

conformity and productivity

Does forming a group to achieve a productive goal actually lead to greater productivity? This depends in large part on the group norms. If those norms favor hard work and productivity, then there will be group pressure in this direction and conformity will be productive. On the other hand, a group of workers getting paid a piece rate, for example, may set a production norm artificially low so that the piece rate will not be lowered. A newcomer might look around and think, "I can work harder and make more money." The group may consider this newcomer a "rate buster" who will force the whole group into lower rates by unusually high productivity. Pressure may then be applied to reduce productivity, and conformity will reflect this. A worker switching to a new job with unfamiliar norms may have an adjustment problem for awhile.

increasing group productivity

Several factors besides conformity favor productivity. These factors may actually help determine the group norms for productivity.

Group-centered Leadership. According to Likert (Dessler, 1980, p. 269) effective groups tend to have group-centered leadership. Each person is considered a responsible member of the group, and his or her contributions are respected. The group collectively participates in all major decisions or activities of the group. In Chapter Fourteen we shall see some of the complications of leadership, however.

Group Size. Increasing the size of a problem-solving group may produce opposing factions in the group, as well as make communication more difficult. A rule of thumb is that the most effective group size is about seven people, give or take a couple. If a group gets much larger than this each person has less total time to participate, a few individuals begin to dominate, and group size inhibits some members' participation. Large groups have also been found to provide less satisfaction for the members.

Cohesiveness. A cohesive group "sticks together," with strong mutual support among the members. Cohesiveness is facilitated by the *attractiveness* of the group, its activities and opportunity for interaction among members, and by the *satisfaction* derived from this interaction. The interrelationship of some of these factors was illustrated shortly after the author's academic department was established. There was initially a small, cohesive group of majors sharing common goals and interests. Word spread about this small, cohesive group with high morale, so a large number of students decided to become psychology majors. Suddenly, the department was relatively large and cohesiveness declined: The characteristic that made the students want to join was damaged by their joining. It was then necessary to make special efforts to do new and interesting things which might appeal to the larger group.

Competition. Just as cooperation within groups may increase productivity, *competition between groups* may also increase productivity. First, competition may increase cohesiveness so the members find their group more enjoyable. Second, competition may increase the overall level of arousal and have a social-facilitation effect. Third, the rewards of winning a competition (self-satisfaction and pride, as well as any external rewards) may provide incentives for increased productivity.

Small Group Processes

We have already seen some of the *dynamics* of small groups, how the individuals interact and what effect that interaction has on performance. A better look at some general processes is useful, however. Robert Bales (e.g., 1950) has developed a system for studying small group activities.

Bales' interaction process analysis

Bales' procedure is to have an observer watch a group during a problem-solving session and make a check mark each time a particular kind of behavior occurs. Figure 13–3 shows Bales' system of categories for doing this scoring. For example, if a subject said "I agree with what George just said," this would get a tally mark in Category 3. A participant who said, "Could you explain that to me a little more?" would get a tally in Category 7.

The categories are further combined into four larger ones:

A. Positive social-emotional (1–3)
B. Attempting answers (4–6)

    C. Seeking information (7–9)

    D. Negative social-emotional (10–12)

The social-emotional categories (A and D) are not directly task-oriented, but set a tone to the proceedings. Categories B and C are task-oriented. The twelve categories are said to be exhaustive: Anything which can be communicated can be categorized. Any kind of observable communication is counted, verbal or nonverbal. A nod of agreement is tallied in Category 3 just as if a person had said "I agree." A sarcastically-lifted eyebrow falls into Category 12 just as much as saying "Now, who could believe *that*"?

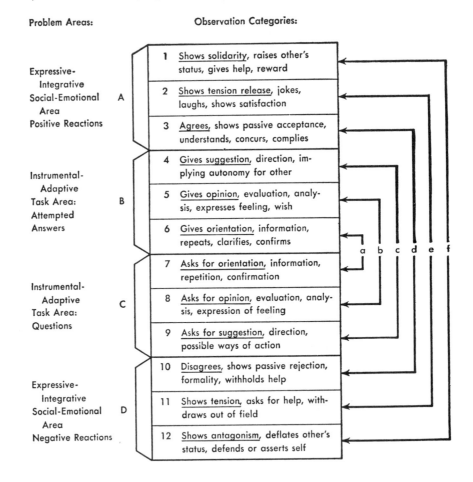

Problem Areas:

Observation Categories:

Expressive-
Integrative
Social-Emotional **A**
Area
Positive Reactions

1 Shows solidarity, raises other's status, gives help, reward

2 Shows tension release, jokes, laughs, shows satisfaction

3 Agrees, shows passive acceptance, understands, concurs, complies

Instrumental-
Adaptive
Task Area: **B**
Attempted
Answers

4 Gives suggestion, direction, implying autonomy for other

5 Gives opinion, evaluation, analysis, expresses feeling, wish

6 Gives orientation, information, repeats, clarifies, confirms

Instrumental-
Adaptive
Task Area: **C**
Questions

7 Asks for orientation, information, repetition, confirmation

8 Asks for opinion, evaluation, analysis, expression of feeling

9 Asks for suggestion, direction, possible ways of action

Expressive-
Integrative
Social-Emotional **D**
Area
Negative Reactions

10 Disagrees, shows passive rejection, formality, withholds help

11 Shows tension, asks for help, withdraws out of field

12 Shows antagonism, deflates other's status, defends or asserts self

a b c d e f

A subclassification of system problems to which each pair of categories is most relevant:

    a Problems of orientation   **d** Problems of decision

    b Problems of evaluation   **e** Problems of tension-management

    c Problems of control   **f** Problems of integration

figure 13–3. Bales Interaction Process Analysis category system for scoring activities in group discussions. (Bales, 1952, Fig. 1. Used by permission of publisher.)

The typical laboratory problem used to study groups with this analysis is a tangled human relations situation in an organization. Each participant has read a summary of case material before a group discussion. Bales sees three communications problems to be solved.

1. *Orientation.* The members of the group are initially uncertain about the situation, whether they have all the information needed, whether it is correct, and so on.

2. *Evaluation.* Participants will typically have different interests and values about what is important to the problem. The group must arrive at some reasonable consensus about values and interests. For example, in a given situation is production valued more highly than human concerns, or vice-versa?

3. *Control.* Participants try to exert influence over each other to arrive at a course of action. A person tries to promote whatever solution he or she thinks is best.

These three communication problems are characteristic of task-oriented groups everywhere, whether in school, industry, civic clubs or church groups. To arrive at a solution a group typically progresses through certain stages involving changes of frequency of the various behaviors described by the scoring categories.

Distribution of Acts. Table 13–2 (Bales, 1950) shows the percentages of responses in the twelve categories by the "most satisfied" and "least satisfied" of sixteen groups in one study. The most noticeable fact is the *similarity* of the groups. There are three interesting points of dissimilarity, however, which make intuitive sense: the satisfied groups showed a much higher level of agreement (#3), more suggestion giving (#5), and less disagreement (#10).

table 13–2

profiles of "satisfied" and "dissatisfied" groups on case discussion task

category	meeting profiles in percentage rates			
	Satisfied	Dissatis-fied	Ave. of the two	Ave. % by sections
1. Shows solidarity	.7	.8	.7	
2. Shows tension release	7.9	6.8	7.3	25.0
3. Agrees	24.9	9.6	17.0	
4. Gives suggestion	8.2	3.6	5.9	
5. Gives opinion	26.7	30.5	28.7	56.7
6. Gives orientation	22.4	21.9	22.1	
7. Asks for orientation	1.7	5.7	3.8	
8. Asks for opinion	1.7	2.2	2.0	6.9
9. Asks for suggestion	.5	1.6	1.1	
10. Disagrees	4.0	12.4	8.3	
11. Shows tension	1.0	2.6	1.8	11.4
12. Shows antagonism	.3	2.2	1.3	

(From Bales, R. 1952. Used with permission of publisher.)

The uniformity of responses across such groups is reliable enough to make good classroom demonstrations. The author has done this many times, both in university and industrial training classes. Some class members discuss a topic of current interest, and others are observer/scorers. With only about ten minutes instruction and no particular case material as background, the results are remarkably like those shown in Table 13–2. In such situations, however, there is a reluctance of the observers to score negative social-emotional behaviors.

Changes over a Session. Figure 13–4 (Bales, 1952) shows changes in kinds of communication over successive thirds of a typical session. Orientation starts off high and decreases. Evaluation stays the same. Attempts to gain control increase, however, as do *both* positive and negative reactions. Attempts to control increase as individuals try to induce others to accept their solutions. Negative reactions may increase because as the session nears an end, the increasing effort for control produces greater tension and possibly antagonism. Negative responses may be a reaction to this. There may also be status struggles

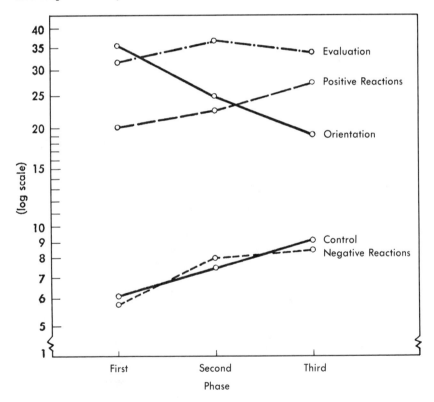

figure 13–4. Percentages of particular types of acts over successive thirds of a discussion session. Based on analysis of 22 sessions. The vertical scale has been adjusted to make the comparisons easier. (From Bales, 1952. Used with permission.)

which lead to tension. The positive reactions probably do not increase quite as steadily as the graph implies. At the very end of a session there is considerable relief when the problem is solved, along with joking and verbal back-slapping. This just gets lumped in with the last third of the session overall.

Who Talks to Whom? Another uniformity of small group behavior is that people who *initiate* talk the most also get talked *to* the most. Conversely, those who do the least initiating also get talked to the least. Figure 13–5 shows how this occurs. Furthermore, when group members rate each other on "productivity," "who has the best ideas," and "whom the members like," the rank order is the same as that for who does the talking. The moral seems clear: The person who does the most talking is likely to have the most influence.

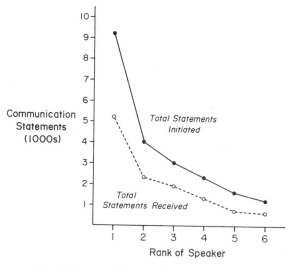

figure 13–5. Who speaks to whom. The total number of communicative acts for 18 sessions of six-man groups. The rank order (1 to 6) for the group members is the same for the amount of communication initiated and received. (From Bales, 1952. Used with permission.)

Usefulness of the Bales Analysis. It is impractical to do formal frequency counts of a group in which we are participating, but a familiarity with the Bales analysis can make us more sensitive to certain kinds of problems. For example, if there were a large amount of positive social-emotional behavior throughout an entire session we might recognize that the group was happy but not necessarily working on the problem at hand. We should expect positive social-emotional behavior to decline after the initial "breaking the ice." Similarly, we might recognize too much negative social-emotional behavior in general, or on the part of a single disruptive person.

Encounter Groups

nature of encounter groups

As compared to problem solving or production groups, encounter groups have a very different purpose, which can be summarized as five goals (Campbell & Dunnette, 1968):

1. Increasing self-awareness,
2. Increasing sensitivity to others,
3. Increasing sensitivity to small group processes,
4. Improving skills in understanding of human relations, and
5. Improving leadership skills.

There are many different specific kinds of groups under the broad heading of encounter groups, but all had a common origin in the industrial group training sessions conducted by the National Training Laboratories. They were first known by the name T-Groups. A major cause for the strong public interest in encounter groups may be that social relations in our society seem to be increasingly less personal. We may interact with more people since we are more mobile, but we may not interact with anyone very intensively. Encounter groups may provide a kind of interaction that many people need. Also, within psychology there has been the so-called humanistic movement, emphasizing psychological growth and freedom as compared to the more traditional clinical concern with recovery from problems generated by frustration and conflict. Carl Rogers' development of non-directive (client-centered) therapy and Abraham Maslow's emphasis on self-actualization were major antecedents of this movement.

An encounter group is typically small, about a dozen or so people, and typically the group isolates itself from the outside world for fairly long periods of time. A group might last an entire weekend, for example, or might meet for several hours at a time over a period of weeks. There are several special emphases in encounter group activity.

1. Members are to deal with their lives and situations as they exist here and now, as opposed to reliving the past or fantasizing the future.
2. Members are urged to *disclose* their own thoughts and feelings and not to put up a "front." A person who feels happy or angry is urged to say so, and to explore *why* he or she feels this way.
3. There is a climate of support for people to say what they are thinking and feeling; members are not rebuked for expressing themselves. This does not mean that everything a person says or does is *approved* by the group, but it is *accepted*. Experimentations with ideas and self-expression is encouraged.
4. There is *feedback* about one's expression. If John says he objects to Mary's acting a certain way in the group, it can be expected that he will be questioned about this. Or, it may be pointed out that this bothers no one else. In any event, *confrontation* or challenge is expected, particularly if there seem to be discrepancies between what a person says and the way that person acts.

criticisms of encounter groups

Since there is such a variety of groups called encounter groups, and since these vary in the degree of professionalism with which they are conducted, the seriousness of the participants, and so on, neither criticism nor praise carries

I FEEL LIKE EXPRESSING MY ANGER HERE AND NOW!

equal weight for all situations. One major criticism is that encounter groups can easily deteriorate into indulgent displays of hostility, exercises in self-pity or indiscriminate praise, or shallow practices of trust in others. For example, one common encounter group exercise has been to lead someone around blindfolded as a means of developing trust in other people (or falling backwards to let someone catch you). This may demonstrate a certain kind of trust, but it has been questioned whether this is really like the kind of trust one develops in a marriage, for example.

It also appears that some have used these groups for sensation-seeking and freedom from normal social restrictions. Nude encounter groups on the beaches of California would perhaps fall into the sensational category. This is not to say that such groups would not, or could not, serve a higher therapeutic purpose, but one could reasonably question whether therapy was a purpose or an excuse.

potential good and bad effects of participation

Many people have found participation in encounter groups so significant to them that they changed their lifestyles, much in the manner of religious conversion. (I have known at least two people who became dedicated encounter group leaders on the basis of their initial experiences with encounter groups.) Such groups can indeed lead to a new understanding of oneself, and of greater sensitivity to others. At the very least such groups can be entertaining and break up monotony, which is an accomplishment not to be belittled.

Harrison (1976) indicates that about 60 percent of encounter group participants believed they had benefitted from the experience. This figure is, however, considerably less than the 90 percent estimate made by group leaders, among whom there seems to be some self-deception about the significance of participa-

FOLLOW ME!

8 FEET

tion to the members. The leaders' biases would hardly be surprising, however, since those people probably became leaders because the experience was good for them.

A major factor in the value of the experience is the leader. If the leader is careful, taking time to explain, interpret, and clarify group procedures, and is truly interested in the group, there are likely to be beneficial effects. If the leader is not really interested in the group, or just lets things go uncontrolled, there is less likely to be a perceived benefit by the participants.

There are some potential dangers. By their nature, encounter groups promote "encounter" and "confrontation," which may be emotionally stressful. If a person is very sensitive and unprepared to cope with challenges to very personal and important parts of his or her life, the experience might be very bad. If someone has established psychological defense mechanisms which serve to keep him or her on an even keel, and these are broken down during the encounter session, the person's anxiety may skyrocket without having anyone really competent present to deal with this anxiety and help that person. Fortunately, the percentage of people who appear to have such truly serious problems stemming from the group seems to be small (less than 1 percent), although the number who report some bad experience is higher (about 10 percent). It is difficult to imagine any group situation which could not sometimes be a bad experience, however, whether encounter group or something much more mundane. It is difficult to make long term analyses of the effects because people who have bad experiences may not show up again to be counted.

advice on joining encounter groups

If a person is interested in joining an encounter group there are several things to do which can minimize potential risk (Shostrom, 1969). First, decide carefully whether or not to join; do not join on impulse. Second, join a group that is not too small nor too large, somewhere between about six and twenty would be right. Third, it is safer to start off with strangers rather than friends. One would not want to lose friends accidentally, or embarrass oneself, in an uncontrolled confrontation. Fourth, avoid groups that are pushing a particular lifestyle (such as eastern religion) unless that lifestyle is something you are already involved in. Fifth, find out the qualifications of the leader. A competent leader will have good professional connections, such as being a member of an academic community, or have a professional license, or be a member of a reputable professional organization. There is more potential risk from bad leaders than from any other cause.

SUMMARY

1. A *group* is a collection of people whose fates are interrelated (for example, they have a common goal) and who recognize a connection with each other.

2. *Social facilitation* refers to the facilitory effect of observers on the behavior of an individual being observed. This may be due to increased *arousal* or to the fact that the group is *evaluating* the individual.

3. Individuals in groups tend to be more *extreme* in whatever individual attitudes or beliefs they previously had.

4. *Groupthink* occurs when groups get "caught up" in an idea and decide to act on it in an unrealistic manner. Factors encouraging groupthink are strong group cohesiveness, isolation from other views, and endorsement of the policy decisions by the group leader.

5. *Conformity* occurs when an individual matches a group norm under pressure from the group. Conformity increases as the number of people following a norm increases, but decreases if the individual has some support from other individuals or if the group itself is divided.

6. *Group productivity* depends on the extent to which group norms favor or disfavor productivity and the pressure to conform to the norms. Group-centered leadership, a small size (five to nine members), cohesiveness, and competition with other groups tend to produce greater productivity.

7. *Bales' Interaction Process Analysis* is a way of analyzing small group behavior in terms of goal-oriented activities (seeking and giving information) and social-emotional activities. Groups show specific patterns of activities which change in a consistent way over time.

8. *Encounter groups* are formed for positive emotional effects rather than productivity. Their goal is to produce greater self-awareness, greater sensitivity to others and improved relations with others. They are usually small groups which isolate themselves for relatively long periods of time, such as a weekend.

EXERCISES

1. When are a bunch of people a "group"? When would a bunch of people not be a "group"? What feelings are associated with group membership?

2. How does group decision-making affect the views of individual members? How and why would a group consensus be different from individual recommendations? What is this called?

3. Think of particular instances of groupthink. Discuss one of these instances in terms of the eight characteristics of groupthink described by Janis.

4. Why do people conform? Can you think of ways in which you conform, and the reasons why you conform?

5. Give examples of dynamic and static conformity. How are they different?

6. How is conformity related to situational characteristics on the one hand and an individual's personality on the other?

7. Form small groups of about four members each. Assign one of Bales' four categories of communication to each member (positive social-emotional, attempting answers, seeking information, and negative social-emotional). Then choose a topic to discuss with each member speaking only according to his or her assigned category. After a brief discussion by this group (say, ten minutes) describe your reactions to each type of communication.

8. What are the three communication problems which Bales thinks group interaction should solve? Did you encounter these in the small group discussion in Question 7?

9. How does the type of communication in a group change over time?

10. What method does Bales use to measure group interaction? Discuss its advantages and disadvantages.

11. Group productivity and conformity depend on group norms. What situations would encourage increased productivity and which would encourage decreased productivity (other than those described in the text)?

12. Think of some group you belong to. Does its leadership, size, cohesiveness, and competitiveness encourage productivity?

13. How are the goals of encounter groups related to the causes of great popular interest in them? How has society contributed to this interest?

14. What are the advantages and disadvantages of encounter group participation, in view of the fact that encounter groups are not necessarily good for everyone?

14

Leadership and Group Effectiveness

(Photo by Bill Henry)

Definitions of Groups and Leaders

We defined a group in Chapter Thirteen as a collection of people who have come together to achieve some goal. A *leader* is a person who *wields influence* over the group in such a way as to achieve certain goals. A leader is not necessarily *formally* identified as such. A manager or supervisor may carry a title which suggests leadership, but the title does not necessarily make him or her a leader. The "real" leader in a group may have no title. In *Mr. Roberts,* for example, the *designated* leader was the captain of the ship, but the *real* leader was his chief officer, Mr. Roberts.

Why Do People Comply with Leaders?

People in positions of leadership seem to command considerable following, and in fact, surprisingly little friction. Why should this be so? DuBrin (1980) suggests several reasons.

The Psychological Contract. It is probably not written clearly for most jobs that an employee is expected to follow orders, except for the military. It is implicit, however, that if you are well-treated by your company you will follow the orders given you within the limits of the implied contract.

Thus, an eight-to-five day may be within the psychological contract, as are occasional compliances to requests for longer time. Similarly, a few days off without penalty is within the psychological contract. Excessive employer demands may bring resistance from the employee, however, just as excessive absence will bring a response from an employer.

Early Cultural Conditioning. Most people accept what they perceive as *legitimate* authority. We learn at an early age to do what we are told, to respect adults (and other authority figures), and so on. There are considerable variations in what people *perceive* as legitimate authority. The poverty stricken, jobless, slum dweller may find it difficult to accept police as legitimate authority, but a neighborhood gang leader may be well accepted. Some males may find it difficult to accept a female "foreman" in occupations traditionally male-dominated (such as construction).

Satisfaction of Dependency Needs. Most of us want to have control over our lives, but we do not always want control over others or the responsibility that goes with independence. It is therefore comforting to have someone else take the leadership role, and then we can depend on him or her. There are considerable differences among people in this regard; some people never want a leadership role, others always want it, and most people fall in between these extremes.

Fear of Consequences of Noncompliance. If a leader has the power to deal out strong punishments, members of a group are more likely to follow orders. The military is a prime example, but many civilian supervisors have the power to hire and fire, and to control salaries, promotions, and work conditions. Federal guidelines are intended to eliminate whimsical use of such power (such as, for sexual favors, or to discriminate against minorities), but the threat of arbitrary use of power is often present, nevertheless.

Are Leaders Distinctively Different from Group Members?

Some leaders seem to have what is called *charisma,* some special feature or features which seem to demand respect. The term *charisma* means "a gift from God." In the entertainment business it is called "star quality." Charismatic political figures have been such people as Charles DeGaulle, Winston Churchill, Martin Luther King, and perhaps John F. Kennedy. One historical view of leadership, then, has been that times are changed by Great Men (or women, such as Joan of Arc) who come along every so often and "have the gift." Certainly Alexander the Great, Christ, Buddha, Julius Caesar, and numerous other persons wrought great change in world politics.

The alternative view, however is that the *social climate* supports particular people at particular times in such a way that they can step into leadership roles which they could not have done at a different time. The deaths of Franklin Roosevelt and John Kennedy paved the way for Harry Truman and Lyndon Johnson. Churchill was a vigorous and effective leader of Great Britain during World War II, but he subsequently could not get re-elected because economic and political conditions had changed.

Realistically, then, we need to look at the characteristics of *leaders* and of *situations* to see how they interact. A major research fallacy, however, would be to focus only on existing leaders to see their characteristics. This ignores all those people who may have the same personal characteristics but perhaps have never had the opportunity to get into a leadership role.

the trait theory of leadership

A popular view of leadership, both in the public mind and that of many researchers and theorists, is the *trait theory,* a milder form of the Great Man theory. According to this approach there are certain characteristics which distinguish leaders and non-leaders. For many years industrial and social psychologists have sought to identify such traits. Many traits have been proposed, but the research is conclusive only in a perverse way: There are no identifiable personality traits which reliably separate leaders from non-leaders for *all* situations.

A number of different characteristics are of some importance, however, although varying with circumstances.

Intelligence. Leaders are typically *somewhat* more intelligent than the groups they lead. If the difference is too great, however, the leader may "lose" the group in "abstract" ideas and consequently not be very effective. This leads to the curious strategem, often seen in politicians of all sorts, of trying to give the *appearance* of not being too much superior to the group in question. The actual level of intelligence required, of course, depends on the situation. Leadership on a construction crew may require a different level of intellect than leadership of a space flight project or an academic department in a university. By the same token, the leaders of these latter groups might be quite ineffective as construction crew leaders because they lack other characteristics.

Sensitivity to a Situation. A good leader needs to be sensitive to what is going on around him or her, within the group, and with the overall situation in which the group is involved. For example, the orderly conduct of many organization meetings is aided by a set of rules called *Roberts Rules of Order.* The moderator of a meeting might recognize that there were undercurrents of feeling and emotion which might best be served by *not* sticking strictly to the rules. This, in fact, would be a higher level understanding of what the rules are *for,* which is to facilitate the work of a meeting and not to have rules for rules' sake.

Productivity. A good leader is productive in helping the group achieve its goals. Productivity, in turn, is a matter of (1) expended effort on the part of the leader, and hence the group; (2) knowledge about the problems the group faces, and (3) effective time management. What is necessary for productivity may change with circumstances; sometime long work hours are required, sometimes proper delegation of authority is necessary, sometimes just knowing who to call for vital information is all that is necessary. The leader needs to see the "big picture" (requiring intelligence and sensitivity) in order to allocate the group's resources most effectively.

Being a Self-starter. Related to productivity is being a self-starter; a good leader anticipates problems before they get out of hand. He or she does not have to be told to do something. Needless to say, it is important to anticipate and work on the *right* problems and to have the correct priorities for the importance of problems at a particular time. A major complaint of many managers is that they spend most of their time "firefighting" rather than productively planning. There is always firefighting (dealing with emergencies) to be done, but one can reasonably question the capability of a leader who never seems to get beyond this.

It is an interesting, perhaps startling, fact that managers seldom have time to sit down and carefully plan things, mulling over big decisions with careful logic and all the necessary facts at their fingertips. A manager in a large corporation, for example, told the author that he was called in on a Saturday morning for a two-hour conference on the basis of which a multi-million dollar decision was made. All the information he had to offer, although not inconsiderable, was "off the top of his head." Managers generally prefer brief reports, often oral, and time studies have shown that most managers seldom work for more than just a few minutes without interruption.

Talkativeness. If you talk a lot at meetings the chances of your being a leader are greater, even if what you say is not terribly profound. As we saw earlier, the people who talk most also get talked *to* the most. An experiment by Sorrentino and Boutillier (1975) found that the quantity of speech was a more important factor in perceived leadership ability than what was actually said. We can certainly relate this to political rhetoric, where style is often more important than content. Much has been written about the "selling of the president," the Madison Avenue approach to political campaigning which emphasizes just about everything *but* ideas.

Over the years various investigators have reported other traits which they believed distinguished leaders from non-leaders, including self-assurance, decisiveness, masculinity, maturity, need for power, and so on, which we have not discussed above. The difficulty has always been that different investigators tend to produce different lists, and those proposed by one investigator based on research in one situation are not found by a different investigator in a different situation.

Styles of Leadership

This approach is more concerned with what the leader *does* than with what some test says he or she *is* (the trait approach). The two are probably related in that some people do some things more readily than others. For example, a person who is sensitive to others is going to behave differently toward his or her subordinates than someone who is lacking in sensitivity to the needs and feelings of others. One approach to behavioral style is the managerial grid.

the managerial grid®

Developed by Blake and Mouton (1964, 1978), the Managerial Grid provides a descriptive framework for managerial styles. It is not in itself a theory of management or of leadership, but provides an outline for thinking about different ways in which managers *can* perform their functions. This is very important, however, because some people rise to (or fall into) managerial positions with preset ideas about how a leader *ought* to behave. One of the most *misused* ideas is that a leader should be decisive and make quick decisions. This is certainly true for relatively small decisions, but one would certainly hesitate to recommend this as a method of approaching foreign policy. Another idea is that leaders should always exert their authority and let their subordinates know who is boss at all times. If in fact a leader *has* authority he or she does not *need* to flaunt it. Such misconceptions as these make it useful to have a broad framework for examining managerial styles.

Figure 14–1 shows the Grid. There are two dimensions: *Concern for Production* and *Concern for People.* Since these are *concerns,* they are attitudes or motives which predispose people to approach certain problems one way rather than another. For example, we might expect that a person with a high need for affiliation might tend to be more concerned with people and one with a high need for achievement to be more concerned with production.

The Grid is arranged from 1 to 9 on each dimension, with verbal descriptions of the managerial "styles" represented by the four extremes and the middle. A given manager may act differently at different times depending on (1) pressures from *within* (such as personal or religious values, pressures related to his or her personal life), (2) pressures from external sources (from the manager's own superiors, from demands of a situation such as a production schedule), and (3) pressures from the institution within which the individual is operating. (Educational institutions have certain values, goals, traditions, and ways of operating which are quite different from manufacturing organizations. Within performing arts institutions there are different traditions yet, and so on.)

Blake and Mouton characterize five "pure" managerial styles, shown in Figure 14–1.

9,1 Managerial Style. This is the lower right-hand corner, a high concern with production and a low concern for people. This is characterized by a strict

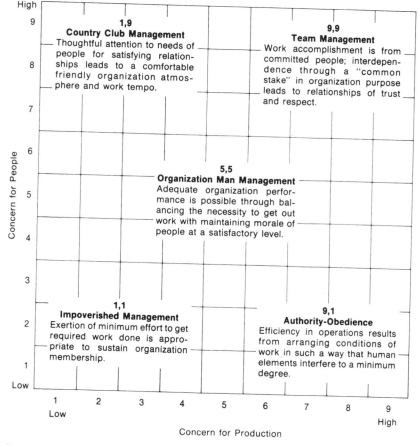

figure 14–1. The New Managerial Grid. (Copyright 1978 by Blake & Mouton, *The New Managerial Grid.* Houston, TX: Gulf. Used with permission.)

"engineering" approach to work, a strong emphasis on the manipulation of things and processes for efficient production and relatively little consideration of the organization or roles of the people who will actually carry out these processes. In terms of motivation we might characterize the 9,1-oriented manager as having a high need for achievement (production) and a low need for affiliation (concern with others). The supervisor-subordinate relationship is one of *authority* and *obedience*. "I'm the boss," this type of manager might say, "I plan how to get things done and give the orders. Sure, I'm concerned about my people. If their morale is low they don't work as well, so I give them a pat on the back occasionally. But if they don't produce I get on them pretty damned quick."

1,9 Managerial Style. This style is diametrically opposed to the 1,9 style just discussed. This extreme managerial style is concerned with maintaining smooth interpersonal relationships and not ruffling anyone's feathers. The attitudes and feelings of the people are more important than production, and indeed, an overemphasis on production may be viewed as bad. This is a very democratic sounding ideal in the tradition of Thomas Jefferson, "He who manages least manages best." The work is fitted to the people (or at least this is the *concern* of this style of management, implemented where possible) rather than fitting the people to the work. In dealing with people the 1,9-oriented manager is more prone to use the carrot than the stick carried by the 9,1-oriented manager. This approach lends itself well to management by objectives (MBO) discussed in Chapter Four because it allows the 1,9-oriented manager freedom to be concerned with his or her people but at the same time to set organizational goals which are to be met. The subordinates of this manager participate in setting objectives, with such catch phrases as "We are all one big happy family."

1,1 Managerial Style. This combines the worst of all managerial approaches, low concern with either people or production. As Blake and Mouton (1964, p. 85) put it, ". . . the person managing 1,1 has learned to be 'out of it,' while remaining in the organization." Little is expected of him or her and little is given. The 1,1-oriented manager is not really managing. This is more common in situations involving routine operations as compared to situations where frequent attention to details by the manager is important. Since Blake and Mouton's introduction of the Managerial Grid, a new concept has developed which beautifully fits the description of the 1,1-oriented manager: *Learned Helplessness,* as discussed in Chapter Two. The classic example of 1,1 behavior is the bureaucrat who is careful not to rock the boat, has no influence and wants none, waits out his or her time to retirement, and presumably finds personal satisfactions outside the job.

There is little concern with goals under 1,1 since there is no concern with production or people. The only real goal is to "save your own tail"; the 1,1 manager wants to look respectable and is moved to action only when his or her own well-being is threatened. A marvelous example of a 1,1-oriented manager was Ensign Pulver in *Mr. Roberts* (played by Jack Lemmon in the movie). For anyone unfortunate enough not to be familiar with *Mr. Roberts,* Ensign Pulver had managed to be a shipboard officer for two years before the captain discovered his presence. Minimal communication, as between Ensign Pulver and the captain, is typical of the 1,1 type. The communication role the 1,1 adopts is that of reliably passing communication between two other parties.

The 5,5 Managerial Style. This managerial style is the hypothetical middle road between low and high concern for both production and people. The guiding assumption here is not to resolve conflicts between people and production regularly one way or the other, but to compromise between the two, to find a middle ground. The 5,5-oriented position is a "delicate balancing act" requiring constant monitoring in order to keep production running smoothly and the workers happy. The 5,5 line of thinking is to lead, to motivate, to communicate what is to be done. Blake and Mouton emphasize that 5,5 types rely more on rules for their own sake and may seem unduly bureaucratic and snarled in red tape.

The concept of *target* exemplifies the 5,5. People aim at certain target production goals, but failure to achieve them is not disastrous (as in 9,1). Nor is failure completely ignored (as in 1,1). In line with the emphasis on rules and regulations, there is tendency for the 5,5 to hide behind opinion polls and committee decisions as a rationale for carrying out certain policies. The 5,5 is self-protective and is indeed probably not very creative. The 5,5 seldom confronts conflicts head-on, because if this is done there is a winner and a loser and the 5,5 approach is to compromise rather than to have winners and losers. The 5,5-oriented manager above all tries to be practical, to get things done "reasonably well" and not have too-high expectations.

The 9,9 Managerial Style. This manager sees no conflict between production goals and people, therefore sees no need for compromises in favor of either one. "Under 9,9 effective integration of people with production is possible by involving them and their ideas in determining the conditions and strategies of work. . . . A basic aim of 9,9 management, then, is to promote the conditions that integrate creativity, high productivity, and high morale through concerted team action." From the point of view of the manager, "My job is not necessarily to *make* sound decisions, but it sure is my job to see that sound decisions are made." (Blake & Mouton, 1964, pp. 142,143).

It is then important to make workers a part of the work, to make sure they understand how organizational goals tie into their personal goals and how they can promote their own welfare through the organization. It is furthermore assumed that there is a basic need of individuals to be involved in pro-

table 14–1

the leader behavior description questionnaire

---

initiating structure

1. He makes his attitudes clear to the staff.
2. He tries out his new ideas with the staff.
3. He rules with an iron hand.[a]
4. He criticizes poor work.
5. He speaks in a manner not to be questioned.
6. He assigns staff members to particular tasks.
7. He works without a plan.[a]
8. He maintains definite standards of performance.
9. He emphasizes the meeting of deadlines.
10. He encourages the use of uniform procedures.
11. He makes sure that his part in the organization is understood by all members.
12. He asks that staff members follow standard rules and regulations.
13. He lets staff members know what is expected of them.
14. He sees to it that staff members are working up to capacity.
15. He sees to it that the work of staff members is coordinated.

consideration

1. He does personal favors for staff members.
2. He does little things to make it pleasant to be a member of the staff.
3. He is easy to understand.
4. He finds time to listen to staff members.
5. He keeps to himself.[a]
6. He looks out for the personal welfare of individual staff members.
7. He refuses to explain his actions.[a]
8. He acts without consulting the staff.[a]
9. He is slow to accept new ideas.[a]
10. He treats all staff members as his equals.
11. He is willing to make changes.
12. He is friendly and approachable.
13. He makes staff members feel at ease when talking with them.
14. He puts suggestions made by the staff into operation.
15. He gets staff approval on important matters before going ahead.

---

[a] Scored negatively. (Reprinted with permission of The Macmillan Company from *Theory and Research in Administration* by Andrew W. Halpin. © Copyright by Andrew W. Halpin, 1966.)

ductive work and that through a high concern for both people and production this need can be met.

To understand all the implications of the Managerial Grid one should read the clearly written Blake and Mouton book. The point here, generally the same as those authors make, is that there are many possible managerial styles and it is worthwhile to reflect on what one does as a manager, whether you already are one or might become one. In some situations it may be best to be a 9,1 (where people basically dislike their jobs but the jobs have to be done). It is conceivable that a 1,1-oriented manager is better than the alternatives: A non-involved manager might be preferable to one who enthusiastically does things wrong. The 9,9 approach sounds best but, as one author put it, it may be difficult to entice escaped prisoners back into the walls with a 9,9 approach.

Consideration and Structure. The two dimensions of leadership embodied in the managerial grid have appeared and reappeared under different names in many approaches to leadership. In particular the words "*consideration* (concern for others) and *initiating structure* (concern for production) have been used. The consideration and structure approach is perhaps of somewhat broader implication than the managerial grid, which primarily has a business orientation. Scales for consideration vs. structure have been devised by Halpin (1966) and are shown in Table 14–1. The scales indicate in a more specific way exactly what is meant by initiating structure and consideration. The two sets of scales are known collectively as the *Leader-Behavior Description Questionnaire* (or LBDQ, for short).

Leader-Situation Interaction

The trait and behavioral style approaches differ, but both emphasize the leader. The interaction approach emphasizes the relationship between leader characteristics and situational characteristics. What may be effective behavior for a leader in one situation may be quite inappropriate in a different situation. Fred Fiedler has developed the most complete and influential theory within this framework (for example, see Fiedler, 1967).

fiedler's contingency model of leadership.

Fiedler's theory is called a *contingency* model (or theory) because its fundamental premise is that *the most effective leadership style is contingent on (depends upon) the specifics of the situation.* Fiedler and others have contributed a vast array of research on many different kinds of groups in real situations (as compared with more contrived laboratory situations). These range from basketball teams

table 14–2

bipolar ratings used in rating least preferred co-worker

Pleasant	8	7	6	5	4	3	2	1	Unpleasant
Friendly	8	7	6	5	4	3	2	1	Unfriendly
Bad	1	2	3	4	5	6	7	8	Good
Distant	1	2	3	4	5	6	7	8	Close
Supportive	8	7	6	5	4	3	2	1	Hostile
Contented	8	7	6	5	4	3	2	1	Discontented
Stubborn	1	2	3	4	5	6	7	8	Not stubborn
Not enterprising	1	2	3	4	5	6	7	8	Enterprising
Tense	1	2	3	4	5	6	7	8	Relaxed
Not studious	1	2	3	4	5	6	7	8	Studious
Unsympathetic	1	2	3	4	5	6	7	8	Sympathetic
Impatient	1	2	3	4	5	6	7	8	Patient
Happy	8	7	6	5	4	3	2	1	Depressed
Unenthusiastic	1	2	3	4	5	6	7	8	Enthusiastic
Not confident	1	2	3	4	5	6	7	8	Confident
Disagreeable	1	2	3	4	5	6	7	8	Agreeable
Unproductive	1	2	3	4	5	6	7	8	Productive
Unadventurous	1	2	3	4	5	6	7	8	Adventurous
Sociable	8	7	6	5	4	3	2	1	Unsociable
Satisfied	8	7	6	5	4	3	2	1	Dissatisfied
Unambitious	1	2	3	4	5	6	7	8	Ambitious

(Adapted from J. G. Hunt, Fiedler's leadership contingency model: An empirical test in three organizations, *Organizational Behavior and Human Performance*, 1967, **2**, 291. Copyright 1967 by Academic Press, Inc. and reprinted by permission.)

to research with the Belgian navy. In general, the results have tended to support the theory.

Fiedler (1978) has a measure of "consideration" or "concern for others" which he calls the *Least Preferred Coworker Score* (LPC score). A research subject thinks of all the coworkers he or she has had in the past and rates the *worst* of these (the least preferred coworker) on the series of scales shown in Table 14–2. These scores are added up to produce a total score. The logic is that a person whose LPC score is positive (his or her Least Preferred Coworker was pleasant, friendly, etc.) is more concerned with people (consideration) than with structure. Conversely, a person whose LPC score is more negative (the LPC was unpleasant, unfriendly, and so forth) has less interest in people and more interest in structure.

Given the LPC score for leadership characteristics, there are then three elements of a situation considered important: leader-member relations, task structure, and leader position power.

Leader-member Relations. In a small group situation (such as, a bomber crew or athletic team) one of the most important factors becomes whether the leader is liked and respected.

Task Structure. Are the goals of the group clear? Is the way to achieve these goals clear? Once a decision has been made is there any good way to verify that the correct decision has been made?

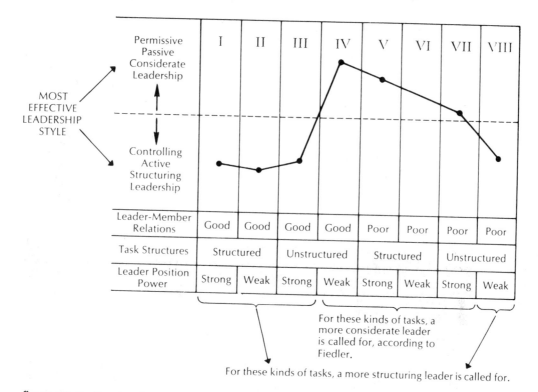

figure 14-2. Results of many tests of Fiedler's contingency theory of leadership. In "very good" (I,II,III) or "very poor" (VIII) situations task-oriented leadership is relatively more effective. In more ambiguous situations (IV, V, VI, VII) consideration for others becomes relatively more important. (Adapted from Fiedler, 1967 by Dessler, 1980. Used with permission.)

Position Power. Does the leader have the authority to dole out rewards and punishments? In a business group the leader might control salaries and working conditions; in a volunteer group, on the other hand, the leader might have little position power.

Figure 14-2 summarizes the results of a large number of studies on many groups of different kinds. Each data point represents an entire research study unto itself. Considering high vs. low for each of the three situational factors there are eight possible combinations of these to indicate favorableness of situation. These are indicated on the baseline. The vertical axis represents correlations between LPC scores and independent measures of how well a particular group performed. The most obvious and interesting result overall is that performance is better with low LPC leaders when conditions are *very favorable* or *very unfavorable*. In the middle range of favorableness, however, leaders with high LPC scores do better. How might this translate into actual situations?

Consider points I, IV, and VIII on the baseline. For I, there are good leader-member relations, a structured task, and strong leader power. A leader concerned with production or winning is more effective here. At the other end of the scale, at VIII, there are poor leader-follower relations, an unstructured task, and low position power. Again, a leader concerned with production or winning is more effective, but for different reasons. In I, everything is so well oiled that the leader *need not* be very concerned about individuals. In VIII everything is so bad that the leader simply *cannot* be overly concerned about the individuals or everything will fall apart. In IV, however, the situation is more ambivalent, the concern for people takes on relatively greater importance. Thus, there are good leader-member relations, but an unstructured task and little position power. By being more concerned with the workers the leader can get more done in this kind of ambiguous situation.

The main point is that the type of leadership which is effective differs according to the situation, but with some predictability. Literally thousands of groups, one of the most ambitious research programs in the history of social psychology, support this approach.

Why Leaders Fail

We can glean from the previous discussion some of the reasons leaders may fail. They may be using the wrong approach at the wrong time with the wrong people. In a highly unfavorable situation, as in Fiedler's theory, for example,

the leader may be *too* people-oriented to get a task done effectively. Or, indeed, the task may be impossible. Jobs such as city manager or athletic coach usually do not have a long survival rate, because it is impossible to satisfy all the demands of all the people who have input into the job.

Warren Bennis (1975) puts the problem in a different light. He says, "Many an institution is very well managed and very poorly led. It may excel in the ability to handle each day all the routine inputs—but may never ask whether the routine should be done at all." (p. 27). The author's daughter was recently describing a college course she was taking. I asked "Why . . ." and she completed the sentence, ". . . am I taking the course"? I replied, "No, why are they *offering* the course?" There was good and sufficient reason, but academic institutions can fall into outmoded traditions as can any other large institution. Indeed, because of their somewhat special status, schools and churches can perhaps become stultified more easily than many other institutions.

The distinction between a leader and a manager is important. Someone who is supposed to be a leader, to set the pace, may become swamped with daily trivia. Bennis notes that leaders often become managers because they take too much on themselves rather than properly delegating responsibility. Consequently they do not have sufficient time to set goals and to develop and implement plans. The title of Bennis' book, *The Unconscious Conspiracy,* aptly conveys the message that in many kinds of large, diffuse organizations it is very difficult to bring about change, even just to keep up. People do not intentionally set out to thwart the leader, by whatever title he or she may be called, but the sheer weight of molehill piled on molehill makes a mountain very difficult for the leader to overcome.

Leadership and Assumptions About Human Nature

In Chapter One we briefly noted some different assumptions about human nature which may generally affect the way we act toward each other. Nowhere are such assumptions more critical, however, than in the way they influence how leaders treat their subordinates. A global example is the case of the Soviet Union, where it is considered that the government in its infinite wisdom always knows that is best for the people: what they shall see and hear, as well as produce and consume. At the time of this writing the workers of Poland were trying to unionize, with limited success, in the face of the threat of Soviet invasion. The paradox is that the communist party is supposed to be the worker's party, but the workers cannot unionize without reprisal from the government.

Schein (1965) has summarized four different approaches to the nature of human beings. Though he characterizes these models with the term "man," they are meant to apply to women as well.

rational-economic man

Developed in the early part of this century, the idea is that people are motivated solely by economic considerations. Therefore, proper manipulation of wages and incentives should be sufficient to control workers. A subsidiary idea is that people would not work unless paid—a natural state of laziness. The feelings of the workers, their hopes, fears and ambitions, were considered irrelevant. This is similar to McGregor's Theory X, discussed in Chapter Four. The ultimate product of this kind of thinking is mindless assembly-line manufacturing. A leader with this belief would be much more concerned with production than with the people who produce.

social man

Stimulated by what were the apparently bizarre results of the Hawthorne Studies (Chapter One), the belief developed that workers are primarily motivated by social needs which are not met by the assembly line approach to work. Workers are considered to be more responsive to their peers than to management, except to the extent that a supervisor can meet the subordinate's social needs. Within this framework was developed worker-participation in goal-setting, involving the workers socially as well as economically.

self-actualizing man

Wrightsman (1972) says "For the leader who adopts the view of man as self-actualizing, concern about his employees is still great, but he is more concerned in making their work meaningful and satisfying than in filling their social needs. . . . "According to the self-actualizing conception, man is seen as intrinsically motivated. . . . He takes pride in his work because it is *his* work (p. 510)." Pride and satisfaction in accomplishment may not be possible in all jobs, so wages and incentives are relatively more important in those situations. But where there is the possibility for personal growth and accomplishment for the worker, a good leader will provide the opportunity. The women's revolution seems as much directed to this issue as to economic independence.

complex man

The preceding views all have some degree of accuracy but are also oversimplified. The Complex Man view recognizes the great variation in motives, emotions, experiences and abilities of different people (male or female), and that *these change over time.* New motives can be learned, new skills may completely change a person's attitude toward a job as well as ability to handle the job. There is no single leadership strategy that will fit; the leader has to be prepared to deal with different people in different ways. This does not say that a leader should be inconsistent, or "waffle" in dealing with subordinates. It does say that the leader has to be sensitive to the differences in needs and motivations of different workers and to deal with these accordingly. As an example of where such recognition did *not* occur, a local industry developed a "motivational" strategy that required workers to sign a card stating that they would have "pride in personal performance." Many of the workers seemed to take this with the grain of salt it probably deserved, but one worker with whom the author talked was totally irate. He said he *always* gave the company everything he had to give and it was a personal insult to have him sign a card which implied that he would do something in the future which he had not done in the past. Somehow, this implication had escaped those who had put the program into force, and they did not anticipate that many of the responses to the program would be ridicule or benign indifference, if not outright hostility.

SUMMARY

1. *A leader is a person* (whether or not designated as a leader) *who wields influence over a group in such a way as to achieve certain goals.*

2. People *comply* with leaders because of unwritten "psychological contracts," early cultural conditioning, satisfaction of dependency needs, and fear of the consequences of noncompliance.

3. *Charisma* is some special feature or features of a person which "demand" respect. The *Great Man view* of history proposes that charismatic leaders change the times in which they live. In contrast, the *social climate view* stresses that a particular situation produces the opportunity for a person to take a leadership role. Under other circumstances that person would not be the same kind of leader. Probably both personal and situational factors are involved.

4. The *trait theory* is a mild form of the charismatic view, stating that there are certain personality traits that differentiate leaders from non-leaders. Traits that may be important, depending on the situation, are intelligence, sensitivity to the situation, productivity, being a self-starter, and talkativeness.

5. The *leadership style* approach is more behavioral, emphasizing what the leader does and how he or she acts. The *Managerial Grid* classifies leaders along the two dimensions of *concern for productivity* and *concern for people.* Vari-

ous combinations of these, such as high concern for productivity and low concern for people are discussed.

6. *Leader-situation interaction* approaches stress the relationship between the characteristics of the leader and the situation. Fiedler's *contingency model of leadership* states that the most effective leadership style depends on the specific situation. The model takes into account leader-member relations, task structure and leader position-power. Some of the reasons leaders *fail* are that (1) they are using the wrong leadership approach for a particular situation, (2) the task is impossible, or (3) they are unable to bring about needed change.

7. How leaders act toward their subordinates is partially determined by their *assumptions about human nature.* Four different views of man see him (or her) as *rational-economic* (motivated solely by economic concerns), *social* (emphasizing social needs), *self-actualizing* (intrinsically motivated), and *complex* (motivation varies greatly between people and within the same person at different times).

EXERCISES

1. When is a leader not really a leader? Make up some specific examples of this kind of situation.

2. Is there a psychological contract in your classroom? What are some of the unwritten rules?

3. Name some charismatic leaders (past or present). What characteristics do they share? How would the social climate view of history account for each of them in their particular situations?

4. Think about the current President of the United States. What leadership traits does he have? Can you think of any circumstances where these traits would be disadvantageous rather than assets? How would you rate the President on intelligence, sensitivity to the situation, productivity, being a self-starter, and talkativeness?

5. Using the Managerial Grid, figure out where a specific leader of some group you belong to (or are familiar with) would fit in terms of managerial style. Does he or she fit exactly into one of the pure categories or somewhere in between?

6. Now think of fictional characters (from literature, T.V., or movies) who would fit into each of the five pure categories of the managerial grid. If you were leader of a group, which style would be more like you?

7. Think about some female leaders, such as Margaret Thatcher of England. Do these differ in their behavior from male leaders?

8. How is the Least Preferred Coworker Score related to leadership, in terms

of both the leader and the situation? What is the basic assumption underlying use of this score?

9. Whom would you describe as failures as leaders? Why do you think they failed?

10. Describe the four assumptions leaders can make about human nature. Which one is most similar to your beliefs? Think of particular leaders who may have held each of these views. How might their beliefs have affected their actions and attitudes?

15

Industrial Organization and Behavior

behavior is a function of the worker and the organization

Let us restate what should already be well-drilled into your mind by now: *Behavior does not occur in a vacuum nor is it totally controlled by external circumstances.* What a person does depends on the person and the environment. In this chapter we consider the organization of business and industry as an environmental influence on the worker, including the way the organization affects job satisfaction. In the next chapter, we consider environments more generally.

To illustrate how different environments might affect work behavior, think about those of a teacher and of a salesperson on weekly commission. The teacher typically contracts for a year's salary and his or her organization (usually a school system) does not allow for immediate financial rewards for a job well done. A brilliant classroom session is followed by the same size check this month as last month or next month. On the other hand, a salesperson who makes a brilliant pitch and a sale can immediately "see" the money in hand. The organizational structure of the teacher's environment does not allow for immediate monetary reward whereas the salesperson's environment is specifically designed for this. Any immediate rewards the teacher gets must be other than monetary, such as pride in a good day's work. Such intangibles may also be important to the salesperson, too, but the two different kinds of environments in which the teacher and the salesperson work just don't pass out rewards the same way. In Chapter Two we saw the importance of immediate reward, or positive feedback, on behavior; some organizational structures provide for this better than others. The teacher-salesperson example illustrates only one of many ways in which organizational structures differ in their influence on the worker.

formal organizations

A very small organization can conduct its affairs in a relatively simple fashion: "You do this and I'll do that." As organizations get bigger, however, they begin to take on a structure of their own, in order to guarantee that necessary work gets done. Assignments are given to particular *positions* in the structure rather than to particular *people*. People may come and go, but a position lingers on.

Figure 15–1 shows a typical organizational chart in abstract form. There are two kinds of functions: *line* and *staff*. People in the line organization have direct authority and responsibility for those below them in the line, whereas the staff people do not have such authority. The president has authority over the vice-president, who has authority over the manager, who controls a supervisor, who controls his or her workers. Staff functions may be at a very high

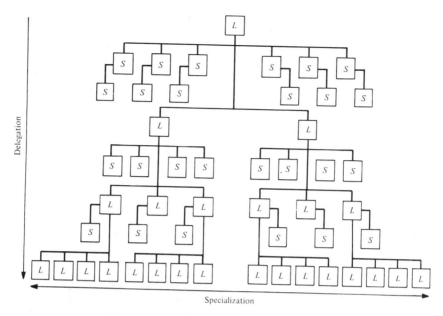

figure 15-1. A representation of specialization and delegation dimensions of a hypothetical organization (L = line; S = staff). (From Landy & Trumbo, 1976, p. 412. Used with permission of publisher.)

level, such as the Pentagon staff or corporate lawyers, but staff personnel have no direct line authority.

Over the years there have evolved different theories of how business and industry, or other groups, might best be organized to operate efficiently. Landy and Trumbo (1976) point out some important differences distinguishing "classical" and "modern" approaches to organization theory.

classic organization theory

The classic approach is to break down an organization into ever smaller components. The original reason for this was to establish a formal framework which could be described objectively so that workers and management alike could see what they were doing and where they could expect to get if they did their work well. The system was supposed to have the advantage that individuals could advance according to merit rather than birthright (the boss's son) or social class (the aristocracy). The characteristics distinguishing one organization from another in this view are the following.

Division of Labor (Specialization). In a manufacturing plant there is fabrication, assembly, finishing, as well as such separate specialities as marketing and financing. A person fits into the particular slot which specializes in a certain function.

Classic organization theory.
(Photo by Bill Henry)

Delegation of Authority. The whole process of development of a product, manufacture, distribution, and sales may require the coordination of thousands of people since the division of labor keeps any single person from doing a 'whole' job. In classic theory this was considered best handled by having some people delegated the authority for getting a job done and coordinated with other activities. In the organization chart in Figure 15–1, each box represents a division of labor and downward lines represent authority. This is a *hierarchical* structure, which each person at a higher level having greater responsibility for more people below.

Structure. This refers to the height of an organization chart relative to its width. Figure 15–2 shows a *tall* structure (many people in the line of authority with few people *directly* under their control in terms of face-to-face contact), and a *flat* structure, with many people directly under the control of a given supervisor.

Span of Control. This is related to structure. In a tall structure there is relatively little span of control (few people reporting directly to a given supervisor), whereas in a flat structure there is a relative large span of control (many people reporting to a given supervisor). It is important to find the best structure and span of control for a given organization. This can be illustrated with a football analogy. A college football coach cannot direct a whole team, so he has offensive and defensive coordinators. These in turn have coaches for differ-

Small Span of Control Company (size = 1000)

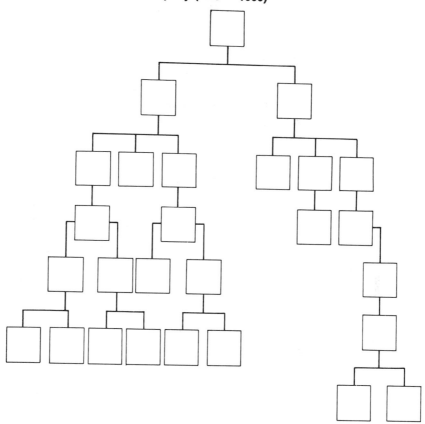

Large Span of Control Company (size = 1000)

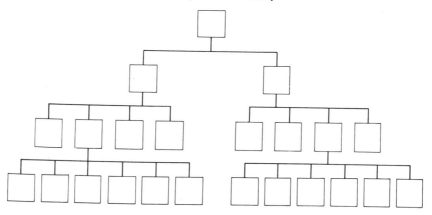

figure 15–2. Small (upper) and large (lower) spans of control. (From Landy & Trumbo, 1976, p. 413. Used with permission of publisher.)

ent positions. If this were carried to an extreme with a tall structure there would be so many people to pass information through that a player on the field might never get a message from the coaches. This problem has been pretty well solved for football teams, but the solution is not so obvious when dealing with a multinational corporate structure which is highly diversified.

The question of the most efficient span of control cannot be answered apart from a specific situation. Thus, it has been suggested that one person can efficiently manage only about seven other people, but this depends on the manager's capacity to handle the information which he or she must deal with. One supervisor might be able to handle only three people and another might be able to handle thirty or fifty. Optimal spans of control seem also to be partly related to the type of job involved.

Joan Woodward (1958) [not the actress] examined span of control in many organizations and distinguished three different types: (1) *small-batch* organizations, (2) *large-batch* and *mass production* organizations, and (3) *continuous process* organizations. Small batch organizations produce specialty products, one type of item at a time, in small batches or runs. For example, there may be chocolate Santa Clauses for the Christmas trade, chocolate hearts for Valentines Day, chocolate bunnies for Easter, and something entirely different for other times of year. She found the average span of control in such organizations was between twenty-one and thirty. In large batch or mass production organizations (such as the auto industry) large numbers of units are routinely produced or assembled, and the average span of control was between forty-one and fifty. In continuous process organizations, with a continual "flow" of a product, such as in oil refining, the average span of control was smallest of all, between eleven and twenty. This may be due to the cost of making mistakes in continuous process procedures. For example, millions of gallons of oil might be incorrectly processed before anybody found the mistake. Woodward was not able to account entirely for her results, although it appears that the span of control is related to how much attention must be paid to day-by-day, or even minute-

by-minute, operations. Other people have not found the same sort of groupings. Nevertheless, Woodward's analysis is considered important in terms of the kinds of things one might look for in order to deal with the problem of optimal span of control. In particular, Woodward's analysis points up the fact that there is no single principle of span of control which is applicable for all situations.

Relatively flat structures are sometimes thought to be better than tall structures because they are more decentralized, less complex, and allow individual workers more responsibility (Landy & Trumbo, 1976, p. 418). But this may not always be the case.

Criticism of Classic Theory. Classic theory puts the *decision-making* under the control of one group of people but requires another group to *implement* those decisions. This runs contrary to several principles discussed in previous chapters, particularly those involving communication, autonomy, ego involvement, need for participation, and so on. We saw, for example, that participation promotes positive attitude change more than simply being told something. Workers commonly complain that management makes unrealistic demands because "they don't understand the problems of the workers." What may appear to a decision-maker to be a simple change in a manufacturing process may seem completely unrealistic to a worker. Overall, the classic approach tends to make the "Economic Man" assumptions about worker motivation, ignoring workers as individuals. It is often too rigid when change is needed.

Informal Organizational Structure. Given that a particular organization has a "paper structure" of the classic variety, does that mean that the organization actually works that way? The answer appears to be a resounding "No!" Workers may get around an organization chart simply by ignoring it where possible. Thus, Mr. Brown may be the formal supervisor but Mrs. Smith is the one who really does the job, so workers in effect report to her. As a graduate student the author was able to get all sorts of monetary assistance for his research by the simple expedient of having the secretary write out purchase orders which the department head signed without looking at them closely. This will all sound very familiar to viewers of M*A*S*H, wherein Corporal Walter (Radar) O'Reilly really ran the 4077. It is common for workers to deal through networks of friends or to find expertise where it exists rather than where the organization chart says it is. This introduces a high degree of flexibility into organizations which would not seem, *on paper*, to have the flexibility. As shown in the original Hawthorne studies, the workers can create their own environment and working conditions within certain limits. Figure 15–3 shows how the lines might be drawn for the way a company really works.

modern organization theory

Many ideas discussed in previous chapters relate to modern organization theory. In particular, modern theory tries to take into account the *attitudes* and

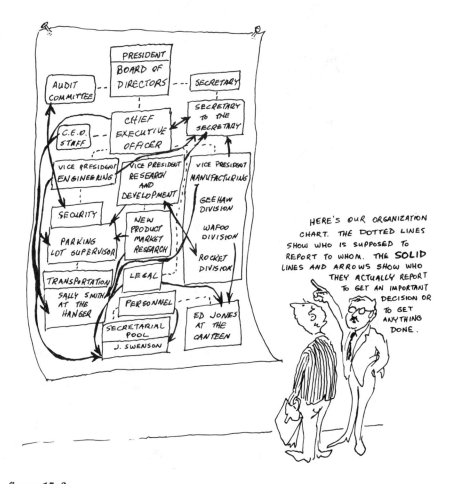

figure 15–3

emotions of the workers, as well as their ability to *think* for themselves. Figure 15–4, from Dessler (1980), compares classic and modern approaches. In rough outline the more modern approach says that if workers have positive attitudes about their jobs (high job satisfaction, discussed in more detail in the next section), this affects how well they perform. Worker attitudes are determined by a variety of things, such as the nature of the work, the goals to be reached, and the resolution of conflicts. In strict classical form, a large corporation might decide for example that Mr. X has to be transferred to Chicago. Mr. X has been working in the south for many years, likes neither large cities nor cold weather, and has children nearly through school, but he is told without regard to any of his personal circumstances "You are being transferred to Chicago." Modern theory would put more emphasis on Mr. X's personal life, under the assumption that he will work better under positive than under negative circumstances. A little search might find a Ms. Right, who has the same qualifications and is eager to live in a big city.

The Organization as Viewed by the Classicists

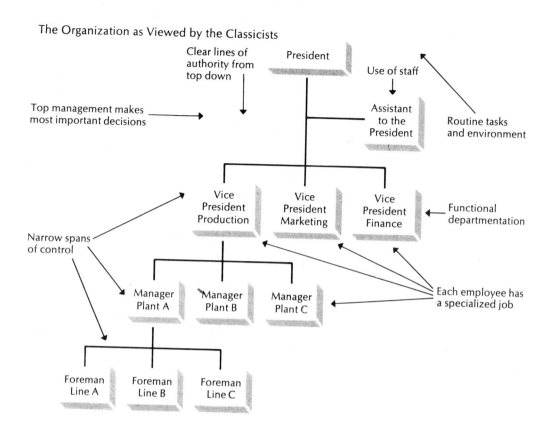

Clear lines of authority from top down

President

Use of staff

Top management makes most important decisions

Assistant to the President

Routine tasks and environment

Vice President Production

Vice President Marketing

Vice President Finance

Functional departmentation

Narrow spans of control

Manager Plant A

Manager Plant B

Manager Plant C

Each employee has a specialized job

Foreman Line A

Foreman Line B

Foreman Line C

The Organization as Seen by Behavioralists

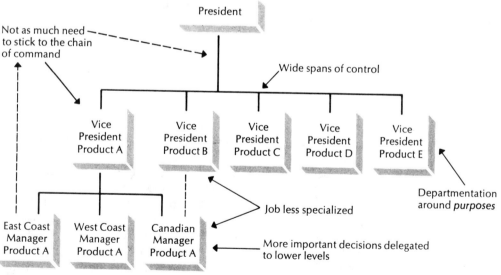

President

Not as much need to stick to the chain of command

Wide spans of control

Vice President Product A

Vice President Product B

Vice President Product C

Vice President Product D

Vice President Product E

Departmentation around *purposes*

Job less specialized

East Coast Manager Product A

West Coast Manager Product A

Canadian Manager Product A

More important decisions delegated to lower levels

figure 15–4. A comparison of two "universal" organization theories: Classical and modern (behavioral). (From Dessler, 1980, p. 327. Used with permission of publisher.)

It is possible to have a division of labor, obviously essential in a large organization, without at the same time completely ignoring individuals in the organization and their needs. Such programs as management by objectives (Chapter Four) or smaller scale variations of employee participation reflect this. So also do approaches to leadership which take into account concern for people as well as concern for structure or production.

organizational climate

Some observers believe that organizations have different "personalities," just as people do. Some people are cold and standoffish; others are warm and receptive. Similarly, some organizations are impersonal while others seem to be caring. Of course, these differences are largely to be observed in the people in the organization, and perhaps some aspects of the physical facilities, since organizations are not real things apart from the people and facilities which comprise them. Organizational climate is often vaguely defined, and it is often not clear just what it is that distinguishes one climate from another or how a particular climate affects the workers.

Litwin and Stringer (1966) described differences in climate in terms of six dimensions:

1. *Structure of the organization,* such as flat versus tall.
2. Amount of *individual responsibility* given to workers.
3. *Rewards,* kind and amount.
4. *Amount of risk* required to do a job effectively.
5. *Warmth and support* exhibited for workers by the company.
6. *Tolerance* for individual differences and *conflict* between individuals or groups within the company.

Other investigators cited by Landy and Trumbo (p. 429) have suggested that there really is no definable "thing" called climate except for degree of job satisfaction. In fact, measures of organizational climate have been derived from measures of job satisfaction. As a positive example that *something* is perceived, however, Schneider (1972) compared the perception of an organization's climate by *potential* employees with those of present employees. He found that if the potential employees' perceptions were similar to those of the present employees, they were more likely to join the organization. Apparently there was something pretty obvious to the potential employees, even if nothing more than "These are (or, are not) my kind of people. I think I would (or would not) like to work here." At present, though the concept of climate is intriguing and deserves study, it is still in its infancy as an approach to describing an organization.

Job Satisfaction

definition

We just saw that organizational climate might represent whatever it is that relates to job satisfaction. The importance attributed to job satisfaction is indicated by the fact that there were over 3,000 *published* studies of job satisfaction between 1935 and 1976, an average of one publication *every five days!* (Locke, 1976). We put job satisfaction under organizational influences because different approaches to management and organization are major (environmental) determinants of satisfaction.

McCormick and Ilgen (1980) define job satisfaction as "the attitude one has toward his or her job" (p. 303). It is an emotional response to the job which can vary from positive to negative in many degrees. This definition is important because everything previously said about attitudes in general (especially in Chapter Seven) is applicable to job satisfaction in particular. The measurement of job satisfaction, the relation of job satisfaction to behavior, and methods of improving job satisfaction are special cases of the same problems raised by the study of attitudes in general.

A job has many characteristics, so job satisfaction is necessarily a summation of worker attitudes about all these characteristics. Good features of a job are balanced against bad features so that job satisfaction "on the whole" is relatively high or low. Table 15–1, adapted from Locke (1976) by McCormick and Ilgen (1980) shows a dozen job dimensions and the components that make up each. Attitudes on each of these (or whatever particular attitude measure is used) are then used to obtain a single overall index of satisfaction which can be used to predict other behaviors.

measurement of job satisfaction

Measures of job satisfaction are designed according to principles used to measure other attitudes. Tables 15–2 through 15–5 illustrate different measures.

Table 15–2 shows a *Thurstone Scale.* The employee indicates which of the statements he or she agrees with. The average of the scale values for the items checked is the individual employee's numerical job satisfaction score.

Table 15–3 shows a *Likert Scale.* A number of extreme statements toward the job, some positive and some negative, are presented. The employee indicates the extent to which he or she agrees or disagrees with each. There are typically five steps, from strong disagreement to strong agreement. Disagreement with a negative item is scored the same as agreement with a positive item.

Table 15–4 shows a set of *Semantic Differential* scales in relation to job satisfaction.

table 15–1

job dimensions typically relevant to job satisfaction

general categories	specific dimension	dimension descriptions
I. Events or Conditions		
1. Work	Work Itself	Includes intrinsic interest, variety, opportunity for learning, difficulty, amount, chances for success, control over work flow, etc.
2. Rewards	Pay	Amount, fairness or equity, basis for pay, etc.
	Promotions	Opportunities for, basis of, fairness of, etc.
	Recognition	Praise, criticism, credit for work done, etc.
3. Context of Work	Working Conditions	Hours, rest pauses, equipment, quality of the workspace, temperature, ventilation, location of plant, etc.
	Benefits	Pensions, medical and life insurance plans, annual leave, vacations, etc.
II. Agents		
1. Self	Self	Values, skills and abilities, etc.
2. Others (In-Company)	Supervision	Supervisory style and influence, technical adequacy, administrative skills, etc.
	Co-Workers	Competence, friendliness, helpfulness, technical competence, etc.
3. Others (Outside Company)	Customers	Technical competence, friendliness, etc.
	Family Members*	Supportiveness, knowledge of job, demands for time, etc.
	Others	Depending upon position, e.g. students, parents, voters

* not included in Locke's discussion
(Adapted from Locke, 1976, p. 1302 by McCormick & Ilgen, 1981. Reprinted with permission of publisher.)

Table 15–5 shows a measure somewhat more specific than the previous measures, the *Job Description Index.* The JDI covers *work, supervision, pay, promotions,* and *co-workers.* The logic of this measure is that if an employee describes his or her job in favorable terms, there is high job satisfaction. This measure has a number of advantages: It is easily administered and understood by the employees, it has obvious relevance to the job, and it has been widely used so that comparisons can be made from one study to another on this measure. Such comparisons have not always been easy because psychologists seem to find it important (or to enjoy) inventing their own attitude measures for particular situations, and the comparability of these different measures is not known.

table 15-2

statements used in a Thurstone scale for measuring employee attitudes toward the company

statement	scale value
I think this company treats its employees better than any other company does	10.4
If I had to do it over again I'd still work for this company	9.5
They don't play favorites in this company	9.3
A person can get ahead in this company if one tries	8.9
The company is sincere in wanting to know what its employees think about it	8.5
On the whole the company treats us about as well as we deserve	7.4
The workers put as much over on the company as the company puts over on them	5.1
The company does too much welfare work	4.4
I do not think applicants for employment are treated courteously	3.6
I believe many good suggestions are killed by the bosses	3.2
My boss gives all the breaks to his lodge and church friends	2.9
You've got to have "pull" with certain people around here to get ahead	1.5
In the long run this company will "put it over" on you	1.5
An honest person fails in this company	0.8

(From Uhrbrock, 1934. Used with permission of publisher.)

table 15-3

Likert-type scales for job satisfaction

1. My work is routine	SA	A	N	D	SD
2. My work is difficult	SA	A	N	D	SD
3. I seem to do many useless things on my job	SA	A	N	D	SD
4. I have the opportunity to be creative in my work	SA	A	N	D	SD

SA = strongly agree; A = agree; N = neutral; D = disagree; SD = strongly disagree. Favorable and unfavorable items are scored from 1 to 5, but in opposite directions so that a high score always means the same thing (e.g. favorable)

table 15-4

semantic differential scales applied to job satisfaction

the work itself	
Fascinating :___:___:___:___:___:___:___:	Boring
Monotonous :___:___:___:___:___:___:___:	Challenging
Simple :___:___:___:___:___:___:___:	Difficult
Creative :___:___:___:___:___:___:___:	Routine
Useless :___:___:___:___:___:___:___:	Useful

table 15–5

sample items from the job description index (part d, work)

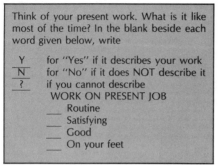

Think of your present work. What is it like most of the time? In the blank beside each word given below, write

Y   for "Yes" if it describes your work
N   for "No" if it does NOT describe it
?   if you cannot describe
      WORK ON PRESENT JOB
___ Routine
___ Satisfying
___ Good
___ On your feet

Source: The scale (Part D, Work) is copyrighted by Bowling Green State University. Information may be obtained from Patricia Cain Smith, Department of Psychology, Bowling Green State University, Bowling Green, O. 43403.

job satisfaction and behavior

General Comment. Although it is something of a truism that happy workers are good workers, this is only *partly* true. There is a relationship between job satisfaction and job performance, but it is not a perfect relationship. There is also an implication that job satisfaction *causes* good performance. Therefore, if we do things to make workers happy, they will perform better. The flaw in this argument is that a *correlation* between job satisfaction and performance

OH, I ADMIT JOB SATISFACTION HAS IMPROVED SINCE YOU BEGAN THESE "SUN TAN BREAKS," BUT, PRODUCTION...

TO SUN DECK

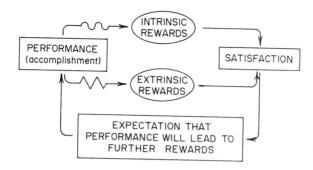

figure 15–5. The Lawler-Porter model of job satisfaction, showing how performance leads to rewards and satisfaction and the expectation of future rewards. (From Lawler & Porter, 1967, Fig. 1. Figure slightly adapted by Dessler, 1980. Used with permission.)

does not prove that satisfaction causes performance. Good performance might lead to high job satisfaction rather than the other way around.

Lawler and Porter (1967) proposed the following model for job satisfaction: *Performance* which leads to *rewards* produces *satisfaction* with the work, *and* the *expectation* that future performance will also lead to rewards. This is shown in Figure 15–5.

Several studies indicate that *there is greater job satisfaction when rewards are specifically related to job performance than when equal rewards are given but not specifically related to job performance.* We can relate this to the discussion of achievement motivation in Chapter Four. Job satisfaction is related to *control* over events. Though organizational attempts to "increase morale" by contrived programs may have some positive effects, they may not necessarily lead to increased performance. It is when the employee perceives the rewards as being the consequence of his or her work that performance and satisfaction *both* increase.

Turnover. Where job satisfaction is high, turnover is low. Turnover is one of the most expensive of personnel problems because of time and money lost in training and retraining. For purely selfish reasons then, businesses need to be concerned about job satisfaction. Measures of job satisfaction can also be used diagnostically to find those aspects of a job which are not satisfying. If these can be corrected, turnover can perhaps be reduced.

Absenteeism. Absenteeism is not consistently related to job satisfaction because many other factors, such as illness or specific work conditions, affect absenteeism. Smith (1977) nicely illustrated both that there is an effect of job satisfaction on absenteeism *and* the difficulties in showing that such a relationship exists. During a bad snowstorm in Chicago, job satisfaction predicted rather well among a large number of managers who would or would not show up for work. Given a good excuse not to come to work, the less satisfied managers in a large corporation did not come to work, but better satisfied managers did. On the same day, in New York City where there was no snowstorm, job satisfaction did *not* at all predict absenteeism among comparable managers. It took a combination of environmental factors (snowstorm) and personal factors (job satisfaction) to predict accurately.

Job Performance. In Chapter Seven we saw some of the difficulties in predicting performance from attitudes, just as we saw above for absenteeism. Many studies have found virtually no relationship between job satisfaction and performance. There may be a relation which is outweighed by other factors, such as employees needing the job, but at present we have to say that the question is still not clearly answered.

Job Satisfaction and Unionization. Hammer and Smith (1978) studied some 88,000 workers in 250 different units of a single industrial organization. Attitude surveys had been taken as a matter of course, and these data were already on hand when subsequent union activity was begun. Half the units had attempts to unionize and 31 did vote in a union. All the units with *no* union activity had higher job satisfaction scores than all those units which *did* have unionizing activity. Other studies have also shown the same general trend, which makes perfectly good sense. A worker who is satisfied with his or her job perceives little reason to bring in a third party and stir things up.

individual and group differences in job satisfaction

Occupational Level. Job satisfaction increases as occupational level increases. This is understandable, since higher occupational levels have higher pay, greater autonomy, greater opportunity for feeling of accomplishment, and so on. There are exceptions, however, sometimes dramatic. Studs Terkel, in his book *Working* (1974), quotes at length from a grave digger who thoroughly enjoys his work. It is outdoors, it is necessary, it is in a pleasant environment, and he takes pride in how well he does it. Locke and Whiting (1974) report that garbage collectors were relatively well-satisfied with their jobs as compared to equally unskilled laborers in other jobs. The moral seems to be that we cannot prejudge that a given job is or is not satisfying. Stockbrokers can have low satisfaction and garbage collectors, high.

Gender. It is to be expected that this whole area may be rapidly changing, but one study of male and female college graduates joining the Prudential Insurance Company (Manhardt, 1972) found that men were more concerned with long range career objectives and women more with comfortable working conditions and good interpersonal relations. More important, perhaps, is that they did *not* differ on many other factors, such as degree of autonomy on the job.

Race. A number of studies have reached the conclusion that blacks and whites consider the same things to be of the same relative importance in jobs but that blacks have lower job satisfaction. This would appear to be because the whites are getting more of the rewards they seek than are the blacks. Again, as in the case of women, the similarities are as important as the differences. The fact that both groups had the same general values with regard to what is important in a job should cut through any *stereotypes* about racial differences in this regard.

Age. There have been two different sets of findings about age (Bass & Ryterband, 1979). One is that job satisfaction is relatively high for young workers, declines in middle age (the 30s and 40s), then increases again with further age. The other is that there is a steady increase in job satisfaction with age. It is well-established that younger workers are more likely to quit their jobs than older workers. A reasonable overall interpretation is that there is relatively low satisfaction at some point early in a career because expectations are not met, and greater satisfaction later because expectations have been reduced. At some point, most workers seem to realize that they have reached some limit and adjust with greater satisfaction to their situation. Very young workers may be satisfied in the belief that they are going to progress and then show a middle-age decline when they do not go as far as they had hoped. The reason for the discrepant results is not understood, except perhaps as a result of studying different individuals or companies or occupational levels. A young person coming out of law school with a degree in hand might be expected to have steadily increasing job satisfaction, whereas a person in business who does not get the desired promotions might well show lower satisfaction before finally "settling in."

theories of job satisfaction

Theories of job satisfaction involve motivational, emotional, and informational components, as do other attitude theories. McCormick and Ilgen (1980) selected the following five general approaches to job satisfaction from the longer list of specific theories presented by Locke (1976).

Comparison Processes. The individual is said to have some reference standard against which he or she judges the actual job. Job satisfaction is then greater or lesser depending on the size and direction of the difference. If the real job is better than the referent, there is a positive attitude and high satisfaction. But if the job is worse than the referent there is a negative attitude and low satisfaction. For example, construction workers might find much satisfaction in a job which lasts for several years, is indoors, and has a boss who is not too bossy. This is in contrast to a reference job (the worker's idea of a typical construction job) which might be short-lived, requires outdoor work in winter, and has strict supervision.

Instrumentality Theory. Job satisfaction is said to be high to the extent that the job is instrumental in getting the worker what he or she values, or wants from the job. This might be pleasure in the work, security, prestige, money, short hours, autonomy, convenient location, or anything else considered valuable.

Social Influence. This proposes that people are influenced by how satisfied they perceive other workers to be with the same job. A person new to a job might not be very happy with it initially, but then change attitudes in a more favorable direction upon discovering that other workers are well-satisfied with the job.

Equity Theory. People generally want to get what they consider a fair (equitable) return for their behavior. This suggests there is greater job satisfaction if the worker perceives that the return for his or her work is equitable. To illustrate, the author listened to the complaint of a steel assembly worker about having to do some welding one day when the regular welder was sick. His complaint was not that he disliked welding or that it was more difficult than his regular job. Rather, he was dissatisfied because welders earn more than his job paid and he considered it unfair that he be asked to weld but be paid at his regular rate. Equity, of course, can involve much more than money. A worker might get a title without increased pay and consider this valuable and fair.

What about the converse, however, the situation where a worker gets *more* than is "deserved" for a job? According to equity theory the worker should feel the pressure of this inequity in his favor as well as inequity not in his favor. There is in fact some direct evidence. Workers in an experimental setting who believed they were overpaid for their work did work harder than others who did not believe they were overpaid. What may happen in practice, however, is that people *adapt* to "overpayment" so that the perceived inequity no longer exists.

Two-factor Theory. This is Herzberg's theory of "satisfiers" and "dissatisfiers" previously discussed in Chapter Four. Herzberg argued that the things which cause satisfaction are not the same as those that cause dissatisfaction. McCormick and Ilgen (1980, p. 380) believe the evidence is firmly against this theory, but it has nevertheless enjoyed considerable popularity.

how to increase job satisfaction

Bass and Ryterband (1979) propose the following three *approaches* to increasing job satisfaction. These follow from the general idea that employees are satisfied to the extent that they perceive their behavior is rewarded on the job.

1. *Increase the expectation that the employee can derive what he or she values by working. Or, increase the value of those rewards which are available.* For example, if an employee values an overseas assignment, the expectation of that assignment can be guaranteed under certain conditions (assuming it is relevant to the job at all). Or, if an overseas assignment is inevitable, its value can be increased by showing the employee how such an assignment is important in the long run and will help the employee to get what he or she ultimately values.

2. *Increase the extent to which an employee believes that he or she has the capability to do the work which will lead to the valued outcomes. Or, increase the value of the outcomes which the employee believes he or she can achieve.* For example, an employee might be assured that her credentials for a particular job are more than adequate (if that is true), thus increasing her expectation of success. Or, those things which the employee can be reasonably expected to achieve (such as pay and security) can be given greater emphasis and made more valuable.

3. *Increase the employee's fullfilment of his or her needs with valued outcomes. Or, make more valuable to the employee those outcomes which fulfill the employee's needs.* For example, if an employee with strong social needs is on a job which requires isolated work for long periods, special efforts can be made to allow social contact other than the actual work itself. Or, meetings about the work might be given more emphasis and value.

Bass and Ryterband suggest that these general propositions lead to three specific principles, which we quote verbatim (p. 119):

1. Design the job to allow people to feel personally responsible for a meaningful portion of their work. The job should provide them with a sense of *autonomy* and 'ownership' of the outcomes of their work.

2. Design the job so that outcomes from working at it are intrinsically meaningful and worthwhile to the jobholder. This can be accomplished by providing *variety* and *task identity* in the work. A job with a variety of activities requires employees to use a variety of skills and abilities, as well as alleviating boredom. A job with task identity has 'meaningful wholeness,' a sense of beginning and end (closure), and involves highly visible 'doing something that really makes a difference.'

3. Design the job so that it gives positive feedback [reward] to the worker.

Job Design: Work and Environment

background

Over the centuries, there have been changes in the design of work and the work environment. Only in this century, however, has there been a conscious attempt to examine work conditions to determine which are better than others, using a scientific approach involving careful research and measurement.

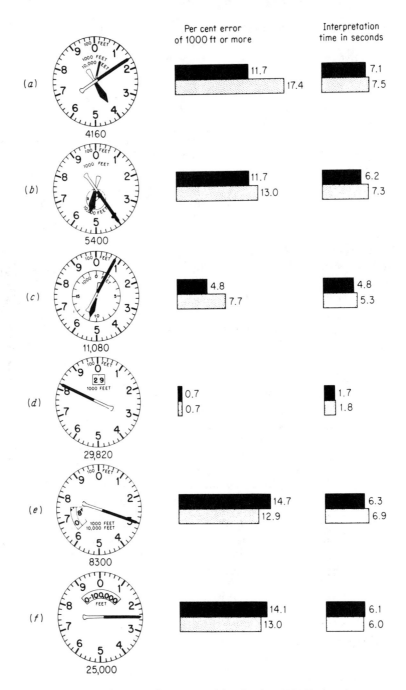

figure 15–6. Altimeter designs used by Grether (1949) showing percentage of errors and interpolation time for United States Air Force pilots and college students. Numbers underneath the dials are correct readings. (From McCormick, 1964, Fig. 6–2. Used with permisssion of publisher.)

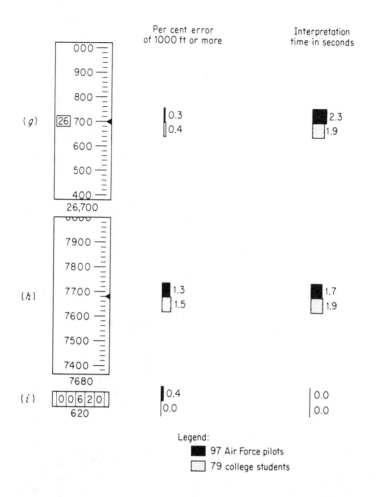

Per cent error
of 1000 ft or more

Interpretation
time in seconds

(g)   26 700

26,700

0.3
0.4

2.3
1.9

(h)   7700

7680

1.3
1.5

1.7
1.9

(i)   0 0 6 2 0

620

0.4
0.0

0.0
0.0

Legend:

■ 97 Air Force pilots
□ 79 college students

McCormick and Ilgen (1980) identify three major approaches to job design.

The first approach is *methods analysis,* an outgrowth of *industrial engineering.* The general idea is crystalized in time and motion studies of work behavior. For example, for a given repetitive job some ways are better than others for making the specific movements needed to do the job (say, attaching a part to another part on an assembly line). Some movements are quicker, less fatiguing, and generally more productive.

The second approach is *human engineering,* or *human factors.* This is commonly a problem of *worker-machine relationships.* For example, what shape pliars work best for a particular job? What shapes and markings of dials make them most readable? What handles on levers make the levers most distinctive so the operator does not confuse them? As an example, look at the different dial displays in Figure 15–6. Some are easy to read and others are difficult. Even the most difficult of these have been used, though, and there have been many errors and accidents with them. Presently, human engineering is concerned with all kinds of *operating systems of which humans are components.* Air traffic control is shared

Two extremely different work environments. Each contains its own approach to job enrichment and job satisfaction. (Building photo by Bill Henry)

between machines (radar screens, computer analysis of the radar) and humans who look at the data generated by the machines. The question in such a system is What can the machine(s) do better and what can the human do better, so that the overall system works best?

The third approach is *job enlargement* and *job enrichment*. This is largely a product of the 1960s and 1970s concern with the "dehumanizing" nature of many jobs. The usual example is the assembly line job, illustrated in the extreme by a worker who does nothing all day but screw the same few screws into the same few places on some object which passes endlessly by on a conveyor. The idea behind job enrichment is that if workers are more satisfied, they will be more productive.

The Dilemma. On the surface, the human factors and job enrichment approaches seem to pose a dilemma in values. The most efficient way to do a job from an engineering standpoint may also be the most boring and unsatisfactory to the worker. If an industry (say, the automotive industry) is to be competitive it must be efficient. On the other hand, if a job is so unsatisfactory that it is only done from sheer necessity, what is the worker living for? In an old joke, an unemployed "bum" asked a businessman why he worked so hard. The businessman replied that if he worked hard for the next twenty-five years he could relax and enjoy himself. But, replied the bum, that's what I'm doing *now*. Unemployment, of course, is not the answer to job satisfaction, but the moral of the story is clear: The quality of life which civilization is supposed to achieve may be better achieved if we enjoy our work.

How is the above dilemma to be resolved? The answer is that there is no single solution, but there are a number of possible ways to look at the problem. One is that there may often be compromise—some jobs can be made more mechanically efficient but still contain elements of autonomy and satisfaction for workers. One company uses workers as tour guides on a rotating basis. Workers can be shifted from one assembly line task to another so they are not permanently bored.

A second point is that there are individual differences in people. Some people may like assembly line work just because it does not tax their capabilities, or they do not want more responsibility. The problem then is to assign people for particular jobs which fit their interests and abilities. Third, we should realize that for much human engineering work there is no conflict. Reducing fatigue or errors or having machines do part of the work is not in conflict with job enrichment. Imagine what air traffic control would be like *without* radar.

measurement of human factors

Four different approaches to the measurement of human factors are commonly used (McCormick, 1964).

1. *Work performance,* such as time to perform a task, speed of responding, accuracy in performing the task, and so on.
2. *Physiological measures,* such as heart rate, oxygen consumption, or metabolic waste products from muscular work. Direct electrical measurements of muscle activity may also be taken to show which muscles are more active for a particular task.
3. *Psychological measures,* such as for job satisfaction. One can also study *preferences* for one job situation over another in terms of comfort or aesthetics. Workers may prefer certain wall colors, seating arrangements, amount of lighting, and so on. If these preferences are not in conflict with the job itself, why not take them into account?
4. *Accidents and injuries.* These may be due to personal factors (such as illness or visual defect) or environmental factors (such as moving equipment). We shall discuss accidents and safety in more detail at the end of this chapter.

stimulus-organism-response and work

We began this chapter with the general point that behavior (response) is a function of the environment (stimulus) and person (organism). To illustrate this approach, let us take the example of a visual display *(stimulus)* which contains information which a worker *(organism)* must perceive and process and *respond* to. Poor performance may be due to difficulties at any of these three points.

Stimulus Factors. Stimulus factors may include displays which are not large enough to be seen at the typical user distance, like supermarket signs which cannot be read from one end of the aisle to the other, or displays which are not bright enough to be easily read, or which have strange lettering systems, and so on.

Figure 15–7 shows three sets of numbers which appear to be rather similar but which vary significantly in their readability (McCormick, 1964, p. 161). With daylight, for example, the NAMEL numbers were misread only half as often as the AND numbers. The differences were less when the numbers were on plastic illuminated from behind (transillumination).

Figure 15–6 showed several different kinds of altimeters, for displaying the altitude of an aircraft, along with the *percentage* of reading errors of 1000 feet or more, and the time in seconds to interpolate between two numbers. Look particularly at a, b, e, or f and imagine yourself in the cockpit of a rapidly descending aircraft trying to figure out how far you are from the ground. It was exactly this sort of problem that gave the field of human engineering its biggest impetus. There are now standard displays for various aircraft functions based on human engineering research.

The human engineer also must consider basic questions of sensory processes. What are the most audible sound frequencies under particular conditions? What colors are most visible under different lighting conditions, and do they vary according to brightness? What size displays can be detected at a given distance (the problem of visual acuity)?

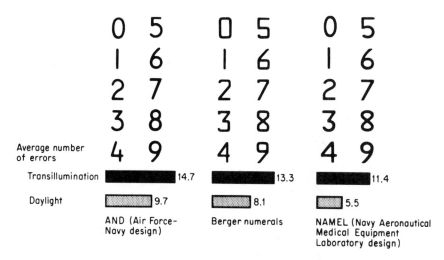

figure 15–7. Three different forms of numerals and average number of errors reading each under two illumination conditions. (From McCormick, 1964, p 1t1, Fig. 6–25, used with permission.)

Organismic Factors. Many individual factors influence responses to visual displays, including fatigue, boredom, distraction, poor vision, color blindness, and the like. We shall look at some of these factors under accidents. What we look at here is the capacity of the person to *process the information* displayed. (The same problem would occur for any sensory modality.)

Absolute vs. Relative Judgments. We may illustrate an *absolute judgment* with the following task: A person has to identify the position of a pointer between two markings. The observer might have to say to the nearest tenth what the marker distance was between 4 and 5, indicating 4.1, 4.2 or whatever. A *relative judgment* involves a *comparison* between two stimuli. For example, which of two lights is brighter, or larger, or which of two sounds is higher or louder, and so on. The amount of information a person can process with these two approaches is vastly different. Most people (not color blind) can distinguish between 100,000 and 300,000 different colors in combinations of *hue* (color), *saturation* (purity) and *brightness.* But, if asked to present by means of some appropriate apparatus any particular color, about fifteen is the limit the individual can do without confusion. In the case of the interpolation of the counter, about ten points is indeed the limit of what can be done accurately. We could tell the person to do the task to the nearest twentieth, but he or she would be unreliable and actually accurate only to about the nearest tenth.

In general, along any single stimulus dimension most people can only identify accurately about seven points, plus or minus two (Miller, 1956). Table 15–6 gives the number of different levels (points) on a given dimension that people can accurately identify by the method of absolute judgment, in several different sensory modalities. Another example of absolute judgment is musical pitch. A musician may set an instrument at A, for example, from memory.

table 15–6

The number of different judgments that can be reliably made on a number of different sensory dimensions. Note especially the differences between the use of single dimensions and the combinations of dimensions.

sensory modality and stimulus dimension	no. of levels which can be discriminated on absolute basis
Vision: single dimensions	
Pointer position on linear scale	9
Pointer position on linear scale	
Short exposure	10
Long exposure	15
Visual size	7
Hue	9
Brightness	5
Vision: combinations of dimensions	
Size, brightness, and hue	17
Hue and saturation	11–15
Position of dot in a square	24
Audition: single dimensions	
Pure tones	5
Loudness	5
Audition: combination of dimensions	
Combination of six variables	150
Odor: single dimension	4
Odor: combination of dimensions	
Kind, intensity, and number	16
Taste	
Saltiness	4
Sweetness	3

(From McCormick, 1964, p. 92, Table 5–1. Used with permission of publisher.)

Trained musicians can set more than seven notes accurately, but even musicians with so-called perfect pitch are considerably short of perfect.

Given the fact that we can make such a relatively small number of absolute judgments on a single dimension, how is it that we can recognize literally hundreds and hundreds of different people's faces? The answer is that we use many different dimensions for such identifications, such as size, shape, and coloring, and in such combinations we can build up a very large number of accurate judgments.

Responses. Human behavior is limited by our genetic inheritance: We cannot fly, we have limited strength and flexibility, limited speed and duration. Much human engineering is concerned with the problems of designing equipment to overcome our limitations. Accurate responding also depends on our ability to detect and process information from the environment. Some responses work better with some displays than other responses. Figure 15–8 shows two different types of display and response requirements (knobs to be turned). The arrangement to the right has greater "compatibility" between the display stimuli and the responses than the one on the left. *Stimulus-response compatibility*

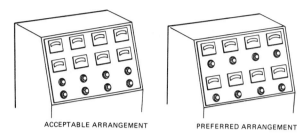

ACCEPTABLE ARRANGEMENT   PREFERRED ARRANGEMENT

figure 15–8. Illustration of spatial compatibility of a set of displays and their corresponding controls. The one at the right is more compatible because of the closer, one-to-one relationship of each pair of displays and controls. The one on the left is still reasonably compatible, however. (From McCormick & Ilgen, 1980, p. 350. Used with permission.)

means that some stimuli and responses "naturally" go together better than others. This is to be determined by research, however; we have already seen that engineering "logic" led to displays like the worst of the altimeters in Figure 15–6.

There are many examples of stimulus-response compatibility, in the home as well as in business and industry. For example, the arrangement of the knobs for the burners on a stove is better done some ways than others. Figure 15–9 shows one very good arrangement and some bad arrangements of these (adapted from Chapanis & Mankin, 1967; Gilmer, 1975). People can learn, of course, to use even the bad arrangement, and errors are not as disastrous as a bad display-response arrangement in an aircraft cockpit or in a nuclear power plant.

Another factor in responding is the shape of the response instrument, such as a lever handle. In an aircraft, a pilot has to watch numerous visual displays while simultaneously pushing and pulling various knobs and levers *without looking at them.* In WWII aircraft, many of these levers had the same

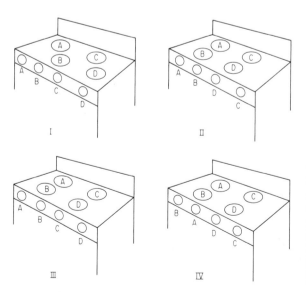

figure 15–9. The control-burner arrangements of a simulated stove in the study of human reactions. There were zero errors for design I in the upper left-hand corner and had the shortest response times. The relationship between stimulus and response is much better than in the other models. (Adapted from Chapanis & Mankin, 1967 by Gilmer, 1975. Used with permission.)

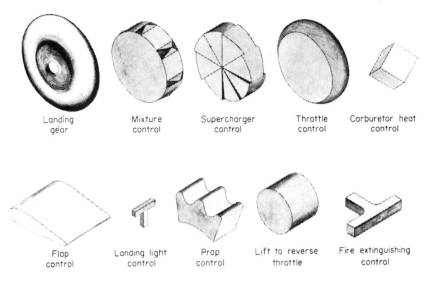

Landing
gear

Mixture
control

Supercharger
control

Throttle
control

Carburetor heat
control

Flap
control

Landing light
control

Prop
control

Lift to reverse
throttle

Fire extinguishing
control

STANDARD KNOB SHAPES

figure 15–10. Standardized shape-coded knobs which are readily distinguishable by touch alone, and which are related to the functions in the aircraft which they control. (From McCormick, 1964, p. 309–310. Used with permission.)

kind of handles and pilots could (and did) easily pull the wrong one, resulting in an accident or near accident. Considerable research resulted in several different sets of handle shapes which were virtually never confused by touch. It is also helpful if the shape of the handle is symbolic of the function it serves. For example, a control for the wheels would be shaped like a wheel. This is illustrated in Fig. 15–10. This along with standardization of location for various kinds of levers with different functions has greatly reduced "human error" in aircraft accidents.

There are many other kinds of response problems, such as the easiest kinds of movements, the least fatiguing, and so on. The reader may look at a standard reference book for information about these.

Accidents and Safety

We may think of an accident as an *unplanned event that interferes with the normal progress of work.* A painter spills a can of paint and has to clean it up, a waiter drops a tray of dishes, a motorist hits a slick spot on the road and spins off, an athlete trips and falls. We are generally most concerned, of course, with accidents that involve injuries or fatalities. This is too narrow a focus for accident *research,* however, because it does not pay enough attention to those *conditions* which *almost* lead to accidents. The painter may have spilled the paint because he or she slipped and almost fell off a scaffold. The near-serious accident might go unreported, however, even though it could be important information relevant to the prevention of future injurious accidents.

the person: human factors in accidents

Is There Such a Thing As Accident Proneness? When research into accidents and safety was seriously begun, in the 1920s, one of the first consistent findings to emerge was that a relatively small proportion of the workers accounted for a relatively large proportion of industrial accidents. This led to the idea that some people were "accident prone," which was considered something like a personality trait. Such a concept is of no value, however, unless we can identify "accident prone" people independently of their accidents. That is, if we say that people have accidents because they are accident prone and we know they are accident prone because they have a lot of accidents, we have said only that "People with a lot of accidents have had a lot of accidents." In other words, we have said nothing by this "circular reasoning."

Consider the following "thought experiment." We put 1000 names in a hat and pull out 500. We replace each name when we have recorded it so that the same name can be drawn as many times as chance allows. The following will happen. At least 500 names will never be drawn at all. A few names will be drawn twice and some may be drawn three, four, or even five times. If these drawings were accidents, we might tend to call those names drawn several times "accident prone," but in fact we know that on the basis of purely random drawings these results are entirely expected.

This analysis can be researched with real data. If we have the accident records for a company for several years, we can see who had the high accident rates in the first year. If we eliminate those high repeaters from the analysis of subsequent years we should expect that the accident rate would go down. Table 15–7 shows that this is not the case; the accident rate is about the same in the second and third years as it was in the first. This means that there must be a steady accident rate which is not accounted for by accident prone individuals. This, and other analyses, all indicate that accident proneness is not a phenomenon of sufficient importance to bother with very much, if in fact there is such a thing as accident proneness at all. More recent research does suggest that there may be some personality characteristics which have a weak association with accidents (such as being "adventuresome"). The identification and treatment, such as by counseling, of such individuals is not very reliable, and it is so expensive that it has not seemed worthwhile to pursue.

Vision. The effect of poor vision depends on the job. An accident with a typewriter is not the same as an accident with a crane. But it has been found over many different kinds of jobs that individuals with poorer vision do have more accidents. Automobile driving is a well-known example.

table 15–7

Accident rates for workers over a three-year period. the ten men with the highest accident rates in the first year were removed from the analysis (lower row) without any significant change in accident rate by the remaining workers over the next two years.

	first year	second year	third year
Mean accident rate for 104 men	.557	.355	.317
After removing 10 men with highest rate in 1st year, i.e., 94 remaining men	.393	.361	.329

(From Arbous & Kerrich, 1953, Table 1. Reprinted by permission of publisher.)

Age. A variety of research (McCormick & Ilgen, 1980) strongly suggests that accident rate increases up to about age twenty-five, with a relatively high level throughout the twenties, then declines steadily. This trend might be partly due to very young and older workers being in jobs which are less accident-liable. The actual accident data themselves, however, are very clear.

Perceptual-motor Skills. Drake (1940) compared individuals whose motor skills were relatively better or worse than their perceptual skills. He concluded that ". . . the person who acts quicker than he can perceive is more likely to have accidents than is the person who can perceive quicker than he can act (1940, p. 339)." It is quite possible that people with good motor skills get themselves into situations of risk with the confidence they can get themselves out safely, but sometimes fail to do so. Conversely, those individuals with less good motor skills are simply more cautious.

Fatigue. The greater the fatigue, the more likely are accidents. During the course of a regular work day, accidents tend to peak about two-thirds of the way through the morning, then decline. In the afternoon, there is the same build-up and decline. Also, workers on night shift tend to have more accidents than those during the day, perhaps because their sleep-waking patterns have not adjusted to the unusual work hours.

the environment: external factors in accidents

Safety Devices. A young woman of the author's acquaintance working in a print shop accidentally cut off several fingers in a paper cutting machine when she was able to hit the "start" mechanism at a time when she should not have done so. One can argue that she should have known better, that she should have been more careful, that she should have been this or that. But the fact remains: Had the safety mechanism for the cutter been designed differently she would not have had the accident. Safety mechanisms are supposedly designed precisely for the purpose of protecting the unaware, the careless, the clumsy, the dizzy, the hasty, or what have you. They are to compensate for otherwise dangerous work environments.

table 15–8

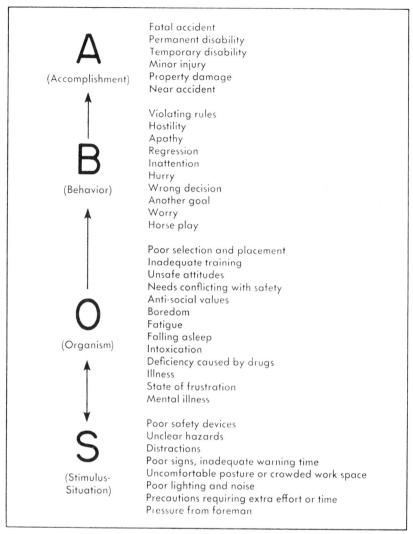

A
(Accomplishment)
- Fatal accident
- Permanent disability
- Temporary disability
- Minor injury
- Property damage
- Near accident

B
(Behavior)
- Violating rules
- Hostility
- Apathy
- Regression
- Inattention
- Hurry
- Wrong decision
- Another goal
- Worry
- Horse play

O
(Organism)
- Poor selection and placement
- Inadequate training
- Unsafe attitudes
- Needs conflicting with safety
- Anti-social values
- Boredom
- Fatigue
- Falling asleep
- Intoxication
- Deficiency caused by drugs
- Illness
- State of frustration
- Mental illness

S
(Stimulus-Situation)
- Poor safety devices
- Unclear hazards
- Distractions
- Poor signs, inadequate warning time
- Uncomfortable posture or crowded work space
- Poor lighting and noise
- Precautions requiring extra effort or time
- Pressure from foreman

(From Maier, 1965. Reprinted with permission of publisher.)

Maier (1965) suggests three rules for good safety devices. *First, they cannot be disengaged.* Automobile seatbelts are mere expensive decorations if not used. In industry, safety devices can be built into machines so there is no way not to use them. *Second, they should be foolproof.* A device that is only 50 percent safe (and probably a random 50 percent at that) may be more dangerous than no safety device at all, since the worker may mistakenly believe it to be completely effective. *Third, they should not interfere with production.* This may not always be entirely possible, but Maier suggests that even if slowed down a little, the fact that a worker is free from worry about safety, and hence able to concentrate on the job better (and perhaps therefore be less fatigued) may more than compensate.

Job Characteristics. There are certain jobs that are inherently dangerous, and specific measures have to be taken to deal with their particular problems. In the fabrication of mobile homes, large sheets of metal with sharp edges are used. The accident rate has been very high because the industry is relatively new and safe methods for handling the materials were not used. Coal mining is a job within a more obviously dangerous environment. There are many precautions to be taken by workers, but unless the environment is made safe, accidents will continue to occur.

Other kinds of job-related illnesses (such as brown lung disease from breathing cotton dust, or lung problems from breathing asbestos) are not called "accidents," but they certainly result from environmental hazards, and from our point of view here they might just as well be considered preventable accidents.

Summary. Table 15–8, from Maier (1965) indicates the kinds of factors involved in accidents, from the S-O-R approach, and shows that accident prevention must consider changes in the environment (working conditions) as well as changes in the individual (such as education or placement into a more appropriate job).

SUMMARY

1. The organizational structure of a business or industry, the work situation, influences work behavior.

2. Organizations have *line functions,* where people have direct authority over those below them, and *staff functions,* which do not have direct authority.

3. *Classic* organization breaks an organization into progressively smaller parts. Such organization varies according to *division of labor* (specialization), *delegation of authority, structure* (tall vs. flat), and *span of control.*

4. Span of control is the number of people who report directly to a given superior. Different spans of control work better in some situations than others. Three different situations in this regard are *small-batch* organizations, *large-batch and mass production* organizations, and *continuous process* organizations.

5. *Modern organization theory* takes into account the workers' *attitudes, emotions,* and *ability to think* for themselves. It therefore gives more responsibility to workers as well as being more sensitive to their needs.

6. *Organizational climate* refers to the particular "personality" of an organization. Six proposed dimensions of climate are (a) structure of the organization, (b) amount of individual responsibility given to the workers, (c) rewards, (d) amount of risk involved in the job, (e) warmth and support

for the workers by the company, and (f) tolerance for individual differences and conflict within the organization.

7. *Job satisfaction* is the *attitude,* or emotional response, one has toward one's job, considering all the different characteristics (good and bad) of the job situation. Job satisfaction is measured by a variety of different attitude scales specifically focused on the job situation.

8. Employee *turnover, absenteeism, performance,* and *unionization* are all related to job satisfaction.

9. Satisfaction is related to differences in *occupational level, sex, race,* and *age.*

10. Job satisfaction is greater when rewards are *specifically related to job performance* than when they are not related to job performance.

11. Several theories attempt to explain job satisfaction. *Comparison process theory* says that satisfaction is determined by comparing the job a person has against some standard for that job. *Instrumentality theory* says that job satisfaction is high to the extent that the job gets the worker what he or she values. *Equity theory* says that job satisfaction is high if the worker perceives that he or she is receiving a fair return for his or her work. Herzberg's *two-factor theory* says that things which satisfy or dissatisfy workers fall into two different categories.

12. To *increase job satisfaction* an employer could set up work situations to allow the worker to perceive greater *autonomy,* make the outcome of work *intrinsically meaningful and worthwhile,* and give the worker *positive feedback* about his or her work.

13. The three major approaches to job design are (a) *methods analysis,* which typically studies the time and motion involved in work, (b) *human engineering,* which deals with worker-machine relationships, and (c) *job enrichment* or enlargement, the aim of which is to make workers more satisfied and therefore more productive.

14. The human factors in job performance can be *measured* by *work performance* (like speed or output), *physiological* measures, *psychological* measures, and *accident and injury records.*

15. *Job performance,* as a behavior, depends on both the work *environment* (stimulus situation) and the *person* (organism). Stimulus factors include such environmental variables as visual displays. Organism variables of importance here deal with the capacity of the person to process relevant information, which varies according to the kinds of judgments a person is required to make. Response factors include finding the easiest, fastest, most accurate, or least fatiguing kinds of movements.

16. An *accident* is an unplanned event that interferes with the normal process of work. The notion that some people are *accident prone* is not well supported by evidence. A number of personal factors are related to accidents, however, such as vision, age, perceptual-motor skills, and fatigue. Some jobs

are inherently more dangerous than others, but safety devices properly designed and used can help prevent accidents.

EXERCISES

1. How is work behavior influenced by organizational structure? What specific qualities are encouraged by the environments of a teacher and a salesperson on commission, respectively (the text examples)? Which type of work situation and reward schedule would you be happiest with?

2. What are line and staff functions in an organization? How are they similar and different? Think of specific types of business that would utilize each function.

3. Compare and contrast the classic and modern theories of organization. What are the advantages and disadvantages of each? If you were a worker, which would you tend to agree with? Which would you agree with more if you were an employer?

4. What are the different types of span of control? Give specific examples of companies that would fit into each category.

5. Using the six dimensions of organization structure, design your ideal organizational climate. Explain why it would best fit into a classic or modern approach or a combination of these.

6. Choose some job you think you would be dissatisfied with. On a piece of scratch paper complete the Likert scale, semantic differential scales, and Thurston Scales with that job in mind. Now think of a job you would very much like to have and fill out the same scales with reference to it. Compare the two sets of results.

7. How are job satisfaction and behavior related? Besides using attitude measures, how might you judge job satisfaction?

8. Discuss the influence of characteristics of the individual (sex, age, race, occupational level) on job satisfaction. How are changes in society affecting these influences?

9. Make up a hypothetical worker (that is, imagine one). Now, using the five theories of job satisfaction describe how his or her job satisfaction might be seen differently according to which theory is applied.

10. Use the guidelines for increasing job satisfaction to arrive at a list of specific steps (motivation courses or investment programs, for example) that could increase job satisfaction, and indicate how these should increase satisfaction.

11. What is the purpose of studying job design? What are three approaches to this study, and exactly what types of problems does each approach deal with?

12. Analyze your classroom in terms of human engineering and come up with two or three possible improvements. Think about how you might design a more efficient kitchen in human engineering terms.

13. Why would an employer be interested in job enrichment for his or her workers? Give at least two possibilities.

14. Think of some examples of stimulus-response compatibility in your home, job, or school environment. In particular, how might various appliances be improved?

15. What are the most dangerous jobs you can think of? How could they be made safer? What principles of job design might be used?

16

Environmental Psychology

In previous chapters we have referred to person-environment interrelations, but we have emphasized people. Now we emphasize the environment. Take a trivial example. You are standing behind a desk and hold out your hand to shake with someone coming toward you. The chances are practically zero that this person will *climb over your desk* to shake your hand. He or she may walk around it or reach over it but hardly climb it. Here we have the presently existing environment plus all the individual's past experiences determining his or her behavior. The desk is an environmental object with a highly predictable effect. In this chapter, we will be concerned with a variety of complex environmental-behavior relations.

Orientation to Environmental Psychology

defining environmental psychology

The authors of the several textbooks on environmental psychology have been near-unanimous in *not* defining the subject matter. A definition should set off this area of psychology from others, but the field is so new that what environmental psychologists *should* do is still unsettled. It is usually said that "environmental psychology is whatever it is that people called environmental psychologists do." There is, of course, an implied relationship between environment and behavior, but that is about the only limitation.

some general assumptions

In the first environmental psychology textbook, (Ittelson, et. al., 1974) there were the following assumptions about people and their relation to the environment.

1. *The environment is experienced as a whole.* There are many parts, but we respond to those collectively, as a whole. This is the Gestalt psychology dictum that "the whole is more than the sum of the parts."
2. *The person also has environmental properties as well as individual psychological properties.* A person is part of his or her own environment, and that of other people. People perceive their own actions, just as they perceive other animate or inanimate objects.
3. *Physical environments are inevitably related to social systems.* The way an environment affects us is partly the result of social learning and social activities of the people in the environment. The social system of a desert nomad affects perception of the Sahara desert very differently than does the social system of an American city dweller.
4. *The degree of influence of the physical environment on behavior depends somewhat on the behavior in question.* Beautiful churches do not necessarily make believers, nor do they necessarily command attendance in the same way that good roads affect driving behavior.

5. *The environment frequently operates below the level of awareness.* We take much of our environment for granted unless there is a change. We don't notice air pressure unless it becomes very different from normal, such as greatly increased humidity or a very strong wind.

6. *The "observed" environment is not necessarily the real environment.* The "real" environment is filtered through our sensory-perceptual systems and what gets filtered varies from person to person (Chapter One). We shall return to this shortly.

7. *The environment is conceived as a set of mental images.* These images depend on our experiences, motives, and so on. We organize the environment in our minds according to what is important to us.

8. *The environment has symbolic value.* Flags, pieces of cloth flapping in the wind, have symbolic value far beyond their actual value. Iron bars may symbolize something different according to which side of them you are on. Homes, cars, desks, offices, medals of honor, and uniforms have important symbolic value. The nation of Israel has a great deal of importance because it is symbolic as the traditional home of the Jews.

perceiving the environment visually

We perceive the environment through all our senses, but visual perception is especially important. The classic problem to puzzle both psychologists and philosophers is how we perceive a three-dimensional world (with depth) when we only have two-dimensional stimuli (height and width) projected through the lens of our eye onto the flat receptor surfaces, the retinae. The answers are not all in, but since the days of renaissance artists we have had some pretty good ideas.

Binocular Cues. Being in slightly different positions, the two eyes have slightly different images of the environment. This is called *binocular disparity.* The familiar stereo slide viewers impress us with the great three-dimensional effects they produce. These two-eye cues do not actually provide the bulk of distance information, however. There have been perfectly competent one-eyed ski jumpers, airplane pilots, and tennis players, all using skills requiring good distance perception. Binocular cues are of special value up to about fifteen feet, roughly the maximum distance a tree-dwelling animal might have to jump from one limb to another. The brain does combine the two images in a special way, but one author has been moved to write that the main advantage of two eyes is that you have twice as many monocular (one-eye) cues.

Monocular Cues. As an object is farther and farther away, the angle between the object and the eyes is less and the more nearly similar the two visual inputs are. A number of important monocular cues then come into play.

1. *Size.* Other things being equal, the larger of two images appears to be the closer.

2. *Linear perspective.* The far end of a building in a photograph (or on the retina) is smaller than the close end. The gradually decreasing apparent size is linear perspective.

3. *Interposition.* If one object blocks off vision of another object, it is perceived as being closer.

4. *Brightness.* Other things equal, a brighter object appears closer. It is possible to pit such cues as size and distance against each other. A smaller circle can be made to look closer by making it brighter.

5. *Aerial perspective.* Things in the distance usually look slightly hazy and have a bluish cast; this is aerial perspective. One of the visual deceptions in the desert is the apparent closeness of mountains. There is little aerial perspective because the air is clear, and size is hard to judge, so mountains appear closer than they actually are.

6. *Texture.* Other things equal, if a surface has a rough texture it seems closer than if it has a fine texture. James Gibson, a well-known researcher in the field of visual perception, has considered texture gradients (changes in texture) to be the best cues available for perceiving distance. Figure 16–1 illustrates the different cues described.

7. *Shadows.* Shadows add depth to a two-dimensional scene because shadows can only exist in a three-dimensional world.

hearing and spatial perception

Next to vision, people most often use hearing to judge distance and direction. Sounds that originate straight ahead, behind, or above are very difficult

figure 16–1. This photograph has virtually all the monocular distance cues. Can you identify them?

to locate because the sound reaches the two ears at the same time. If there is only a tiny fraction of a second difference in arrival time at the two ears, we can detect quite accurately that the sound is coming from the direction of first arrival. In practice, we usually keep cocking our head in different directions until we get a sound located. Stereo recording/playback systems allow sound perception closer to that of live music than do monaural systems. Instruments seem to be located in the direction of the speaker they come first from (or loudest from). Direction and loudness can also be competing cues, like size and brightness.

increasing social change and environmental impact

That people have long been concerned with their surroundings is exemplified in the unmatched architecture, formal gardens, and art of the pre-Christian era. Toward the middle of this century, however, there has been a new kind of interest, legitimized, for example, by the formation of the Environmental Protection Agency, planning organizations and citizens groups. All this has been necessitated by the twin problems of increasing population and decreasing resources. To feed and house more people, we appropriate the habitats of other species, as well as cutting forests for wood, strip mining for minerals, and polluting oceans with oil and waste.

Americans have been especially wasteful of natural resources, only slowly realizing the actual cost which Western Europe has long known. High gas prices and shortages are very familiar to the rest of the world. We will have to re-evaluate the kind of housing possible in the future. Almost certainly, houses will be smaller, more fuel efficient, have smaller lots (perhaps used as gardens), and there will be more multiple unit dwellings.

The increasing age of population will also affect housing needs. In 1900 about 4 percent of Americans were sixty-five or older but by the year 2000 this will increase to about 12 percent—about thirty million people with relatively low incomes and specialized demands related to aesthetics, functions, and economics. Part of all the process will be in changing perception of the environment.

Cognition and Environment

the cities of the mind: cognitive maps

The di Barbari Map of Venice. In 1500, Jacopo di Barbari published a remarkable map of Venice, Italy. It is a composite of six woodcuts. Jacopo (Jacob, the Barbarian—Renaissance Italians considered *all* Germans barbarians) was a superb draftsman and cartographer, and the detail in his woodcuts is

figure 16–2. Di Barbari map of Venice circa 1500.

exquisite. What makes his map so notable, however, is that it is an *aerial* view, as if taken from about 4,000 feet above the Venice lagoon. But the highest places that Jacopo or his aides could reach were the belltowers of the cathedrals of St. Mark and St. George, both of which are seen from far above in his map. By combining all the information he had from city plans and sketches taken from many viewpoints, as well as by making meticulous measurements, Jacopo arrived at a map of the city from a single visual location whose accuracy was subsequently verified several centuries later. Jacopo's map was a creation, his mental image of the city of canals transferred to woodcuts and paper.

Cognitive Maps in Rats and Humans. Leaping forward about 450 years we find Edward Chace Tolman, a psychologist at the University of California, publishing a scientifically charming paper called "Cognitive maps in rats and

men" (Tolman, 1948). Tolman argued that much of what people (and rats) learn is the relationships between events and places in their environments. Some things are near, others far; some are to the right, others left, some are up and others down. But, every one also has his or her *private* viewpoint, which includes emotional and cognitive understandings beyond mere map locations. Not everyone in Venice saw the city from Jacopo's lofty perches. Venice had a unique social stratification. The impoverished near-slaves who toiled for the wealthy merchants and nobility lived on the ground floors of the palaces along the Grand Canal, within reach of the high tides and always damp. The merchants inhabited the warm, dry, upper floors. The middle floors were rented to whoever could afford them. The picturesque city must have been perceived very differently depending on which floor one inhabited. Similarly, the isle of Manhattan must look very different to those who live on the Upper East Side (where there is a congregation of wealth and talent) than it does to the residents of the Lower East Side (where talent may abound, but not money). A city is, in fact, a city of the mind.

Psychologists are increasingly interested in cognitive maps, those internal representations of reality. What is the cognitive map of the United States for a New Yorker? A Chicagoan? A poor southern Italian?

The U.S. as viewed by as East-coast inhabitant.

The Value of Cognitive Maps. How are cognitive maps valuable? Tolman argued that they are mental images of how to get to *valued things,* representing paths, goals, and landmarks between. What, however, is the usefulness of getting to valued things? The answer is *survival.* We earlier pointed out (Chapter Three) that we strive both for *needed* goals and *wanted* goals. But surely the needed goals (food, water, air) had evolutionary priority. As our cerebral hemispheres grew we could develop more complex cognitive maps and more complex goals to reach with those maps. But underneath this veneer of civilization is survival. We are frequently reminded how easy it is to strip this veneer. Nowadays, groups of people calling themselves *survivalists,* prepared with stored supplies and weapons for what they believe is the inevitable crumble of civilization, are ready to fight their neighbors.

Several Views of the Environment. Cognitive maps are related to other more specific ideas and perceptions of the environment and hence, how we treat the environment.

1. *Religious Views.* One view has it that the environment is part of our dominion, to do with as we will since we are created in God's image. Another view is that we are but brief transients and should leave our environment, like a guest room, as clean as we found it.

2. *Political Views.* Empires are assembled and destroyed as the result of political views. A particular river or mountain range may be seen as a natural boundary between countries with border disputes which persist for centuries. Related to the political views are military strategy and economics. Parts of Europe, rich in natural resources, have been invaded over and over by political regimes hoping to gain advantage for their own people.

3. *Economic Views.* A real estate developer may look at an unspoiled beach and envision only high rise hotels. The next thing we know, we have Miami Beach. A well-known actor, praised for his conservation work, was involved in land development operations for resorts in the North Carolina mountains. His resolution to this apparent conflict was that "everybody has to live somewhere."

4. *Aesthetic Views.* The artist in all of us can appreciate the aesthetic value of an unbroken beach line, an undeveloped mountain, an untouched forest, or a crystal clear lake. We can also appreciate the beauty of artificial structures, from the magnificent cathedral of Notre Dame to a tastefully designed and decorated restaurant.

5. *Scientific Views.* Physical scientists view the world (from their professional perspective) as atoms and molecules, radiation and energy. The same air contaminants that produce a golden sunset cause the scientist to wonder about the coming of the next ice age because the sun's rays will not reach the earth as effectively through the haze. The scientist Galileo conflicted with the church because Galileo could see things through his telescope which religion then said were impossible.

6. *Biological Views.* Biologists see life forms existing on earth in a delicate balance. The food chain from plants to herbivorous animals to meat-eating animals can be broken by changes in the environment. A highway through a species' natural range can be as disruptive as a subdivision. *Ecology* is that subdivision of biology concerned with the interactions between life and the environment.

7. *Poetic Views.* William Blake, in his depressive moods, could write:

Tiger, tiger burning bright
In the forest of the night
What immortal hand or eye
Could frame thy fearful symmetry?

Blake was not literally writing of the environment, but he invoked a frightening image of a world not understood. More romantic poets could see "sermons in rocks" and understanding of the universe through contemplation of pastoral scenes. Walden Pond, as a body of water, is now barely a memory, but the beautiful imagery of country life invoked by Henry David Thoreau may be everlasting.

Said Thoreau:

I went to the woods because I wished to live
deliberately, to front only the essential facts
of life, and see if I could not learn what it had to teach,
and not, when I came to die, discover that I had not lived.
Walden

Conflicting Images. The "cities of the mind" are powerful; people will work to maintain their images and will experience conflict with people having different images. An act of Congress was necessary to keep a dam from destroying an area on the New River, near the North Carolina—Virginia border. Thousands of hours and dollars were spent in conflict between citizens groups and the power company. Congress did finally pass the bill declaring the place a national wilderness area, but the heart of the struggle was the question of how to use an important part of our environment. In my home town, surely like yours in this regard, there are continual battles between developers on the one hand and the city planning board and citizens groups on the other, about how land should be zoned. One large fight has been over the location of a cross-town highway which everyone agrees is needed—but not in *their* neighborhood. The challenge of environmental psychology is to understand how people perceive their environment, how their perceptions relate to their actions, how to protect the environment, and how to live in it most pleasantly, given all the problems to be faced.

learning the environment: active participation

We learn about the environment through all of our senses. We see buildings, smell a bakery, or feel a footpath. Yet, consider the following. You ride several times as an automobile passenger along a route previously unfamiliar to you. Then you have to drive it, and discover that you don't know it as

Joggers should develop very good cognitive maps of their environments because there is much active participation in the learning.

well as you thought. This fairly common experience illustrates a major fact: *active involvement and muscle movements are important in learning even about visual space.* In numerous experiments, humans have worn glasses which displaced a visual image several degrees to the side. The subject has simply to touch a target. Just having a hand passively placed on such a displaced target is not sufficient for the subject to adjust to the displacement. The subject has to actively make the correct adjustments before significant learning occurs. (Similar results have also been found in the *development* of visual-motor coordination in kittens (Held, 1965.) Our mental representation of the environment is based on movement and activity as well as what we usually consider sensory inputs.

symbolic properties of space

We have seen the symbolic importance of objects, but space in itself is also symbolic. In business, the higher the level of your job, the more office space you have. A "spacious" home is a sign of "success," and, the more land area surrounding it the greater is the apparent success, particularly in cities. Within an office the following are indicators of status: (1) windows, (2) a rug, the larger the better, (3) a private office, (4) the type of chair and the size and style desk. (A *really* important executive may not even have a desk, but a luxurious table or a "communications center"), (5) general decor, such as pictures lamps, or supplementary furniture, and (6) a private washroom, or direct access to the "executive washroom."

Such symbols do not *directly* enhance work performance unless the job

(Photo by Bill Henry) [of Bill Henry]

involves impressing someone or because people will work harder to obtain such visible signs of status. Because they are visible, they automatically confer in the possessor power and prestige.

Environment and Emotion

environmental load

Environmental psychologists have used the concept *environmental load* to describe environments in relatively simple form. Load is defined in terms of the amount of information an individual must use to deal with the environment. A highly complex, changing environment, or one which is novel and full of surprises, requires much effort to keep up with and has *high load.* A relatively unchanging, simple, repetitive environment has *low load.*

The following pairs of adjectives have been used to rate the load of an environment (Mehrabian, 1976, p. 12) and illustrate more precisely what load refers to: uncertain-certain; varied-redundant; complex-simple; dense-sparse; intermittent-continuous; surprising-usual; heterogeneous-homogeneous; crowded-uncrowded; asymmetrical-symmetrical; immediate-distant; moving-still; rare-common; random-patterned; and improbable-probable. The left-hand adjective in each pair represents a high-load environment and those on the right refer to low load environments. New York City is typically a high-load environment, a small rural town would typically be a low-load environ-

*This Venetian "street scene" suggests a very low-load environment as compared with the hustle and bustle of motor traffic in most cities. (**Bottom** photo by Bill Henry)*

ment. There are, naturally, many little pockets of variation in either the large city or the small town.

emotions

Mehrabian uses the three emotional dimensions of arousal-nonarousal, pleasantness-unpleasantness, and dominance-submission (also commonly referred to as control-lack of control) as the ingredients from which all other emotions are manufactured. In general, *approach behavior* is related to an optimum level of arousal, pleasantness, and dominance. *Avoidance behavior* is related to too-low or too-high arousal, unpleasantness, and submissiveness (lack of control). The dimension of arousal-nonarousal is most closely related to environmental load: the higher the load the greater the arousal.

Individual Differences: Screeners and Nonscreeners. People can be characterized according to their typical levels along each emotional dimension. Some people typically have pleasant dispositions and find pleasure in many things. Some people are typically in control (dominant) and others are not (submissive). The most important differentiating characteristic in Mehrabian's scheme, however, is related to arousal. He distinguishes what he calls *screeners* and *nonscreeners*. The screeners are very sensitive to selected parts of their environment and to load changes; they are quickly aroused but their arousal subsides quickly when the load reduces. The nonscreeners are less selective in what they respond to, they take in more stimuli, they are aroused by a greater variety of things, and they stay aroused longer after the load has been reduced. A screener, then, recovers more quickly from an environmental load than a nonscreener and is ready to "take on" the environment again sooner.[1]

putting the pieces together

The stronger the environmental conditions for arousing approach behavior, the less is the environmental load; the stronger the conditions for avoidance behavior, the greater the environmental load. People try to average out situations so that over some period of time, such as a day or a week, the *average* load best suited to them is achieved. Any environment is far too complex to be completely described in all its detail, but in Mehrabian's view, environments can be described relatively simply in terms of load and the effects of load on the different emotional "types" described above, particularly on screeners and nonscreeners.

---

[1] The distinction between a screener and a nonscreener is very similar to the distinction between an introvert and extravert, as put forth by Hans Eysenck (for example, 1973). Introverts are more excitable and hence seek less stimulating environments, whereas extraverts are less excitable and seek more stimulating environments.

Let us take two examples of environments with different loads and see how they relate to behavior. George is an advertising salesman for a radio station. He is always on the go, feels he must always be "up" for his clients, is continually under a heavy environmental load and is therefore highly aroused at work. The circumstances are not too pleasant and not really very much under his control. Alice, his wife, does not work outside the home. Her work there requires little time, effort, or intellectual demand. Her arousal level is very low, is not particularly pleasant for her, and she is often at loose ends (little control). George arrives home in the evening and wants to reduce his load (and lower his arousal level) by sitting down with the paper, having a couple of drinks, relaxing, and not thinking about anything stimulating. Alice, on the other hand, wants to increase her environmental load, to get a more optimal level of arousal for her. She wants to talk, or go out, or do something active.

So George and Alice may be in conflict with each other's interests. This fictitious example is not unlike the experience of many traditional couples. The situation would be modified, however, according to whether George was a screener or a nonscreener. If he were a screener, he might be able to "come down" in a half-hour or so and be ready to go again. But if he were a nonscreener it might take him all evening to come down. For Alice's sake we hope he is a screener.

To generalize the above example, if people tend to average out their environmental loads for whatever their individual optimal level is, we could make some reasonable predictions about the kinds of activities they might engage in if we knew for any given person (1) the optimal load level, (2) whether he or she was a screener or nonscreener, and (3) something about the load levels of the various situations in which this person might be involved. In the abstract we would predict that individuals would choose higher load levels if their typical situation were below their preferred load level, but opt

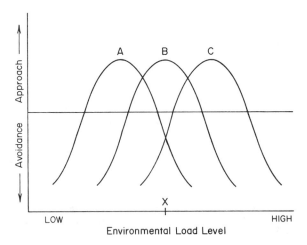

figure 16-3. The effects of the same environmental load level (arousal) on three different people. The level at point "X" is too high for person A, too low for C and about right for B. A seeks an environment with a lower road level than X, C seeks a higher level than X and B is relatively satisfied.

for lower load levels if their typical situations were above their preferred level. We would fine tune the predictions according to whether they were screeners or nonscreeners. This is illustrated in Figure 16–3. Even without this detailed information, however, we can *understand* better, for example, why some people want vacations full of excitement and others just want to have a quiet two weeks away from everything.

The Natural Environment and Behavior[2]

use and conservation

Those who view the environment as a tool favor its exploitation as being essential to human welfare. If aesthetics and recreation suffer, so be it; it is necessary. *Necessity,* however, is dictated by what people *believe* is important, the way they perceive the environment.

The conservationist view is to question the long-term cost of economic development. The argument is simple: If we use up our natural resources (including clean air and water), then what? The larger problem is well illustrated on a smaller scale by the *Tragedy of the Commons* (Hardin, 1968). In Britain, sheep owners grazed their flocks in a public "common" area, to which everyone had a right. This worked well with a small number of sheep. But the herds grew larger and everyone still claimed his right. As we know, sheep bite grass off very close to the ground and readily *overgraze* in a confined area. The sheep owners were not willing to restrict their rights to the common grazing ground, and as a result all the grass was eaten and the commons destroyed so that no one could graze any sheep there. Conservation is an economic necessity. Air, water, and oil are *not* unlimited. People flying over the southwest United States look at the vast stretches of land and say "We've got no land problem, this could all be settled." It is no accident that the government put the Navajos on this land; it has *no water* either. Entire states argue over who has the rights to the water coming down the continental divide in the Rockies. California wants water from Colorado. There is no guarantee that we will develop practical alternative energy sources before our present ones run out. The energy from the sun is vast, but so is the wind in a hurricane. The trick is to capture it and transfer it into something we can use—electricity.

natural hazards

When nature becomes unusually violent, almost incomprehensible power is released. If the impact of floods, hurricanes, earthquakes, and lightning is

---

[2] Much of this section is organized around the excellent discussion by Ittelson, et al. (1974, Chapter Ten).

lessened, life is considerably easier. In California, residents repeatedly rebuild homes in areas subjected to forest fires and mudslides. In India, periodic floods drown thousands of people, there is mass evacuation, and when the waters recede the survivors go right back again. In both cases, people continue to put themselves into jeopardy, indicating the very strong environmental influence on behavior.

In some ways we invite national disasters. If forest cover is removed, by fires or development, the natural drainage and absorption of water by land are changed. This produces erosion and flooding. When rivers are dammed for flood control, as up and down the Mississippi, there is simply a displacement of the flood problem from one location to another. A "major spring recreation" in the author's birthplace, built on hills overlooking the Mississippi, is to go watch the river flood above the local dam. About 200 U.S. cities are built on flood plains, land "reclaimed" by filling and surrounding with levees.

How do people adjust to natural disasters? In the early 1960's Yellowstone Park was hit with a major earthquake in the middle of the night.[3] A cliff crumbled onto a campground near the West Gate, burying all the occupants. The immediate reaction of many people in the area was to pack up at midnight and leave. The roads were jammed. But where did the people think they were going? They did not know where the quake was centered or where the greatest danger was. They simply panicked and did *not* think. This is not unusual. A number of studies, both of civilians and military personnel, have shown that only about one person in four is very rational in severe emergencies.

Such disasters as earthquakes and floods are rare for most people. The *psychological* ways of reacting to such stress situations depend on such factors as frequency, recency, and severity of previous disaster(s) in individual cases. One reaction is *denial* ("It can't happen here." or "It can't happen again.") Denial, of course, leaves a person very vulnerable because he or she is not likely to do much in anticipation of disaster.

Another reaction is to *reduce the uncertainty* (if not the uncontrollability) of natural disasters. For example, "locusts come every seven years, so relax." Or there will be a drought every so many years, or a hard spring freeze, and so on. This reduces the surprise and may initiate some action in preparation for an expected setback or disaster. Americans were caught totally off guard by the Arab oil embargo in 1972 and did not know how to react. We will no longer be surprised in such matters.

A third mechanism is to *give responsibility for doing something to someone else*, including God and the government. In one of the humorous scenes in the movie *Patton,* the general orders the chaplain to write a weather prayer to stop a snowstorm so Patton's forces can get air cover. The weather changes for the better and Patton has the chaplain decorated!

---

[3] I am indebted to Prof. L. I. O'Kelly, an astute observer of behavior and a camper in the park that night, for a first-hand description of events.

All these mechanisms, like defense mechanisms in general (Chapter Six), involve reducing anxiety about disaster. They represent different ways of perceiving the situation. At earlier times people might have tried to cope by offering sacrifices to the gods of wind, fire, or water.

recreation

Why do people choose to go camping as recreation? The virtues of "getting away from it all" and "getting back to nature" are commonly stated. But what does the usual campground look like? There is as little inconvenience as possible. Campgrounds are often crowded, dirty, filled with recreation vehicles, trailers, and house-size tents which have everything, *including* the kitchen sink. It is commonly suggested that outdoor recreation gives an immediate sense of accomplishment in terms of survival as we imagine it to have been in the past. The image of the lone survivor at the frontier, doing all his or her own chores and briefly being in *control* of things, may be achieved at least temporarily (even in the crowded campground) in a way that is often *not* achieved in usual daily pursuits. Most people go through many days in which their activities are almost completely controlled by outside agencies such as one's job or the family transportation needs. Any kind of camping is a break from most of this.

Who Uses Natural Areas for Recreation? The national park system and wilderness areas, started in the mid-1800s, have steadily increased in size and use, now occupying about forty million acres or about 2 percent of the continental United States (Stanley, 1969). What kind of people use the wilderness areas?

One study (Outdoor Recreation Resource Review Commission, 1962) characterized the "typical" wilderness user as a professional person with high education, above average income, living in an urban area with more than 200,000 people. There are a number of possible explanations for this. One is that the wilderness is chosen because it is so different from usual work and living conditions—it has a lower environmental load. Another is that it *does* take money to get there. Those who have less money or who live in more rural areas may get outdoor recreation in their own "backyard."

Not everyone, of course, likes wilderness areas. A steady rain or a leaky tent may challenge some, but for others it simply reaffirms the value of civilization. Catten and others (1969) found the main reason for wilderness camping reported by campers in the Pacific Northwest was what the authors call "Spartanism"—a setting for the display of manliness and fortitude. The second reason was a rejection of commercial "improvements" in the wilderness. (Thus they did not use the more popular campgrounds.) Third was enjoyment of the environment in its primitive state. We thus can distinguish two kinds of "campers"—those who hang stereo speakers on trees outside their recreational vehicles and those who use only what they can carry on their back.

Privacy and Personal Space

nature of personal space

A notable characteristic of groups of organisms is that they do not occupy space randomly. Individuals in a group tend to maintain a relatively constant distance between each other. The distance may get smaller as the number of occupants increases, but it tends to remain proportional. For example, if two people were ten feet apart a third person might tend to stand five feet from each, and so on.

Territorial spacing by pigeons and by people. *(Photos by Bill Henry)*

There are two major interpretations for why we space ourselves as we do (Bell, et. al., 1978, pp. 142–144): *protection* and *communication*. We try to protect ourselves from *overstimulation* produced by too-close contact with others. The most prominent theory accounting for the periodic rise and fall of animal populations is *not* fluctuating food supply, but rather that as populations increase there is less individual space and hence greater stress from inter-animal contact. Among the various internal responses (see Chapter Five) are hormonal changes and a lowering of the survival rate. Secondly, we try to protect a feeling of freedom and to maintain control of our own behavior. Territorial spacing helps protect this feeling. The communication function of interpersonal distance, such as by varying closeness, operates by giving nonverbal messages about us.

what determines the size of personal space?

In Chapter Nine we saw that different kinds of communication are related to different interpersonal distances. Though there are considerable individual differences among people in this regard, many Americans seem aware at least of the socially expected distances. Recall the four zones labelled by Hall as *intimate* (0–18 inches), *personal* (1.5 to 4 feet), *social* (4 to 12 feet) and *public* (beyond 12 feet). Hall's observational studies were provocative and stimulated research which has indeed supported his ideas. However, there are a number of different factors which also account for individual differences in the size of personal spaces.

Attraction and Interpersonal Space. The greater the attraction between two people the smaller the physical distance between them. This seems to be due to females moving closer to their opposite sex friends, however (Edwards, 1972). Interpersonal distance between males does not vary with liking as it does with females, at least in the U.S. Fairly obvious interpretations are that females are socialized to be more intimate and males are not. There is also fear of homosexual connotations with other males. People watching couples infer greater liking when the couple is closer together (for example, Mehrabian, 1968).

Similarity. People who are more similar to each other tend to have greater liking and maintain a closer distance between themselves. This has been found for people with similar personality and attitude characteristics, as well as with such group similarities as age, race, and social or business status. This may be because people anticipate more favorable reactions from people who are similar to them (Bell, et. al., 1978, p. 150).

Type of Interaction. Pleasant interactions are generally conducted at closer distances than unpleasant ones. The exception is angry interactions, where we can picture two antagonists standing eyeball to eyeball.

Racial and Cultural Factors. Some cultures, for example, Latin Americans, French, Greeks, and Arabs, use closer interpersonal distances than others such as American, English, Swedish, and Swiss (Bell, et al., p. 152).

Sex Differences. Overall, quite separate from interpersonal attraction, women tend to maintain closer distances.

Age. There is relatively little research here (Bell, et. al.). Adult patterns of spatial behavior do not appear until puberty, however.

Personality. A number of personality characteristics have been related to interpersonal distance *preference*. Briefly, (1) People who believe more in external control of events desire more distance from others than do people who believe in internal control. (2) Schizophrenics require more space than "normals." (3) Emotionally disturbed children in a play situation put dolls farther apart than did non-disturbed children. (4) Extroverts maintain less space than introverts. (5) Violent prisoners required three times as much space to feel comfortable than did nonviolent prisoners (Bell, et al., p. 155).

Territory and Crowding

territory

We have seen that certain distances are maintained between individuals, which we thought of as *invisible, individual-centered personal spaces*. Now we turn to *permanent, identifiable geographic areas* which individuals mark as their *territory*. If you have a pet dog it has a territory marked by its urine, especially around your yard, and perhaps your car. Your dog and the other dogs around know where the territory is and respect it: Even a small dog can defend its own territory against larger dogs. There may be border disputes, as between neighboring dogs, but these are usually settled without too much difficulty. The advantage of territory is that it does minimize disputes. Many animals have territories, perhaps less obvious than the dog's. Some birds, for example, are highly territorial, but it is harder to identify the boundaries, or even the proprietor.

It is a big jump from the animal research to say that territorial defense is instinctive in humans, as some have argued (e.g., Ardrey, 1966). Much of American law, however, is based on the concept of the inviolability of private property. There are few instances where someone can *take* your land or trespass into another's home without legal consequences. Breaking and entering, for example, is a major offense, especially if firearms are involved. Many people feel they have the right to defend their homes to whatever extent necessary.

Kinds of Territory. Altman (1975) has distinguished three kinds of territory.

1. *Primary territory* is "owned," such as a house or office. The owner has complete control and intrusion is a serious breach of etiquette, if not of law.
2. *Secondary territory*, like a classroom, is not individually owned, but at certain times a given person has temporary authority and "ownership." From nine to ten A.M. on Monday, Wednesday, and Friday, my classroom is *mine* and no one would think of intruding. Campsites in public campgrounds are quickly marked by new occupants and thereafter are avoided by other newcomers.
3. *Public territory*, such as a beach or library table, are not owned and are difficult to control. There are many tricks for marking such territory, however, such as leaving towels and beach umbrellas, or books, to "save" the space temporarily. Defining occupancy of public territory is considered important as a way of holding down the environmental load.

Group Territorial Behavior in Humans. There are many identifiable group territories, such as churches, schools, or businesses. More dramatic, however, are gang territories in cities. Suttles (1968) studied territoriality in ethnic groups in Chicago. He found that territories are clearly identified by such boundaries as streets and are vigorously defended by their occupants. On a grander scale are the political boundaries separating states or nations. Legal jurisdiction in one area does not carry over to another except by treaty. Were the police from East St. Louis (Illinois) to start operating in St. Louis (Missouri), or vice-versa, there would be tremendous disputes.

crowding

Calhoun (for example, 1962) has shown that if rodents are allowed unlimited food and water supply, but limited space in which to live and breed, the population will increase, then level off well below the theoretical limit. There is a disastrous drop in birth rate, high infant mortality rate, homosexuality, heightened aggressiveness, and cannibalism. The animals also show physiological signs of stress. A *behavioral sink* is established, a place with a particularly high density of animals, usually around the food source. Social problems are particularly severe in this area. Such results have been found reliably enough with animals to raise concern whether they would also occur with humans. Increasing population coupled with the trend to greater urban living make this a realistic concern.

Human Crowding. Fortunately, human research does not bear out all the pessimistic predictions from animal research. Some cities with very high density (such as Hong Kong and Tokyo) have much lower crime rates than cities of much lower density. This suggests that the ill effects of crowding can be modified, probably by social controls. Some of the negative effects of crowding on humans are as follows (Bell et al., Chapter Six):

1. People working under crowded conditions report more feelings of discomfort than those under less crowded conditions, more so for males than females.
2. Males show high physiological arousal, such as higher blood pressure, under crowded conditions, but females do not.
3. Individuals living in crowded conditions are more prone to illness, possibly a joint consequence of greater transmission of illness and less resistance due to stress.
4. People living under crowded conditions are less attracted to others; again, this is more true of males than of females.
5. People tend to withdraw from high density situations.
6. The greater the density, such as in an apartment building, the less likely people are to help each other. This extends generally to people living in cities as compared to more rural areas.
7. Research on aggression and density gives inconsistent results.

There are several possible interpretations for these results. One of these is the *environmental load* concept. Excessive crowding is a high load (high arousal) condition which is eventually unpleasant. Secondly, behavior is more *restricted* in crowds and this reduced freedom is aversive.

built environments and behavior

Cities. As cities get bigger they become more complex, noisier, more polluted, and more demanding of time and inconvenience (for example, commuting time, and waiting in lines). Individuals living in cities may become adapted to these environmental characteristics so that they either are not as bothered by them or do not recognize them as inconveniences. People migrating from small towns to New York, for example, notice such things more than do people migrating from other large cities (Wohlwill & Kohn, 1973). Even if not consciously recognized, however, the environmental load (high arousal) of a city may induce coping behavior to deal with the situation. People may learn to deal with property crime by multi-locked doors and being more vigilant in general. And perhaps they learn to be screeners to cut out some of the environment.

There is also an apparent decrease in desire to associate with strangers, lest there be stressful encounters. For example, there is less direct eye contact between commuters in a central city area than in a suburb of the same city (McCauley, Coleman & DeFusco, 1977). Contact with *friends,* however, does not seem to be much different in cities than in small towns. Many people have talked about the deficiency of helping behavior in big cities, but this is apparently an exaggeration. Helping behavior depends on whether a person has the skills to help, as well as the willingness, and sometimes big-city people do indeed have more skills for some situations. People in cities tend to say they would rather live in the suburbs, escaping from the noise and crowding and pollution, but they typically want to be close to the city for the many real advantages in terms of jobs, shopping, and entertainment.

Housing and Building Design. Tradition plays a large role in the design of houses and apartment buildings. Tradition is partly dictated by economics (some designs are cheaper than others), but also by cultural factors. For example, *modern tradition* has it that the bath and toilet are in the same room, even though some of us remember bathing in the kitchen in the winter because that is where the stove was. As we noted earlier, economics may force a rethinking of housing design—a greater trend to apartment dwelling, for example. This may meet with some resistance since many people have been familiar only with the housing conditions under which they were raised. There is, in fact, little real departure from the way houses are constructed now and how they were a hundred years ago.

Housing Projects. Whether they are publicly or privately financed, we have gained some valuable information about what *not* to do in the design of apartment dwellings. The most infamous case in point was the Pruitt-Igoe project in St. Louis. Completed in 1954 with forty-three buildings eleven stories high for a total of 12,000 people, the project was essentially dead within fifteen years. The essence of the design principle was *efficiency:* there was no wasted space and there were vandal-resistant walls, fixtures, and plumbing. It was an almost instant slum with high incidences of rape, pillage, plunder, and vandalism. The project was eventually demolished as a failure. What went wrong? There are a number of explanations, but two of the main ones offered were that (1) the space was organized so that people were kept isolated; there were no communal meeting places for informal groups, and (2) stairwells and dark dead-end corridors were breeding places for all kinds of illicit activities and mischief out of the sight of any of the apartment dwellers and therefore anonymous. In brief, the whole project was constructed so that no community ties could be established between neighbors and so that asocial behavior was made easier. There are a number of possible solutions to this problem, which we cannot detail here, so suffice it to say that designers are now much more aware of the importance of open, common areas where social interactions are easy, where a sense of community can develop, and where people or things are not easy targets for crime or vandalism.

SUMMARY

1. Environmental psychology deals with the *relationship between the environment and its occupants.* Some of its basic assumptions are that the environment is experienced as a whole and often operates below the level of awareness, physical environments are inevitably related to social systems, and that the environment is conceived of as a set of mental images and has symbolic value.

2. *Three-dimensional vision* is very important in our perception of the environment. Monocular cues, like interposition, and binocular cues, like binocular disparity, help us convert 2-dimensional sensory input into depth perception.

3. Increasing population and decreasing natural resources are putting strain on the environment and Americans are realizing the necessity for conserving our resources and developing further social programs.

4. The *real environment* and the *perceived environment* are not always the same. Internal representations of reality are called cognitive maps and they are influenced by a wide range of viewpoints including religious, political, and scientific views. Active participation in the environment facilitates learning about it.

5. *Environmental load* refers to the amount of information an individual must use to deal with the environment. A high load environment is complex and changing. A low load environment is relatively simple and unchanging.

6. People can be classified according to their arousal level in relation to environmental load. *Screeners* are people who are very sensitive to selected parts of their environment and to load changes. They are aroused quickly but their arousal subsides rapidly when the load is reduced. *Non screeners* are less selective in what they respond to, are aroused by more things, and stay aroused longer.

7. *Natural disasters* and opportunities for outdoor *recreation* are two ways in which the environment influences behavior. People try to reduce the anxiety involved with natural disasters in different ways depending on their perception of the situation. These include denial, reducing the uncertainty around them, or attributing the responsibility for them to someone else.

8. Different *interpersonal distances* are preferred for various types of communication. The size of a particular *personal space* is related to communication and protection, and is affected by a number of factors like attraction, similarity, type of interaction, age, and sex.

9. *Territories are permanent, identifiable geographic areas* which, individuals mark as their own to different extents. Primary territory is individually owned, secondary territory is temporarily owned, and public territory is temporarily occupied but not individually owned.

10. *Built environments* influence human behavior in a number of ways. As cities grow larger they become more complex and behavior changes accordingly, perhaps to reduce arousal. Crowding produces heightened stress and can result in several different problems. Building design can also either facilitate or obstruct social interaction.

EXERCISES

1. What aspects of your immediate environment are influencing your behavior right now? How strong an influence do you feel the environment exerts on your behavior?

2. Fix your gaze on a distant object. Which of the visual cues, binocular and/or monocular, do you think are making you perceive distance, and how?

3. In what ways has your perception of the environment changed in the past several years? What resources are in greater or lesser abundance? Have those conditions affected your lifestyle?

4. What would *your* cognitive map of the U.S. look like? What areas are most important to you? Compare your perception with your classmates' ideas and try to explain the differences.

5. Describe how your own personal cognitive map of the environment influences a couple of the following views: Religious, political, economic, aesthetic, scientific, biological, literary (or others you prefer). Why are cognitive maps useful?

6. What are the symbolic aspects of the "space" in your classroom? What nonverbal messages might it convey? If you were the most important person in the class how would you redistribute the space and why?

7. Is the city or town you live in a high or low load environment? What characteristics of it lead you to that conclusion? How is your optimal level of arousal affected by that particular environmental load?

8. What natural resources are conservationists presently concerned about and why?

9. What type of natural disasters affect your area of the country? What adjustments in behavior are made because of that threat?

10. At what interpersonal distance do you feel most comfortable in informal conversation? Do you know others whose personal space requirement is very different? Why might that be?

11. What do you consider your primary territory, secondary territory, and public territory? How are they different (in terms of ownership)?

12. Think of some crowded situation that made you feel negatively. How could you rearrange the environment to solve the problem? What underlying causes are you alleviating in your solution? How would you *feel* in the most crowded situation you know of?

VI

Toward the Future:
Creative Problem Solving

Nature of Creative Problem Solving
Definition
The Problem Situation
Guilford's Dimensions of Creative Thinking
Originality
Relationship of Creativity and Humor

Blocks to Creative Problem Solving
Lack of Knowledge About a Problem
Habit
Faulty Perception
Motivational Blocks
Cultural Blocks
Set
Over Reliance on Authority and Tradition

Steps in Problem Solving
Problem Definition
Defining the Problem
Making the Problem Statement More Precise
Getting Subproblems
The Importance of Information

17

Problem Solving I:
The Broad Attack

Nature of Creative Problem Solving

definition

Everyone has problems, great or little. You may have to find a new way to get to work during a fuel shortage. You may have to accommodate unexpected dinner guests. The same basic *psychological processes* underlie all problem solving, however. It is from this common psychological viewpoint that we discuss problem solving here.

the problem situation

A problem situation has three components: (1) a motivated person, (2) a goal this person is trying to achieve, and (3) a barrier to achievement. The goal may be going to a movie, getting a date, or reaching a higher level of work output. If there are *no* barriers to these goals, there are no problems.

Sometimes aggressive behavior is effective in our effort to overpower the barrier. If a door won't open, we might force it open. This may work for doors, but brute force is usually not effective. The heart of creative problem solving is finding effective alternatives.

One definition of creative problem solving is "the application of new solutions to old problems." A similar definition is "putting two or more previously unrelated elements together to arrive at a solution." For example, freeze drying is an old process but its application to the food industry is relatively new. There are more factors involved in creative problem solving to be considered, however.

guilford's dimensions of creative thinking

J. P. Guilford (1950), a pioneer investigator in this field, arrived at four dimensions of creative thinking: problem sensitivity, flexibility, fluency, and originality.

Problem Sensitivity. Problems are what we perceive them to be. If we are insensitive to a problem developing along a production line, it is not now a problem to us. If we do not foresee an energy shortage, the world energy situation poses no particular threat. If we fail to recognize "the times are a changing," our company may continue manufacturing a product that people want less and less. If we are sensitive to problems, we may anticipate them or react more quickly to solve them.

Problem sensitivity depends on our perception of a situation. Perception depends on our past experience, our immediate "set" to see a situation a particular way, our motives, and our emotions. If we have lived through the depression of the 1930s, we have a different perception of economic indicators than someone who has not (past experience). If we are told "Watch out for machine number four, it's been acting up," we are more likely to respond quickly to unusual noises emanating from number four (our immediate "set"). If we are hungry, we notice signs for eateries (motivation); if we are alone and afraid, we pay more attention to creaky sounds (emotion).

Guilford devised a test of problem sensitivity. It consists of a series of "What's wrong with . . . ?" questions. For example, what's wrong with the common incandescent light bulb? What's wrong with the government? The more ideas about what's wrong, the greater the problem sensitivity. This test, like others used to measure different aspects of creative thinking, is a *research* test, however, and not good enough to *select* people in or out of jobs or schools.

How could this common household toaster be improved?

Flexibility. We may be getting nowhere on a problem and then solve it easily by a different approach. A cleat broke off in my son's soccer shoe, and I couldn't remove it from the underside of the shoe. Someone suggested removing the lining and working from inside the shoe. It was repaired in two minutes. Trying different approaches is flexibility. Figure 17–1 gives some simple problems requiring flexibility. A commercial example is the "Weed Eater." Reel mowers work like scissors and power mowers use a rigid blade like a knife, but the Weed Eater uses flexible nylon line. It is less dangerous than other cutters, light weight, energy efficient, and can reach hard to get places.

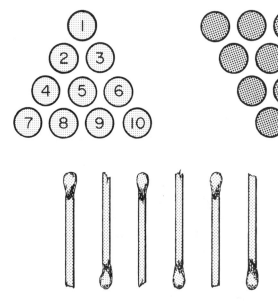

figure 17–1. Problems requiring flexibility to solve. *A.* Using 10 pennies, turn the triangle in 1 upside down so that it looks like that in 2, by moving 3 and only 3 of the pennies. *B.* With six identical matchsticks make 4 and only 4 equilateral triangles. (Solution on page 442.)

Fluency. The more solutions we think of, the more likely we are to find a workable one. Fluency is the number of ideas about a particular problem, regardless of their ultimate merit. Guilford has tests for four different kinds of fluency. These are

1. *Word Fluency:* Write all the words you can within a 2-minute period which contain a specified letter of the alphabet. For example, words with the letter "O" might be: *lot, to, over, on, open,* and so on.
2. *Ideational Fluency:* Name things that belong to certain classes. For example, name FLUIDS that will BURN. These might include *gasoline, kerosene, hydrogen,* and *alcohol.*
3. *Expressional Fluency:* Write a series of four-word sentences, with the first letter of each word being the same. You cannot, however, repeat any word. Thus:

L___	G___	H___	N___
Losers	Go	Home	Now
Lumbermen	Get	Heavy	Nails
Little	Garlands	Hang	Nicely

4. *Associational Fluency:* Write words similar in meaning to a given word. Write words similar to the word GOOD: These might include *kind, tasty, moral,* or *pleasant.*

originality

Originality is commonly defined as "putting together two or more previously unrelated ideas to achieve some purpose." The restriction "to achieve some purpose" is intended to eliminate completely random associations. The Remote Associations Test, originally devised by Sarnoff Mednick (1962) illustrates this.

Remote Associations Test. If asked to give the first word you could think of in response to the word HOUSE, you might say, YARD. In response to HORSE, you might say RUN. Now suppose you were asked to give a word which had a *common association* for both HOUSE and HORSE. This would take longer, but you might come up with FLY (house fly or horse fly). "Fly" would probably be a weak association for either HOUSE or HORSE, but it is a *remote association* linking the two stimulus words. Table 17–1 gives a two-word remote association test devised by the author, which correlates well with Mednick's version. Fill in the answers as per the instructions. The answers given in the key on page 423 are the most likely, but you may think of others.

table 17–1

remote associations

Given below are four pairs of words with a third word which serves as an association for each of the pairs in parentheses.

Example 1.	(fly)	House:Horse
Example 2.	(first)	Aid:Hand
Example 3.	(White)	House:Bob
Example 4.	(Handle)	Bar:Door

Thus we have: (1) House fly: Horse fly (2) First aid: first hand (3) White House: Bob White (4) Handle-Bar: Door Handle.

Given below are 24 additional pairs. Fill in the blank space in front of each pair with a word that associates with each member of the pair. You have 10 minutes to work. Do not expect to complete all of them. The common answers are on the next page.

1.	_____	Tie:Rain	13.	_____	Set:Up
2.	_____	Board:Blade	14.	_____	Shrinker:Pin
3.	_____	Air:Coat	15.	_____	Out:Off
4.	_____	News:Doll	16.	_____	Barrel:Smith
5.	_____	Floor:Street	17.	_____	Light:Hold
6.	_____	Mate:Foul	18.	_____	Man:Show
7.	_____	Ball:Piano	19.	_____	Spelling:Honey
8.	_____	Bone:Horse	20.	_____	House:Fish
9.	_____	Ring:Cauliflower	21.	_____	Stone:Bottle
10.	_____	Glass:House	22.	_____	Stone:Soft
11.	_____	Worm:Note	23.	_____	Ball:Play
12.	_____	Key:Task	24.	_____	Plaid:Whiskey

Uncommonness of Response. Creative people tend to give *unusual* responses if free to do so. Two tests are the Unusual Uses Test and the Quick Responses Test.

- *Unusual Uses Test.* Think of all the uses you can for a common ordinary safety pin. People usually start off with common responses and then move on to less common ones. Maltzman et. al. (1960) categorized common and uncommon uses for several familiar objects, including the safety pin. Common responses included pricking the skin, punching a hole, opening a lock, or removing a splinter. Uncommon uses, occurring very rarely, were such things as making doorbells stick, cork opener, using to demonstrate a magnate, hook for a lanyard, food decoration, and poison dart.

  Uncommon responses in one group of people might be common in an-

table 17–1a

scoring key for remote associations test

1.	Bow	Tie:Rain	13.	On or Back	Set:Up
2.	Switch	Board:Blade	14.	Head	Shrinker:Pin
3.	Pocket	Air:Coat	15.	Side or Cast	Out:Off
4.	Paper	News:Doll	16.	Gun	Barrel:Smith
5.	Walker	Floor:Street	17.	House	Light:Hold
6.	Play	Mate:Foul	18.	Boat or Show	Man:Show
7.	Grand or Player	Ball:Piano	19.	Bee	Spelling:Honey
8.	Collar	Bone:Horse	20.	Cat or Dog	House:Fish
9.	Ear	Ring:Cauliflower	21.	Cap	Stone:Bottle
10.	Ware	Glass:House	22.	Soap	Stone:Soft
11.	Book	Worm:Note	23.	Fair or Foul	Ball:Play
12.	Master	Key:Task	24.	Scotch	Plaid:Whiskey

other group. Engineers commonly think of safety pin uses which would be rare for artists, such as to replace a fuse or use as an electric probe. Artists, on the other hand, might think of using them to dab on minute quantities of paint, rare tasks for engineers. It is therefore necessary in research to find out what responses are unique and which are common among the particular subjects being studied.

- *Quick Responses Test.* A series of stimulus words is given to a group and each person records the first word associated with each stimulus word. There is usually a time limit of five seconds per word. The score is based on the statistical frequency of the responses. For example, the predominant response to the word SALT might be PEPPER. If someone said MINE (for salt mine) or ARMS (for Strategic Arms Limitation Talks), these might be unique responses in the sample being studied and therefore receive high scores. Table 17–2 contains a list of stimulus words. Write down the first response you think of to each and then compare these with the rest of your class. How many unique ones did you have?

table 17–2

quick responses test—instructions: read each of the following words and write down as quickly as possible the first word that comes to mind in association to each of these stimulus words in column a, then go back and repeat the task for column b, and then go back for column c. but *do not repeat any words in your association.*

	a	b	c
1. Pencil			
2. Shut			
3. Dark			
4. Scissors			
5. White			
6. Black			
7. Sour			
8. Blue			
9. Boy			
10. Butter			
11. Table			
12. Window			
13. Frog			
14. Swift			
15. Tobacco			
16. Blossom			
17. Yellow			
18. Back			
19. Hammer			
20. Rough			
21. Loud			
22. Hot			
23. Brown			
24. Sweet			
25. City			

cleverness

Cleverness is judged more subjectively than the previous tasks, so two or more judges usually rate each idea. The scoring might be as simple as "clever" or "not clever" for each idea. If there is high agreement between the judges, both judges must be responding to the same aspect of the ideas.

Cartoon Captions. Subjects may also write their own captions for cartoons. These are scored for cleverness. Figure 17–2 shows two cartoons. Write a caption for each of these. You might get several people outside class to write captions and then bring them back to class for anonymous evaluation. Do class members agree very well on which captions are clever?

Plot Titles. Subjects are given two brief stories and asked to write as many relevant titles as possible in, say, five minutes for each story. Two stories are given so that the results do not depend on the details of one story. Two measures are obtained: *fluency,* the total number of titles; and *cleverness,* based on judges' ratings. Look at the stories and their titles as given by two actual subjects in Table 17–3. You assign each title a score of "1" (for clever) or "0" (for not clever).

figure 17-2. Write captions for each of the above cartoons. Have several other people write captions for them. Can you detect any noticeable differences in the cleverness of the various captions?

table 17-3

samples of plot titles test

---

story one

"In London, England, a bicyclist and an automobile driver almost had a collision at an intersection. Each stopped his respective vehicle. The cyclist walked over to the car and bashed in a headlight without saying a word. Equally silent, the auto driver knocked the horn off the bicycle. Without passing a word, the two remounted their vehicles and went their opposite directions."

Subject A's Titles	*Subject B's Titles*
"The Cyclist and the Motorist"	"A London Exchange"
"A London Scene"	"Bicycle vs. Automobile: Round 1"
	"Near Miss Results in a Hit"
	"Trade Fair of Destruction"
	"Selective Collision—The New Way to . . ."
	(subject ran out of time here)

story two

Many years ago, a poor beggar, weary from traveling on the road all day, approached the entrance of an inn known by the name of "St. George and the Dragon." The poor wretch knocked on the door. His knock was promptly answered by a large, overbearing female with the sourest of dispositions. "Could you spare a poor man a bite to eat?" he pleaded. "Get away from here you no-good-beggar," she spat at him, "before I call the dogs on you." And she slammed the door in his face with a resounding bang. The man hesitated for a moment, then knocked again. The door opened a crack and before the woman could say a word, the beggar asked: "Ma'am, could I speak with George now?"

Subject A's Titles	*Subject B's Titles*
The Beggar	The Lady (Dragon) and the Tramp
St. George and the Dragon	Pity St. George
Turned Away	An Episode from "My Favorite Dragon"
A Poor Man's Travels	Don Quixote goes "Tramp."
	George's Landlady

Which subject, A or B, do *you* say had the more clever titles? Add up the scores for each subject from both stories, and compare your scores with those of someone else. Subject B comes out ahead in fluency (B = 10, A = 6), but what about cleverness?

relationship of creativity and humor

What is it that makes something funny? This is not easy to answer and many TV programs have floundered because they were not funny. One clear element in much humor, however, is the unexpected twist. For example:

> *Question:* Do you believe in clubs for boys?
> *Answer:* Only if reason fails.

The humor depends on the listener attributing one meaning to "clubs" (such as Boys Scouts) and then finding that it refers to big sticks. Such incongruities are also at the heart of ethnic jokes. For example:

> *Question:* How many Californians does it take to change a light bulb?
> *Answer:* Three. One to screw in the bulb and two to enjoy the experience.

Many of the same elements that constitute originality (unusual associations) also constitute humor. Since they share these common elements, it is not surprising that original ideas often seem funny at first. ("They laughed at Thomas Edison, too.")

Blocks to Creative Problem Solving

Often the crucial barriers to our achieving goals are *within ourselves.* Removing these internal barriers is a major step in the direction of better problem solving.

lack of knowledge about a problem

Lack of knowledge is a major barrier. If we don't have materials to work with, we cannot build much; if we don't have information about a problem, we will be lucky to solve it. The person most immersed in a problem is most likely to solve it because he or she knows the *requirements* of the problem. Sir Alexander Fleming may have accidentally found that mold killed his biological cultures, but surely this had been seen many times before. It took someone as knowledgeable as Fleming about the *meaning* of this observation to develop penicillin.

habit

Experience makes us all creatures of habit to some degree. When we learn about gravity we are automatically less likely to believe that heavy objects can spontaneously rise into the air (except for aircraft). The exercise in Box 17–1 illustrates the role of habit. Work the problem before reading further.

box 17–1

digit-symbol substitution—in the following simple arithmetic problems a (+) sign means to multiply, a (÷) sign means to add, a (−) sign means to divide, and a (×) means to subtract.

complete these problems following the above directions:	
8 + 2 =	14 ÷ 7 =
9 + 11 =	6 × 5 +
4 × 3 =	8 + 3 =
6 ÷ 2 =	7 × 2 =
9 − 3 =	9 + 2 =
7 × 4 =	8 − 4 =
4 + 4 =	9 + 6 =
8 − 4 =	1 ÷ 1 =
12 × 2 =	8 × 7 =
20 − 10 =	13 − 1 =
9 − 1 =	16 − 4 =
5 + 6 =	8 × 2 =
2 × 1 =	9 ÷ 9 =
10 − 5 =	6 × 2 =
12 + 2 =	8 + 4 =
6 ÷ 6 =	10 − 2 =
8 + 5 =	4 − 1 =
6 + 6 =	18 − 3 =
17 × 2 =	8 ÷ 2 =
14 ÷ 7 =	15 × 3 =

Now that you have completed the exercise, answer this question: Did you work the individual problems *consecutively* or did you do all the adding first, then all the subtraction, and so on? Most people do the problems consecutively, but skipping through them four times is really more efficient. This habit of going through things one-by-one is very strong because it often *is* appropriate. The symbol substitution task is just not one of those situations. We might frequently ask ourselves then: "Am I doing something the *best* way or just because I've always done it this way?"

faulty perception

Experience often *forces* us to perceive events in ways that are difficult to overcome. For example, subjects (college students) were supposed to get a ping pong ball out of a deep rusty pipe which was bolted upright to the floor. In

An adult may see only a bun warmer here. But to a small child it is just as readily a helmet. How many things can you perceive the bun warmer to be?

the room there were hammers, pliers, rulers, soda straws, strings, bent pins and an old bucket of dirty wash water. After fishing around with the various tools, most subjects finally "saw" the solution; they poured the dirty water into the pipe and floated the ball to the top and picked it up.

The problem was presented differently to other subjects. Instead of the bucket there was a crystal pitcher, full of fresh ice water, surrounded by shining crystal glasses, all on a table with a clean white cloth. It was much more difficult to "see" the solution. The rusty pipe and the water just didn't "go together" the way they had in the first condition.

Figure 17–3 is another problem for you. There are nine dots in a rectangular array. The task is to join the nine dots with four straight connected lines without retracing any line and without lifting your pencil from the page. The solution is on page 441. If you have difficulty, consider the following questions. Are you putting any *unnecessary restrictions* on yourself because of the way you perceive the problem? Are you trying to work the problem entirely by drawing the four lines *within the four corners* of the nine-dot matrix?

There is no simple way to avoid perceptual blocks. They come at inopportune times and would not even be perceptual blocks if we could immediately see past them. The most important thing is to realize that such blocks occur and try to look at problems in different ways when we run into difficulty.

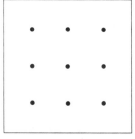

figure 17–3. Join all nine dots by four straight connected lines without retracing and without lifting the pencil from the page. If you have difficulty (which you probably will) draw several sets of dots on a separate sheet of paper. Do not hesitate to try all kinds of "strange" solutions. (The solution is on page 441.)

motivational blocks

Low Motivation: The Path of Least Resistance. My wife used to ask me if I could fix a broken door. The least work was to say "no." She has gotten wiser, however, and now asks, "How can you fix that door?" I am caught up in the problem unless I think fast enough to say "I can't" (an admis-

sion I am loathe to make). If our motivation for solving a particular problem is not very high (the door doesn't bother *us*), we may simply shy away from the problem.

Can you write down the names of twenty different kinds of birds? You think not? Okay. Do it. Don't say you can't. Write them down on a sheet of paper. Take about five minutes.

How far did you get in five minutes? Most people *can* in fact do this problem (in perhaps a little more time), although they *say* they cannot. Virtually everyone can recognize many more than twenty birds. Table 17–4 gives a list of thirty birds. Are *any* unfamiliar?

table 17–4

thirty different kinds of birds. are there any not already familiar to you?

1. Robin	11. Chicken	21. Red Winged Blackbird
2. Wren	12. Pheasant	22. Albatross
3. Duck	13. Eagle	23. Egret
4. Goose	14. Hawk	24. Flamingo
5. Blue Bird	15. Buzzard	25. Sea Gull
6. Blue Jay	16. Heron	26. Swan
7. Red Bird	17. Parrot	27. Sparrow
8. Cardinal	18. Parakeet	28. Mocking Bird
9. Blackbird	19. Canary	29. Cowbird
10. Crow	20. Ostrich	30. Quail

Motivation Too Strong. If we are too concerned about a problem, we may be overly anxious and dwell on the consequences of failure. High anxiety hinders our best efforts on complex tasks. We may also be too highly aroused by other people observing us (as in stage fright) or may try too hard to be successful (as in front of a person we like of the opposite sex).

Resistance to Change. Resistance to change may result from a fear of the unknown, of what *might* happen to us when the change is made. Under a new manufacturing system, we might lose status or not be able to keep up.

Optimal Level of Motivation. Many observations indicate that a medium level of motivation, not too low or high, is optimal for problem solving. This is shown diagramatically in Figure 17–4 and is recognizable as activation theory (Chapter Three). It is difficult to specify in objective terms just what too low or too high is. We may, however, recognize at a given time that we are too tense and nervous about a job to do it well and need to relax.

Similarly, if we see someone else not doing their job effectively, this might not imply low motivation, but rather that the job makes the individual too anxious to do it well. We might consider the need to calm someone down or bolster their confidence, rather than automatically trying to *increase* their motivation.

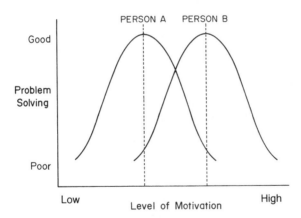

figure 17–4. Inverted-U relations for level of motivation and problem solving for two different people. What is optimal for one person may be above or below that for another person.

cultural blocks

We often do things "because that's the way they are done." We eat three times a day and consider different foods appropriate for breakfast, lunch and dinner because this is how it is done in *our* culture. We want to get along with others so we tend not to depart too much from cultural norms for dress, for speech, or for behavior. It may not even occur to us that there is another way. Cultural norms influence most everything we do, including our choice of a mate. It is interesting to ponder how many things we do one way simply because that's the way they are done in our corner of the world. Could we have done them differently?

set

A set is a *temporary readiness to respond* in a certain way. If I say "*add* eight and two," you will answer "ten." If I say "*divide* eight and two," you will say "four." If I say "subtract" or "multiply" you will give different answers for the same two numbers. The set to respond in one way ("add") can be changed in an instant to a different set ("subtract") and is therefore different from a habit.

Sometimes sets are helpful, as in the example, but they can be blocks to problem solving. If a football defense is set for a pass and there is a run, the defense gets burned. Consider this: An elevator starts at the ground floor with no passengers. As it goes up it stops and lets on five passengers, then stops and lets on three and lets off two, then stops and lets on four and lets off six, then stops and lets on five and lets off four. Question: How many stops did the elevator make? Most people try to keep track of the number of *passengers,* even though never actually told to do this more difficult task. Sets are tricky because we seldom recognize them at the critical time.

over-reliance on authority and tradition

The history of science is filled with examples of reliance on authorities who were nevertheless wrong in particular instances. For example:

- According to the ancient astronomer Ptolemy (and to religious authority of medieval times) the earth is the center of the universe.
- According to the Greek philosopher Aristotle, an object remains in motion only as long as there is something pushing it (as contrasted to the later view of Galileo that objects in motion remain in motion until something—friction, another object—stops them).

These assertions were authoritative in their time, and people depended heavily on either tradition or religious authority to answer all questions. The greatest contribution of modern science has been to encourage skepticism of authority and to encourage the active search for answers in nature. We often need authorities (such as doctors or dentists), but the fallibility of authority must be recognized.

Steps in Problem Solving

We shall consider five steps in the problem solving process overall:

1. Problem definition
2. Finding alternative courses of action

3. Making decisions among the alternatives
4. Technical implementation of the solution(s)
5. Social implementation of the solution(s)

This is a *logical* sequence which in practice may be rearranged, repeated or modified in a particular problem. For a simple problem, we might accept the first solution we can (for example, what tie to wear in the morning); for a very complex and costly business problem we might spend years carefully going through many refinements of each step.

problem definition

Mess Problems Versus Improvement Problems. Rarely are we handed a well-defined problem. We usually face "situations" where something is wrong and we have to define the problem for ourselves. Johnny may be doing poorly in school, but why? Production is snagged someplace along the line, but where? Furthermore, somebody else's "solution" to a problem may simply be to hand us the "mess." We may "solve" our problems by getting someone else (the plumber, the automechanic, the doctor) to solve them for us. We recognize the "mess," the loosely defined problem *situation,* but we have to have help to define the problem carefully enough to actually solve it.

It is often hard to define the exact problem. We may see only bits and pieces, have bad information or hear many different viewpoints from other people. A problem well-defined *is* half solved.

The *improvement problem* is different. We may manufacture a product that is reasonably cheap, reliable, and efficient—but there is always the possibility of making it better. New manufacturing techniques, materials, and designs are always close at hand. Perma press fabrics, frozen foods, and aerosol sprays are all in some way improvements over the "old" ways of doing things. Transistors, diodes, and printed circuits have revolutionized manufacturing and information handling problems.

Perception and Problem Definition. We can apply principles of perception to problem definition.

1. *The situation is different for every viewer.* If a product is not getting out on time to meet orders, the salesman sees the situation one way, the accountant differently, the line foreman a third way and the line worker a fourth. The stockholder doesn't care about any of this except to get things moving.
2. *Our sensitivity to problems, and the way we define and approach them depends on our perception, not on the objective situation alone.* To the extent that the objective situation determines our perceptions, our perceptions are more accurate, but still not completely determined by the situation. If people mutually engaged in solving

a problem don't see the problem the same way, they are not working on the same problem. Labor and management may negotiate, but are perhaps not trying to solve the same problem.

3. *Our perception of problems is determined by past experience, temporary set, motives and emotions.* Past experience may be from reading, hearing about, or direct involvement. Many potentially dangerous situations are easily handled if one has the necessary knowledge.

As we have already seen, "set" refers to a temporary readiness to respond to a situation a certain way. The runner gets "on the mark," then "set," and is ready to "go" as quickly as possible when the gun sounds. Verbal instructions are commonly used to establish sets.

When a person is hungry (motivated) or fearful or angry (emotional), he or she may see a problem very differently than otherwise.

We may solve a problem as *we* see it, but *others* seeing it differently are unhappy with our solution. We may properly ask *why* others see the problem differently than we do. Or, how *do* they see it? We try to look at the same situation from different points of view and arrive at a mutually satisfactory solution.

defining the problem

Defining a problem well involves several steps.

- Broadening the problem statement from a narrow viewpoint to look at the larger problem in which our particular "target problem" is imbedded.
- Making the problem statement more precise.
- Breaking the larger problem into more manageable subproblems.

Broadening the Problem: Shall I Fire Joe? A manager is periodically faced with the question of firing someone. But "Shall I fire Joe" is a restrictive "yes-no" *decision* problem with only two alternatives. Why do we *want* to fire Joe? Because he's not getting his job done? This suggests a new way to look at the problem. What we want is to get the job done. So, the problem can be more broadly defined as How can we get Joe's job done? This leads to such alternatives as having someone trade jobs with Joe, giving Joe some assistance, giving Joe additional time or training, or, maybe, actually firing Joe and replacing him.

Any one of several solutions might be better than firing Joe, but we also need information. Why isn't Joe getting the job done? Is he ill? Does he have family problems? Is there more work than one person can handle? Is he properly trained? (Has the job changed since he took it?) We might define the problem even more broadly than before by asking "How can we get the big job done?" Here we are just thinking of *Joe's* job as a separate thing. Asking *"why?"* and phrasing the problem definition more broadly provides the possibility for more creative solutions. Consider the following three problems in brief form.

1. Problem Definition #1   Shall I fire Joe?
    Question: Why do I want to fire Joe?
    Answer: So Joe's job will get done.
    Problem Definition #2   How can I get Joe's job done?

2. Problem Definition #1   How can we get rid of Fidel Castro?
    Question: Why do we want to get rid of Castro?
    Answer: To contain communism in the Western Hemisphere.
    Problem Definition #2   How can we contain communism?

3. Problem Definition #1   How can I build a better mousetrap?
    Question: Why a better mousetrap?
    Answer: To get rid of mice.
    Problem Definition #2   How can I get rid of more mice?

Each of these examples has an initial problem definition which led into a *broader* problem definition. However, the broader definition never *excluded* the original problem statement, but rather it added the possibility of many more solutions. Problems are best stated in the form of questions which permit

The problem of land pollution cannot be isolated from the broader problem of pollution in general. If solving the land pollution problem simply increases the air pollution (by burning) or water pollution (by dumping) problems, then our solution is inadequate.

many possible answers. We may represent increasingly broader problem statements diagramatically, as shown in Figure 17–5.

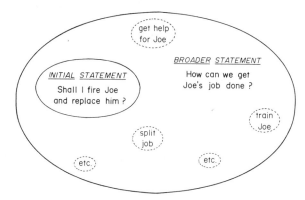

figure **17–5.** Increasingly broader problem statements which still contain the initial problem statement. The broader statement still includes the possibility of "firing Joe" as a solution, but also has other potential solutions (dotted circles). It would be important to have more information about Joe, about the job and any other relevant circumstances before settling on a problem statement or a solution.

Synonyms. It is often useful to play with a problem definition by stating it in a different way. What might appear to be the same definition may have very different implications. For example:

Where is the bottle opener?
or
Where is something to open the bottle?

Something to open the bottle could range from a belt buckle to a fire ax.
Sometimes "synonomous statements" lead the same direction as the ques-

tion "why?" But sometimes they give an entirely different outlook. For example, people working in a tall building complained about the slowness of the elevator. The problem of speeding up the elevator was mulled over for a while until it occurred that the problem was not to speed the elevator but to slow the complaints. With this new definition, the solution was to put floor-to-ceiling mirrors on three sides of the elevator. The complaining stopped immediately.

making the problem statement more precise

A problem should be defined as *precisely* as possible. This does not conflict with defining a problem as broadly as possible. Imprecise language just fuzzes a problem, narrow or broad. If we say we want to manufacture a "better" product, we must ask what constitutes "better?" Bigger? Faster? Cheaper? If we have a problem definition with ambiguous words, we may indeed be defining the problem ambiguously. Even if *we* understand, it may be ambiguous for someone else who should understand it.

Knowing When We Have Reached the Solution. With a clear problem statement we can more easily tell when we have the solution. We might define a fund-raising problem as "raise a lot of money" or "raise $10,000." Few of us would define a problem in the first way because we all recognize the ambiguity in "a lot of money." We would want to know how much money to raise so we could tell when we achieved our goal.

If we are specific, it may even turn out that a problem does not exist. Suppose we think we ought to spend less time cutting the grass. If we consider how much time we are willing to spend, we may discover that we are not spending more time than that now. The problem disappears when we see it clearly. We may sit down to work out a budget and find we are better off financially than we thought.

A Difference That Makes a Difference. Suppose we spend two hours a week cutting grass with a push mower and believe we need a riding mower. We discover a riding mower will save thirty minutes a week. Over an estimated twenty-four-week grass season, we could save twelve hours. The riding mower costs $400, for a savings of twelve hours a year for, say, five years. This would be more than $6 an hour for using the mower, not counting upkeep, inflation, and lost interest on our money. Maybe we don't have the problem we thought we did!

Specifications. Specifications are precise problem definitions. A piece of equipment should be so many inches each dimension and have certain operating characteristics and lifespan. This is the definition of the thing to be built. Von Fange (1959) notes, however, that we even have to be careful with specifications. A piece of equipment is supposed to have a certain life in salt spray, but *field conditions* of spray might be quite different than *laboratory tests*. The specifications should state that the equipment operate under specified laboratory-controlled conditions. The buyer might have one set of conditions and the manufacturer another. Conditions should be firmly established to avoid misunderstanding.

getting subproblems

Having a precise, broad problem definition, we may find that we cannot handle it all at once. We have to divide it so we can deal with the parts one at a time. These parts are *subproblems,* parts of the whole which can be dealt with separately.

Back to the grass. Our major problem is keeping our yard neat and attractive. There are a number of fairly obvious subproblems: keeping the ground properly seeded, fertilizing, watering, weeding, cutting, and trimming. We can diagram this as shown in Figure 17–6.

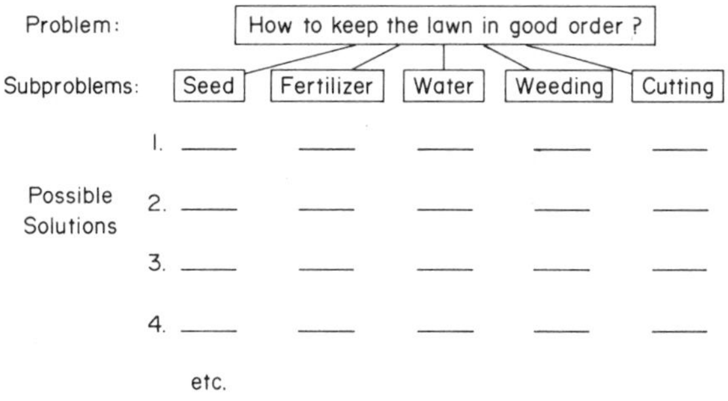

figure 17–6. Block diagram of broad problem statement, subproblems, and spaces for possible solutions.

There may even be subproblems of subproblems. For example, we may have the subproblems of selecting the fertilizer, transporting it, and spreading it.

A really creative solution to the problem might be to plow up the grass and replace it with ground cover and pine bark. We would still have a neat and attractive lawn, and we could spend Saturday afternoons with a good book.

If a problem is very broad, it may have to be parceled out to several individuals, or groups, working on different subproblems. In building a house, we have the masonry, plumbing, carpentry, and electrical work subcontracted to different individuals.

At this stage, people often ask if this problem definition business is getting to be more burdensome that it's worth? If we did this with every problem, would we not spend all our time defining problems and never getting any further? There are several answers to this.

First, the process is *not* really so time consuming. Once practiced it is easier. If we really are plagued by a problem (mice or rats, say, in a warehouse full of wheat), the solution is worth whatever time it takes.

Second, we naturally do a certain amount of definition anyway. If we approach the definition more systematically, we can do it more efficiently.

Third, some individual judgment is necessary to determine how far we should go with problem definition. A business decision involving millions of dollars may be worth weeks or months. For a few dollars, on the other hand, a businessperson might do well to avoid wasting his or her time.

How far should one broaden a problem and get subproblems? There is no set answer to this, but the following rule of thumb is reasonable: Carrying the definition to some broader level than the problem solver can deal with sets the problem solver's *limits* more clearly and gives a better *perspective* on the problem at the level he or she *can* deal with it. A Peace Corps worker may have the immediate problem of teaching a farmer how to dig a proper ditch, but at the same time be dealing with the broader problem of "containing communism."

The same principle holds for subproblems. The problem solver works down to a lower level than he or she is going to deal with. Though the building contractor may know what kind of plumbing is necessary for the job, doing the acutal plumbing is left with a subcontractor.

the importance of information

At every stage of problem solving, one must have facts, such as how much money was spent last year for advertising, how much for expansion, how much for wages, taxes. What we sometimes think are facts are often less than we suppose, however.

According to the American College Dictionary, the meanings of the word "fact" are (1) What has really happened or is the case, truth, reality; (2) Something known to have happened, a truth known by actual experience or observation; and (3) Something said to be true or supposed to have happened. We might have thought that the difference between fact and assumption would be very clear, but the third dictionary definition of "fact" immediately clouds the distinction. Furthermore, since different people often "see" the same "objective" situation in different ways, they may argue that the "facts" are different. A fact, then, is whatever we believe to be a fact at a given time. We should therefore check "facts" just as we would check assumptions.

Hodnett (1955) illustrates the problem of facts and assumptions as follows.

Be skeptical of assertions of fact that start, 'J. Irving Allerdyce, the tax expert says. . . .' There are at least ten ways in which these facts may not be valid. (1) Allerdyce may not have made the statement at all. (2) He may have made an error. (3) He may be misquoted. (4) He may have been quoted only in part. (5) What he said may have applied to a different context. (6) He may have been joking or ironical. (7) He may have been exaggerating. (8) What he said may be generally true but not true in this exceptional situation. (9) He may not be a tax expert at all. (10) He may not be an authority in this phase of taxation.

Now, having seen something of the basic nature of the creative problem-solving process and having taken the giant step of defining a problem, let us move on to techniques for finding solutions.

SUMMARY

1. A *problem situation* consists of a *motivated* person, a *goal* to be achieved, and a *barrier* to achievement.

2. There are a number of possible definitions for creative problem solving, but all contain the idea of using new or unusual solutions or combinations of solutions for a problem.

3. Four dimensions of creative *thinking* are (a) *problem sensitivity*, the ability to see problems in their early stages; (b) *fluency*, having many ideas; (c) *flexibility*, the ability or willingness to try different approaches to arrive at a solution; and (d) *originality*, putting together previously unrelated ideas to achieve some purpose.

4. The major *blocks to problem solving* are often *within ourselves*. These include

(a) lack of knowledge about a problem; (b) habit; (c) faulty perception of a problem; (d) inappropriate levels of motivation, either too high or too low; (e) culture block, that is, doing things a certain way because that is how they are usually done in our culture; (f) "sets" to respond in one way rather than another; and (g) over-reliance on authority and tradition.

5. *Problem definition* includes (a) *being sensitive* to the existence of a problem, which depends on perceptions which are different from person to person; (b) *broadening the problem,* trying to see if there is a bigger, more important problem of which the problem we initially see is but a part; (c) dividing and conquering, breaking the overall problem into component parts, or *subproblems,* which can be more readily attacked one at a time; (d) making the problem statement as *precise* as possible, to clarify the problem and to help know when a solution has been reached.

6. At every stage of problem solving, *information* relevant to the problem is vital. It is important that we determine that the information is reliable and not confuse *assumptions* about a situation with *facts* about the situation. "Facts" are often less than supposed.

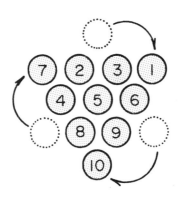

Solution to problems in Figure 17–1.

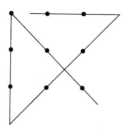

Solution to problem in Figure 17–3.

18

Problem Solving II:
Solutions and Decisions

A number of complementary "techniques" can assist us in creative problem solving. These techniques are not all equally applicable in every situation, and they do not guarantee that all problems can be solved any more than exercise in weight lifting qualifies a person to do any feat of strength. However, the person practiced in the techniques described here may better solve *more* problems. We will examine the following five techniques:

1. Brainstorming (Group and Individual)
2. Attribute Analysis
3. Morphological Analysis (Matrix Analysis)
4. Checklisting
5. Analogies

Brainstorming: Deferment of Critical Judgment

an example

Suppose we have a group of eight people pretend they represent an advertising firm for the Ajax Safety Pin account. We tell them, "Sales have been lagging and the company wants to promote new uses for safety pins. Your job is to think of all the *good* uses you can for safety pins to use in the advertising campaign. We want to think of as many *good* ideas as we can in the next 20 minutes. Let's go. Let's think up those *good* ideas."

A group of eight engineers typically comes up with something like 30 to 50 ideas. The group then compares its results with those of an equivalent group only to discover that the other group has 100 to 150 ideas. Furthermore, practically all the ideas that the first group had are included in the larger number of the second group.

The first group is at a loss to explain the difference, and with good humor may suggest that the members of the other group are geniuses. Someone in the lower-idea group will eventually say, "I thought of some of those things, but there was so much emphasis on 'good ideas' that I didn't say them." The other members of his group concur, and it is brought out that there *was* a difference in instructions. The high idea group was told to give *all* the ideas they could think of and not to worry about whether their ideas were good or bad, nor to take any time evaluating them.

This result has been obtained many times as a demonstration, as well as in carefully controlled experiments. People working under "brainstorm" or "non-critical" instructions produce more and better ideas than do those working under instructions to have good ideas. Since most of us work in situations where we want to do well, often we are working under a *critical set*, which is a block to problem solving. We must then conclude that most of us are often not problem solving at our best, so let us look at brainstorming in more detail.

the suspension of critical judgment

Alex Osborn (1957) developed brainstorming as the group technique we have described, and he has outlined factors which he believes to be necessary. A substantial body of research, however, indicates that *it is the suspension of critical judgment which is important, not group activity in and of itself.* For example, Dunnette, Campbell, and Jaastad (1963) presented problems to forty-eight research personnel and forty-eight advertising personnel. Each subject brainstormed some problems individually or as members of a four-person team. Individuals produced more ideas than groups and without sacrificing quality. Four persons working individually and combining their output do better than four individuals working together as a group. Group participation apparently contains certain inhibitory influences, even in brainstorming. However, either groups or individuals working under suspension-of-judgment conditions perform better than under critical conditions. For *training* purposes, however, the individual *can learn more from group activity because he or she can see what others are doing.* One can see the good and bad points of one's own activities and those of others, can have one's own work examined, and can develop the enthusiasm which is, initially at least, more likely to come from group effort.

basic principles

Osborn has considered the following two principles indispensable to brainstorming.

1. *Deferment of judgment.* You can think up more good ideas in the same length of time if you defer judgment until after you have created an adequate checklist of possible leads to solutions.
2. *Quantity Breeds Quality.* The more ideas you have, the more likely you are to arrive at the potentially best leads to solution.

Osborn quotes from Friedrich Schiller, the German poet, as follows:

> In the sense of a creative mind, it seems to me, the intellect has withdrawn its watchers from the gates, and the ideas rush pell-mell, and only then does it review and inspect the multitude. You worthy critics, or whatever you may call yourselves, are ashamed or afraid of the momentary and passing madness which is found in all real creators, the longer or shorter duration of which distinguishes the thinking artist from the dreamer. Hence your complaints of unfruitfulness, for you reject too soon and discriminate too severely.

Why *should* individuals judge themselves, or others, too soon and too severely? If a person has in the past been ridiculed for "dreamer's ideas," he or she is less likely to express "dreamer's ideas" again. Punished acts are less likely to occur again. A person may then keep quiet until he or she decides that what is said will be "worthy." These "good" ideas are then rewarded by attention and appreciation. As adults, we are hesitant even to "play" with *words* which are not "safe" or "certain."

The notion that "quantity breeds quality" is that our *initial* solutions to problems are more *likely* to be "common" or "obvious" solutions. A "good" idea is workable, but not necessarily immediately obvious. If it were immediately obvious there would be no problem. In brainstorming many ideas are not very good, but the process is analogous to that of mining: 10 percent ore is a high yield. A lot of brainstormed ideas are rock but the 10 percent gold is well worthwhile.

"rules" for brainstorming

Adverse Criticism is Taboo. It is imperative to have a "ground rule" that one should not criticize others. Criticism is punishing and defeats the entire purpose of the brainstorm session. Criticism can take many forms. It may be a blatant, "It will never work." It may be sarcastic laughter. It can be just lifted eyebrows, or turning away from the speaker.

The environment for brainstorming should be one where *ideas are accepted, not judged.* The individual brainstormer must be free to express thoughts on the problem at hand. If criticism is allowed, others than the individual criticized will tend to be less open since they too can anticipate criticism. One individual should not take advantage of this permissiveness and dominate the entire session, but this is a problem for the group leader. Finally, it is assumed that an individual accepted into a brainstorming situation has contributions to make. It is better not to have him or her there in the first place rather than criticize.

Free Wheeling is Welcomed. "The wilder the idea, the better; it is easier to tame down than to think up" (Osborn, 1963, p. 156).

Quantity is Wanted. The greater the number of ideas, the more the likelihood of useful ideas.

Combination and Improvement Are Sought. "In addition to contributing ideas of their own, participants should suggest how ideas of others can be turned into better ideas, or how two or more ideas can be joined into still another idea" (Osborn, 1963, p. 156). One cannot be concerned in the brainstorming session with priority or credit. Individual identity is submerged into the group.

No Editorializing. Don't try to elaborate or defend ideas, but simply state them as quickly as possible and go on. If the individual feels compelled to elaborate or defend his or her ideas, either there is some anticipated criticism or the session is being diverted from its primary goal—getting ideas for problem solutions. This can be a rather potent inhibitor and may be harder to detect than more blatant types of criticism. Any distracting influences are to be avoided.

Don't Overlook the Obvious. If an idea is not stated because it is obvious, there is self-criticism. It may *not* be obvious to everyone. It may be possible to twist an "obvious" idea into something not obvious. The obvious solution may, in fact, *be* the best solution.

Don't Fear Repetition. In their initial experiences with brainstorming, groups spend considerable time trying to remember if a given idea had been presented earlier. Actually, it makes no difference, and "jumping on" someone for being repetitive is an obvious criticism. Furthermore, if a particular idea

were presented first, no one might have any association to it. If presented again as the seventy-fifth idea, it might trigger a valuable response.

individual brainstorming

There is one other particular advantage of individual brainstorming: If other people with whom you deal are *not* accustomed to the idea of brainstorming, they may not allow themselves to be involved in it, or may be highly critical of it. *Your* boss or teacher may be this way. This does not keep *you* from brainstorming individually. *The only restrictions you have as an individual brainstorming are the ones you put on yourself.* As long as you are self critical, it doesn't make much difference whether you are working individually or in a group. If you can suspend judgment of yourself, you can brainstorm and then criticize so that your "finished output" is polished, sensible, and defensible. No one else need know how you arrived at your final solution(s).

Attribute Analysis

Attribute analysis involves the *analysis* of an object or situation into its components or functions. The following two questions are divisible into two subquestions:

What else can we do with this object or process? If we have a particular product (for example, Polaroid cameras) or process (such as electroplating), we could very well ask such a question, as we did for the safety pin problem. We can arrive at even more possibilities, however, if we ask the following two questions:

1. What are the attributes (characteristics) of this object or process?
2. Taking each of the attributes in turn, or in their various possible combinations, how else can they be used?

How else can we do it? We have a particular job to do and want (or need) to do it differently than in the past. What are alternative methods? Breaking the question into two questions, we expand the range of possibilities.

1. What are the *necessary* attributes of the object (or process) that we have been using to get the job done?
2. Given just these necessary attributes, how else could we do the job?

By looking at the attributes as properties *divorced from the object as it was intended to be used,* we free ourselves of a narrow conception of the object. A good example is the *steam iron.*

What else could we do with a steam iron?

1. What are the attributes of the common household steam iron?
   - weight
   - heat
   - smooth surface
   - shiny surface
   - has a cord
   - has a plug
   - can hold things (has a container for water)
   - has a thermostatic control
   - has a point
   - contains copper (wire)
   - contains steel
   - produces steam
2. Taking each attribute in turn, what else could we use the steam iron for?
   - *Weight:* Paper weight, book end, plumb bob, boat anchor, weapon, fishline sinker, for stretching something, for a unit of measure, etc.
   - *Heat:* cooking, take to bed on a cold night, mounting pictures, welding, melting plastics, evaporating water, heating water, as a branding iron, an instrument of torture, sealing a wound (cauterize), etc.
   - *Smooth surface:* writing surface (desk), _____ _____ (fill in your own)
   - *Shiny surface:* face mirror, reflector for sending signals, for attracting moths, _____ , _____ , _____ .

Finish out the list at this point and find other uses based on the remaining attributes.

The attribution listing technique is especially valuable in situations where there may be multiple product uses, or utilization of part processes separately. If we manufacture heating elements for steam irons, the same production techniques could be used for something else. The technique also applies to people. If you discover the attributes (skills, talents) a person has, you might find that he or she could do things that you might not have thought of before. This is part of the problem of personnel administration.

How else could we do the job the steam iron was intended to do? This sort of question probably faces us more often. We may have a job to do at home or work and are not equipped to do it the usual way. We may want to make a process faster, make a part more cheaply, eliminate parts, and so on.

1. What are the *necessary* functional attributes of the steam iron for it to perform as intended—to steam press clothes? These *might* be as follows (but there are invariably some disagreements among engineers):

   - Have heat
   - Have pressure
   - Have a smooth surface
   - Have water

You might consider other attributes necessary, or you might not think all these four are necessary. There is no easy way to settle such arguments, although some technical knowledge helps. The point, however, remains: *The necessary attributes are far fewer than the actual attributes of the object listed earlier.*

2. *How else can we "steam iron"?* We could look for any source(s) of heat, pressure, smooth surface, and water. For example:

   - Wrap the material to be pressed around a smooth surface steam boiler while wet. (Note that it is irrelevant that it is a *steam boiler* as long as it is hot.)
   - Heat a pie pan and press it against the damp material.
   - Put hot sand into aluminum foil, wrap around with a damp silk cloth, and press against the material. (Holding it might provide some problem but we can solve that!)

You can undoubtedly think of many other possibilities. The point is that entire new vistas are opened when we divorce ourselves from the specific object normally used and look at the problem more abstractly. The steam

iron is a good example just because it *is* such a common object. The trick is to keep an eye on the job to be done, not on some fixed thing to do it with. The Sears-Roebuck catalog can even become a useful "scientific instrument" catalog.

An exercise we have used frequently is the attribute analysis of a portable ice chest. Take five minutes for each of the following questions and see what you can come up with.

What other uses can we find for the portable ice chest (the common kind of chest used for camping)?

- What are the attributes of the ice chest? (5 min)
- Taking the attributes in turn, what else can we do with the chest? (5 min)

How else can we get done the particular job the chest is supposed to do?

- What are the necessary attributes of the chest? (5 min)
- Given the necessary attributes, how else can we do the same job? (5 min)

Morphological (Matrix) Analysis

A variation of attribute analysis is *morphological analysis.* We will also call it matrix analysis because it is based on the following principle. If we flip a coin, how many outcomes can there be? Two, of course, head (H) or tail (T). If we flip two coins, how many outcomes can there be for the two coins taken jointly? Four is the answer: HH, HT, TH, and TT. We can put this into the following table.

		coin one	
		H	*T*
coin two	*H*	HH	HT
	T	TH	TT

Each coin has two attributes, H and T. The number of possible combinations with two coins is the product of the two multiplied together. If we increase the number of attributes, the number of possible outcomes also increases. Suppose we used dice rather than coins. One die has six possible outcomes for the face up. Two dice thrown together have thirty-six possible outcomes (six times six).

The important point about morphological analysis is that it is easier to see what all the possible combinations for the two dice are if we put them into tabular (or matrix) form, as we did with the coins. The dice example is easy but it is still hard to remember all the possible combinations without

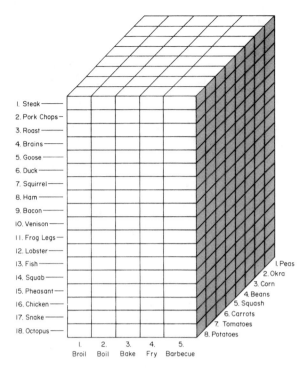

1. Steak
2. Pork Chops
3. Roast
4. Brains
5. Goose
6. Duck
7. Squirrel
8. Ham
9. Bacon
10. Venison
11. Frog Legs
12. Lobster
13. Fish
14. Squab
15. Pheasant
16. Chicken
17. Snake
18. Octopus

1. Broil 2. Boil 3. Bake 4. Fry 5. Barbecue

1. Peas
2. Okra
3. Corn
4. Beans
5. Squash
6. Carrots
7. Tomatoes
8. Potatoes

figure 18–1. Morphological Analysis: 720 different meals.

writing them down. You can see them all instantly, however, if you put them in a matrix.

Remember that our purpose is to find many alternatives from which to choose. Mr. Brown says he has run out of ideas for the meat dish for supper and wants us to help. What are the kinds of meat we might have? Possibly, the following: steak, pork chops, roast, brains, goose, duck, squirrel, ham, bacon, venison, frog legs, lobster, shrimp, sea fish, squab, pheasant, chicken, snake and octopus. Now, what are all the ways we can *cook* meat dishes? We might broil, boil, bake, fry, barbecue. This makes a matrix of ninety combinations (five times eighteen), some of which are rather unusual. Palatability is a matter of judgment, which we are deferring.

If we add a third dimension, such as a single vegetable to go with the meat dish, we might have carrots, corn, squash, peas, potatoes, tomatoes, okra, beans. These 8 multiplied by the 90 above, give us 720 possible combinations, enough for a different dinner every night for two years. This is illustrated in Figure 18–1. If we multiply ways of cooking the vegetables, different desserts, and so on, we can expand almost indefinitely. We cannot easily go beyond three dimensions on paper, of course, but we can break the problem into subparts and do it that way.

An automobile dealer, or any other business, could also check *inventory* in such a fashion. If there are eight body types and four motor sizes, there are thirty-two possible combinations, and the dealer could quickly see which of these he had or needed by checking the table. The matrix technique thus has two different uses: finding unusual combinations and "inventory control." We are mainly concerned with the first here, but the second is very useful.

Check Lists

Just as the aircraft pilot checks off the necessary activities for takeoff, we might have check lists to help us take off on new ideas. Such check lists do not give us the solution directly, but they provide leads. The following examples are "general purpose" check lists. You will be able to invent other check lists better suited to your needs.

Osborn suggested the following, especially applicable to manufacturing and sales:

Put to other uses?	Substitute?
Adapt?	Rearrange?
Modify?	Reverse?
Magnify?	Combine?
Minify?	

A list suggested by Kohberg and Bagnall (1974) involves "manipulative verbs," such as multiply, divide, eliminate, subdue, invert, separate, transpose, unify, distort, rotate, flatten, squeeze, complement, submerge, freeze, soften, fluff-up, by-pass, add, subtract, lighten, repeat, thicken, stretch, extrude, repel, protect, segregate, integrate, symbolize, abstract, dissect.

We might, for example, magnify a truck, minify a car, soften a food, add an ingredient, combine a clock and a radio. There are many, many possibilities which you can work on as an exercise.

Analogies

Another time-honored approach to finding new relationships is to use analogies. Analogies often clarify the meaning of something. For example, we might say that the lake was smooth as glass, or that person is sly as a fox. In his book *Synectics* (1961), William Gordon talks about using analogies to *make the familiar strange* (to get a different perspective) and *to make the strange familiar* (so we can deal with it).

Gordon describes four kinds of analogy.

1. *Parallel analogy*—a direct translation of particular principle from one situation to another. Biological analogies can be especially interesting. Sonar detection devices designed in World War II were based on the principle of echolocation used by bats and porpoises.

2. *Personal analogy*—solving a problem the way the problem-solver him or herself would do it. For example, I might say, "If I wanted to get up to that tree,

Biological analogies are widely used. Radar and sonar systems copy the sonar principles used by bats and porpoises to navigate without vision.

I'd leap up and grab a limb with my hands and pull myself up." This might suggest a claw, or hand-like trap mechanism, that would be raised to a crossbar, upon contact with the bar would close and grasp the bar, and then would pull something up.

3. *Symbolic analogy*—pictorial representations of molecules are symbolic analogies used to understand and predict the behavior of molecules.

4. *Fantasy analogy*—if this were the best of all possible worlds, in which anything could happen, how might we solve a particular problem? Earlier science fiction writers merely fantasized about doing things with a beam of light, but present day engineers actually use beams of light (lasers) for tasks ranging from welding loose retinas in eyes to measuring the distance a discus is thrown in a track meet.

Decision Making

the rational person model: maximizing

Having generated possible alternatives, we must make decisions among them. Such decisions are based on the *expected gains and losses associated with each alternative.* Gains are monetary or personal benefits, and losses are such disadvantages as increased expense, danger, lack of consumer appeal, or difficulty of manufacture. Formal mathematical ways to reach such decisions constitute the field of *operations research.* Here we shall just introduce some useful basic ideas.

table 18–1

decision making by assigning positive and negative values to each alternative, exemplified with a choice of lawnmowers. By this analysis the push mower "wins," but for a different situation the riding mower might come out ahead.

push mower		riding mower	
Advantages(+)	Disadvantages(−)	Advantages(+)	Disadvantages(−)
Low purchase cost	Slow	Fast	High purchase price
	Hard work	Easy work	Higher operating cost
Low operating cost		Better than what I have now	
Gets around trees and bushes easily			Cannot work in close spaces
			Cannot store easily
Better than what I have now			
5+	2− = 3+	3+	4− = 1−

Counting Advantages and Disadvantages. In the lawnmower problem, suppose we have two alternatives, a push-type power mower and a riding mower. We might see the advantages and disadvantages as shown in Table 18–1.

We can add up the pluses and minuses associated with these two alternatives. Thus: Push mower has five plus and two minus, for a net of three pluses. The riding mower has three pluses and four minuses for a net of one minus. By this analysis, the pushmower wins. But should not some things count more than others? Maybe cost should count more than time. We can handle this straightforwardly. A really great advantage counts five pluses and a really great disadvantage counts five minuses. Smaller numbers of pluses or minuses would be smaller advantages or disadvantages. We can *add up* all the pluses and minuses to everyone's agreement but the *initial assignment* of pluses and minuses is subjective. It makes a difference whether you are an athletic twenty-five-year-old or a lame sixty-year-old, or whether the yard is large or small. It also makes a difference whether you have the money to buy a riding mower.

Overriding Factors. An overriding factor is *some factor that is so important that it supersedes everything else.* If you cannot spend more than $75, you can probably forget the riding mower. If a manufacturing process is so dangerous that employees are likely to be injured or made ill, that process is eliminated.

Personal Values. If you have always wanted a riding mower, even just for fun, you should take this into account, just like money. The question you alone can answer is how much you should weigh this factor. Maybe it gets two pluses. This might or might not swing the decision to the riding mower, but after you complete your analysis you can say that whatever is

I ALWAYS WANTED A BIG POWER MOWER...

RUMBLE RATTLE

CHUG CHUG

LAWN BERSERKER

SLASH!

YIPE! YIPE!

WHIRRRRRRR

Z-Z-Z-ZAP

important to you has been accounted for. The analysis does not *always* favor what we "want," since it includes economics, but if you explicitly include your personal values you should be more satisfied with whatever the outcome is.

Typical Factors to be Evaluated. Many possible factors are evaluated in making a decision, each of which requires relevant information. Imaginative thinking may be necessary to determine what these are because we are talking about the values of *future* outcomes. Typical factors might be cost, size, shape, speed, temperature, strength, material, process, appearance, safety, standardization, interchangeability, acceptability, and sales appeal. What is a major factor in one place may not be critical in another. Buying an exotic foreign car in a small town involves service difficulties different from what you might encounter in a large city.

Relevant Information.

1. *Effect on other people.* If other people are significantly affected by your decision, you need to know this. For example, use of hazardous materials, new medical research procedures, or new technology which might produce increased unemployment would all involve "people considerations" about which information would be needed.

2. *Missing or incomplete information.* If you lack necessary information, you can do several things: ask somebody who knows, go to the library, or make the best assumptions possible. Making assumptions can be very useful. You might ask, "What is the *worst possible* thing that could happen if I decided to do such and such?" The worst possible outcome may not be too bad. Remember

also that reference librarians in your public library are hired just to help you find information.

3. *Reliability of information.* Some sources are more reliable than others. Advertising is one of the least reliable sources of information, since it is often misleading if not outright deceptive. The statement that "No other product has been shown to be superior to our product" also means "Our product is not shown to be better than any other product." That is, they are all equally effective, as is true with aspirin, for example.

Though advertising gives you some ideas, a source like *Consumer's Guide* presents a more unbiased view and may consider factors you might not have thought of (such as the reliability of certain parts in an automobile). The most *unbiased* source of information you can find is likely to be the most reliable. You do not want to be blinded by authority, but you do want information from a knowledgeable source. You would usually do better to ask an auto mechanic about a car than to ask a housepainter.

Difficulties with the Maximizing Approach. In creative problem solving there is no guarantee that your solution is the best. No one always makes perfect decisions. You do the best you can. In baseball, a .300 batting average is really good and .400 is fantastic, even though there is only a 10 percent difference between the two and both are less than half. Harrison (1975) suggests that there are three major problems with the maximizing approach, particularly if applied to large and complex business or other problems.

1. Businesses or other organizations might not really *want* to reach maximal decisions. For example, there may be conflicts of interests about what the important goals are which are to be maximized.
2. It may be very difficult to assign numerical values to various alternatives in a complex organization, again because of conflicting interests. Further, there is no guarantee that doing this will necessarily lead to the most preferred outcome.
3. Getting *all* the relevant information may turn out to be a formidable, or even impossible task, because of time and money limits.

Because of these kinds of problems, maximizing is not necessarily the best way to approach decisioning making for all situations. It does have the important value, however, that it forces us to think in more precise terms about what we want to achieve.

satisficing

If we may never have all the appropriate information and could not process it "correctly" if we did, what alternative decision approach do we have? Herbert Simon, Nobel prize winner for his work in organizational behavior, proposed an alternative called satisficing. Instead of setting out everything there is to know about a problem and its alternative solutions you determine *the minimum acceptable characteristics of a solution.* This may be vastly quicker, and if we consider time important, then satisficing has two advantages: We can accept more than

This house was named "Satisficer" because it was purchased almost instantly as the first one which met the buyer's minimum criteria.
(Photo courtesy of John Compere)

one possible solution (not even looking for the single "best" solution), and we can do it relatively quickly.

Suppose you are looking for a used car, usually a chancy business. If you lined up all the criteria you want to fulfill, got information on all the used cars in town, then carefully chose, it is very likely that the car of your choice would be sold while you were fiddling with pencil, paper, and pocket calculator. Using the satisficing approach, you could set a number of criteria (which are as much up to you as in the maximizing approach) and then look until you found a car that met those criteria. For example, you might want a car to drive to school (or one for your child to drive). The criteria might be

1. have less than 80,000 miles on it
2. cost less than $1,000
3. not need major repairs, as far as is visible
4. gets 18 mpg or better.

The first car that meets these criteria you could buy on the spot (or after having it checked by a mechanic to make sure it is what it seems). The criteria might be adjusted according to circumstances, such as paying a little more for a car that gets exceptionally good mileage, or accepting one that gets not such good mileage but is in exceptionally good condition and is inexpensive.

To summarize, the main idea of satisficing is to set the minimum criteria, whatever you want them to be, and then take the first solution that passes this test. The savings in time and worry alone make this approach very useful, especially with the confidence of knowing that the maximizing approach simply is not very applicable to many problems. For either approach to be effective, however, you have to know what it is you want—which was the reason for emphasizing problem definition so much in chapter seventeen.

Technical Implementation of Solutions

Once an idea or course of action has been elected, it has to be implemented. Technical implementation refers to the technical requirements for accomplishing a task. If it is decided to build a certain piece of equipment, the design must be made, it must be tested, and then manufacturing set up for production. In our lawn mower example, technical implementation would mean going out and buying the mower. Technical implementation in itself might set off a whole new set of problems to be solved (where to get the money, how to transport the mower home). Since the means of implementation depend on the problem, different details have to be dealt with for different problems.

Social Implementation of Solutions

It is easy to say that when a workable idea has been discovered the problem is solved, but what if no one *accepts* the solution? We might buy the lawnmower, expecting our children will be eager to use it, but they may have to be persuaded. This is part of social implementation. A company may decide to diversify and then discover there is no market for the new product. And then there was the Edsel, a car nobody wanted. Marketing research, advertising, and sales-people are parts of the social implementation process in business. Selling an idea to the congress is part of the social implementation process of the presidency. Until an idea or product is accepted by somebody it has not solved the problem which prompted it.

Training for Creative Problem Solving

If you have done the suggested exercises in Chapters Seventeen and Eighteen, you have completed a mini-course in creative problem solving. These chapters contain the material commonly used in training courses in business, industry,

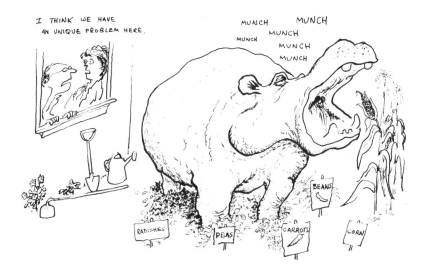

and schools. Engineering knowledge, for example, becomes outmoded so fast that today's graduate will not be able to solve many problems five years from now on the basis of his or her engineering education. Therefore, creative problem solving is very important skill.

The same can be said for most of us. Until very recently, a young person could follow in his or her parents' footsteps with little difficulty. In some parts of the world, farming may still be done as it was thousands of years ago, but few people in the United States can farm as their parents did. Nor can the rest of us easily engage in our parents' occupations. The problems inherent in the accelerated change of pace have been thoughtfully discussed by Alvin Toffler in *Future Shock* (1970). We must all be prepared to learn continually and to adjust repeatedly to different situations. This is education's big problem: We cannot educate for the future solely by teaching the past.

SUMMARY

1. *Brainstorming* involves "thinking up" as many ideas (potential solutions) as possible *without* simultaneously judging them. The two basic principles of brainstorming are (a) *Defer critical judgment* of ideas, and (b) *Quantity breeds quality,* therefore get as many ideas as possible.

2. Brainstorming can be done either in *groups* or *individually.* Groups tend to have an inhibitory influence, however, and a combination of individual and group brainstorming on a particular problem is useful.

3. *Attribute analysis* involves looking at an object, process or person in terms of separate attributes rather than as a whole. The intent is to see things in a new way, so that (a) by determining the *minimum necessary attributes* of an object or process new ways can be found to perform its functions, or (b) by looking at the *actual attributes* of an object, new uses for that object can be found.

4. *Morphological (matrix) analysis* uses multiple dimensions in forced combinations to arrive at new possibilities, such as all the possible ways of cooking meat times all the possible meats one could serve. This puts many combinations into view that might otherwise be overlooked.

5. *Check lists* can be used to make sure that one has looked at a particular problem in many ways.

6. *Analogies* (for example, from biological principles to mechanical principles, such as echolocation by bats to radar) are often helpful ways of finding new solutions to problems.

7. After a number of potential solutions have been found, a *decision* from among the alternatives must be made. This can be done in terms of the expected gains and risks associated with each alternative.

8. *Technical implementation* involves the demonstration that a proposed solution is technically feasible, that it would actually work. This may involve an actual demonstration of a model, of a new engine for example.

9. *Social implementation* is the process of selling the solution so it will actually be used. A solution which no one will use is no solution.

Bibliography

ADORNO, T., FRENKEL-BRUNSWIK, E., LEVINSON, D., & SANFORD, R. *The authoritarian personality.* New York: Harper & Row, 1950.

ALLEN, V. L., & LEVINE, J. M. Consensus and conformity. *Journal of Experimental Social Psychology,* 1969, *5,* 383–399.

ALLPORT, F. H. The J-Curve hypothesis of conforming behavior. *Journal of Social Psychology,* 1934, *5,* 141–183.

ALLPORT, G. W. Functional autonomy of motives. *American Journal of Psychology,* 1937, *50,* 141–156.

ALLPORT, G. W., & POSTMAN, L. *The psychology of rumor.* New York: Holt, Rinehart, & Winston, 1947.

ALTMAN, I. *The environment and social behavior.* Monterey, CA: Brooks/Cole, 1975.

ARBOUS, A. G. & KERRICH, J. E. Accident statistics and the concept of accident provenness. *Biometrics,* 1951, *7,* 340–432.

ARDREY, R. *The territorial imperative.* New York: Atheneum, 1966.

ARGYLE, M., & DEAN, J. Eye contact, distance, and affiliation. *Sociometry,* 1965, *28,* 289–304.

ASCH, S. E. Effects of group pressure upon the modification and distortion of judgement. In Z. H. Guetzkow (Ed.), *Groups, leadership, and men.* Pittsburgh: Carnegie, 1951.

ASCH, S. E. Forming impressions of personality. *Journal of Abnormal and Social Psychology,* 1946, *41,* 258–290.

ASCH, S. E. *Social psychology.* Englewood Cliffs, NJ: Prentice-Hall, 1952.

ASCH, S. E. Studies of independence and conformity: A minority of one against a unanimous majority. *Psychological Monographs,* 1956, *70* (9, Whole No. 416).

ATKINSON, J. W. *An introduction to motivation.* New York: Van Nostrand, 1964.

ATKINSON, J. W., & WALKER, E. L. The affiliation motive and perceptual sensitivity to focus. *Journal of Abnormal and Social Psychology,* 1956, *53,* 38–41.

AZRIN, N. H., & HOLZ, W. C. Punishment. In W. K. Honig (Ed.), *Operant behavior: Areas of research and application.* New York: Appleton-Century-Crofts, 1966.

BALES, A. F. *Interaction process analysis: A method for the study of small groups.* Reading, MA: Addison-Wesley, 1950.

BALES, R. F. Some uniformities of behavior in small social systems. In G. E. Swanson, T. M. Newcomb, & E. L. Hartley (Eds.), *Readings in social psychology.* New York: Henry Holt and Company, 1952.

BANDURA, A. *Social learning theory.* Englewood Cliffs, NJ: Prentice-Hall, 1977.

BANDURA, A., ROSS, D., & ROSS, S. A. A comparative test of the status envy, social power, and secondary reinforcement theories of identification learning. *Journal of Abnormal and Social Psychology,* 1963, *67,* 527–534. (a)

BANDURA, A., ROSS, D., & ROSS, S. A. Imitation of film-mediated aggressive models. *Journal of Abnormal and Social Psychology,* 1963, *66,* 3–11. (b)

BARBER, T. X. *Hypnosis: A scientific approach.* New York: Van Nostrand Reinhold, 1969.

BARON, R. A., & BYRNE, D. *Social psychology: Understanding human interaction.* Boston: Allyn and Bacon, 1977.

BASS, B. M., & RYTERBAND, E. C. *Organizational psychology.* Boston: Allyn and Bacon, 1979.

BECK, A. T. *Depression: Clinical, experimental, and theoretical aspects.* New York: Hoeber Medical Division, Harper & Row, 1967.

BECK, R. C. *Motivation: Theories and principles.* Englewood Cliffs, NJ: Prentice-Hall, 1978.

BECK, R. C., & DAVIS, J. V. Effects of real vs. pretend shock on semantic differential judgements and the GSR in some classical conditioning paradigms. *Journal of Research in Personality,* 1974, *8,* 33–44.

BELL, P. A., FISHER, J. D., LOOMIS, R. J. *Environmental psychology.* Philadelphia: W. B. Saunders Co., 1978.

BEM, D. J. Self-perception theory. In L. Berkowitz (Ed.), *Advances in experimental social psychology* (Vol. 6). New York: Academic Press, 1972.

BENNIS, W. *The unconscious conspiracy: Why leaders can't lead.* New York: AMACOM, 1976.

BENSON, H. *Relaxation response.* New York: Morrow, 1975.

BENTHAM, J. The principles of morals and legislation [1789]. In E. A. Burtt (Ed.), *The English philosophies from Bacon to Mill.* New York: Modern Library, 1936.

BERKOWITZ, L. Some determinants of impulsive aggression: Role of mediated associations with reinforcements for aggression. *Psychological Review,* 1974, *81,* 165–176.

BERKOWITZ, L., & LEPAGE, A. Weapons as aggression-eliciting stimuli. *Journal of Personality and Social Psychology.* 1967, *7,* 202–207.

BERLEW, D. E. Interpersonal sensitivity and motive strength. *Journal of Abnormal and Social Psychology,* 1961, *63,* 390–394.

BERLYNE, D. E. *Conflict, arousal, and curiosity.* New York: McGraw-Hill, 1960.

BERNE, E. *Games people play.* New York: Grove Press, 1964.

BERSCHEID, E., & WALSTER, E. Physical attractiveness. In L. Berkowitz (Ed.), *Advances in experimental social psychology* (Vol. 7). New York: Academic Press, 1974.

BEST D. L., WILLIAMS, J. E., CLOUD, J. M., DAVIS, S. W., ROBERTSON, L. S., EDWARDS, J. R., GILES, H., & FOWLES, J. Development of sex-trait stereotypes among young children in the United States, England, and Ireland. *Child Development,* 1977, *48,* 1375–1384.

BLAKE, R. R., & MOUTON, J. S. *The managerial grid.* Houston, TX: Gulf, 1964.

BLAKE, R. R. & MOUTON, J. S. *The New Managerial Grid.* Houston, TX: Gulf, 1978.

BOGARDUS, E. S. Measuring social distance. *Journal of Applied Sociology,* 1925, *9,* 299–308.

BOYATZIS, R. E. Affiliation motivation. In D. C. McClelland & R. S. Steel (Eds.), *Human motivation: A book of readings.* Morristown, NJ: General Learning Press, 1973.

BRANNON, R. Attitudes and the prediction of behavior. In B. Seidenberg & A. Snadowsky, *Social psychology.* New York: The Free Press, 1976.

BRIDGES, K. M. B. Emotional development in early infancy. *Child Development,* 1932, *3,* 324–341.

BROWN, J. S. *The motivation of behavior.* New York: McGraw-Hill, 1961.

BROWN, R. Further comment on the risky shift. *American Psychologist,* 1974, *29,* 468–470.

BROWN, R *Social psychology.* New York: Free Press, 1965.

BRYAN, J. H., & TEST, M. A. Models and helping: Naturalistic studies in aiding behavior. *Journal of Personality and Social Psychology,* 1967, *6,* 400–407.

BURGER, J. M. *Effectance motivation and the overjustification effect.* Unpublished doctoral dissertion, Univeristy of Missouri-Columbia, 1980.

BYRNE, D., FISHER, J. D., LAMBERTH, J., & MITCHELL, H. E. Evaluations of erotica: Facts or feelings? *Journal of Personality and Social Psychology,* 1974, *29,* 111–116.

BYRNE, D., & LAMBERTH, J. The effect of erotic stimuli on sex arousal, evaluative responses, and subsequent behavior. In *Technical Report of the Commission on Obscenity and Pornography,* Vol. 8. Washington, D.C.: U.S. Government Printing Office, 1971.

CALHOUN, J. B. Population density and social pathology. *Scientific American* 1962, *206,* 139–148.

CAMPBELL, J., & DUNNETTE, M. Effectiveness of T-group experiences in managerial training and development. *Psychological Bulletin,* 1968, *70, 73*–104.

CANNON, W. B. *Bodily changes in pain, hunger, fear, and rage* (2nd ed.). New York: Appleton-Century-Crofts, 1929.

CANNON, W. B. The James-Lange theory of emotions: A critical examination and an alternative theory. *American Journal of Psychology,* 1927, *39,* 106–124.

CASTANEDA, C. *The teachings of Don Juan: A Yaqui way of knowledge.* New York: Ballantine, 1968.

CATTON, W. R., JR., HENDEE, J. C., & STEINBRUN, T. W. *Urbanism and the natural environment.* Unpublished manuscript, Institute for Sociological Research, University of Washington, 1969.

CHAPANIS, A., & MANKIN, D. A. Tests of ten control-display linkages. *Human Factors,* 1967, *9,* 119–126.

CHRISTIE, R., & GEIS, F. L. *Studies in Machiavellianism.* New York: Academic Press, 1970.

Commission on Obscenity and Pornography. *The report of the Commission on Obscenity and Pornography.* Washington, DC: U.S. Government Printing Office, 1970.

CSIKSZENTMIHALYI, M. Intrinsic rewards and emergent motivation. In M. R. Lepper & D. Greene (Eds.), *The hidden costs of reward.* New York: Lawrence Erlbaum Associates, 1978.

DAHLE, T. L. Transmitting information to employees: A study of five methods. *Personnel,* 1954, *31,* 243–246.

DARLEY, J. M., & BATSON, C. D. From Jerusalem to Jericho: A study of situational and dispositional variables in helping behavior. *Journal of Personality and Social Psychology,* 1973, *27,* 100–108.

DARWIN, C. R. *Expression of the emotions in man and animals.* London: Murray, 1872. (American edition, D. Appleton Co., 1873).

DE CHARMS, R. Affiliation motivation and productivity in small groups. *Journal of Abnormal and Social Psychology,* 1957, *55,* 222–226.

DE CHARMS, R. *Personal causation: The internal affective determinants of behavior.* New York: Academic Press, 1968.

DECI, E. L. *Intrinsic motivation.* New York: Plenum, 1975.

DENENBERG, V. H. Early experience and emotional development. *Scientific American,* 1963, *208,* 138–146.

DESSLER, G. *Human behavior: Improving performance at work.* Reston, VA: Reston Publishing Co., 1980.

DOLLARD, J., DOOB, L., MILLER, N. E., MOWRER, O. H., & SEARS, R. *Frustration and aggression.* New Haven, CT: Yale University Press, 1939.

DRAKE, C. A. Accident proneness: A hypothesis. *Character and Personality,* 1940, *8,* 335–341.

DUBIN, R. Stability of human organizations. In M. Haire (Ed.), *Modern organizational theory.* New York: Wiley, 1959; 1962.

DUBRIN, A. J. *Effective business psychology.* Reston, VA: Reston Publishing Company, Inc., 1980.

DUFFY, E. Emotion: An example of the need for reorientation in psychology. *Psychological Review,* 1934, *41,* 184–198.

DUNNETTE M. D., CAMPBELL, J., & JAASTAD, L. The effect of group participation on problem-solving. *Journal of Applied Psychology,* 1963, *47,* 30–37.

DUTTON, D G., & LENNOX, V. L. Effect of prior "token" compliance on subsequent interracial behavior. *Journal of Personality and Social Psychology,* 1974, *29,* 65–71.

EDWARDS, D. J. A. Approaching the unfamiliar: A study of human interaction distances. *Journal of Behavioral Sciences,* 1972, *1,* 249–250.

EKMAN, P., & FRIESEN, W. V. Constants across cultures in the face and emotion. *Journal of Personality and Social Psychology,* 1971, *17,* 124–129.

EKMAN, P., & OSTER, H. Facial expressions of emotion. In M. R. Rosenzwerg & L. W. Porter (Eds.), *Annual Review of Psychology.* Palo Alto, CA: Annual Reviews, Inc., 1979.

ELLIS, A. Rational-emotive therapy. In R. J. Coisini (Ed.), *Current psychotherapies.* Itasca, IL: Peacock Publishers, 1973.

ELLSWORTH, P. C., CARLSMITH, J. M., & HENSON, A. The stare as a stimulus to flight in human subjects: A series of field experiments. *Journal of Personality and Social Psychology,* 1972, *21,* 302–311.

EMSWILLER, T., DEAUX, K., & WILLITS, J. E. Similarity, sex, and requests for small favors. *Journal of Applied Social Psychology,* 1971, *1,* 284–291.

EPLEY, S. W. Reduction of the behavioral effects of aversive stimulation by the presence of companions. *Psychological Bulletin,* 1974, *81,* 271–281.

EPSTEIN, S. Toward a unified theory of anxiety. In B. Maher (Ed.), *Progress in experimental personality research.* New York: Academic Press, 1967.

ERIKSON, E. H. *Childhood and society* (2nd ed.). New York: Norton, 1963.

ERON, L. D., LEFKOWITZ, M. M., HUESMANN, L. R., & WALDER, L. Q. Does television violence cause aggression? *American Psychologist,* 1972, *27,* 253–263.

EYSENCK, H. J. *The biological basis of personality.* Springfield, IL: C. C. Thomas, 1967.

EYSENCK, H. J. *Eysenck on extroversion.* New York: Wiley, 1973.

FALKENBERG, P. R. *15 days to study power.* Winton-Salem, N.C.: Greencrest Press, 1981.

FAST, J. *Body language.* New York: M. Evans, 1970.

FESTINGER, L. *A theory of cognitive dissonance.* Evanston, IL: Row, Peterson, 1957.

FESTINGER, L. A theory of social comparison processes. *Human Relations,* 1954, *7,* 117–140.

FESTINGER, L., & CARLSMITH, J. Cognitive consequences of forced compliance. *Journal of Abnormal and Social Psychology,* 1959, *58,* 203–210.

FIEDLER, F. E. *A theory of leadership effectiveness.* New York: McGraw-Hill, 1967.

FIEDLER, F. E. Validation and extension of the contingency model of leadership effectiveness: A review of empirical findings. *Psychological Bulletin,* 1971, *76,* 128–148.

FREUD, S. *A general introduction to psycho-analysis.* New York: Liveright, 1935. Originally published 1920.

FREUD, S. Three contributions to the theory of sex. In A. A. Brill (Ed.), *The basic writings of Sigmund Freud.* New York: Random House, 1938.

FRIEDMAN, M., & ROSENMAN, R. H. *Type A behavior and your heart.* New York: Knopf, 1974.

FRY, D. *Homo loquens: Man as a talking animal.* Cambridge, England: Cambridge University Press, 1977.

GELFLAND, D. M., GELFLAND, S., & DOBSON, N. R. Unprogrammed reinforcement of patients' behaviour in a mental hospital. *Behaviour Research and Therapy,* 1967, *5,* 201–207.

GLASS, D. C. Changes in liking as a means of reducing cognitive discrepancies between self-esteem and aggression. *Journal of Personality,* 1964, *32,* 531–549.

GOLDSTEIN, M. The relationship between coping and avoiding behavior and response to fear-arousing propaganda. *Journal of Abnormal and Social Psychology,* 1959, *58,* 247–252.

GORANSON, R., & BERKOWITZ, L. Reciprocity and responsibility reactions to prior help. *Journal of Personality and Social Psychology,* 1966, *3,* 227–232.

GORDON, W. J. J. *Synectics: The development of creative capacity.* New York: Harper & Row, 1961.

GOUGH, H., & HEILBRUN, A. B. *Adjective Check List manual.* Palo Alto, CA: Consulting Psychologists Press, 1965.

GUILFORD, J. P. Creativity. *American Psychologist,* 1950, *5,* 444–454.

HALL, E. T. *The hidden dimension.* New York: Doubleday, 1966.

HALPIN, A. W. *Theory and research in administration.* New York: Macmillan, 1966.

HAMMER, W. C., & SMITH, F. Work attitudes as predictors of unionization activity. *Journal of Applied Psychology,* 1978, *63,* 415–421.

HANSEL, C. E. M. *ESP: A scientific evaluation.* New York: Scribners, 1966.

HARDIN, G. The tragedy of the commons. *Science,* 1968, *162,* 1243–1248.

HARDING, J., PROSHANSKY, H., KUTNER, B., & CHEIN, I. Prejudice and ethnic relations. In G. Lindzey & E. Aronson (Eds.), *Handbook of social psychology* (2nd ed.) Vol. 5. Reading, MA: Addison-Wesley, 1969.

HARLOW, H. F. *Learning to love.* San Francisco: Albion, 1971.

HARRIS, T. A. *I'm o.k., you're o.k.* New York: Harper & Row, 1967.

HARRISON, A. A. *Individuals and groups.* Monterey, CA: Brooks/Cole, 1976.

HARRISON, E. E. *The managerial decision-making process.* Boston: Houghton Mifflin Co., 1975.

HEBB, D. O. Drives and the CNS (conceptual nervous system). *Psychological Review,* 1955, *62,* 243–254.

HEBB, D. O. On the nature of fear. *Psychological Review,* 1946, *53,* 259–276.

HEIDER, F. *The psychology of interpersonal relations.* New York: Wiley, 1958.

HELD, R. Plasticity in sensory-motor systems. *Scientific American,* 1965, *213,* 84–94.

HELLER, J. F., PALLAK, M. S., & PICEK, J. M. The interactive affects of intent and threat on boomerang attitude change. *Journal of Personality and Social Psychology,* 1973, *26,* 273–279.

HERZBERG, F. One more time: How do you motivate employees? *Harvard Business Review* (January-February), 1968.

HILGARD, E. R. A neodissociation interpretation of pain reduction in hypnosis. *Psychological Review,* 1973, *80,* 396–411.

HILGARD, E. R. *The experience of hypnosis.* New York: Harcourt-Brace-Jovanovich, 1968.

HILGARD, E. R., ATKINSON, R. C., & ATKINSON, R. L. *Introduction to psychology,* New York: Harcourt-Brace-Jovanovich, 1975.

HODNETT, E. *The art of problem solving.* New York: Harper & Row, 1955.

HOKANSON, J. E. Psychophysiological evaluation of the catharsis hypothesis. In E. I Megargee & J. E. Hokanson (Eds.), *The dynamics of aggression.* New York: Harper & Row, 1970.

HOLMES, T. H., & RAHE, R. H. The social readjustment rating scale. *Journal of Psychosomatic Research,* 1967, *11,* 213–218.

HORNER, M. *Sex differences in achievement motivation and performance in competitive and noncompetitive situations.* Unpublished doctoral dissertation, University of Michigan, 1968.

HOVLAND, C. I. *Communication and persuasion.* New Haven, CT: Yale University Press, 1953.

HOVLAND, C. I., & WEISS, W. The influence of source credibility on communication effectiveness. *Public Opinion Quarterly*, 1951, *15*, 635–650.

HULL, C. L. *Principles of behavior.* New York: Appleton-Century-Crofts, 1943.

HUNT, J. McV. Intrinsic motivation and its role in psychological development. In D. Levine (Ed.), *Nebraska symposium on motivation.* Lincoln: University of Nebraska Press, 1965.

HUNT, M. *Sexual behavior in the 1970s.* Chicago: Playboy, 1974.

ITTELSON, W. H., PROSHANSKY, H. M., RIVLIN, L. G., & WINKEL, G. H. *An introduction to environmental psychology.* New York: Holt, Rinehart, and Winston, 1974.

IZARD, C. E. *Human emotions.* New York: Plenum Press, 1977.

JACOBSON, E. *Progressive relaxation.* Chicago: University of Chicago Press, 1939.

JAMES, W. What is an emotion? *Mind*, 1884, *9*, 188–205.

JANIS, I. L. *Victims of groupthink.* Boston: Houghton Mifflin Co., 1972.

JANIS, I. L., MAHL, G. F., KAGAN, J., & HOLT, R. R. *Personality.* New York: Harcourt-Brace-Jovanovich, 1969.

JELLISON, J. M. Communicator credibility: A social comparison of abilities interpretation. In A. A. Harrison (Ed.), *Explorations in psychology.* Monterey, CA: Brooks/Cole, 1974.

JOHNSON, R. J. *Aggression in man and animals.* Philadelphia: Saunders, 1972.

JONES, M. C. The elimination of children's fears. *Journal of Experimental Psychology*, 1924, *7*, 382–390.

KATZ, D., & BRALY, K. Racial stereotypes in one hundred college students. *Journal of Abnormal and Social Psychology*, 1933, *28*, 280–290.

KELLEY, H. H. The warm-cold variable in first impressions. *Journal of Personality*, 1950, *18*, 431–439.

KESEY, K. *One flew over the cuckoo's nest.* New York: Viking Press, 1962.

KIMMEL, H. D., & HILL, F. A. Operant conditioning of the GSR. *Psychological Reports*, 1960, *7*, 555–562.

KINSEY, A. C., POMEROY, W. B., & MARTIN, C. E. *Sexual behavior in the human male.* Philadelphia: Saunders, 1948.

KINSEY, A. C., POMEROY, W. B., MARTIN, C. E., & GEBHARD, P. H. *Sexual behavior in the human female.* Philadelphia: Saunders, 1953.

KOBERG, D., & BAGNALL, J. *The universal traveler. A soft-systems guidebook to: Creativity, problem-solving, and the process of design.* Los Altos, CA: William Kaufmann, Inc., 1974.

KOHLBERG, L. Development of moral character and moral ideology. In M. L Hoffman & L. W. Hoffman (Eds.), *Review of child development research* (Vol. 1). New York: Russel Sage Foundation, 1964.

LANDY, F. J., & TRUMBO, D. A. *Psychology of work behavior.* Homewood: Dorsey Press, 1976.

LA PIERE, R. T. Attitudes and actions. *Social Forces*, 1934, *13*, 230–237.

LATANÉ, B., & DARLEY, J. M. *The unresponsive bystander: Why doesn't he help?* New York: Appleton-Century-Crofts, 1970.

LATHAM, G. P., & BALDES, J. J. The "practical significance" in Locke's Theory of Goal Setting. *Journal of Applied Psychology*, 1975, *60*, 122–124.

LAWLER, E. E., & PORTER, L. W. The effects of performance on job satisfaction. *Industrial Relations*, 1967, *20*, 20–28.

LAZARUS, R. S. *Psychological stress and the coping process.* New York: McGraw-Hill, 1966.

LEAVITT, H. J. Some effects of certain communication patterns on group performance. *Journal of Abnormal and Social Psychology*, 1951, *46*, 38–50.

LEAVITT, H. J., & MUELLER, R. Some effects of feedback on communication. *Human Relations,* 1951, *4,* 401–410.

LEEPER, R. W., & MADISON, P. *Toward understanding human personalities.* New York: Appleton-Century-Crofts, 1959.

LEFCOURT, H. M. *Locus of control.* Hillsdale, NJ: Lawrence Erlbaum Associates, 1976.

LEONARD, W. E. *The locomotive God.* New York: Appleton-Century-Crofts, Inc., 1927.

LEVINE, S. Stimulation in infancy. *Scientific American,* 1960, *202,* 80–86.

LEWIN, K. Group decision and social change. In G. E. Swanson, T. M. Newcomb, & E. L. Hartley (Eds.), *Readings in social psychology.* New York: Henry Holt and Company, 1952.

LIKERT, R. A. A technique for the measurement of attitudes. *Archives of Psychology,* 1932, No. 4.

LINDSLEY, D. B. Emotion. In S. S. Stevens (Ed.), *Handbook of experimental psychology.* New York: Wiley, 1951.

LITWIN, G. H., & STRINGER, R. I. *The influence of organizational climate on human motivation.* Paper presented at a conference on organizational climate, Foundation for Research on Human Behavior, Ann Arbor, MI, March, 1961. Cited in Landy, F. J., & Trumbo, D. A., *Psychology of work behavior.* Homewood: Dorsey Press, 1976.

LOCKE, E. A. The nature and causes of job satisfaction. In M. D. Dunnette (Ed.), *Handbook of industrial and organizational psychology.* Chicago: Rand McNally, 1976.

LOCKE, E. A. Toward a theory of task motivation and incentives. *Organizational Behavior and Human Performance,* 1968, *3,* 157–189.

LOCKE, E. A., & WHITING, R. J. Sources of satisfaction and dissatisfaction among solid waste management employees. *Journal of Applied Psychology,* 1974, *59,* 145–156.

LORENZ, K. Z. *On aggression.* New York: Harcourt-Brace-Jovanovich, 1966.

LYKKEN, D. T. Psychology and the lie detector industry. *American Psychologist,* 1974, *29,* 725–739.

MACHIAVELLI, N. *The prince and the discourses.* New York: The Modern Library, 1950 (1513).

MAIER, N. R. F.*Psychology in industry.* Boston: Houghton Mifflin, 1965.

MALTZMAN, I., BOGARTZ, W., & BREGER, L. A procedure for increasing word association originality and its transfer effects. *Journal of experimental psychology,* 1958, *56,* 392–98.

MALTZMAN, I., SIMON, S., RASKIN, D., & LICHT, L. Experimental studies in the training of originality. *Psychological Monographs,* 1960, *74*(6), 1–23.

MANDLER, G. Emotions. In T. M. Newcomb (Ed.), *New directions in psychology.* New York: Holt, Rinehart and Winston, 1962.

MANHARDT, P. J. Job orientation of male and female college graduates in business. *Personnel Psychology,* 1972, *25,* 361–368.

MARK, V. H., & ERVIN, F. R. *Violence and the brain.* New York: Harper & Row, 1970.

MASTERS, W. H., & JOHNSON, V. *Human sexual response.* Boston: Little, Brown, 1966.

McCAULEY, C., COLEMAN, G., & DE FUSCO, P. *Commuters' eye contact with strangers in city and suburban train stations: Evidence of short-term adaptation to interpersonal overload in the city.* Unpublished manuscript, Bryn Mawr College, 1977.

McCLELLAND, D. C. *The achieving society.* Princeton: Van Nostrand, 1961.

McCORMICK, E. J. *Human factors engineering.* New York: McGraw-Hill, 1964.

McCORMICK, E. J., & ILGEN, D. R. *Industrial psychology* (7th ed.). Englewood Cliffs, NJ: Prentice-Hall, Inc. 1980.

McGregor, D. The human side of enterprise. In E. Deci, B. von Haller Gilmer, & H. Karn, *Readings in industrial and organizational psychology*. New York: McGraw-Hill, 1972.

McGuire, W. J. The nature of attitudes and attitude change. In G. Lindzey & E. Aronson (Eds.), *Handbook of social psychology* (2nd ed.), Vol. 3. Reading, MA: Addison-Wesley, 1969.

McKeachie, W. J., Lin, Y., Milholland, J., & Issacson, R. Student affiliation motives, teacher warmth, and academic achievement. *Journal of Personality and Social Psychology*, 1966, *4*, 457–461.

Mednick, S. A. The associative basis of the creative process. *Psychological Review*, 1962, *69*, 220–232.

Mehrabian, A. Questionnaire measures of affiliative tendency and sensitivity to rejection. *Psychological Reports*, 1976, *38*, 199–209.

Mehrabian, A. *Public spaces and private places*. New York: Basic Books, 1976.

Mehrabian, A., & Russell, J. A. *An approach to environmental psychology*. Cambridge, MA: M.I.T. Press, 1974.

Meichenbaum, D. *Cognitive-behavior modification: An integrative approach*. New York: Plenum Press, 1977.

Milgram, S. *Obedience to authority: An experimental view*. New York: Harper & Row, 1974.

Miller, G. A. The magical number seven plus or minus two: some limits on our capacity for processing information. *Psychological Review*, 1956, *63*, 81–97.

Moss, M. K., & Page, R. A. Reinforcement and helping behavior. *Journal of Applied Social Psychology*, 1972, *2*, 360–371.

Mowrer, O. H. A stimulus-response analysis of anxiety and its role as a reinforcing agent. *Psychological Review*, 1939, *46*, 553–564.

Mowrer, O. H. *Learning theory and behavior*. New York: Wiley, 1960.

Mullahy, P. *Oedipus: Myth and complex*. New York: Grove Press, 1948.

Murray, H. A. *Explorations in personality*. New York: Oxford University Press, 1938.

Öhman, A., & Dimberg, U. Facial expressions as conditioned stimuli for electrodermal responses: A case of "preparedness"? *Journal of Personality and Social Psychology*, 1978, *36*, 1251–1258.

Osborn, A. F. *Applied imagination*. New York: Scribner's, 1963.

Osgood, C. E., Suci, G. J., & Tannenbaum, P. H. *The measurement of meaning*. Urbana: University of Illinois Press, 1957.

Outdoor Recreation Resources Review Commission. *Wilderness and recreation: A report on resources, values, and problems*. Report No. 3, The Wildland Research Center, University of California. Washington, DC: U.S. Government Printing Office, 1962.

Ovid. *The art of love*. In H. Gregory (Trans.), *Love poems of Ovid*. New York: The New American Library, 1964.

Owen, D. R. The 47, XYY male: A review. *Psychological Bulletin*, 1972, *78*, 209–233.

Pavlov, I. P. *Conditioned reflexes* (translated by G. V. Anrep). London and New York: Oxford University Press, 1927.

Peterson, L. R., & Peterson, M. J. Short-term retention of individual verbal items. *Journal of Experimental Psychology*, 1959, *58*, 193–198.

Phares, E. J. *Locus of control in personality*. Morristown, NJ: General Learning Press, 1976.

Piliavin, I., Rodin, J., & Piliavin, J. Good samaritanism: An underground phenomenon? *Journal of Personality and Social Psychology*, 1969, *13*, 289–299.

RACHMAN, S. Sexual fetishism: An experimental analogue. *Psychological Record,* 1966, *16,* 293–296.

REGAN, D. T., & CHENG, J. B. Distraction and attitude change: A resolution. *Journal of Experimental Social Psychology,* 1973, *9,* 138–147.

ROETHLISBERGER, F. J., & DICKSON, W. J. *Management and the worker.* Cambridge, MA: Harvard University Press, 1947.

ROGERS, C. R. *Client-centered therapy.* Boston: Houghton Mifflin, 1951.

ROSENTHAL, R., HALL, J. A., ARCHER, D., DI MATTEO, M. R., & ROGERS, P. L. The PONS test: Measuring sensitivity to nonverbal cues. In S. Weitz (Ed.) *Nonverbal communications.* New York: Oxford University Press, 1979.

RODIN, J. Current status of the internal-external hypothesis for obesity. *American psychologist,* 1981, *36,* 361–372.

ROTTER, J. B. Generalized expectancies for internal versus external control of reinforcement. *Psychological Monographs,* 1966, *80*(Whole No. 609).

ROTTER, J. B. *Social learning and clinical psychology.* Englewood Cliffs, NJ: Prentice-Hall, 1954.

RUBIN, Z. *Liking and loving: An invitation to social psychology.* New York: Holt, Rinehart and Winston, 1973.

RUNYON, R. P. & HABER, A. *Fundamentals of behavioral statistics.* Menlo Park: Addison Wesley, 1980.

SADE, D. A. F. (called Marquis de). Philosophy in the bedroom. In R. Seaver & Wainhonse, A. (compiled and translated), *The complete Justine Philosophy in the bedroom, and other writings.* New York: Grove Press, 1966.

SCHACHTER, S. Deviation, rejection, and communication. *Journal of Abnormal and Social Psychology,* 1951, *46,* 190–207.

SCHACHTER, S., & RODIN, J. *Obese humans and rats.* Potomac, MD: Lawrence Erlbaum Associates, 1974.

SCHACHTER, S., & SINGER, J. E. Cognitive, social, and physiological determinants of emotional state. *Psychological Review,* 1962, *69,* 379–399.

SCHEFLEN, A. E. Quasi-courtship behavior in psychotherapy. *Psychiatry,* 1965, *28,* 245–257.

SCHEIN, E. H. *Organizational psychology.* Englewood Cliffs, NJ: Prentice-Hall, 1965.

SCHNEIDER, B. Organizational climate: Individual preferences and organizational realities. *Journal of Applied Psychology,* 1972, *56,* 211–217.

SCHWARTZ, S. Words, deeds, and the perception of consequences and responsibility in action situations. *Journal of Personality and Social Psychology,* 1968, *10,* 232–242.

SCHWARTZ, S., & CLAUSEN, G. Responsibility, norms, and helping in an emergency. *Journal of Personality and Social Psychology,* 1970, 16, 299–310.

SECORD, P. F., & BACKMAN, C. W. *Social psychology.* New York: McGraw-Hill, 1974.

SEIDENBERG, B., & SNADOWSKY, A. *Social psychology.* New York: Macmillan, 1976.

SELIGMAN, M. E. P. *Helplessness: On depression, development, and death.* San Francisco: W. H. Freeman and Co., 1975.

SELIGMAN, M. E. P. On the generality of the laws of learning. *Psychological Review,* 1970, *77,* 406–418.

SELYE, H. *The stress of life.* New York: McGraw-Hill, 1956. 1976 (2nd edition).

SHERIF, C. W. *Orientation in social psychology.* New York: Harper & Row, 1976.

SHERIF, M. A study of some social factors in perception. *Archives of Psychology,* 1935, No. 187.

SHERIF, M. *In common predicament: Social psychology of intergroup conflict and cooperation.* Boston: Houghton Mifflin, 1966.

SHERIF, M., HARVEY, O., WHITE, B., HOOD, W., & SHERIF, C. *Intergroup conflict and cooperation: The robbers' cave experiment.* Norman, OK: Institute of Group Relations, University of Oklahoma, 1961.

SHIPLEY, T. E., & VEROFF, J. A projective measure of need for affiliation. *Journal of Experimental Psychology,* 1952, *43,* 349–356.

SHOSTROM, E. L. Group therapy: Let the buyer beware. *Psychology Today,* 1969, *4,* 37–40.

SKINNER, B. F. *Science and human behavior.* New York: Macmillan, 1953.

SMITH, F. J. Work attitudes as predictors of attendance on a specific day. *Journal of Applied Psychology,* 1977, *62,* 16–19.

SMITH, P. C., KENDALL, L. M., & HULIN, C. L. *The measurement of satisfaction in work and retirement.* Chicago: Rand McNally, 1969.

SOAL, S. G., & BATEMAN, F. *Modern experiments in telepathy.* New Haven, CT: Yale University Press, 1954.

SOLANO, CECILIA H. Variable self and constant other. Unpublished doctoral dissertation, Johns Hopkins University, 1977.

SOLOMON, R. L., & CORBIT, J. D. An opponent-process theory of motivation: I. Temporal dynamics of affect. *Psychological Review,* 1974, *81,* 119–145.

SORRENTINO, R. M., & BOUTILLIER, R. G. The effect of quantity and quality of verbal interaction on ratings of leadership ability. *Journal of Experimental Social Psychology,* 1975, *11,* 403–411.

SPIELBERGER, C. D. The effects of manifest anxiety on the academic achievement of college students. *Mental Hygiene,* 1962, *46,* 420–426.

SPIELBERGER, C. D. Theory and research on anxiety. In C. D. Spielberger (Ed.), *Anxiety and behavior.* New York: Academic Press, 1966.

SPIELBERGER, C. D., ANTON, W. D., & BEDELL, J. The nature and treatment of test anxiety. In M. Zuckerman, & C. D. Spielberger (Eds.), *Emotions and anxiety:* New concepts, methods, and applications. New York: Lawrence Erlbaum Associates, 1976.

STANLEY, G. H. Myths of wilderness use and management. Review draft. Missoula, MT: Intermountain Forest and Range Experiment Station, 1969.

STUART, R. B., & DAVIS, B. *Slim chance in a fat world.* Champaign, IL: Research Press, 1972.

SUTTLES, G. D. *The social order of the slum.* Chicago: University of Chicago Press, 1968.

TERKEL, S. *Working.* New York: Pantheon Books, 1974.

THAYER, R. E. Toward a psychological theory of multidimensional activation (arousal). *Motivation and Emotion,* 1978, *2,* 1–34.

THIGPEN, C. H., & CLECKLEY, H. *The three faces of Eve.* New York: McGraw-Hill, 1957.

THOREAU, H. D. *Walden.* Garden City, NY: Anchor Press, 1973.

THORNDIKE, E. L. *The psychology of learning.* New York: Teachers College, 1913.

THURSTONE, L. L. & CHAVE, E. J. *The measurement of attitude.* Chicago: University of Chicago Press, 1929.

Time. Satchel Paige's rules for coping. 1953, *41*(24), 49. (June 15, 1953, issue.)

TOFFLER, A. *Future shock.* New York: Bantam Books, 1970.

TOLMAN, E. C. Cognitive maps in rats and men. *Psychological Review,* 1948, *55,* 189–208.

TULVING, E. Episodic and semantic memory. In E. Tulving & W. Donaldson (Eds.), *Organization of memory.* New York: Academic Press, 1972.

UHRBROCK, R. S. Attitudes of 4,430 employees. *Journal of Social Psychology,* 1934, *5,* 365–377.

VALENSTEIN, E. *Brain control: A critical examination of brain stimulation and psychosurgery.* New York: Wiley, 1973.

VIDMAR, N., & ROKEACH, M. Archie Bunker's bigotry: A study in selective perception and exposure. *Journal of Communication,* 1974, *24,* 36–47.

VON FANGE, E. K. *Professional creativity.* Englewood Cliffs, NJ: Prentice-Hall, 1959.

WALLACE, D. H., & WEHMER, G. Evaluation of visual erotica by sexual liberals and conservatives. *Journal of Sex Research,* 1972, *8,* 147–153.

WALLACE, R. K., & BENSON, H. The physiology of meditation. *Scientific American,* 1972, *226,* 84–90.

WALSTER, E., ARONSON, V., ABRAMS, D., & ROTTMAN, L. Importance of physical attractiveness in dating behavior. *Journal of Personality and Social Psychology,* 1966, *4,* 508–516.

WALSTER, E., & WALSTER, G. W. Interpersonal attraction. In B. Seidenberg & A. Snadowsky (Eds.), *Social psychology.* New York: The Free Press, 1976.

WATSON, J. B. *Psychology from the standpoint of a behaviorist.* Philadelphia: Lippincott, 1924 (2nd ed.).

WATSON, J. B. & RAYNER, R. Conditioned emotional reactions. *Journal of Experimental Psychology,* 1920, *3,* 1–14.

WEBER, M. *The Protestant ethic and the spirit of capitalism* (T. Parsons, Trans.). New York: Scribner, 1930. Originally published, 1904.

WEINER, M. J., & WRIGHT, F. E. Effects of undergoing arbitrary discrimination upon subsequent attitudes toward a minority group. *Journal of Applied Social Psychology,* 1973, *3,* 94–102.

WEITZ, S. (Ed.). *Nonverbal communication* (2nd ed.). New York: Oxford University Press, 1979.

WELLS, W. D., GOI, F. J., & SEADER, S. A. A change in a product image. *Journal of Applied Psychology,* 1958, *42,* 120–121.

WHITE, R. W. Motivation reconsidered: The concept of competence. *Psychological Review,* 1959, *66,* 297–333.

WILLIAMS, J. E., & BENNETT, S. M. The defintion of sex stereotypes via the Adjective Check List. *Sex Roles,* 1975, *1,* 327–337.

WILLIAMS, J. E., & BEST, D. L. *Sex stereotypes around the world: Findings in 30 countries.* Book in preparation.

WILLIAMS, J. E., GILES, H., EDWARDS, J. R., BEST, D. L., & DAWS, J. T. Sex-trait stereotypes in England, Ireland, and the United States. *British Journal of Social and Clinical Psychology,* 1977, *16,* 303–309.

WILLIAMS, J. E., & MORLAND, J. K. *Race, color, and the young child.* Chapel Hill, NC: University of North Carolina Press, 1976.

WINTER, D. G. *The power motive.* New York: Free Press, 1973.

WITKIN, H. A., MEDNICK, S. A., SCHULSINGER, F., BAKKESTRØM, E., CHRISTIANSEN, K. O., GOODENOUGH, D. R., HIRSCHHORN, K., LUNDSTEEN, C., OWEN, D. R., PHILIP, J., RUBIN, D. B., & STOCKING, M. Criminality in XYY and XXY men. *Science,* 1976, *193,* 547–555.

WOLHWILL, J., & KOHN, I. The environment as experienced by the migrant: An adaptation-level view. *Representative Research in Social Psychology,* 1973, *4,* 135–164.

WOLFGANG, M. E. Victim-precipitated criminal homicide. *Journal of Criminal Law, Criminology, and Police Science,* 1957, *48,* 1–11.

WOODWARD, J. *Management and technology.* London: Her Majesty's Stationery Office, 1958.

WOODWORTH, R. S. *Dynamic psychology.* New York: Columbia University Press, 1918.

WRIGHTSMAN, L. S. Effects of waiting with others on changes in level of felt anxiety. *Journal of Abnormal and Social Psychology,* 1960, *61,* 216–222.

WRIGHTSMAN, L. S. *Social psychology in the seventies.* Monterey, CA: Brooks/Cole, 1972.

YERKES, R. M., & DODSON, J. D. The relation of strength of stimulus to rapidity of habit-formation. *Journal of Comparative and Neurological Psychology,* 1908, *18,* 459–482.

ZAJONC, R. B. Attitudinal effects of mere exposure. *Journal of Personality and Social Psychology Monograph Supplements,* 1968, *9*(2, Pt. 2), 1–27.

ZAJONC, R. B. Social facilitation. *Science,* 1965, *149,* 269–274.

ZELLNER, M. Self-esteem, reception, and influenceability. *Journal of Personality and Social Psychology,* 1970, *15,* 87–93.

ZIMBARDO, P. G. The human choice: Individuation, reason, and order versus deindividuation, impulse, and chaos. In W. J. Arnold & D. Levine (Eds.), *Nebraska symposium on motivation.* Lincoln: University of Nebraska Press, 1969.

ZIMBARDO, P. G., EBBESEN, E. B., & MASLACH, C. *Influencing attitudes and changing behavior.* Reading, MA: Addison-Wesley Publishing Company, 1977.

Index

Ebbesen, E. B., 240, 241
Ecology, 396
Edison, T., 98
Education, 75, 241
Edwards, D. J. A., 407
Edwards, J. R., 174, 199
Ego, 182, 232–33, 235–36, 301
Ekman, P., 123
Electrocardiogram (EKG), 114
Elliot, J., 209
Ellsworth, P. C., 221
Emotion, 112, 117–22, 136, 137, 248–49, 253, 274, 275–77, 279, 280, 399–403
Emotional experience, early, 123–24, 137
Emotional expression, 122–24, 137
Emotional recognition, 122–24
Employee participation, 106, 108
Employment screening, 116–17
Emswiller, T., 299
Encoding, 214, 226–27, 235, 242
Encounter groups, 325–29
Endorphins, 71, 81
Enkephalins, 71
Environment, 5–8, 22, 39, 393–405, 410–11, 412, 413
Environment psychology, 390–93, 412
Epley, S. W., 259
Epstein, S., 125
Equilibrium, 93
Equity theory, 263–64, 279, 370, 384
Erikson, E., 195
Eron, L. D., 293
Erotica, 277, 278, 280
Ervin, F. R., 296
Escape, 127, 134, 137, 221
Estrogen, 70
Ethnocentrism, 202, 207, 210
Evaluation apprehension, 314
Exhaustion, 131, 137
Experimental methods, 15–16, 22
Exploitation, 263–64
Exploration, 72–73, 81
External cues, 67, 81
External locus, 95, 107
External justification, 94
Extrasensory perception (ESP), 19–21, 22
Extroverts, 408
Eye contact, 220–21, 235, 411
Eysenck, H., 401

Facial expression, 119–20, 121, 122–23, 137, 219, 220–21, 226, 235
Facial features, 17
Fact, vs. assumption, 438–39, 440
Falsification, intentional, 19, 22
Familiarity, 177–78, 187, 261, 266–67, 279
Fast, J., 219
Fatigue, 381, 385
Fear, 89–90, 107, 119, 120, 122, 125–29, 133, 137, 178, 181–82, 240, 248–49, 252, 259, 278
Feedback, 214, 216, 228, 231, 235

Festinger, L., 93, 260, 261
Fetishes, 275, 280
Fiedler, F., 343–46, 349
Field experiment, 15, 22, 437
First impressions, 270, 279
Fisher, J. D., 276
Fixation, 134, 137
Fixed interval (FI) schedule, 38, 58
Fixed ratio (FR) schedule, 37, 58
Fleming, A., 427
Flexibility, 420, 421–22, 440
Food preferences, 68–69, 81
Ford, G., 99, 187
Forgetting, 51–52, 59
Formal organizations, 354–55
Fowles, J., 174
Free association, 150
Freedom of choice, 11, 22, 241, 251
Free wheeling, 446–47
Freud, S., 11, 52, 65, 73, 79–80, 82, 95, 112, 125, 142, 149, 219, 272, 284, 301, 302, 306
Freudian theory, 80, 123, 137, 153, 232
Friedman, M., 131
Friesen, W. V., 123
Frigidity, 151, 277, 280
Frustration, 133–34, 137, 268, 294
Frustration-aggression hypothesis, 284–87, 305
Fry, D., 48
Functional autonomy of motives, 86

Galen, 117
Galileo, 396, 432
Galton, F., 54, 55
Galton's Walk, 54–55, 59
Galvanic skin response (GSR), 28–29, 30, 116, 122, 133, 136
Gandhi, M., 98
Gebhard, P. H., 272
Geis, F. L., 100
Gelfand, D. M., 40, 41
Gelfand, S., 40, 41
General adaptation syndrome (GAS), 129, 131, 137
Generalized expectancies, 97
Genetics, 5–6, 296, 305
Genital stage, 123
Genocide, 202
Genovese, K., 297, 301
Gestalt therapy, 152, 153, 162
Gesture, 219, 221–23, 226, 235
Gibson, J., 392
Giles, H., 174, 199
Gilmer, D. von H., 378
Glands, 113, 115
Glass, D. C., 262
Goals, 64, 79, 80, 102–106, 108, 134, 137, 286
Goi, F. J., 201
Goldstein, M., 182
Goranson, R., 300
Gordon, T., 195
Gordon, W., 453

Polygraph, 116, 136
Pomeroy, W. B., 272
Pornography, 272, 276–77, 280
Porter, L. W., 367
Positive emotional arousal, 182
Positive reinforcer, 32
Positive transfer, 51
Post-decisional dissonance, 183–84
Postman, L., 7, 217
Power, 98–100, 107, 204, 209, 221, 344, 345, 349
Precognition, 20
Predictive methods, unconventional, 16–19, 22
Prejudice, 201, 204–209, 210
Preschool Racial Attitude Measure (PRAM), 173–74
Pretest-posttest procedure, 179–80, 187
Primacy effect, 246, 248, 270, 279
Primary territory, 409, 412
Privacy, 406–408
Prison violence, 408
Proactive interference, 52
Problem solving (*see also* Analogies; Attribute analysis; Brainstorming; Checklisting; Decision making; Morphological analysis)
  creative, 418–40, 459–60
  steps in, 432–39
  solutions, 458–59
Production vs. people, 338–46, 348, 349
Productivity, 320–21, 329, 337, 349
Profile of Nonverbal Sensitivity (PONS), 225–26
Progesterone, 70, 296
Projection, 88, 143
Prolactin, 71
Promoters, 18, 22
Propaganda, 241
Proshansky, H., 208
Prosocial behavior, 297–305, 306
Protestant ethic, 90
Proxemics, 223, 235
Proximity behaviors, 219, 223–25, 235, 261, 266–67, 279
Proxmire, W., 297
Psychiatric patients, 226
Psychic determinism, 79
Psychoanalysis, 149–50, 161–62, 301–302, 306
Psychological contract, 335, 349
Psychological minority, 204
Psychological reactance, 251, 253
Psychological resistance, 251
Psychological Stress Evaluator, 223
Psychoses, 146, 161
Psychosomatic disorders, 114, 149, 161
Psychosurgery, 295–96, 305
Psychotherapies, traditional, 149–53
Psychotics, 152
Ptolemy, 432
Punishers, 31–32, 42–43
Punishment, 33, 42–45, 58, 90, 133, 175, 177, 187, 286, 305, 445–46
Punishment-agression cycle, 296–97
Pupil size change, 116
Public space, 224

Public territory, 409, 412
Public zone, 407

Quantity-breeds-quality principle, 445, 446, 460
Quick Responses Test, 423, 424–25

Race (see Stereotypes)
Rachman, S., 275
Rahe, R. H., 129
Random sample, 13, 174–175
Rational-economic man, 347–48, 350
Rational-emotive therapy, 150, 162
Rationalization, 144
Rational person model, 454–57
Rayner, R., 121, 122
Reaction formation, 143
Recall, 217–18, 230
Recency effect, 246, 248
Reciprocity, 300
Recreation, outdoor, 405, 412
Regan, D. T., 248
Regression, 134, 143
Rehearsal, 46, 47, 48
Reik, T., 231
Reinforcement, 30, 36–39, 58
Reinforcement theory, 263, 302, 306
Rejection, 268
Relative judgment, 376
Relaxation, 71, 81, 128–29, 133, 151, 156–58, 162
Remote Associations Test, 420, 423–24
Repetition, 447–48
Representative sample, 13–14
Repression, 52, 142, 161
Reproduction, human, 273–74, 275, 279
Research methods, 12–19, 22
Respiration rate, 116, 136
Respect, 264, 279
Responsibility, diffusion of, 298, 306
Reticular activating system, 118, 136
Reward, 31–32, 33, 34, 35–42, 43, 76, 133, 175, 187
Rhine, J. B., 19
Rimm, D. C., 157
Risk takers, 89–90, 107
Risky shift effect, 315
Robertson, L. S., 174
Rodin, J., 67, 298
Roethlisberger, F. J., 4
Rogers, C., 150, 326
Rokeach, M., 208
Role playing, 182–83, 187
Roles, 192–95, 209, 210
Romantic love, 258, 265–68, 279
Roosevelt, E., 176
Roosevelt, T., 143
Rosenman, R. H., 131
Rosenthal, R., 225
Ross, D., 292, 293
Ross, S. A., 292, 293
Rotter, J., 96, 97, 98, 107

Rottman, L., 265
Rubin, Z., 263, 264, 267, 279
Rumor transmission, 217–18, 235
Runyon, R. P., 14
Ryterband, E. C., 369, 370

Sadness, 120, 122, 137
Safety devices, 381–83, 385
Sampling, 13, 174–175
Satisficing, 457–58
Satisfiers, 100, 107, 370
Scatterplots, 14
Schacter, S., 67, 118, 136, 318
Schein, E. H., 347
Schlefen, A. E., 223
Schiller, F., 445
Schizophrenic disorders, 147–48, 161, 408
Schneider, B., 362
Schwartz, S., 299
Screeners, 400–403, 410, 412
Seader, S. A., 201
Secondary gain, 145
Secondary reinforcers, 33
Secondary territory, 409, 412
Secord, P. F., 181, 218
Seidenberg, B., 318
Selective attention, 19, 22
Self-actualizing man, 348, 350
Self-concept, 9–10, 22
Self-consistency, 9–10, 22
Self-disclosure, 232
Self-esteem, 250, 262, 298
Self-evaluation, 259, 260, 261, 278, 279
Self-fulfilling prophecy, 18, 22, 202
Self-perception theory, 184, 188
Self-punitive behavior, 44–45
Self-report, 200
Self-starter, 337, 349
Self-starvation, 68, 81
Seligman, M., 45, 121
Selye, H., 129, 131
Semantic differential, 172, 173, 363, 365
Senility, 149, 161
Sensory stimulation, 124, 137
Sequencing items, 56, 59
Serial position effect, 52
Set, 271, 279, 431, 440
Sex differences, 292, 293, 296, 368, 408, 410
Sexuality, human, 70–71, 81, 258, 264–68, 272–77, 279, 280, 296
Shaping, 35–36, 58, 152
Sherif, C., 207
Sherif, M., 206, 252
Shipley, T. E., 259
Shostrom, E. L., 328
Signal, 215, 227, 235
Simon, H., 457
Singer, J., 118, 136
Single complex response, 75, 81
Single dominant response, 75, 81

Skinner, B. F., 31, 36
Skinnerian terminology, 32
Skin temperature, 116
Sleep learning, 52
Smith, F., 367, 368
Smooth muscle, 113
Snadowsky, A., 318
Soal, S. G., 21
Soap, 204
Social change, 393, 412
Social comparison, 316
Social comparison, theory, 260, 261, 279
Social Distance Scale, 171, 172
Social exchange theory, 262–63, 279
Social facilitation, 74–76, 313–14, 323
Social filtering, 266–67
Social implementation, 459, 460
Social influence, 266–67, 279, 298, 306
Social interactions, 5, 21
Socialization, 208–209
Social learning, 208, 210
Social learning theory, 98, 107, 291–94, 305
Social man assumption, 348, 350
Social pressure, 4, 316–317
Social support, 252, 253, 319, 320
Social zone, 407
Solano, C., 200
Solomon, R. L., 132
Somatic nervous system, 113, 114
Sorrentino, R. M., 337
South Africa, 170, 204–205
Soviet Union, 245, 290, 347
Space, 223–25, 235, 398–99, 406, 407–408, 412
Spatial perception, 392–93
Specialization, 355, 383
Specifications, 437
Spielberger, 75, 126, 128, 129
Spinal cord, 113, 114, 115
SQ3R method of learning, 53
Stanley, G. H., 405
Stereotyping, 195–204, 206, 209, 210, 217, 271–72, 279, 368
Stimuli, 28–30, 32–33, 34, 42, 43, 58, 71, 81, 121–22, 376–77
Stimulus-response compatibility, 377–78
Stoner, J., 315
Stress, 114, 129–33, 137, 410
Stringer, R. I., 362
Sublimation, 143
Subproblems, 437–38, 440
Successive approximation, 35–36, 58
Suci, G. J., 173
Superego, 301–302, 306
"Supermale," 296, 305
Surprise, 119, 120, 122, 137
Surveys, 13–14, 22
Survival, 396
Suttles, G. D., 409
Symbionese Liberation Army, 240, 241, 242, 252
Sympathetic nervous system, 113, 114, 115